Euroscepticism in Contempo
British Politics

- How can we explain the ebb and flow of opposition to European integration in the Labour and Conservative parties?
- What has been the effect of opposition to Europe on British policy formation?
- How is Euroscepticism becoming 'a new faith'?
- Is there a higher loyalty than party loyalty – to one's country?

In a study examining Euroscepticism since 1945, this book argues that opposition to Europe has been shaped decisively by the opportunities available to sceptics to oppose government policy and the arena in which European policies have been made.

The book argues that opponents to European integration have evolved from a group of anti-Europeans, into anti-Marketeers and finally into a mainstream group of Eurosceptics committed to opposing Political, Economic and Monetary Union agendas.

Anthony Forster is Director of Research at the Defence Studies Department, King's College, London. Since 1997 he has been Professor Invité at the Institut Supérieur des affaires de défense, Université Panthéon Assas (Université Paris II). He is the author of *Britain and Maastricht Negotiations* (Macmillan: 1999); and *The Making of Britain's European Foreign Policy* (Longman: 2001) with Alasdair Blair.

Euroscepticism in Contemporary British Politics

Opposition to Europe in the British
Conservative and Labour Parties
since 1945

Anthony Forster

To Andrew, I hope this
is a very good read!
with best wishes

28 June 2017

London and New York

First published 2002
by Routledge
11 New Fetter Lane, London EC4P 4EE

Simultaneously published in the USA and Canada
by Routledge
29 West 35th Street, New York, NY 10001

Routledge is an imprint of the Taylor & Francis Group

Typeset in Times by
HWA Text and Data Management, Tunbridge Wells
Printed and bound in Great Britain by
MPG Books Ltd, Bodmin

British Library Cataloguing in Publication Data
A catalogue record for this book is available from the British Library

Library of Congress Cataloging in Publication Data
A catalog record for this book has been applied for

ISBN 0–415–28731–6 (hbk)
ISBN 0–415–28732–4 (pbk)

To VJC

Contents

Acknowledgements

This work has drawn on several research projects over the last decade which have explored the impact of Europe on Britain's political processes. In addition to the citations in the book, I would like to thank a number of individuals who have been interviewed during this period: William Cash, George Gardiner, Teresa Gorman, Michael Howard, Lord Lamont of Lerwick, Graham Mather, Sir Teddy Taylor, Anthony Teasdale and Michael Welsh.

I would also like to thank Lord Harrison, Lord Powell of Bayswater, the late Lord Shore of Stepney and Lord Williamson of Horton for whom I have been fortunate to work as a specialist adviser on the House of Lords Select Committee on European Affairs, Sub-Committee C (CFSP). Lynton Harrison was a Labour MEP from 1989–1997 when the Labour Party was moving from a sceptical to a pro-European position. Charles Powell was Margaret Thatcher's foreign affairs private secretary for six years from 1984–1990 and responsible for the drafting of the Bruges speech. Peter Shore, a longstanding Labour critic of the EC/EU, articulated in the 1970s many of the arguments Eurosceptics would embrace 20 years later. David Williamson was a senior Europe adviser to Margaret Thatcher and Secretary General of the European Commission. On a Eurostar trip to Paris in July 2001 – which as a consequence of various delays lasted seven hours – their lordships were kind enough to respond to some of the key arguments in this book, and offered an impromptu master class in understanding opposition to closer European integration. I am solely responsible for both matters of interpretation and argument, but I am deeply grateful to them for their critical advice. I would like to thank the British Council Paris, for funding part of the research through Alliance award number PN99.115.

Colleagues who have debated various ideas in this volume include Alasdair Blair, Philip Budden, Agnès Alexandre-Collier, Oliver Daddow, Anne Deighton, Erik Jones, Pauline Schnapper, Helen Wallace and William Wallace. Thanks also go to the staff at Taylor and Francis, especially Craig Fowlie, Jennifer Lovel and Grace McInnes for their unfailing assistance. In addition, I would like to thank those Nottingham University second and third year students who took the Britain and the European Union course from 1997–2000 and who to varying degrees were exposed to and assisted with developing and refining some of the arguments contained within this book. My greatest debt of gratitude, however, is to Victoria Child, who has endured much in the research and writing of this book and without whom it could not have been completed. The book is dedicated to her.

The analysis, opinions and conclusions expressed or implied in this book are those of the author and do not necessarily represent the views of the JSCSC, the UK MOD or any other government agency.

1 Defining and explaining Euroscepticism

Introduction

One of the most striking features both of contemporary British politics and of Britain's attitude towards European integration is the emergence of a phenomenon termed Euroscepticism. This phenomenon has deeply divided the two major British political parties, with the Labour Party splitting over European policy in the 1980s and the Conservative Party emerging from the 1990s gravely wounded. This study is concerned with the impact of scepticism, both on the parties themselves and through them on Britain's policy towards Europe. In addition, it is concerned with how we can account for the ebb and flow of opposition to Britain's involvement in the European integration project in the period since the Second World War.

This study is not therefore an attempt to present a history of scepticism or indeed of Britain's relationship with Europe since 1945 and public attitudes to it. Rather, the focus is on key events in British policy towards the European integration project, in order to cast a spotlight on the activities and influence of the sceptics within the two main political parties and to present an introductory overview of the issues. To this end, Chapter 2 examines the *volte face* which led to the first two applications for membership of the European Communities (EC) in 1961 and 1967;[1] Chapter 3 examines the passage of the European Community Bill in 1970 to 1972; Chapter 4 examines the referendum on continued membership of the EC in 1975; Chapter 5 examines the Single European Act of 1986; Chapter 6 examines attitudes towards the Political Union agenda of the Maastricht Treaty; and Chapter 7 examines opposition to British entry into the single currency (the Euro). The final chapter explores the patterns and trends in scepticism and reflects on the reasons behind the ebb and flow of scepticism over the last half century.

Clearly, the term 'Euroscepticism' is not without difficulties, both in terms of its analytical purchase and as a descriptive tool. It has routinely been employed and misemployed in the popular press. Often it is used to express a derogatory value judgement and as a term of abuse, but rarely has the term been rigorously defined by the academic community. The *Oxford English Dictionary* defines a sceptic as a person who doubts truth of, or is inclined to question truth of facts, statements or claims.[2] However, generally the term Euroscepticism has been employed as a generic label that defines a negative point of view towards the European Union (EU).

For Agnès Alexandre-Collier, a Eurosceptic is someone who doubts the utility and viability of Economic and Political Union. There are three important aspects to this definition (Alexandre-Collier, 1998:17). First, it assumes that opposition focuses on two interconnected processes, economic and political integration within Europe; second, it directly links this opposition to the transformation of the EC into the EU in 1993; and third, it implies that Eurosceptics are to be found only within the Conservative Party and not in other political parties. In this sense the term is used to describe opponents of European integration whether principled or opportunist, who were first galvanised by Prime Minister Thatcher's Bruges speech in September 1988 and who came to prominence in the ratification of the Maastricht Treaty between December 1991 and July 1993, but more generally during the second Major administration of 1992 to 1997. Many of these MPs now occupy leading positions in the Shadow Cabinet or as frontbench spokesmen for the Conservative Party.

This study seeks to expand this rather narrow and contemporary understanding of Euroscepticism, by arguing that the term needs to be seen as a particular manifestation of a school of sceptical thought about the value of Britain's involvement with moves towards supranational European integration. This scepticism has moreover been a feature of both main political parties. Thus there are important similarities and continuities in terms of the arguments sceptics have deployed since the Second World War. While these have developed growing sophistication, and their exact combination has varied, they share many of the same core concerns, above all in terms of a focus on sovereignty, national identity and the need for economic and political independence. There has also been a remarkable continuity amongst those individuals opposed to European integration. Thus alongside a new generation of sceptics, old hands such as Peter Shore, Barbara Castle, Tony Benn, Richard Body, Peter Walker and Teddy Taylor continue to play a role. These points highlight the danger of 'presentism', viewing the situation without reference to the historical context in which current political and intellectual issues are debated. It is therefore too simplistic to view Euroscepticism as a phenomenon of the 1990s, triggered by the Maastricht Treaty and rooted solely in the Conservative Party, without setting it in a wider perspective and historical context.

A key to the way in which scepticism has evolved over time has been its multi-faceted nature. There is hence a thought-action spectrum of scepticism. This spectrum ranges from a relatively latent questioning of the value of involvement with the European integration project; to doubts about the benefits of EC/EU membership; to active scepticism advocating opt-outs and partial exemptions from particular parts of the EC/EU competence; to a position which favours disengagement and outright withdrawal. But although the multi-faceted nature of scepticism has been a key to its longevity, this study argues that it has also been a source of division among sceptics. In particular, the impact of scepticism has been deeply affected by the prior party political allegiances of its adherents. It was party loyalty that undermined its chances of success in securing a 'No' vote on continued British membership of the EC in the 1975 referendum, when the cross-party National Referendum Campaign was weakened by party political tensions. Indeed, partly as a product of the ongoing problems caused by ideological differences, a recent trend has been the creation of more apolitical groupings, such as the New Europe group formed to resist moves towards the adoption of the Euro.

This study therefore argues that the Euroscepticism which emerged following the Bruges speech has a long lineage with three key formative periods. The first was bounded by the Macmillan government's application to join the European Community in 1961 and the end of the referendum in 1975. The second period, from 1979 to 1990 and the Bruges speech of September 1988, which re-ignited the European issue when Margaret Thatcher re-defined the terms of the debate. This marked the opening of the third period, dominated by opposition to the Maastricht agenda of Political and Monetary Union and the re-emergence of the question as to whether Britain should remain a member of the EU.

The academic context

Despite their growing prominence, the question of the influence of sceptics and the reason for it has not hitherto been directly addressed in the scholarly literature. In so far as it has received academic treatment, this has largely been as a by-product of the analysis of Britain's troubled historical relationship with Europe. Here the debate is dominated by the conventional wisdom that Britain is 'an awkward partner' or '*mauvais élève*' in its management of its relations with, and participation in, the European integration project (George, 1992; George, 1998; Schnapper, 2000). Five competing explanations have been advanced for this problematic relationship, but all fall short in their explanation of scepticism, presenting at best a partial and at worst a misleading picture of its influence (Bulpitt, 1992:258–75; Buller, 1995:33–42). Part of the explanation is the predominance of pro-integrationists in the academic community, especially in the field of European integration, which for a variety of reasons has treated Euroscepticism in an asymmetrical way to pro-integration groups such as the European Movement. The academic community has therefore routinely overlooked Eurosceptics and Euroscepticism and by design or default has often failed to treat it as a serious phenomenon or object of study.[3]

First, a 'behaviouralist' school has focused on the importance of leadership behaviour and placed emphasis on the way in which key players have viewed the world, their attitudes and values. This rather cosmopolitan school has highlighted the weak motivations of British governments in applying to join the EC (Baker and Seawright, 1998:1); thus Northedge for instance argues that there was little public or elite commitment to membership, which was a decision of last resort when all other alternatives had been explored (Northedge, 1983:26). Against this background, sustaining support for EU membership was always going to be difficult. Developing this theme, Christopher Lord and Henrik Larsen focus on the discourse through which the European question has been presented and debated. Lord argues that in the initial application in 1961 and subsequent applications in

1967 and 1970, the membership debate centred around the concept of parliamentary sovereignty, which obscured an open and honest debate on the costs and benefits of joining the Common Market. The political elite therefore failed to build up a solid majority in the country in favour of Community membership and a broad and stable domestic platform upon which Britain's European policy could be based (Lord, 1993:99; Larsen, 1997). However, what these contributions overlook is important party and institutional considerations leading to British scepticism and the importance of political economy issues in shaping attitudes towards European integration.

A second 'party' school has focused on political parties as the source of the difficulties in Britain's relationship with Europe. Geoffrey Howe argues that the nature of divisions inside both the Labour and Conservative Parties inhibited a thoroughgoing discussion on Europe (Howe, 1994). The instruments of party discipline deployed to shore up support only ever succeeded in masking the deep divisions inside the major political parties concerning the European question, but never fully resolved it. Once in the EC, the pace and direction of integration undermined many of the initial assurances given that further developments would be minimal. In this view, the unambiguous development of a political dimension to the process of European integration, epitomised by the transformation of the Community from a Common Market to a Union with a single currency and common foreign and security policy, has further compounded these initial difficulties (Baker and Seawright, 1998:2). Elsewhere, I have argued that the changing nature of the integration project makes it difficult for British Labour and Conservative party leaders to justify and explain the development of the EU to their own supporters (Forster, 1998a; Forster, 1998b). This problem has become even more difficult as integration has touched on defence, border controls, citizenship and money which are part of the core functions of a state and which are particularly sensitive symbols of national sovereignty (Forster and Wallace, 2000b:411). Whilst this school usefully locates the European issue within the political arena, it has often overlooked or in some cases inadequately explored the inter-party nature of the European question and opposition to it, along with the broader context within which the European issue has been managed and debated.

A third 'institutionalist' group of scholars highlights structural explanations as the cause of Britain's problematic relationship with the integration project. Stuart Wilks for instance points to the particular situation created by British political institutional structures (Wilks, 1996). Here, blame is directed at the electoral system which disproportionately rewards the winning party in Parliament, and the adversarial nature of British politics in which the role of the opposition is to oppose the government even where agreement exists between them on the substance of policy (George, 1998). Armstrong and Bulmer have developed a historical institutionalist account, which seeks to offer an analysis of formal multi-layered power structures as well as informal procedures and practices, socialisation and norms (Bulmer, 1994:351; Armstrong and Bulmer, 1998). More recently, Mark Aspinwall has focused on the first past the post electoral system which he argues creates centrifugal forces within the party system where the general public do not appear to share a similar concern with Europe (Aspinwall, 2000:415). Simon Usherwood contends that to cope with this mismatch political parties have externalised the problem, leading to extra party groupings and the development of radical opposition movements (Usherwood, 2001). Usherwood thus brings to the institutionalist approach explanations which draw on some of the findings of the first and second schools in understanding the ebb and flow of scepticism, but to date institutionalists still fail to offer adequate explanations of Euroscepticical influence on British European policies.

A fourth and emerging 'international political economy' (IPE) school argues that British economic structures clash with European models of industrial organisation. In moving away from examining British political institutions, Andrew Gamble for instance focuses on the political economy of Britain's European relationship, and argues that the difficulty posed for Britain by the European question arises from the long-term development of the British state and its preference for an alternative economic model – free trade and deregulated markets (Gamble, 1998). The IPE contribution is therefore more of a corrective to issues overlooked in other approaches than a free-standing approach to explaining and understanding scepticism.

A fifth 'conjuncture' group of scholars has offered a series of more contingent and eclectic explanations to account for British governments' reluctance to participate in the European integration project. David Gowland and Arthur Turner point towards the interplay between domestic and international factors, especially the changing role and importance of Britain's declining power in the world, the evolving concerns of policymakers, the influence of national politics, the activities of interest groups and economic trends (Gowland and Turner, 2000:7). Robert Lieber argues that group influence was central to understanding why the British government was reluctant to join the EC in 1957. Low levels of party and public attention and the conscious choices of government leaders have allowed economic and business groups to play a dominant role in shaping the calculations of the costs and benefits by governments. However, once the issue of EC membership was politicised, governments were motivated by considerations of the national interest rather than material advantage (Leiber, 1970:viii). These explanations attempt to take account of the complexity of, but fall short of offering any systematic explanations for, the role and influence of sceptical opposition groups on government policy.

These conventional explanations of the British relationship with Europe thus have a number of important shared and individual weaknesses as a means of determining the impact and influence of scepticism. In particular, these explanations neglect the paradox that whilst all governments come into office as relatively supportive of integration, by the end of their period in office they are far more sceptical. In addition, they fail to assist our understanding of why it is that a high profile does not always translate into a high degree of sceptic influence on government policy. The key problem, however, is that they fail to adequately focus on scepticism and sceptical groups, which are often treated as of tangential interest to most studies. Little is therefore offered in terms of an explanation of the ebb and flow of scepticism.

This study takes as its point of departure the position that while debates and policy-decisions at the EC/EU level are important, it is mainly the domestic arena where battles are fought. From this start point, it seeks to address the shortcomings in the existing analysis of scepticism by arguing that five key factors explain the influence and changing impact of scepticism on the political parties and on British European policy. These are the identity of the sceptics themselves, the opportunities available to them for opposition, the arena in which opposition occurs, and closely related with the latter, the resources and information available to sceptics to advance their cause. It is these factors which comprise the core considerations and shape the structure of each of the following chapters.

As regards the first factor of the identity of the sceptics, a central concern of the study is how their party political and other allegiances prompted them to view the European issue and its context. A key question for supporters and opponents alike has been the exact implications of closer European integration for domestic Conservative and Labour political programmes. Here a major issue has been the extent to which the political elite is willing to subordinate concerns about sovereignty and autonomy in return for securing domestic political objectives.

However, what complicates partisan approaches to the EC/EU, is that what it 'is' in policy terms is not fixed, but evolving, posing on-going problems for political parties in reaching a judgement on the utility and implications of integration to domestic party agendas. In the 1970s many Labour sceptics opposed the EC as a capitalist club; in the late 1980s Mrs Thatcher famously denounced the EC as trying to impose socialism through the backdoor and castigated its regulatory approach to policy-making (Majone, 1993:153). In the 1990s, the issue of Economic and Monetary Union has drawn fire from right-wing sceptics.

In terms of expressing their objections, however, the principal argument of this study is that for most of the post-war period, opponents of closer integration fought their battles inside their own political parties. For a variety of reasons, including the fear of the charge of disloyalty, their parliamentary tactics mainly comprised the tabling of Early Day Motions (EDMs), and voting with the opposition party was highly exceptional. However, as deference to party leadership has declined and at least for some the European issue became one of conscience, the bonds of party loyalty have been loosened. Nonetheless, party tribalism remains a powerful constraint both real and imagined in shaping sceptical opposition. But the study further argues that the increasing appropriation of the political sceptic agenda by the right, as almost all levels of the Conservative Party have embraced a sceptical position, was by the late 1990s affecting the picture in two particular ways. These were the emergence of non-partisan sceptical groups concerned especially with the issue of the Euro, and in which remaining Labour sceptics have found an outlet for their views, and the development of opposition groups outside Parliament.

As regards the second factor which has shaped the influence of scepticism since the Second World War, that of the opportunities available for sceptics to oppose European integration, the study argues that if opportunities to oppose government policy are limited and the chance of success small, then the scale of opposition will be small and will rarely expand beyond a hard core of principled opponents. If the opportunities to oppose government policy are clear cut or numerous and the chance of success perceived to be high, then opposition has the potential to be much greater.

Between 1945 and 1969, there were few set-piece opportunities to oppose integration apart from the failed membership applications of 1961 and 1967. However, in the 1970s, major legislative battles over EC membership gave opponents ample scope to make their case, as did the June 1975 referendum which placed the European question before the public for the first time. From the mid-1980s, the growing frequency of Intergovernmental Conferences (IGCs) and the need to ratify major EC/EU treaties in Parliament has increased the opportunities to oppose government policy. Between 1955 and 1985 there was one IGC – the Messina Conference – to establish the European Economic Communities and the European Atomic Energy Community (EURATOM). Between 1985 and 2001 there were four IGCs and at decreasing intervals of five, four and three years respectively.[4] Moreover, the decision of both the Labour and Conservative parties to hold a referendum on British adoption of the Euro has been important in providing a new opportunity to garner support from the wider electorate.

Following on from this is the third factor which shapes the influence and impact of sceptics, the arena where the issue will be decided. The study argues that if the arena is Parliament, on the floor of the House of Commons or House of Lords, this significantly constrains the possibilities for dissent. To be successful the key instruments are the ability to defeat a government motion or to damage the government's reputation, or as a minimum register a significant protest vote from the government's own supporters. In the chamber, this requires the government's own supporters to vote against or abstain from backing the government, or to register protest through EDMs. Whether this happens or not depends on MPs themselves, and relates to their willingness to risk developing a reputation for being disloyal, how they assess the security of their own position within the party, and whether their constituency associations will support them. It also depends on the quality of the party's leadership, party management skills, and a willingness of government backbenchers to side with the opposition. Above all, the study argues that outright success – defeating the government – is crucially dependent on the size of the majority of the government and the actions of the opposition parties, since even if a protest takes place it will not change policy unless the parliamentary arithmetic works against the in-built executive dominance of the legislature.

If the issue is decided outside Parliament, for example through a referendum or there is a clear choice over a European issue in a general or a European election, then other factors come into play. In this arena, the government finds it much more difficult to manage the process since voters rarely owe loyalty to the government in quite the same way as its own MPs do. Here, access to resources to fund publicity campaigns and mobilise a mass organisation are important in delivering votes. In addition, the role of the media is also clearly very important in providing access to information, disseminating it to voters and lending credibility to arguments. Resources and information are thus the final factors which shape the impact of sceptics.

As regards the fourth factor of resources, the study argues that, in the 1960s and 1970s, sceptics lacked the resources to provide an effective challenge to the government of the day. The ability of Eurosceptics to create and subsequently harness resources has been a major factor in mounting an effective public campaign against government policy. The Eurosceptical groupings now have access to a range of resources, including financial, social and political, which allow them to challenge pro-European integration groups. The consequence has been a professionalisation of the effectiveness of Eurosceptics as a campaigning force. In this they have been assisted by a number of developments, including access to the organisational resources of the Conservative Party, the increasingly sceptical tone of elements of the print news, and growing support from a number of important business figures. All have done much to enhance the credibility and reach of the sceptic message.

As regards the final key factor which has shaped the influence of scepticism, the general argument is that sceptical groupings have increasingly gained access to, and made intelligent use of, information on European integration. In the past, the technical and legalistic language in which European integration was discussed made the substance of decisions very difficult to understand for those beyond a closed policy-making elite centred on Whitehall and Westminster. With a handful of notable exceptions, sceptics did not, until the late 1980s, really take seriously the need to fully understand the technical nature of European integration – their knowledge levels were rather low since they themselves needed little convincing of their own rectitude. There has, however, been an important change particularly since the watershed Maastricht Treaty on European Union of 1993, with serious Eurosceptic groupings now seeking to develop a capacity to provide autonomous analysis of policy-making, decisions and Treaty outcomes. This has allowed them to challenge the British government in a way that has never been done before.

Overall, in terms of the impact of Euroscepticism on British policy, this study draws a distinction between direct and indirect effects. Despite little direct success in defeating major parliamentary legislation – the EC Bill of 1972, the Single European Act, and the Maastricht Treaty – scepticism has had important indirect effects on British policy. In particular, sceptics have been sufficiently vocal in challenging pro-integrationists to make a significant contribution to shaping and constricting the character of the British debate on Europe. Sceptics have also been influential enough to destabilise political parties, comprising at various times sizeable factions in both the Labour and the Conservative parties with serious consequences for each. Perhaps most importantly, however, they have been instrumental in manoeuvring both the Labour Party and the Conservative Party into commitments to hold a referendum on the Euro, and so explicitly to put the European question before the electorate for a second time. But the extent to which the Eurosceptics can grasp this opportunity will crucially depend on their ability to draw on the experiences discussed by this study and circumvent the partisan dimension which has dominated so much of British European policy-making.

Conclusions

So far as the impact of scepticism on the two main political parties, and through them on Britain's European policy, is concerned, the study argues that the policy preferences of domestic actors, the institutional arenas in which policy preferences are contested, the availability of resources and distribution of information among domestic groups, are central to explaining both the ebb and flow of groups opposing Europe and the influence these groups can exert. In particular, however, the study suggests that Eurosceptics themselves have increasingly made an important contribution to the changing centre of gravity in the country on the European issue. They appear to be learning better and quicker from the lessons of history than their Europhile counterparts. Access to a wide range of resources – not just financial – has facilitated an increasingly credible sceptical challenge to governments of all political persuasions. In addition, Eurosceptics are becoming increasingly adept at creating as well as reacting to opportunities to oppose the European project.

An underlying question, to which this study will return in Chapter 8 is, however, the extent to which scepticism exhibits the characteristics of a faith amongst its adherents. In this regard, while identifying core concerns amongst Eurosceptics, and so the makings of what might be termed a creed, the study highlights the fact that opponents to British membership of the EC/EU and closer European integration have generally failed to articulate a positive and shared alternative vision to Britain's involvement with the European integration project. In addition, its multi-faceted nature, while contributing in important ways to its adaptability, longevity and reach, has also left scepticism prone to divisions, and vulnerable to the counter-pull of another faith of sorts, that of party political allegiance.

Notes

1   The term European Communities comprises the European Coal and Steel Community (founded in 1951); European Economic Communities (founded in 1957); and the European Atomic Energy Community (founded in 1957). In 1965 a merger Treaty made each legally distinct organisation share common institutions and, in 1993, the Treaty on European Union renamed the European Economic Community the European Community. It also created a European Union (Bainbridge and Teasdale, 1996:168 and 315).

2   The full entry is as follows: '**sceptic**/skeptic/n. person who doubts truth of (esp. religious) doctrine or theory etc.; a person inclined to question truth of facts or statements or claims; philosopher who questions the possibility of knowledge; **scepticism** n [F f, Lf. Gk (skeptomai = observe)]'.

3   For example J. Young, 1993; George, 1998; all fail to have an index reference to Eurosceptics or Euroscepticism but many include index references to the European Movement. Other studies have simply overlooked Euroscepticism altogether. An important exception is Baker and Seawright, 1998.

4   The Luxembourg Conference took place in December 1985, leading to the Single European Act which came into effect in 1987. The twin Maastricht IGCs on Economic and Monetary Union and Political Union took place between 1990 and 1991 culminating in the Maastricht Treaty on European Union which came into effect in 1993. The Amsterdam IGC took place from 1996 to 1997, culminating in the Amsterdam Treaty which came into effect in 1999. The Nice IGC took place in December 2000, and is as yet unratified.

2 Opposition to Europe, 1945–1969

Introduction

In the first quarter of a century after the Second World War, two distinct periods of opposition to closer European integration were evident. The dominant theme of the first period, from 1945 to 1961, was one of scepticism, a feeling shared by the Labour government of 1945 to 1951, the Conservative governments of 1951 to 1961, and the majority of their MPs, constituency chairs and party activists alike. In this period, substantive policy differences on Europe were rare and anti-Europeanism – a rejection of anything to do with supranational Europe – was widespread. The second period saw the shattering of this consensus when, on 31 July 1961, Harold Macmillan announced to the House of Commons that the government would open talks to explore whether satisfactory terms for joining the European Economic Community could be negotiated. Macmillan's policy was opposed by the Labour Party, but following the rejection of Macmillan's bid and Labour's return to power on 31 March 1966, it too embarked on its own ultimately unsuccessful application for membership. Within the course of a decade, the issue of Europe had thus risen to the top of the political agenda, with dramatic consequences both for relations between the two main parties, but also within them.

In the first period between 1945 and 1961, an exclusive focus on Europe and the possibility of the government participating in supranational integration were unthinkable to most in the political establishment. Even following the Messina talks which began in June 1955 to explore how to create the Economic Communities, what little discussion that took place was confined to the political elite, and internalised within the major political parties at Westminster and key Whitehall departments, sometimes reaching the floor of the House of Commons, but rarely aired in the public domain. Notwithstanding the fact that a sceptical view dominated Parliament, tensions were, however, evident in the views of opponents of involvement in moves towards supranational integration. These differences of emphasis and motivation in opposing supranationalism evident in the first period, manifested themselves more fully in the second period from 1961.

Once Macmillan had announced his intention to open negotiations there was a refinement of the rather generalised anti-European arguments used to reject British entanglement in Europe. In particular, the declining value of the Empire Commonwealth raised the spectre of anti-Europeans being unable to agree on and advance any alternative solutions. This in turn led to the emergence of anti-Marketeers who advanced arguments more closely focused on a rejection of membership of the EC and all that it stood for.

Whereas during the first period considered by this chapter sceptics had enjoyed considerable influence and support, those who rejected British involvement with the European integration project faced a steep learning curve in the period after 1961. The switch in the official policy position of first the Conservative Party and then the Labour Party to support for membership of the EC, deprived them of a key power base, and indeed, in the end, it was to be the veto of de Gaulle in January 1963 and again in November 1967, and not the influence and actions of the sceptics, that ultimately ensured that there would be no British membership of the European Communities. However, sceptics did retain influential adherents within both parties, and above all within the now deeply divided Labour Party, and this was to provide them with an ongoing and highly disruptive source of strength.

Opportunity

In looking at the period between 1945 and 1961, the first point to make is that the end of the Second World War did not mark a radical rethinking of Britain's relationship with Europe. The key to British foreign policy during this period was instead captured by the metaphor which Churchill offered in 1947 of three interlocking circles, with Britain at the heart of three centres of power: the Atlantic world, the Empire and Commonwealth, and the West European world. Only after a commitment to the Empire and the Commonwealth and the English-speaking world, did Western Europe figure as an arena for British engagement. The fundamentals of British policy in this arena were shared across the frontbenches: Britain would provide a leadership role in Western Europe, but stand aside from European regional co-operation based along federalist lines.

Inspired by these considerations, the Labour government was nevertheless active in four initiatives. All were of a strictly intergovernmental nature, but did provide a degree of scope and ammunition for the development of sceptic arguments. The first initiative was the Dunkirk Treaty signed in March 1947, a defensive pact between Britain and France that in 1948 was extended to include the BENELUX countries and transformed into the Brussels Treaty organisation. The second initiative was the creation of the Washington Treaty in 1949 linking the United States and Canada to Western European security, and the third the creation of the Organisation for European Economic Co-operation (OEEC), established in April 1948 to oversee American economic assistance in the form of Marshall Aid. The final project was the creation of the Council of Europe in May 1949.

When returned to power in November 1951, the substance of the Conservative government's policy was little different from that of its Labour predecessor. Part of the explanation was that the West Europeans had become clearer about their own willingness to accept the principle of supranationalism, and to insist on it as a precondition for participation in negotiations. This made the earlier Conservative strategy of direct participation in negotiations to channel them towards inter-governmental solutions, unviable as a means of securing British interests. The Conservative government therefore endorsed, but did not participate in, the negotiations to create a European Defence Community (EDC), establishing a European army under the authority of a European defence minister and assembly. British support took the form of a pledge of wholehearted backing for the EDC within a broad Atlantic framework. To this end, in March 1952 the Foreign Secretary, Anthony Eden, proposed that all existing West European communities, namely the European Coal and Steel Community (ECSC) and EDC, should come under the authority of the intergovernmental Council of Europe.

By now, however, the British had lost the trust of their partners, in part because of their spoiling tactics both inside the OEEC and Council of Europe, and on the sidelines of other initiatives like that of the ECSC and the EDC. The Eden Plan was viewed with suspicion, 'as a method of granting Britain the advantages of participation without its responsibilities' (Lieber, 1970:24). In 1954, capitalising on the failure of the supranational plans for an EDC, the Conservative government was temporarily successful in an initiative to salvage West European defence co-operation by creating Western European Union (a proposal expanding the Brussels Pact to include West Germany and Italy and which paved the way for their membership of NATO). However, this British success was an aberration, only possible because of the sensitivities that had been shown to exist in the field of supranational defence integration. In June 1955, the founders of the ECSC committed themselves to supranationalism and the pooling of sovereignty, and this initiative culminated in the 1957 Treaties of Rome, creating a European Economic Community and European Atomic Energy Community. In the wake of this development, the British government was left to form an intergovernmental Free Trade Area for those European countries unable or unwilling to join the Six.

With the Conservative government's volte face of 1961, the landscape in which opponents of supranational integration operated changed markedly. Yet, while the applications for EC membership of 1961 and 1967 created opportunities for opposition by bringing the issues into clearer focus and giving opponents a clear target of membership against which to campaign, in practice the scope to oppose government policy was surprisingly limited. When in August 1961 Harold Macmillan applied for negotiations for EC membership, his request comprised not an unconditional commitment to membership, but was instead merely an enquiry about the possibility of applying. This made it rather difficult to confront the government and defeat its policy. Indeed, it was not sceptic action, but the veto of President de Gaulle in January 1963 which effectively foreclosed the issue.

Similarly, Harold Wilson's application to open negotiations was made on comparable grounds to that of Macmillan, and was merely an exploration of the possibility of applying. Once again, the veto of de Gaulle brought the issue to a close in November 1967. A telling feature of the strategy used by both Wilson and Macmillan was that it diverted the energy of opponents of the applications into consideration of the nature of the terms of membership, and so helped to keep the opposition divided. Thus, in the absence of a concrete proposal it was difficult for opponents to engage with either the Conservative or Labour governments. Instead, the spotlight fell on sketching out arguments that might convince colleagues in the sceptics' parties that the terms which might be secured would make British EC membership unacceptable.

Opponents: who were they?

From the moment West Europeans began to organise themselves into various regional groupings, differences in emphasis between opponents of supranational integration were evident. In the Labour Party in the period between 1945 and 1961, there was a spectrum of scepticism which can be characterised as anti-European. Most, like Clement Attlee, Ernest Bevin and Sir Stafford Cripps were committed to preserving British parliamentary sovereignty and highlighted this, as well as British exceptionalism, as reasons for standing aside from European supranational integration.

Whether the alternative should be strong ties with the United States, the creation of an Anglo-European third force equidistant from the United States and the Soviet Union or the development of the Commonwealth was, however, fiercely contested. Bevin adopted and promoted the idea of strong Atlantic links from his position as Foreign Secretary, though he muddied the water by being the author of the third force idea. To Bevin, however, the point about the third force was that it would act as a bridge to the US. Bevin therefore opposed the creation of the Council of Europe and championed the idea of an Atlantic alliance, and this view was strongly supported by a group of Labour MPs who were essentially Atlanticist. Drawn from the right of the Labour Party, the group included Herbert Morrison and numbered around eighty. A second group by contrast took up the idea of a third force and pushed it in a Socialist direction that had strong anti-American characteristics. This variant drew support from left-wingers like Richard Crossman, Michael Foot, Tom Driberg and Barbara Castle, based on the goal of what Fred Peart, for example, called for a 'Socialist foreign policy ... in a Socialist world' (Morgan, 1984:236).

Another group inside the Labour Party simply had a dislike of foreigners and a concomitant pride in everything which was British. For example, Kenneth Morgan has noted that Hugh Dalton, who was the head of the British delegation to develop the concept of the Council of Europe, 'was notoriously amongst the most prejudiced and anti-European of all the Labour ministers' (Morgan 1984:395). Dalton was vigorously supported by John Strachey who in his role as Secretary of State for War, in July 1950, 'made a vigorously anti-European speech', leading to his being publicly rebuked by Prime Minister Attlee (J. Young, 1984:163). A strong anti-German feeling was a central aspect of this form of anti-Europeanism and, indeed, was actively advanced by Attlee in relation to the issue of West German rearmament in the early 1950s, albeit in a more respectable form than that of many grass roots activists. Lynton Robins notes that even in Parliament where by convention criticism of allies was limited, John Snow remarked in October 1960, 'I cannot bring myself to adopt a soft attitude towards Germany either politically or economically and I do not agree with some Hon. Members including … one of my Right Hon. Friends, who feel that Germany is our normal ally and that there is no anti-German prejudice. If there is not there ought to be' (Robins, 1979:25).

In the period up to 1961, a striking feature of Labour's anti-Europeanism was the way it drew its strength from general left-wing groups such as Keep Left (and its successor Keeping Left), Victory for Socialism, the Tribune group and the Campaign for Nuclear Disarmament. The Keep Left group was led by Woodrow Wyatt, Tom Driberg, Ian Mikardo, Richard Crossman and, after 1951, Aneurin Bevan. It numbered some fifty backbenchers and also included a small number of Marxists such as K. Zilliacus and John Platt-Mills on the extreme left (Berrington, 1973:55). Similarly, the Campaign for Nuclear Disarmament (CND) opposed European entanglement and saw NATO, the European Defence Community and in time the EC as, 'the economic reflection of NATO … NATO translated from the military field to the political' (Robins, 1979:17).

In the Conservative Party during the period 1945 to 1961, sceptical groups as such did not exist. In fact, it was the enthusiasts who most notably formed a group, the so-called Strasbourg Tories, who advocated British full participation in European organisations and were led by Churchill's son-in-law, the backbench MP Duncan Sandys. By contrast among the rest of the party there were simply individuals and arguments against closer European engagement. Most prominent here were the pro-Empire-Commonwealthers led by R.A. Butler on the frontbench, and Max Aitken and Major Harry Legge-Bourke, with support from Colonel Hutchinson and J.S. Maclay on the backbenches. The advocates of the Empire-Commonwealth were further backed by the 'out and out antis' who had no particular alternative to promote, but instinctively shared Eden's fears of the consequences of federal integration (Onslow, 1997:32). The Commonwealth Industries Association comprising a number of Conservative MPs also played a key organisational role in mobilising its parliamentary supporters (Kahler, 1984:135). Amongst its members were to be found the major opponents of European integration, including Robin Turton, Peter Walker and Sir Derek Walker-Smith (Aughey, 1996a:204).

As regards the Labour Party in the period between 1961 and 1969, three groupings that took a specifically anti-Market stance were formed following Macmillan's decision that Britain should open negotiations. One of these was the Forward Britain Movement (FBM). This was founded by Richard Briginshaw, a print union activist, and was London-based with quite a wide target audience, publishing a newsletter and pamphlets and organising conferences. Its aims were wide reaching, including reducing arms, increasing education expenditure, rejecting nuclear testing and opposing British membership of the EC. Thus FBM's anti-Market stance was not its sole focus, but it was, 'the task in hand at that moment' (Robins, 1979:35). However, FBM lacked serious sponsorship from among senior Labour Party politicians. Moreover, Robins suggests that it also failed to attract recruits because of its 'blatant chauvinism, threatening language and wider political platform' (Robins, 1979:35).

In 1965 the Britain and the Common Market Group was founded with strong support from the left in the Labour Party. Its parliamentary members included

Douglas Jay, Barbara Castle, Emmanuel Shinwell and Richard Marsh, but the *Guardian* described this group as, 'almost lifeless' by 1967 with only 17 individuals attending meetings (Robins, 1979:51). The rapid rise and decline of Britain and the Common Market requires some comment. The problem for the Labour sceptics was that the death of Gaitskell, in 1963, had robbed them of a leader who commanded respect and whose position had finally been made clear by his resolute opposition to EDC membership and rejection of closer integration at the 1962 Labour Party conference. Wilson's more pragmatic approach – an application hedged with safeguards – shifted the debate away from outright opposition to the nature of terms which might be secured.

Nevertheless, the second application of May 1967 did further mobilise Labour anti-Marketeers, who now became more numerous and vocal. One key result was the foundation of the Labour Committee for the Five Safeguards on the Common Market by another print union activist, Ron Leighton, in 1967, on the basis that membership should only take place if Britain's interests could be safeguarded. The aim was therefore to campaign on behalf of ordinary voters to keep Harold Wilson true to Labour's pledge not to join the EC unless five conditions were observed. These five safeguards had been set out by Hugh Gaitskell in 1962 and were: protection of trade with the Commonwealth, protection of EFTA relations, freedom of economic planning, safeguards for British agriculture, and freedom to pursue an independent foreign policy. In a short period of time the Safeguards Committee recruited Barbara Castle, Richard Crossman and Peter Shore and emerged as the leading Labour Party campaign group within Parliament. It should be noted that the formal aims, which implied that membership might be possible subject to certain terms, belied the fact that this was an anti-entry parliamentary group.

Between 1961 and 1969, Conservative Party opponents similarly became more active and began to coalesce around two organisations. The Anti-Common Market League (ACML) was created in June 1961 by the Conservative MP, Peter Walker. It at least threatened the prospect of mobilising left-wing Conservative opinion which, whatever the state of the Commonwealth, was resistant to any further weakening of it. If this group had also been able to reach out to those on the right of the party, especially what John Ramsden terms 'the old colonial hands and domestic interest groups', it might have been able to develop into a significant internal pressure group (Ramsden, 1996:153). However, the resignation of Anthony Eden in 1957 and the rise of Macmillan robbed the anti-Europeans of a senior cabinet figure to lend weight and credibility to the initiative and altered the balance of power within the party. Despite this weakness, the ACML did actively campaign inside the party and Ramsden notes that it circulated as much literature on the European issue as the Conservative Party itself between 1961 and 1962, supplementing this with a series of public meetings (Ramsden, 1996:153). Keep Britain Out (KBO) was a similar type of group, founded in 1962 by Oliver Smedley and S.W. Alexander. KBO was a people's movement typified by an anti-establishment tone and had a brief high profile role, but quickly fell into decline following de Gaulle's veto in January 1963.

Given the similarity of views amongst the majority of Labour and Conservative politicians, it is surprising that between 1945 and 1969 there was no cross-party collaboration. The challenge for the sceptics was that there were major tensions over the reasons for opposing European integration and no consensus on the preferred alternative policy – whether Empire-Commonwealth or Atlanticist – which prevented a cohesive sceptical movement within each of the parties, let alone between them. In addition to this, in the period up to 1961 anti-Europeans did not link up along cross-party lines in order to strengthen their influence, since their focus was principally on internal battles to hold their respective parties to a sceptical position.

In many ways there was considerable complacency in failing to make these connections but, on the other hand, the bonds of party loyalty were simply too strong and the stakes did not appear to be very high, not least because to varying degrees until 1961 the governments of Attlee, Churchill and Macmillan appeared to be similarly sceptical as to the value of British membership of the supranational institutions. As Sue Onslow notes, so long as the government did not have to take Europe seriously, attacks on government policy 'were mere undercurrents of opinion (Onslow, 1997:32). In the period between 1961 and 1969, on the other hand, cross-party collaboration did not occur since the majority of Conservatives saw a pro-membership position in the context of a winning electoral strategy to beat the Labour Party. This limited the willingness of Conservatives to enter into any kind of collaboration, vulnerable as they were to the pull of party loyalty and the parallel fear of the charge of disloyalty.

However, one common theme in the Labour and Conservative parties was the fact that the identity of opponents did noticeably change between the first and the second periods. In the period up to 1961 the most active sceptics largely comprised an aging generation of parliamentarians. In the aftermath of Macmillan's and then Wilson's application, new and more specifically targeted groups were created to advance Labour and Conservative opposition to EC membership. As is discussed in detail in the next section, the shift from an anti-Europeanism which permeated the establishment to a specifically anti-Market position was thus a crucial difference between sceptics in the first and second periods.

Arguments

As we have seen there was broad agreement in the period from 1945 to 1961 on both left and right of the political spectrum, and indeed across almost the whole of Whitehall, that Britain could not and should not directly participate in any form of supranational integration. Underpinning this consensus, however, there were a number of different arguments. Most attitudes to Europe were shaped by attitudes and commitments on other foreign policy issues, and above all the issues of the US and the Commonwealth. Another controversial area was the extent to which Britain could participate in intergovernmental as opposed to supranational European structures. These differing strands of opinion were an early indication of the disparate views and motivations which were to characterise sceptical thinking over the next half century, widening its reach but also doing much to dilute its effectiveness. In particular, whilst it became increasingly clear what sceptics opposed, it remained unclear what exactly they stood for.

The first argument against involvement in supranational European integration, and the one which was most widely shared, focused on the issue of sovereignty. There was a predominant view that since so many had sacrificed their lives during the Second Wolrd War to ensure Westminster's parliamentary sovereignty along with British territorial integrity, it was neither desirable nor politically feasible voluntarily to surrender these symbols of independence. Often the importance of parliamentary sovereignty was combined with the idea of British distinctiveness; thus according to John Young, 'it seemed unlikely that, with her overseas commitments and her special relationship with America, the United Kingdom could ever merge her own in some European sovereignty' (J. Young, 1984:109). Many anti-Europeans therefore argued that even participation in intergovernmental structures represented the thin end of the wedge, since slowly but surely Britain would be tricked into accepting supranational measures by stealth. Bevin's reaction to the proposal in 1948 to make the Council of Europe a political union was fairly typical, 'I don't like it. When you open that Pandora's Box you will find it full of Trojan horses' (quoted in J. Young, 1984:109).

The bipartisan nature of the commitment to British parliamentary sovereignty was on the face of it somewhat surprising, since as Richard Rose notes, 'for more than 30 years British Socialists had urged a supranational authority to control the vested interests of the capitalist nation states'. However, as Rose goes on to point out, 'when the Labour government came into office, it found that British workers, as well as capitalists, had a vested interest in national sovereignty. The electoral plea, "Put the Nation first" had an unintended double meaning' (Rose, 1950; Dejak, 1993:57). Moreover, from 1945 as the Labour Party settled into government it became increasingly keen to protect the national arrangements that had led to full employment and the creation of a national welfare state system.

The Schuman Plan of 1950 creating the ECSC sharpened some of the key arguments, not least because, out of office, Churchill indicated that participation might be a possibility. In the Labour Party, anti-Europeans argued that membership of the ECSC would damage the British coal and steel industry. On a more general level, it was also argued that membership would hamper a global multilateral approach to economic problems (George, 1998:21). By 1950, and at some cost, the Labour government had completed its nationalisation programme for the coal and steel industries. There was a general feeling that the Schuman Plan would undo Labour's policies and that the ECSC would directly challenge the potential benefits of nationalisation. Moreover, the coal and steel policy sectors contained two of the most influential trade union groups in British industry, and the unions as a whole would not readily acquiesce in participation in the Schuman Plan. As Herbert Morrison, a leading Labour minister, famously remarked, 'it's no damn good – the Durham miners won't wear it' (quoted in Morgan, 1984:420 and J. Young, 1984:156).

A second argument, and one which again had support from both the left and the right of the political spectrum rejected supranational integration but at the same time highlighted the desirability of British leadership in Europe. It was contended that British exceptionalism and especially Britain's global responsibilities required her to lead Europe, as well as the Empire-Commonwealth (Gamble, 1998:14). Indeed, at least part of the opposition to the Schuman Plan stemmed from the fact that the initiative came from Paris and Bonn and did not place Britain at the very centre of developments.

Coupled with the wide consensus against involvement with supranational European integration, there was, however, considerable debate about the relative merits of supporting an Atlantic circle rather than giving preference to the Empire-Commonwealth, along with the appropriate means to achieve the primary goal. Different stances in this debate had an important impact on the kinds of arguments which were advanced against integration (Larres, 1993:85). Thus a group of Bevinites from within the Labour Party argued that a strong link to the United States was absolutely paramount. Accordingly, as Klaus Larres notes, Bevin's interest in Western European Union as a means to ensure that a Europe led by Britain would be able to play the role of a third force in world affairs, was always regarded as a second best alternative to the preferred option of an American commitment to Europe. As soon as the US announced the Marshall Plan and it became clear that American political and military involvement might be forthcoming, Bevin's interest in creating a West European third force quickly waned as well (Larres, 1993:85).

A different set of arguments was advanced by a heterogeneous group that saw the Empire-Commonwealth as a major source of future British political influence and economic well-being. It should be noted that, throughout the late 1940s and most of the 1950s, anti-Europeans of this Empire-Commonwealth school found an important source of support in the economic ministries within Whitehall. Here the predominant view was that Britain could secure its economic well-being without having to sacrifice any economic sovereignty, through the expansion of world trade that would allow Britain to revive its exports and pay for imports.

Within the Labour Party, part of the motivation for support of the Empire-Commonwealth line was that Labour had invested a great deal of effort in establishing the Commonwealth through the independence of India, Pakistan and Ceylon. Activists 'valued the Commonwealth because of its multiracial, non-aligned and non-capitalist nature' (Robins, 1979:21). From 1947 onwards, many Labour MPs therefore opposed the level of effort invested in European negotiations, criticising the government for becoming too engrossed in Europe at the expense of nurturing the Commonwealth (Lieber, 1970:140).

A further spin on this, however, came from the Keep Left group. Here, since Labour's foreign policy was considered 'half-heartedly Socialist and driven into a dangerous dependence on the USA' (Berrington, 1973:59), a Socialist multicultural Commonwealth was the preferred goal. Kenneth Morgan notes that there were some in the Labour Party who seemed to think that the Commonwealth might serve as an intermediate force in world affairs, especially when reinforced by an independent India led by Socialists such as Nehru and Krishna Menon. However, the changing global electoral fortunes of Socialists evidenced by the voting out of

Chifley in Australia and Fraser in New Zealand undermined this particular strand of the argument in relation to the old (white) Commonwealth and attention moved to the new Commonwealth countries (Morgan, 1984:237).

As the above suggests, supporters of the Empire-Commonwealth alternative also tended to exhibit a strong sense of anti-Americanism. Fred Peart, for instance, confessed that 'he was suspicious and disturbed about the American monopoly of capitalism' (Berrington, 1973:53). There was also general suspicion of America's support for European integration and its sponsorship of the United Nations organisation, both perceived as a means to assert global political leadership. This viewpoint had strong support from within the Labour government, and especially from the Chancellor, Hugh Dalton, and Sir Stafford Cripps, President of the Board of Trade. Dalton and Cripps feared, for example, that the customs union suggested in 1947 would both annoy the Commonwealth and lead to the end of British economic independence. As Morgan notes, Cripps in particular was anxious for Britain to pay its way and to regulate its own affairs untrammelled by outside commercial and economic considerations, and was generally hostile to the European idea. His basic loyalty was to the sterling area (Morgan, 1984:391). The economic arguments were therefore vital in establishing the parameters of initial British engagement with the issue of European integration.

Support for the Empire-Commonwealth and a parallel rejection of supranational integration was also evident within the Conservative Party. The Conservatives retained a strong emotional commitment to the white dominions and the Empire which R.A. Butler suggested was still 'the main religion of the Tory party' (Onslow, 1997:31). Hugh Berrington notes that the Empire-Commonwealth wing was characterised by hints of nostalgia for Empire, and tended to comprise urban rather than rural members, with Cambridge better represented than Oxford (Berrington, 1973:172). Paradoxically, given the subsequent right-wing sceptical commitment to 'Americanism' as an antidote to 'Europeanism', this group's belief in the idea of Empire inevitably led them to oppose greater involvement not only in European integration, but also in Atlanticism. In 1951, Captain R.E.B. Ryder and sixty other backbench MPs signed an Early Day Motion (EDM) welcoming the creation of NATO, but noting that the longstanding association of the Commonwealth and Empire remained, 'the first consideration of this country' (Berrington, 1973:172). Whilst this Conservative group shared Labour anti-Europeans' preference for the Empire-Commonwealth as the major forum for the pursuit of British political objectives, they were, however, also keen to maintain the asymmetry of the Empire, balanced in favour of British interests. With one or two notable exceptions, the general view was heavily biased towards English nationalism, holding that the Empire should be transformed into a Commonwealth, but should still remain in the service of English national interests.

Further key arguments against involvement in supranational integration were advanced, in particular by Anthony Eden. Eden was instinctively anti-European and considered Churchill and his pro-European allies within the Conservative Party overly sentimental rather than practical. In Eden's view the British government could not influence West European integration and 'there was no need for

Britain to strive for leadership in Europe to divert attention from federalism' (Onslow, 1997:105). Eden also thought many 'pro-Europeans' like Macmillan too preoccupied with the fear that Germany might soon become resurgent. Eden argued that this fear was misplaced and not something for which it was worth sacrificing British sovereignty. The key to Eden's thinking was that intergovernmentalism was the only acceptable form of integration, and it was this which formed the basis of the Eden Plan of 1952.

But there was also a clear economic underpinning to Eden's thinking. Eden rejected free trade and a common market in favour of imperial preference, an economic principle central to the maintenance of the Empire-Commonwealth as an economic and trading block. Within the Conservative Party, Eden therefore spoke for a large proportion of backbench MPs who opposed Churchill's pro-integration sentiments. In fact, Eden's position was therefore very similar to that of Bevin. Both rejected blue prints and grand designs. Both wanted a united continent but only along intergovernmental lines, to be constructed under British influence and subordinated to and associated with the British Commonwealth. By contrast, Churchill considered there was no contradiction between the Empire-Commonwealth on the one hand, and active support of European federal integration on the other.[1] The loss of Eden following the Suez crisis inflicted a heavy blow on the sceptics' ability to present arguments from the centre of the Conservative Party and with one or two notable exceptions, Eden's departure in 1957 robbed the Conservative anti-Europeans of the first, and arguably last, powerful advocate with mainstream appeal.

Thus the arguments advanced in the period from 1945 to 1961 had many different strands and contained a number of contradictions. These did not, however, come to the surface, first because Europe was not a priority for the governments of this period, and second because a consensus around the rejection of supranational integration masked the divisions amongst anti-Europeans. However, many of the arguments were not fully thought through and lacked a degree of sophistication in advancing a coherent critique of closer British integration in Europe. In particular, xenophobia and an anti-German feeling were a feature of this period and under-pinned a number of arguments, both implicitly and on occasions explicitly.

In the period between 1961 and 1969, and in the face of two applications for membership of the EC, opponents on both left and right of the political spectrum tried – notwithstanding growing economic evidence to the contrary – to breathe fresh life into the idea of the Commonwealth as an alternative international organisation to the EC and the natural focus of British trade (Aughey, 1996a:206). In particular, the Conservative Empire-Commonwealth group played on the economic arguments and sought, 'to construct an alternative political economy around what remained of imperial preference and the need to bind the Commonwealth together' (Gamble, 1998:16). A second argument emphasised the Commonwealth as a world-wide political organisation. In 1962 Patrick Gordon-Walker and Peter Walker published a pamphlet entitled *A Call to the Commonwealth*, which offered an alternative strategy by contending that the first role of Conservative foreign policy should be to strengthen the Commonwealth by using it as a bridge between the first and third worlds 'sacrificing neither the Commonwealth nor national sovereignty' (Aughey, 1996a:202).

These sentiments were echoed in the Labour Party, where Harold Wilson argued that 'we are not entitled to sell our friends and kinsmen down the river for a problematical and marginal advantage in selling washing machines in Dusseldorf' (H. Young, 1999:157). Likewise, in Hugh Gaitskell's speech to the Labour Party conference in 1962 introducing the National Executive Committee (NEC) statement, *Labour and the Common Market*, Commonwealth arguments were a key feature. Gaitskell argued that it was extraordinary 'that some people should be ready, no sooner is it created, to cast it aside!' (Gaitskell, 1996:28). To Gaitskell, 'this remarkable, multiracial association, of independent nations stretching across five continents, covering every race, is something of immense value to the world', and was a significant vehicle of British international influence (Gaitskell, 1996:28). However, by the mid-1960s it was clear that the Commonwealth could not be the economic driver of an alternative international organisation (Aughey, 1996a:207).

As the idea of EC membership moved from the realm of theoretical possibility to that of practical reality, so too the arguments against it evolved and became more substantive. The economic dimension remained the most central and many of the arguments in the period from 1961 to 1969 therefore focused on an economic cost–benefit analysis of whether it really was in Britain's economic interest to join. Thus, in his landmark speech at the 1962 Brighton conference, Gaitskell also focused on the supposed economic benefits of the Common Market which were in his view sufficiently weak not to justify entry.

In addition, however, the sovereignty argument continued to be important. Conservatives like Sir Derek Walker-Smith and Neil Marten were attentive to the issue, with the former pointing out that to relegate arguments concerning sovereignty 'to a sort of postscript to an economic arrangement' was misguided. Foreshadowing the arguments of Enoch Powell a decade later, and in a prophetic warning to Conservatives dazzled in the 1980s by the opportunity to achieve a Single Market with the free movement of goods, capital services and labour, Walker-Smith argued 'there are considerations here which go beyond the considerations of the counting house' (H. Young, 1999:155). These anti-Marketeers also challenged the notion that, once inside the Common Market, Britain could shape it towards her own interests. On the contrary, Neil Marten argued that, 'once in the Common Market the pressure for Britain to become a state in the United States of Europe will be on. The Common Market of the Six only really makes sense if it be federal with a directly elected Parliament' (Aughey, 1996:208). Gaitskell too embraced and advanced arguments concerning the political ramifications of EC membership. He increasingly contended that the political implications of joining the Common Market were as important as any economic arguments and potentially very serious indeed. Concluding that federation, if not the most likely form for the EC, was at least a realistic possibility, he thus gave his famous warning that 'we must be clear about this: it does mean if this is the idea, the end of Britain as an independent European state. I make no apology for repeating it. It means the end of a thousand years of history' (Gaitskell, 1996:23).

A second aspect of the sovereignty argument was based around British exceptionalism. Richard Body was particularly concerned with the agriculture issue, the development of the EC's Common Agricultural Policy (CAP) and its impact on British farming practices. Reginald Maudling and R.A. Butler were broadly sceptical that British interest would be served by any European solutions to Britain's economic situation – whether through EFTA or the EC (Barnes and Cockett, 1994:350). From a historical perspective, Sir Derek Walker-Smith argued that the evolution of the states of Europe was fundamentally dissimilar to that of Britain whose past was 'insular and imperial' rather than 'continental and collective' (H. Young, 1999:1154). A closely related contention was that since Britain was different from other 'continental' European countries, the Common Market would be unable to serve both the Six's own and Britain's political and economic interests.

The arguments deployed in this period also retained a clearly anti-European strand. This was a card that even the most respectable of sceptics, despite their better judgement, could not help playing. Robins notes that evidence from Labour Party documentation suggests that until 1962 anti-German feeling was an important underpinning of European policy (Robins, 1979:20). For example, Gaitskell referred to Europe having, 'a great glorious civilisation' but, in the same breath, noted the 'evil features in European history too – Hitler and Mussolini and today the attitude of some Europeans ...' (Gaitskell, 1996:21). With the exception of one or two notable opponents of closer integration, including the Conservatives, Sir Derek Walker-Smith and Enoch Powell, this was to remain a feature of the discourse, though over the years it was to become increasingly relegated to populist debates in the media.[2]

Arena

Between 1945 and 1961 opposition to closer involvement with European integration projects was confined almost exclusively to the arena of Parliament. The issue of Europe remained the province of the political elite with no public engagement to speak of, in part because it was not regarded as a pressing concern, and in part because what importance it had derived from other issues. It was only in 1961 when Macmillan's decision to launch a membership application broke the bipartisan consensus on opposition to Europe that the issue began to be raised in the public arena for the first time.

Within Parliament, the initial source of criticism in this period came from the Conservative Empire-Commonwealth group and centred on two arguments: that assisting the Europeans to federate would detract and draw attention away from the Empire and Commonwealth and that national sovereignty would be affected by European moves to federate. For example, in the debate in the House of Commons on the first cross-party EDM (33/47) calling on Britain as a long-term policy to join a federal Europe, Anthony Eden argued that the Empire and Commonwealth should always have first consideration. In the foreign affairs debate in January 1948, the concerns of Commonwealth and Europe supporters were again clearly evident inside the Conservative Party, with two amendments tabled attracting fifteen Conservative signatories, one noting anxieties about sovereignty and the other rejecting a federal union (Onslow, 1997:169).

However, at the same time, through Conservative chiding of the Labour government for not participating in the Schuman Plan for a Coal and Steel Community and through Churchill's speeches, the Conservatives gave the impression at home and abroad in the late 1940s that a Conservative government would be a more active and co-operative European partner. The election of October 1951 returned the Conservatives to power under Churchill's first peacetime administration. There was therefore some concern among anti-Europeans that Churchill would adopt a more pro-European stance, and when steps were taken in 1950 to create the explicitly supranational ECSC, and in 1951 to create an EDC, followed by the creation of the EC in 1957, anti-Europeans had to think seriously not only about their own arguments, but also about taking action (Onslow, 1997:31). In the event, there was no real break in policy of Britain standing aside from European integration for three reasons.

First, in the run-up to the February 1950 general election, pressure from Tory grandees was exerted on Churchill to tone down his pro-Europeanism, as the Labour majority was cut to six, the possibility of government became a reality and as doubts about the electoral wisdom of a pro-European stance intensified (Onslow, 1997:55). Second, opposition was also muted because, in government, Churchill was willing to follow Eden's less interventionist line on Europe.[3] In part, this was a direct consequence of divisions within the Conservative leadership over the level of British involvement in Europe, since no Conservative was ready to advocate outright membership of the EC until 1961 (Lieber, 1970:142). Churchill advocated federal integration in Europe with which Britain would be associated, but not a part. Eden, his leading opponent with support from the majority of government ministers and almost all the senior Cabinet ministers, especially R.A. Butler and Reginald Maudling, took a more agnostic position on Europe, which clearly limited Churchill's room for manoeuvre. In part, too, Churchill simply lost interest in leading the pro-Europe group within the Conservative Party. This left the field open for Eden and the Foreign Office, who remained sceptical about the value of closer European engagement. Finally, many in the Conservative Party accepted the principle behind Attlee's argument that it was not reasonable to join in negotiations and then to pull out.

Yet, despite these developments and the apparent strength of the sceptical consensus in both parties, the tide was increasingly to turn in a pro-integrationist direction between 1951 and 1961, influenced by four key factors. First, the government's policy was based on Prime Minister Churchill's loss of interest in the European issue and his willingness to defer to Eden as Foreign Secretary. With the eventual succession of Harold Macmillan in 1957, the pro-Europeans in the Conservative Party got a leader who was willing to take an active role in shaping British European policy and in Sir Alec Douglas-Home, a Foreign Secretary who was more willing to defer to the Prime Minister.

Second, most Conservative parliamentarians, and especially those who opposed British involvement in European supranational integration, were of an older generation. The new intake of 1950 to 1951, 1955 and 1959 had a much greater proportion of pro- than anti-Europeans, including David Eccles, Quintin Hogg, and Edward Heath. Thus, as Peter Thorneycroft noted over the ECSC parliamentary debates, 'the brains of the younger generation were on one side' (H. Young, 1999:67).[4] Whilst they overwhelmingly lost that particular battle, it was the first indication that the new generation was increasingly willing to give serious consideration to closer British engagement in European structures and this slowly began to change the balance of opinion within the parliamentary Conservative Party. Interestingly, in the Labour Party, this generational renewal was a later process, occurring principally in the 1960s, and the effect was much more mixed with a more sceptical anti-Market generation slightly more predominant than pro-Marketeers. That said, the pro-Marketeers were increasingly committed and influential figures such as William Rodgers, Shirley Williams and, above all, Roy Jenkins were to be a source of growing tension and division within the party.

With the advent of the Suez crisis, the psychological impact of the resignation of Anthony Eden, the leading anti-European of his time, was a significant loss to the sceptical cause. Gladwyn Jebb suggests that, 'something like a collective nervous breakdown' of the political elite now took place, culminating in a loss of nerve, and that it was here that the major sources of the shift from anti- to a pro-membership position were to be found (Shore, 2000:55–7). The failure of Britain (and France) in the Suez War raised serious doubts about the ability of the British government to exercise influence in the foreign policy field without US support. With the loss too of the older generation from senior positions in the civil service, the tide was beginning to turn, especially as influential voices in the major departments shifted positions from guarded opposition to forthright endorsement of an application to the EC (H. Young, 1999:172).

The third symptom of the weakness of the bipartisan sceptical position was that there was little or no strategic investment in developing the economic arguments that underpinned anti-European positions. The principal economic basis of opposition to Europe was the role of sterling and imperial preference and this became the key battleground for pro-Europeans. Peter Thorneycroft, the President of the Board of Trade, specifically took on the Conservative Party in this area in 1954 and defeated a conference motion that was critical of the General Agreement on Tariffs and Trade (GATT). Combined with the ending of imperial preferences and the declining importance of Commonwealth trade, these moves steadily undermined an economic alternative to supranational integration. For the Labour anti-Europeans a similar weakness was evident. From the mid-1950s, EC membership seemed so unlikely that they were unwilling to invest intellectual effort in seeking out viable alternative options.

Finally, there was a political failure to identify alternatives to the supranational institutions that further undermined the case for staying out. Kaiser argues, 'that before Suez and the second wave of decolonisation after 1957, the Commonwealth had helped to compensate for Britain's quite dramatic economic and political decline. While the significance of its economic arrangements had long been questioned within Whitehall, by 1961 it was obvious that the Commonwealth also lacked any political cohesion' (Kaiser, 1993:148). In this regard, Peter Shore remarked that Wilson had a '... genuine concern and feeling for the Commonwealth but found in his dealings with them in the mid sixties and after increasing tension and estrangement'; in something of an understatement he further noted that meetings of Commonwealth heads of government 'were increasingly fraught and unhappy events' (Shore, 2000:70). For Britain to retain what was still perceived as world power status and a 'special relationship' with the United States, for some it now seemed inevitable that the European Communities needed to be substituted for the Commonwealth.

Hence, despite the prevailing antipathy towards the idea of European integration, and the low priority assigned to it, apparently further confirmed by the creation of the European Free Trade Area in 1960, the position of the sceptics particularly within the Conservative Party was being increasingly undermined by the late 1950s. Against this backdrop, the effect of Macmillan's declaration in July 1961 that Britain would apply for membership of the EC was to bring the hitherto suppressed divisions over Europe both within and between the parties into the open. Indeed the arena in which the struggle against EC membership took place between 1961 and 1969 was the political parties themselves. All the leading parties treated the issue of membership as important, and this led to considerable intra-party debate on the government and opposition benches alike. In addition, whilst a treaty could be passed using Crown powers, at some stage the decision to join would require implementing legislation and at this point opponents could try and defeat the policy within the arena of Parliament. Thus, 'by embarking formally on negotiations for entry the party leadership had broken the crust on a seething pot of sentiment and commitment' (Turner, 1996:336).

Macmillan's scope for manoeuvre should certainly have been circumscribed by the group of sceptical Tory MPs who opposed the decision, the majority of activists within the Conservative Party and the Cabinet, quite apart of course from the Labour Party. However, the anti-Europeans were outflanked by the context in which they found themselves and the tactics of the Prime Minister. In terms of the economic context in particular, the circumstances were now difficult. As we have noted, despite emotional attachment to the Commonwealth, by 1961 it was not a serious economic alternative. Moreover, the argument that the Commonwealth would not accept British membership was undermined when a tour by several ministers to Commonwealth countries in early summer 1961 showed that opposition to Britain's entry into the EC was not as clear cut as many had thought.

In addition, the economic ministries in Whitehall were starting to recognise that the *status quo* was looking increasingly unattractive. The Ministry of Agriculture, Fisheries and Food was convinced that the old subsidy system was too costly and that joining a common market in agriculture would curb imports from the Commonwealth and thereby strengthen home production. In Cabinet, the new Minister of Agriculture, Christopher Soames, 'argued that the strong opposition by the National Farmers Union (NFU) was only directed against joining the EC without derogations. As there would not necessarily be a decrease in their net income the farmers who, of course, constituted an influential section of the Conservative Party, could surely be convinced of the necessity of a different system of subsidies' (Kaiser, 1993:148). Some influential interest groups, especially the City and a majority of business and industry were also supportive of the government applying for membership.

In terms of tactical considerations, early resistance to the change in policy was exceptionally difficult. In part this was because the Prime Minister cleverly neutralised opposition by announcing that the government would merely start negotiations with the Community to explore the possibility of a formal application if acceptable terms could be secured. For opponents in both parties this cautious approach was difficult to confront head-on. Moreover, the Conservative anti-Europeans were unwilling to threaten a Cabinet schism since to them the most likely outcome was a breakdown in the negotiations or a French veto.

A second reason for the rather muted opposition was the Prime Minister's decision not to treat the change in policy as one based on political grounds. Instead, Macmillan chose to portray it in public and to the Conservative Party as an essentially economic move. Peter Morris argues that Macmillan was acutely aware of the consequences of intra-party disputes on Britain's role in the world economy, and that he 'responded by underplaying the political significance of Common Market membership and by emphasising that his vision of the future had no place for the federalist ambitions of some continental Conservatives' (Morris, 1996:127). Stephen George goes further in suggesting that Macmillan deliberately gave the impression through the cautious tone of his announcement that the decision was made without enthusiasm and was one that was necessary, but not welcome (George, 1998:33).

Third, while Macmillan raised the issue of a membership application, it was left to the personal commitment and the energy of Edward Heath, as the second in command in the Foreign Office, to promote the shift in government policy towards membership. In this way, Macmillan could present himself as a sort of honest broker between different strands of opinion, whilst in reality aiding and abetting the pro-membership faction. Fourth, the caution of Conservative anti-Europeans was in part also dictated by the fact that, while Macmillan's three rivals for the leadership of the party, Butler, Hogg and Maudling, all opposed entry, they were acutely sensitive to the need to avoid Conservative Party disputes on Britain's role in the world economy. In this regard, the spectre of the historic divisions over the Corn Laws and tariff reform loomed large over them. The newly created ACML was to suffer directly from the resulting unwillingness of Cabinet ministers to mobilise against the application. Whilst then it may have looked as though the leadership of the Conservative Party shared remarkable solidarity over the application, Kaiser argues that the position was in reality 'the beginning of the famous "agreement to differ" policy of the 1975 referendum' (Kaiser, 1993:153). One important corollary was that Macmillan dealt with internal opposition 'in a very emollient way and made no attempt to coerce the dissidents' (Morris, 1996:128).

Closely connected with this, however, was Macmillan's use of his position as Prime Minister to manage the balance of power within the Cabinet. In July 1960, Macmillan ensured that the three most sensitive Cabinet posts dealing with Europe went to supporters of membership. Edward Heath became Lord Privy Seal and deputy to the Foreign Secretary with responsibility for European diplomacy, Christopher Soames was appointed Minister of Agriculture and Duncan Sandys was made Head of the Commonwealth Relations Office. Perhaps more importantly, Macmillan neutralised opposition to the European project within the Cabinet by appointing R.A. Butler as chairman of the Cabinet committee considering the details of the negotiations, 'thus depriving Butler of his capacity to campaign against the European project' (Pinto-Dutchinsky, 1987:159).

There was also a partisan dimension to opposition to the initiative. It was the Conservatives' policy, designed in part to put some clear blue water between themselves and Labour and to refresh Conservative Party ideas. This put a premium on Tory dissidents' loyalty, as did the approaching 1964 general election – although ironically Europe was not, in the event, to feature as an issue in this election (Barnes and Cockett, 1994; Morris, 1996:127). Equally, therefore, the Labour Party was not instinctively inclined to assist them. However, the shock of Macmillan's announcement caught the Labour Party unprepared and the leadership took some time to formulate an appropriate response, not least in view of the tensions within the party's own ranks stemming from the growing influence of pro-Market individuals. More quick to react were the backbench MPs, and the left-wing factions inside the Labour Party rapidly mobilised support for an anti-Common Market position. The Victory for Socialism Group issued a manifesto demanding that the party oppose membership as reactionary and capitalist. Ultimately, it was the sceptics who prevailed, and between 1961 and 1962, the party took up a stance of opposition to membership except in the unlikely event that acceptable terms could be reached on the five conditions set out by the NEC.

In the initial parliamentary divisions, few Tory MPs had the courage to vote with the opposition party in opposing the talk about talks. Only one Conservative MP, Anthony Fell, was willing to vote against the proposal, together with four Labour MPs who defied their own party instructions to abstain.[5] Nevertheless, over twenty Tory MPs were prepared to abstain on the first vote on the issue. In time, as the campaign developed momentum, forty-seven Conservative MPs signed an anti-Common Market motion in December 1962, though once again few were willing to cross-vote in the debates themselves. Despite this, the Conservative 'antis' had at least indicated a propensity to rebel and this was enough to encourage the Macmillan government to restrain its enthusiasm and to moderate the language that it used in public. Yet, as Ramsden remarks, 'if the government's rhetoric was inhibited, the will to carry through the policy did not waver. Indeed, the longer that negotiations went on at Brussels, the more prestige it had to invest in ultimate success' (Ramsden, 1996:153).

Robert Lieber notes that the membership application was justified in terms of the economic and commercial circumstances rather than on the basis of a commitment to the idea of a united Europe. Through this means, Macmillan opened up the opportunity for sectoral producer and consumer groups to support a pro-membership policy (Lieber, 1970:166). With the issue of membership now beginning to enter the public arena, the mass media and interest groups as well as the major political parties became involved in the debate, and a number of opportunities arose in which public opinion could be expressed. The issue of Europe figured prominently in several by-elections, for instance, while a wide range of well-publicised public opinion polls also allowed the arguments to be rehearsed. Overall, however, public attitudes continued to fluctuate throughout the decade, giving the overriding impression of searching for leadership on the issue. Ultimately, then, it was not to be public resistance any more than the opposition of the parliamentary sceptics which halted the progress of Macmilllan's application, but rather the veto of General de Gaulle in January 1963.

Perhaps the most remarkable aspect of this second period, however, was not the cautiousness of the Macmillan government of 1957 to 1964, but the second attempt to join the EC made by the Wilson government of 1964 to 1967. What was so surprising was that despite the increasing influence of the Labour pro-Marketeers, Wilson was not from the pro-European wing of the Labour Party. Moreover, the majority of his party were opposed to EC membership, and Wilson was widely considered, as John Campbell summarised it, to be '… thoroughly conservative in his personal tastes and habits and a devout little Englander at heart' (Campbell, 1993:163). Notwithstanding all these apparent strengths, what the anti-Europeans in the Labour Party crucially failed to do was to secure a commitment in principle to oppose membership. Against the backdrop of a series of external pressures and by deploying an internal strategy that effectively constrained opponents within the party, especially in Cabinet, Wilson therefore managed to outflank very senior anti-Marketeers who included Tony Crosland, Denis Healey and Peter Shore. In particular, however, there were three reasons why anti-Marketeers were unable to make an impact.

First, so long as the power of the sceptics within the party was dependent on the Prime Minister, opposition to a second application was built on weak foundations. The toleration, if not acceptance, by the sceptics of Wilson's preference for running the government through a kitchen cabinet effectively circumvented the sceptical majority inside the Cabinet. Despite the presence of serious political anti-Marketeers such as Richard Crossman and Barbara Castle inside the kitchen Cabinet, there were few other sceptics within this grouping, and the most influential member, Marcia Williams, was as pragmatic on the European issue as the Prime Minister was known to be.

Second, Wilson was ultimately willing to use the European issue to his own and to the Labour Party's advantage and this gave him great flexibility. For Wilson, the 1967 application served three purposes: it stole a leading Conservative policy commitment; it was a means to unite the Labour Party; and it diverted attention away from a series of mounting policy disasters at home and abroad, including balance of payments and immigration problems, and growing tensions inside the Commonwealth, especially over Rhodesia's Unilateral Declaration of Independence and India/Pakistan relations. In the view of Uwe Kitzinger, the application was 'a device that looked and sounded like business'. Above all it was, as Lieber comments, a consequence of a 'collapse of alternatives' for Labour's foreign policy that led a pragmatic Prime Minister to apply (Lieber, 1970:260). What sceptics in the Cabinet failed to do was to raise the stakes sufficiently that the Prime Minister did not feel able to play (Kitzinger, 1973:280; Ponting, 1989:213).

Third, there was complacency amongst the sceptics that took two forms. First, a number of Cabinet ministers felt that Wilson's application was not serious and that outright opposition would be unnecessary. In his autobiography, Peter Shore, Secretary of State for Economic Affairs between 1967 and 1969, argued there was good reason to believe that Wilson's decision to probe the EC in 1967 was motivated not by any shift in personal conviction, but by a desire to outwit both Edward Heath and the pro-Marketeers in the Cabinet led by George Brown '… by demonstrating that no tolerable conditions of entry were possible' (Shaw, 1994:99). Another group led by Crossman and Jay came to a similar view that the application was not very serious. Crossman blamed the application on a small group around the Prime Minister, commenting that 'all the decisions are taken by the Prime Minister and his little group behind the scenes' and dismissing it as a 'silly gimmick' (Crossman, 1991:206). For Douglas Jay, Wilson was obsessed with his public image and feared the pro-Market chairman of the Mirror group (Cecil King) who in collusion with George Brown 'coerced' Wilson into making the application (Jay, 1980:367–8).

At the same time, a second strand of complacency amongst the sceptics related to de Gaulle. Many sceptics simply considered the success of the application unlikely whilst de Gaulle remained the French president. As Oliver Daddow notes, the anti-Marketeers – Crossman, Jay, Healey and Crosland – 'were willing if not exactly happy to let Wilson proceed because they predicted that either no acceptable terms could be found or de Gaulle would destroy this European initiative with a veto' (Daddow, 2002).

The effort invested by the Prime Minister in controlling the whole application process should at a tactical level have been sufficient to trigger greater sceptical reflection. In the period after April 1966, Barbara Castle noted in her diary that the initiative was 'ruthlessly stage-managed, under the cover of the soothing phrase: "It is of course for Cabinet to decide"' (Castle, 1984:125). Through avoiding any vote on the formal decision to apply, Wilson lured the Cabinet into debating the terms of an application rather than the principle of membership. As Chris Wrigley notes, 'eventually those confronting him found it was hard to go into reverse, having gone so far' (Wrigley, 1993:130). Moreover, Wilson by-passed normal policy making procedures and personally organised the production and circulation of papers through the Cabinet Office. Through suppression of dissenting papers, for example Crossman's paper on the economic costs and benefits of joining, written in March 1967, the views of opponents of the application were not fully aired (Ponting, 1989:205). Indeed, Peter Shore contended that the appointment as Private Secretary of the 'ardent Europhile', Michael Pallister, 'made certain that no Euro-sceptic critique or argument went unchallenged' (Shore, 2000:71).

Despite these tactics, that were undoubtedly important, some responsibility for failing to oppose the policy as a matter of principle rests with leading sceptical Cabinet ministers. At a key Cabinet meeting to discuss the application, Douglas Jay put a number of counter-arguments to membership, but in his diary entry

'… wondered afterwards whether I should have said more' which at least hints at a recognition of this point (Jay, 1980:384). Ultimately, no Cabinet minister was willing directly to challenge the Prime Minister who had chosen 'to identify the bid firmly with himself'. Moreover, in the final analysis, no anti-Market Cabinet minister was willing to resign over the issue of membership (Hitchens, 1993:9). Once again, therefore, it was not sceptic opposition, but the veto of de Gaulle in November 1967, which put paid to Wilson's application bid.

Conclusion

In looking back at the quarter century after the Second World War for signs of opposition to closer European integration, the specific issues that concerned anti-Europeans between 1945 and 1961 were of a second order nature. They related chiefly to the waste of scarce governmental energy in focusing on the European arena and the opportunity cost of neglecting the Empire-Commonwealth. In many ways these arguments were genuinely anti-European – this was not a rejection merely of the European Economic Community since it was not debated until 1955 and only came into existence in 1957. Opponents held views of outright opposition to any involvement in Europe that might come at the expense of the Empire-Commonwealth. Once the EC was created, and particularly after Macmillan's application bid, the target of the sceptics' opposition came into clearer focus and most anti-Europeans shifted to an anti-Market position within their respective parties. However, to this group were added new anti-Marketeers who had never been anti-European, but specifically opposed the EC and British entanglement with it.

In terms of the opportunities to oppose government policy, on initial scrutiny, the first period offered few opportunities to oppose policy that was anyway essentially sceptical of closer supranational integration. However, complacency gave both Macmillan and Wilson sufficient leeway to make applications, albeit applications hedged with safeguards. By the mid-1960s the failure of sceptics to articulate any serious alternative to membership and the parlous state of the British economy made their own position on Britain and the EC much less secure than may have been evident to them at the time. What is also striking is just how pervasive party loyalties were in preventing a more unified opposition to applications from both Conservative and Labour governments. Some were more vocal in the House of Commons than others, but few were willing to vote against their party whip on the issue of Europe.

Thus the absence of an organised opposition to closer European integration and, above all, the absence of advocacy of realistic alternatives to membership, as well as complacency, were the keys to explaining why sceptics lost control of the agenda so quickly in the 1960s. A corollary of this was that the sceptics failed to fight for the information and resources which might have strengthened their position. As the respective Prime Ministers personally committed themselves to membership the weakness of the sceptics' position quickly became apparent.

Nevertheless, the sceptics emerged from this period having learnt a number of important lessons. A key lesson was the need to fight and advocate more loudly over the European issue to counter the fickleness of Prime Ministers who might be tempted to use the European issue to their own personal and party electoral advantage, drawing on the support of uncommitted MPs who would follow their leadership if the policy shift was managed competently. Second, sceptics quickly recognised the need to develop arguments in two areas: to indicate there were alternatives to membership and to highlight its costs to the country and to individual voters. This also led to the third lesson, the need to move the debate beyond Westminster into the public domain where a more natural sceptical constituency could be directly engaged on the question of whether Britain should join the EC. The extent to which sceptics were successful in implementing these lessons is the subject of Chapters 3 and 4.

Notes

1 A number of prominent supporters of Empire such as Robert Boothby and Leo Amery also took this line (see Berrington, 1973:168).

2 See, for example, Powell's Britain and Europe speech in which he drew attention to the fact that he was not anti-European and had therefore suffered at the hands of the 'East of Suez brigade' (Powell, 1996:77).

3 Onslow notes that a further reason for this was that from 1951 European integration became entangled with the issue of German rearmament and few political figures were willing to advocate British membership of the EDC (Onslow, 1997:225).

4 Interestingly, even young devotees of the Empire and Commonwealth were beginning to argue that imperial preferences required active participation in the EC.

5 The MPs were Michael Foot, Emrys Hughes, Konni Zilliacus and S.O. Davies (Lieber, 1970:170).

3 British entry to the Common Market, 1970–1974

As the last chapter discussed, once the leadership of both major political parties had committed Britain to exploring the possibility of membership of the European Communities, the stakes and nature of opposing closer European integration began to change dramatically. Between 1970 and 1972, this opposition underwent a further set of changes. In examining these issues this chapter covers the period of office of the Conservative government between 18 June 1970 and 28 February 1974, but focuses on the set piece opportunity that emerged for anti-Marketeers to oppose British membership of the European Communities.[1] This occurred when in October 1971 after nearly seven months of negotiations the government of Edward Heath put to a vote the principle of entry followed by the presentation of the European Communities Bill before Parliament for ratification. The ratification process took a further nine months and eventually culminated in a vote on 13 July 1972 in which the House of Commons passed the European Communities Act by 301 votes to 284.

Edward Heath managed to secure approval for the policy of Common Market membership only through the exploitation of a range of government resources to deliver successful votes in Parliament. However, the failure of the anti-Marketeers during this period cannot be attributed solely to the actions of the leadership of the Conservative Party. On the one hand, sceptics were undone by the willingness of nearly seventy pro-Market Labour MPs to conspire with the government, and ultimately to vote against their own party in supporting the principle of membership and delivering parliamentary ratification of the European Communities Bill. By contrast, the reluctance of most Conservative anti-Marketeers to place the European issue above that of party loyalty and their unwillingness to vote against their own party, or to forge an alliance with the Labour Party, significantly limited the effectiveness of their opposition and ultimately condemned them to failure. In addition to this, Labour anti-Marketeers were constrained by the actions of Harold Wilson who imposed an official Labour Party position of abstention on the parliamentary party, further limiting the ability of anti-Marketeers to defeat the government.

As we shall see in Chapters 6 and 7, the weak foundations upon which Britain's continued membership was built, the presence of a group of anti-Marketeers inside the political elite who were unreconciled to membership, and the way the European issue was subsequently handled, eventually rebounded on the leadership of both the Labour and Conservative Parties.

Opportunity

The opening of accession negotiations by Edward Heath's government on 30 June 1970 signalled the final British attempt to join the European Communities. The negotiations lasted from the end of June 1970 until 22 January 1972 when Edward Heath signed the accession treaty in Brussels. Following parliamentary ratification in July 1972, Britain along with Ireland and Denmark became members of the EC on 1 January 1973.

During the negotiations, the government briefly flirted with the idea of a referendum, but Heath took the view that Parliament was most likely to deliver a supportive vote. Official justifications for this line included the un-British nature of a referendum and the reliability of a Parliament that was the envy of the world in doing the matter justice (Butler and Kitzinger, 1976:11). Heath was supported in this view by Jeremy Thorpe, the leader of the Liberal Party, and Harold Wilson, both of whom drew on work of Edmund Burke to argue that MPs were elected to decide on issues on behalf of their constituents. This left open the question as to when and how Parliament should approve Britain's membership. In theory, international treaties could be approved by Crown prerogative, but Heath was reluctant to take this path. It was finally decided to handle the issue of membership through enabling legislation that took the form of the 1972 European Communities Act. In effect, this would change the domestic laws of the land to include the forty volumes of EC regulations that had to be incorporated into British law. Through this means and at a stroke Britain adopted the directives and regulations accumulated over the fifteen years the Community had been in existence (Butler and Kitzinger, 1976:23).

The parliamentary arena offered a significant opportunity for anti-Marketeers to defeat the government. Edward Heath's majority of only thirty set against the fact that Neil Marten, a leading anti-Marketeer, estimated the Conservative opponents as numbering between seventy and eighty, meant that anti-Marketeers held an influential position within the party (Norton, 1978:67). When Conservative sceptics were added to the strength of anti-Market feeling in the Labour Party, the numerical strength of anti-Marketeers in Parliament meant that any vote should have provided an opportunity to defeat the government. The launch of a third attempt to join the Community took place against an unstable political and economic background. Another application was not popular amongst the electorate and public opinion polls indicated that more than half opposed the negotiations (Jowell and Spence, 1975). There was therefore good reason to think that though public opinion was volatile there was a strong possibility that most would vote against membership, either because they were not much interested in Europe or because of nationalistic prejudices. In fact, as defeat of the anti-Marketeers in Parliament loomed, the idea of a referendum became increasingly important as means of trying to thwart the Conservative government's plans and the pusillanimous response of the Labour frontbench.

Opponents: who were they?

In the face of the high degree of public uncertainty about entry, the Conservative Party's 1970 manifesto stepped back from its previous unconditional commitment to membership, and offered a more modest commitment 'to negotiate, no more no less' (H. Young, 1999:223). In addition to this, however, the pro-entry policy lacked broad consensus inside the Conservative Party and received no mention from nearly two-thirds of Conservative candidates in their own 1970 election addresses. Indeed, about a tenth had stated either their outright opposition or major reservations to Britain joining the EC (Ramsden, 1996:335). The Conservative government's commitment to membership was therefore built on quite insecure party foundations. Indeed, the opening of negotiations some twelve days after the general election in which Europe was hardly mentioned caught many Conservative backbenchers by surprise.

Heath coupled the rapid opening of negotiations with a strategy of excluding known sceptics from government, with Enoch Powell the most notable casualty. Of those who were approached, only one, Neil Marten, refused Heath's invitation to join the government. Where sceptics' standing in the Conservative Party meant they could not be ignored, Heath appointed them to posts remote from the negotiations and day-to-day contact with EC institutions (Kitzinger 1973:154). So successful was this strategy that Teddy Taylor, who joined the administration as a junior minister in 1970, and Jasper More, a whip, were the only MPs on the government payroll to resign over Europe in 1971. Most anti-Marketeers were therefore to be found on the Conservative backbenches rather than in the Cabinet.

In this way the Cabinet remained remarkably cohesive on the issue whilst a sizeable minority of around sixty MPs, amounting to some ten per cent of the Conservative parliamentary party, were opposed (S. Young, 1973:275). There were approximately thirty to forty Conservative backbench MPs who since the 1960s had been longstanding opponents to British entry; approximately twenty new MPs who, as the negotiations progressed, expressed anti-Market views, '... and a number of others who were also known to have doubts on the issue' (Norton 1978:66).[2] Since the Conservative manifesto's commitment was 'to negotiate, no more no less', it was difficult for the government to argue that the sceptics' position was inconsistent with party policy. However, there was a hard core of these MPs who were willing to clash with the party leadership on the issue of membership. An indication of the size of this group was an Early Day Motion signed by 44 MPs opposing British entry and indicating that no terms could be secured which could be deemed acceptable. For Heath, by contrast, the terms were of less importance than the principle of membership. Since the size of this group was larger than the government's majority, there was thus the real prospect of Conservative anti-Marketeers defeating the government in Parliament if they remained resolute.

Interestingly, members of this group were also united on other issues as well. There was, for example, a high degree of overlap between those opposing Common Market entry and those opposing sanctions against Rhodesia, the 1972 immigration rules, the government's 1973 Middle East policy, the 1973 Counter-Inflation Bill (amendment to clause four) and, to a lesser extent, the Northern Ireland (Temporary Provisions) Bill (H. Young, 1999:222). Many of these MPs clustered around Enoch Powell who had been sacked from the shadow cabinet in April 1968 and who as a former leadership contender against Edward Heath gave this dissenting group a wider purpose of challenging the Prime Minister's leadership of the party.

Further complicating the picture was the fact that there were several sceptical groupings inside the parliamentary party. Many of the more established MPs were supporters of the Anti-Common Market League (ACML), founded by Peter Walker in 1961 to oppose Macmillan's bid for membership, as discussed in Chapter 2. ACML remained a Conservative grouping, not least owing to its righ-wing critique of the Conservative party leadership (Kitzinger, 1973:233). There was also a large overlap with the backbench 1970 Group that was registered with the whips to prevent charges of conspiracy against the leadership. The 1970 Group met as a dining club under the chairmanship of Sir Derek Walker-Smith with parliamentary activists numbering just over fifty. Its members, directed by Neil Marten and linked to Powell, became active as soon as the third application bid was announced at the end of June 1970 and made a point of tabling hostile questions to their own government, especially at question time.

In the Labour Party, opposition to the Common Market was more widespread, although in many ways more fragmented, with more of a crossover between parliamentary and non-parliamentary groupings. A longstanding force outside Parliament was the Forward Britain Movement (FBM), created by Richard Briginshaw in 1961. The Labour Safeguards Committee founded in 1967 eventually transformed into the Labour Committee for Safeguards on the Common Market (CSCM), unifying with the parliamentary group Britain and the Common Market which included Douglas Jay, Barbara Castle, Emmanuel Shinwell and Richard Marsh and which had some limited support outside Parliament. The CSCM recruited Labour Party members directly and this group enjoyed a surge of support after the February 1970 White Paper *Costs and Benefits of Entry* (Cmnd 4289) and the June 1970 election. A further indication of the strength of Labour anti-Market feeling in Parliament was a statement in the left-wing *Tribune* weekly paper of seventy-four Labour MPs opposing Common Market membership on any grounds, organised by John Stonehouse and William Blyton.

Other groups broadly on the left of the party supported these Labour anti-Marketeers. The Tribune Group, which gained significantly in numerical strength after the 1970 and 1974 general elections, was resolutely opposed to EC membership (Robins, 1979:87). Anthony King notes, however, that 'though most left-wingers were anti-European, not all anti-Common Market MPs were left-wingers' (King 1977: 34). A substantial minority of moderates were also against membership, including Douglas Jay, Peter Shore and Barbara Castle, all senior party figures. The Labour Party was therefore more anti-Market than the Conservative Party, but it was also more divided at every level of the parliamentary party, on the frontbench as well as the backbenches (Robins, 1979:85).[3]

Outside Parliament there were a number of other anti-Market groups. Ann Kerr, a Tribune MP until 1970, founded Women Against the Common Market (WACM) to highlight increases in sugar, tea, coffee and lamb prices. WACM aimed to raise the consciousness of women who were not members of a trade union, to encourage them to influence '... their trade-unionist husbands into taking anti-Market steps' (Robins, 1979:108). Trades Unions Against the Common Market (TUACM) had similar origins to the Forward Britain Movement and had as its purpose convincing uncommitted trades unions that EC membership was not in their interest. Lynton Robins argues that TUACM played an important role as an organisation through which anti-Market activists could operate. David Bolton and Dai Francis both members of the Communist Party and members of TUACM were, for instance, influential in securing an anti-Market position in the National Union of Mineworkers and in turn this ensured that the block votes of the TUC were delivered against membership (Robins, 1979:109).

Although a hard core of Conservative backbenchers and Labour frontbenchers were opposed to Heath's opening of negotiations on membership, the shadow of the broader party struggle made co-operation to oppose Heath extremely difficult. Nevertheless, with the partisan struggle of the 1970 general election overcome, minds were concentrated by the prospect of membership becoming a reality. Anti-Marketeers in both parties initially hoped that their respective groups, the Conservative Anti-Common Market League and the Labour Safeguards Committee, might move to incorporate the other. This gave way to a feeling that what was really needed was an umbrella inter-party organisation which would allow the partisan groups in each of the main parties to co-exist, yet unify them in a common cause against membership. This would dampen the criticism of disloyalty to the party, since the Conservative and Labour sceptic groups would continue as distinct entities inside and outside Parliament. It would have the added advantage of better spreading the message of opposition to membership to party groups and yet at the same time improve access to round tables and women's groups which did not want speakers with specific party political labels.

The result was the creation of the first all-party sceptic group, the Common Market Safeguards Campaign (CMSC) which was launched in February 1970 with Douglas Jay as its chairman and Ron Leighton its full time director (Robins, 1979:107). Its parliamentary members formed an all-party Safeguards Group with Sir Robin Turton as chairman and the secretary a Liberal MP providing administrative support. The contrast between the sceptic groups and the cluster of inter-party organisations dedicated to securing British membership was striking. The pro-European groups had existed in various forms for over two decades. The merger of the UK Council of the European Movement and Britain in Europe into the British Council of the European Movement combined two pre-existing organisations with different comparative advantages. In addition, the pro-membership campaign was launched well in advance of both the government's own campaign and the anti-Marketeers' campaign (Kitzinger, 1977:190).

Once an umbrella group had been created, moreover, partisan differences directly limited the effectiveness of the sceptics' campaign objectives in several ways. The group's name was minimalist in order to appeal to as many opponents of membership of differing political hue as possible. But the fact that the name was taken from one of the Labour Party's leading sceptic groupings betrayed the fact that Labour supporters dominated it. Hence although the Common Market Safeguards Campaign had both Labour and Conservative leaders and comprised twenty-two Conservative and thirty-eight Labour MPs, the perception was of Labour dominance and the group never overcame its difficulties in recruiting Conservative MPs.

CMSC also lacked the solidarity of the pro-membership inter-party groups. In part this was a consequence of attempting to be as inclusive as possible by admitting as members both those who genuinely wanted to open negotiations to see if acceptable terms could be reached, and those who opposed entry outright and knew that the safeguards they wanted could never be secured as the EC stood (Kitzinger, 1977:238). By concentrating on the unacceptable nature of the terms of entry rather than on the principle of membership, the anti-Marketeers hoped to build a broad-based alliance (Butler and Kitzinger, 1976:15). But this robbed the anti-Marketeers of a single focus and the anti-Market camp remained fundamentally divided in a way in which pro-integration members were not, since the latter were united and focused on a single objective: British membership of the EC.

In addition, CMSC had great difficulty in securing sufficient resources to mount an effective campaign against Common Market membership. Kitzinger notes that, in part, company directors feared opposing government policy and risking government disapproval in the form of the withholding of licences, grants and contracts and even honours (Kitzinger, 1977:236). But the problem was exacerbated by a lack of central direction and professional fundraisers to generate and deploy resources, and the overall impression being one of amateurism.

A further problem was that on the issue of its aims and objectives, CMSC was torn between two strategies: whether to focus on the parliamentary arena or whether to concentrate on persuading the electorate that membership was not in its interest. In the parliamentary arena, energies were directed towards three groupings: the government, in order to secure the safeguards on membership; the Labour opposition, to persuade them to swing against entry; and backbenchers of both parties, to deliver anti-Market votes. The tactics used in relation to the latter included either direct appeals or the indirect approach of encouraging constituency associations to put pressure on their MPs. The alternative more populist strategy was to focus on the mass public through direct appeals via the press and broadcasting. The all-party Common Market Safeguards Campaign eventually settled on an elite focused parliamentary strategy, while arguing that a decision of Parliament was not enough in and of itself. By contrast, the pro-Europeans were clear in their two-pronged focus on the party leadership and parliamentarians as well as the country at large, and they had at their disposal considerable sums of money to pursue both these objectives simultaneously.

A second campaign group of quite a different character to CMSC was Keep Britain Out (KBO) founded in 1962. This group became dormant after the failure of the first and launch of the second application but was reinvigorated by Christopher Frere-Smith who became its chairman in 1966. Frere-Smith was a former Liberal who stood as an anti-Market candidate in the 1966 general election, but who, having failed to be elected, changed strategies to form a cross-party alliance through KBO. The group was committed to free trade and saw the Common Market as a protectionist organisation. It brought together a diverse range of outright opponents to membership, ranging from right-wingers and Conservative diehards to left-wing Labour activists. Its committee included backbench MPs, notably the Conservative Richard Body, the Scottish nationalist Donald Stewart, and Oliver Smedley, a former Liberal Vice-President and co-founder of the Institute for Economic Affairs. However, KBO was essentially a people's movement. The diversity of KBO made co-ordination impossible. It was grass roots in nature, with little central direction and was based on local initiatives. It aimed at proving that the political elite was wrong to press for membership, that the will of the people and their institutions were being violated by their leaders' betrayal, and that it was inappropriate to confine a decision on these matters to Parliament. All members had to contribute £1, but activities were left to local action groups (Butler and Kitzinger, 1976:110).

Butler and Kitzinger argue that the clear targeting of KBO's campaign on the general public rather than opinion formers was the source of some friction with parliamentary groups such as the ACML, which were sensitive about their own ineffective public campaign and hampered by the reluctance of MPs to put the principle of membership before their own commitment to party and personal advancement (Butler and Kitzinger, 1976:110). KBO was the only group formally committed to a referendum and therefore pursued a different strategy to that of CMSC which focused on ensuring that the safeguards were made known to all MPs if there should be a parliamentary vote on membership. Thus the anti-Market campaign was, with the exception of KBO, generally an elite focused exercise, and the Westminster centred British political culture led to the predominance of the House of Commons as the principal arena of activity.

Arguments

Part of the difficulty faced by all groupings of anti-Marketeers was the fact that the attitude of the general public on the issue of membership was not fully engaged and therefore fluid. Membership had already been the subject of two failed applications and it was no longer novel. By the time of the third application, there was a tendency to regard membership as a rather tiresome issue that now needed to be resolved one way or the other so that more pressing questions could be addressed. In addition, the level of complexity of the issues involved, covering constitutional law, agricultural economics, international political economy and budgetary matters, made it particularly difficult to involve the public fully in the debate.

Nevertheless, the arguments against the Common Market now used were noticeably different from and more sophisticated than those deployed during either of the applications of the 1960s. In the earlier period, the tone and many of the arguments had been explicitly anti-European and often xenophobic. By the early 1970s, the fragility of the British economy, balance of payments crises, hyperinflation and industrial action had undermined the argument that Britain was distinct and had a successful economy which could rely on its unique geographical location and global trading relationships. National stereotypes were also beginning to wane in their value as means to highlight British separateness. In part, the emergence of European package holidays as well as the better economic performance and higher standard of living of other European countries undermined the effectiveness of using stereotypes. As a consequence, in mainland Britain, arguments based on xenophobia, racial or religious prejudices were now not made explicitly despite a certain unease with the ways of continental Europeans. In addition, whereas in the earlier period concerns about sovereignty had been central, by the early 1970s the public was more worried about prices, the cost of living and their economic well-being.

On the right, the prime focus of the anti-Market case was now on commerce and trading issues. In addition to promoting the Commonwealth as the alternative to the EC, there was also a shift to a new set of arguments focused on the detrimental effects of membership on Britain and criticism of the Brussels bureaucracy (King, 1977:37). The one key political figure on the right who used a different set of arguments to explain his opposition to Common Market membership was Enoch Powell. Powell had been a leading member of the shadow cabinet, but was forced to step down after a controversial speech on racial issues in April 1968 and resigned from the Conservative Party over the European issue in 1974, becoming an Ulster Unionist MP for South Down.

It was true that Powell did flag up the issue of the economic costs of membership, highlighting the facts that food prices would rise and that initially at least there would be a negative impact on the British balance of payments. However, Powell's main concern and driving motivation was the issue of sovereignty, and it was he who became '... the godfather of the successor tribe to whom nation was not just something but everything' (H. Young, 1999:240). Powell became the leading Conservative critic of membership, arguing that it would destroy British sovereignty or at best transform it beyond recognition. In parallel with this, Powell argued that membership of the Common Market would end self-government and, above all, British parliamentary democracy. From a sceptic point of view, Powell was one of the first to argue that the Commonwealth was no longer the alternative organisation many had hoped for in the 1950s and 1960s and was 'no more than an intellectual fig leaf for Empire' (Barnes, 1994:342). For Powell, it was now time to focus on sovereignty and nationhood as the key intellectual arguments for standing aside from EC membership.

In the main, however, Powell's was a lone voice, matched only by Tony Benn and to some extent Peter Shore on the Labour side, who likewise highlighted the sovereignty issue. As Hugo Young notes, Britain was joining an economic community in which the political dimension was very immature. The Luxembourg Compromise had enshrined the use of the veto in defence of vital national interests and even some former sceptics like Sir Harry Legge-Bourke and Angus Maude were convinced that there was no longer any 'serious risk of a major or total loss of sovereignty' (H. Young, 1999:253). Indeed, arguments about sovereignty were not to be heard in the mainstream of the debate again until the late 1980s (King, 1977:29; Butler and Kitzinger, 1976:22).

Powell made three further, more general, contributions that became important for a successor generation of Eurosceptics in the late 1980s and 1990s. The first contribution was the justification Powell used for moving from a position of support for membership to outright opposition. Powell was amongst the first to put forward an argument that his initial support was based on gross deception as to the nature of Community membership which he had thought was based on free trade. Second, and closely related with this, Powell argued that economic co-operation did not require political union: a real Common Market did not require political institutions and, in aspiring to political institutions, the EC was bidding to create a single centralised political power. Third, Powell fused together the idea of the free market with the idea of sovereignty, thus creating a new and more potent critique of the Common Market. This argument was quite different from most other critiques of the 1970s and early 1980s that centred on various alternative forms of protectionism or global trade to that offered by the Common Market. Powell instead offered what can be termed a 'free market nationalist right' critique that became the bench-mark of right-wing scepticism in the later 1980s (Gamble, 1998:18).

On the left of the political spectrum, the focus of anti-Market arguments was on bread and butter issues, with Women Against the Common Market, the London Co-operative Society and Trades Unions Against the Common Market campaigning against 'savage increases in the prices of sugar, tea, coffee, lamb, cheese, butter, clothes, beef that entry would bring' (Robins, 1971:108). It was feared that Heath's terms could damage the Commonwealth, increase food prices and lead to deflationary policies. Moreover, as a capitalist club the Common Market would harm working class interests and damage trade with developing countries by stopping them selling agricultural produce in Europe.

Yet there was more to these arguments than met the eye, since Europe by the early 1970s had in fact become a surrogate issue, of more importance to the struggle over the ideological direction of the Labour Party, than the question of Britain's future *per se*. Thus by 1971 the volatile state of the Labour Party spilled over into the party's stance on the European issue. Between 1970 and 1972, furthermore, a change took place '... which was the most decisive shift to the left in the Labour Party's history' (King, 1977:48). Having adhered to a moderate pro-membership position in 1970, it was quite clear by October 1971 that scepticism was dominant 'emotionally and numerically' with support from activists and antipathy from the trade unions (H. Young, 1999:278). In this internal power struggle, the commitment of Social Democrats like Roy Jenkins to Europe was, as Hugo Young notes '... as much a matter of what would happen to their faction as what would happen to their cause' (H. Young, 1999:276). One bone of contention was the issue of a referendum on membership for which Tony Benn joined the call in March 1972 on the grounds that the issue was too important for the party to decide and that the people needed to participate if they were to take the decision seriously (Butler and Kitzinger, 1976:12).[4] So far as the Social Democratic wing of the party were concerned, this was a self-serving ploy motivated by the populists' desire to appeal to the electorate to secure a mandate that did not exist within the parliamentary Labour Party to pursue a more radical Socialist agenda (Lazar, 1976:259–77).

Characteristically, the referendum issue was handled by Wilson as a party management problem rather than in terms of fixed principle or on the basis of the arguments deployed.[5] The party management issue was, however, further complicated for Wilson by the fact that his three chief rivals for the leadership supported different policies on EC membership. Healey was opposed to membership and favoured a referendum. James Callaghan, Wilson's most public rival and the shadow chancellor, had always been explicit that the Common Market was of secondary importance to party unity and mooted the possibility of re-negotiation and, if necessary, a referendum as 'a life-raft into which the whole party [might] one day have to climb' (Kitzinger, 1977:236; King, 1977:65). The Social Democrat, Roy Jenkins, on the other hand, Wilson's deputy, was open in his support of membership and argued passionately against the referendum device.

Thus Wilson's shift to a position of supporting membership to a position of not ruling entry out but questioning the terms 'seems to have been designed simply to hold [a fractious] Labour [party] together' (S. Young, 1973:275). By concentrating on Heath's terms, Wilson could hope to appease those who wanted to attack the Conservative government, but also keep Social Democrats like Roy Jenkins loyal because this did not rule out membership indefinitely (Kitzinger, 1973:300). But while this policy bought Wilson a breathing space, it was not enough to satisfy the most convinced sceptics, who therefore continued to pursue their strategy on two fronts: in Parliament, where they voted against the EC Bill, and in the party, where they attempted at a series of conferences to secure motions opposing membership as a matter of principle. In particular, they persisted in their call for a referendum as a means to ensure the full-hearted consent of Parliament and the people to membership.

For the anti-Marketeers the attraction of a referendum was that it would allow the people to decide on an issue that the Labour Party found so difficult to resolve and that it would embarrass the Conservative government by making it look elitist and anti-democratic. The anti-Marketeers would also stand a better chance of defeating the government by extra-parliamentary means through an appeal to the 'nationalistic prejudices of the British people' (George, 1998:88). Wilson was initially opposed to the idea since it had the disadvantage to a party leader of surrendering control of the issue, and anyway it had never been used in British mainland politics before. As the EC Bill moved through the parliamentary arena in the following twelve months, Powell and Marten put down an amendment asking for a consultative referendum before entry could take effect. Benn took up this idea on 15 March 1972 and put it to the National Executive, and with Shadow Cabinet endorsement, the referendum became official Labour policy on 10 April, at the expense of the resignation of Roy Jenkins as deputy leader (Butler and Kitzinger, 1976:18).

Thus, for the Labour leadership, support for the negotiations was always conditional on securing 'the right terms' (George, 1998:89). Once the Conservatives had negotiated entry, the Labour frontbench opposed the government by supporting the principle of membership, but opposing the specific terms secured by the Conservatives. Wilson's motivations were several, but first and foremost he viewed the issue through the prism of the internal politics of the Labour Party. His lukewarm position was not one of principled scepticism. As a means of reconciling a deeply divided political party, Wilson therefore settled on the policy that a Labour government would seek to re-negotiate British membership and put this to a referendum. If this failed, Britain would leave the Community.

Arena

Notwithstanding the activities of Labour sceptics in attempting to garner the support of the wider party, and the role of such grass roots movements as Keep Britain Out, the energy of opponents to entry was chiefly focused on the parliamentary arena between 1970 and 1974. The bottom line was that Heath had rejected the notion of a referendum and that it was in Parliament that the battle to pass the EC Bill would be fought and won. This suited the anti-Marketeers, who were confident that they could defeat the government. As late as September 1970, Powell for instance commented that the government could never succeed in getting support from Parliament since a majority opposed membership. In the event, however, there were a number of reasons why the Conservative pro-Marketeers managed to outflank their opponents, even though the government majority was only thirty. First and foremost, the government controlled how the issue was handled, and could capitalise on three important resources. These were the facts that it controlled the timing of the process, that it could control the nature of the debates, and that it could use the instruments of party management to deliver support for the paving motion and the Bill.

As regards the timing issue, parliamentary managers introduced a motion to approve entry into the EC on the terms negotiated on 28 October 1971, at a time that the government hoped to ensure maximum parliamentary support. Moreover, though nearly fifty per cent of the electorate were opposed to entry, few felt strongly one way or the other about this, and the number of people mentioning the Common Market as important rarely exceeded ten per cent in the opinion polls in the period between 1970 and 1972. 'Most voters knew little about Europe and cared less' (King, 1977:25). The government won a majority of 112 approving the principle of joining the EC with thirty-nine Conservative MPs voting against and two (du Cann and Wolrige-Gordon) abstaining.

As regards the nature of the debates, the White Paper *The United Kingdom and the European Communities* (Cmnd 4715) published on 7 July 1971 at one level appeared to be remarkably even handed. As Hugo Young perceptively notes, it acknowledged that Britain would have to pay a sizeable amount into the Community budget, that food prices would increase and that Commonwealth trade would be damaged. On the other hand it stated more boldly, though without explanation, that entry would improve Britain's economic performance. However, riders and qualifications hedged almost all the negative statements. For instance, a statement closely followed the British budgetary question on the need to reform the Common Agricultural Policy, it was noted that food prices would only increase in the short term and that there was an undertaking to press for development aid to the Commonwealth. In general, Heath and his ministers preferred to focus on economic arguments rather than political issues.

The White Paper was most elusive on the issue of the impact on British sovereignty, stating that 'there is no question of any erosion of essential national sovereignty'. As Hugo Young notes, this acknowledged that membership would transform traditional notions of the character and capacity of an independent nation state. On the other hand, the introduction of the qualifying adjective 'essential' deliberately muddied the waters. It implied that whilst some sovereignty would be transformed the essence of it would not. At the same time, it left open to readers to decide which aspects would be affected and which would not (H. Young, 1999: 246). Young suggests that this offered deniability, and on many occasions in the debates on the floor of the House of Commons government ministers did fall back on the theoretical point that no Parliament could bind its successor; what Parliament had passed it could also repeal. In this way the direct consequences of membership on a routine basis were neatly sidestepped, as were almost all the implications for sovereignty.

The government also drafted the White Paper in such a way as to avoid any discussion of the supremacy of Community law over that of Britain. Although supremacy of Community law had already been established in the 1963 supremacy ruling and the 1969 direct effect rulings of the European Court of Justice (ECJ), the government and pro-Marketeers feared that a statement setting out the detail of the relationship between British and EC law would seriously damage the Bill's prospects. Ultimately, for pro-Marketeers like Heath, the terms of entry were of secondary importance and subordinate to the overall aim of securing membership (H. Young, 1999:239).

Opponents were also outflanked by the presentational means used by the government to secure parliamentary approval. 'In drafting the enabling legislation the government compromised between a one-clause enabling Bill and a 1,000-clause Bill making all the necessary legislative amendments to previous legislation entailed by entry, and produced a Bill comprising twelve clauses and four schedules, manageable in terms of the parliamentary timetable – the committee stage having to be taken on the floor of the House – without being too derisory to the principle of parliamentary scrutiny and approval' (Norton, 1978:73). Thus the Bill was crafted with only twelve clauses that simply accepted all past EC regulations, the Treaties of Rome and the terms of entry negotiated by the government (Butler and Kitzinger, 1976:23)

Quite apart from these tactics, however, the anti-Marketeers also proved themselves incapable of seizing control of the agenda. On the one hand, they complained that the Bill made a mockery of the complex legal, financial and constitutional issues involved. But with the exception of Enoch Powell and Tony Benn, they failed in over 300 hours of debate to successfully focus on the paucity of the government's case for entry. Instead, most argued that the Common Market would be economically damaging. Geoffrey Howe conceded some twenty years later that 'I remain at least plausibly exposed to the charge that less of [our] thinking than was appropriate was explicitly exposed to the House of Commons at the time the Bill was being passed' (H. Young, 1999:250).

Since the government controlled the agenda and timing of the Bill, it held significant advantages over its opponents. However, the government also placed the dissidents on the defensive by clever use of the instruments of party management available to it. In particular, the government initially insisted that the vote on the paving bill should be a three-line whip. This meant that the main effort of the Conservative dissidents was directed at pressing for free vote, which would allow them to oppose EC entry without incurring a charge of disloyalty. When eventually the decision came before Parliament, twenty-four hours before the vote on the principle of membership on 28 October 1971, the government, however, wrong footed the dissidents by declaring a free vote afterall. While the bulk of the Conservative Party voted for membership, thirty-nine Conservative backbenchers voted against the government and a further two abstained, an 'act of defiance [which] exceeded even the Conservative rebellion over the Maastricht Bill' (Baker and Seawright, 1998:58). Nevertheless, by removing the whip and declaring a free vote, the government outflanked the rebels by securing sixty-nine votes from the Labour benches, with a further twenty Labour abstentions.

Throughout the Bill's passage the Conservative anti-Marketeers remained persistent in their opposition. The 1970 Group continued to convene, with Enoch Powell, John Biffen and Neil Marten meeting frequently to discuss tactics. John Biffen acted as an unofficial whip, keeping a record of divisions and interviewing anti-Marketeers about their voting intentions. The scale of dissent should not be underestimated but its effectiveness was questionable since the government never lost a division. The leading rebel was Powell who voted against the government eighty times, with John Biffen and Neil Marten doing so in seventy-eight and sixty-nine divisions respectively (Norton, 1978:80).[6]

Despite the efforts of anti-Marketeers the government whips worked assiduously to ensure a majority for every division, and the Bill emerged unamended from the Committee stage onto the floor of the House of Commons and onto the statute books. In the second reading the government carried the Bill by 309 votes to 301. Despite fifteen Conservative MPs voting with Labour and four abstaining and at the third reading it was carried by 301 votes to 284, a majority of seventeen with sixteen Conservatives voting against and four abstaining. Part of the failure of the dissenters therefore lies in the effect the whips and constituency associations had on MPs. In particular, the number of dissenters dropped from the vote on the principle of entry in October 1971 to the vote on the EC Bill itself. As Norton points out, 'of the forty-one to vote against, or abstain on, the vote on the principle of entry in 1971, fourteen cast no vote at all against the EC Bill' (Norton, 1978: 185).[7]

A further reason for the Conservative dissenters' lack of success was Wilson's tactical opposition to membership on the basis of Heath's terms, that many considered Wilson would have been willing to accept if he had negotiated them himself. Wilson's actions were widely perceived by Tories as opportunistic and unprincipled but also as shameless electioneering. After the paving motion had been endorsed, the anti-Marketeers managed to force a further eighty-five divisions, but on each one the rebels were unable to defeat the government, since as Wilson's opposition to the Bill became stronger, it weakened the strength of anti-Market feeling on the Conservative side. It also meant that Labour anti-Marketeers were less likely to make common cause with Conservative sceptics since, as Robins notes, there was a widespread grass roots feeling 'that Labour MPs were elected to fight the Conservatives, not to fraternise with them' (Robins, 1979:83).

Wilson's actions also had an equal and opposite effect on Labour's pro-Market rebels who were committed to membership as a matter of principle and were not willing to be intimidated by his opportunism. These Labour pro-Marketeers voted with the government ensuring that Heath had a majority for the Bill at all the key moments. Through backroom deals with the Labour rebels, the government managed to secure a majority of 112 for the paving motion with Roy Jenkins leading sixty-nine Labour MPs into the Conservative lobby. The decision of the Labour Shadow Cabinet to endorse the idea of a referendum on 10 April 1972 led to the resignation of Jenkins, leaving the government sure that the Labour anti-Marketeers had over-played their hand. Indeed, although parliamentary managers continued to need to resort to cutting short debates by the use of a guillotine, as Kitzinger comments, 'from Monday 10 April 1972 onwards, the eventual passage of the European Communities Bill was almost assured' (Kitzinger, 1977:395). At times the government's majority fell to single figures, but on each occasion through abstention or voting with the government, the Labour rebels operating hand in glove with the Conservative whips prevented defeat.

Conclusion

In analysing the period 1970 to 1972, a key question is what the anti-Marketeers achieved in the debates that led to British membership. First, as regards the Conservative Party, sceptics succeeded in establishing a crack though not yet a split in the unity of the Conservative Party over the European issue. On the European issue forty-one opponents of Common Market membership proved themselves willing to defy their party. Moreover, as the party managers noted, theirs was a sustained campaign and it was only brought to an end through the mechanism of a guillotine motion introduced by the government that was secured by a majority of eleven, with fifteen Conservatives voting with Labour and eight abstaining.

However, while most of the Conservative rebels were willing to oppose the government in the lobbies of the House of Commons, most did not want to bring the government down on the issue. Only Enoch Powell was considered by his anti-Market colleagues as willing to defeat the government at all cost (Norton, 1978:79). In addition, only he supported the Labour Party because it promised re-negotiation and withdrawal in both the elections of 1974 when Powell made it explicit that the issue transcended party loyalty. Many sceptics did not go this far, but after 1972 they were routinely willing at least to defy their government on the European issue.

Second, there was growing solidarity amongst the Conservative dissenters emanating from what may loosely be termed the party's right-wing. In this period, Kitzinger notes, there was no great similarity between anti-Marketeers in terms of educational background, constituency representation, size of majority or date of first return to Parliament (Norton, 1978:80). However, the sceptics had become a distinct group of individual MPs within the Conservative Party. The passage of the EC Bill translated their position from abstract to concrete opposition. Through Powell's '…articulation of an alternative view to Government policy, in opposition both to Mr Heath's policies and to his style of government, Mr Powell thus helped facilitate and strengthen the expression of intra-party dissent within the parliamentary party' (Norton, 1978:253).

Third, it should not be overlooked that the majority of anti-Marketeers at this time were on the Labour Party benches in Parliament. However, Europe was the issue that fundamentally divided the Labour Party, with one-third of its MPs anti-Market, one-third neutral and one-third pro-membership. The failure of the sceptics' parliamentary campaign was in essence a consequence of Labour's failure to unify around an anti-Market position – and as a corollary, a willingness by the pro-membership faction to put their own commitment to this issue above party loyalty.

Fourth, while it was true that the anti-Marketeers' attempt to prevent or at best slow down the legislation failed, with the principle of membership supported by 356 votes, the implementing legislation passed with wafer-thin majorities that were well short of the 'full-hearted consent' for which Heath had hoped. Indeed, as noted above, the second reading of the Bill was only secured with a majority of eight. Opponents thus forced the government to build membership of the EC on shaky foundations. Despite being unable to change the substance of the Bill, by consistently voting against the government, the anti-Marketeers ensured that there was always the possibility of a government defeat, forcing it to rely on Labour and Liberal abstainers throughout the Bill's passage. Hugo Young correctly notes that the effect of this was paradoxical. In particular, it pushed alarmed ministers to dissemble about what they were doing and to avoid some important issues that should have been debated in Parliament (H. Young, 1999:376). This was to have important consequences, with subsequent Eurosceptics arguing that the government had evaded directly addressing the issue of legal supremacy of Community law over British law and that the political implications of membership had been sidestepped.

Notes

1 For a further discussion of the nomenclature see endnote 2 chapter 1.

2 Philip Norton summarises the state of the Conservative Party as 194 pro-entry, seventy uncertain and sixty-two hostile (Norton, 1978).

3 For the conversion of Eric Heffer to an anti-Market stance, see Heffer in the *New Statesman*, 17 April 1970.

4 See, for example, Tony Benn's letter to his Bristol constituents which outlined his thinking (Benn, 1996:38–41).

5 For alternative views, see Austen Morgan who argues that Wilson's key objective was to prevent the Labour Party from definitively ruling out membership (J. Young, 1993:115).

6   Figures for other rebels were as follows: Sir Robin Turton, sixty-eight; Richard Body, sixty-five; Roger Moate, sixty-five; Sir Derek Walker-Smith, sixty-four; Anthony Fell, fifty; Michael Clarke Hutchison, forty-eight; James Molyneaux, forty-six; John Maginnis, thirty-one; John Jennings, thirty; Stanley McMaster, twenty-seven; James Kilfedder, twenty-four; John Farr, fifteen and Sir Ronald Russell, fourteen (Norton, 1978:292). It is interesting to compare this with the passage of the Maastricht Treaty Bill in 1992–3 in which the leading rebel Bill Cash, voted sixty times against the government, rebelling forty-seven times and abstaining on three occasions.

7   These MPs were: William Clarke; Edward du Cann; Toby Jessel; Sir Donald Kaberry; Carol Mather; Angus Maude; Colin Mitchell; Jasper More; Geraint Morgan; Sir Harmar Nicholls; Sally Oppenheim; Harold Soref; Robert Taylor and Patrick Wolrige-Gordon (Norton, 1978:293); Norton argues that local constituency associations generally underscored the leadership line, a position which was only to change in the 1990s.

4 The referendum on Britain's continued membership of the European Community

Introduction

On 5 June 1975 the anti-Marketeers secured the prize they had increasingly sought, with the holding of a referendum on Britain's continued membership of the European Community. However, the outcome was a major defeat for the sceptical cause, since the electorate voted by seventeen million to eight million in favour of membership. Although covering the period of office of the Labour governments from February 1974 to May 1979, the central focus of this chapter is thus the paradox of the referendum, an experience which was to have far-reaching consequences for sceptical thought and action.

Despite a majority of Labour MPs opposing membership, anti-Marketeers were continually wrong footed by Harold Wilson who moved the European issue into different arenas and used the information and resources at his disposal to outmanoeuvre opponents. The failure to create an effective trans-party anti-Market group, and so to overcome the ideological partisan dimension which divided parties, left the anti-Marketeers unable to exploit the volatile mood of the public on the issue of membership. The divided nature of the anti-Marketeer camp impacted not only on the clarity of their message and the quality of their referendum campaign, but also resulted in their being denied access to the information and financial and political resources available to the advocates of membership. Ultimately, the public voted in force in favour of continued membership, but without any great enthusiasm. As Andrew Duff points out, however, 'the question asked in the referendum concerned the United Kingdom's membership of the European Economic Community, not the kind of Community the British people wanted' and this allowed the anti-Marketeers to sustain the hope that the struggle might continue (Duff, 1976:120).

Opportunity

The return of Harold Wilson as Prime Minister in late February 1974 provided the anti-Marketeers with two key opportunities to advance their case. First, since April 1972 Wilson had committed himself to a re-negotiation of the terms of entry to the EC secured by Edward Heath. This re-negotiation was targeted on seven areas: a zero VAT rating on basic items; protection of Britain's balance of payments by limiting capital movements with the EC; criticism of Economic and Monetary Union (EMU); reform of the Common Agricultural Policy (CAP) to benefit third world producers and lower food prices; assistance to Commonwealth exporters; freedom of manoeuvre for Britain's regional and industrial policies; and reduction of the British budgetary contribution. The initial hope of the anti-Marketeers was therefore that re-negotiation would be impossible, and that if it did prove possible, the terms sought by the government could not be secured.

However, the second key opportunity for the sceptics comprised the fact that, whether or not it deemed the re-negotiated terms acceptable, the Labour government was committed to a consultative referendum on the issue of membership. Since July 1972 when the EC Bill received its third reading with a majority of seventeen, it was clear that the parliamentary battle on membership was lost, the referendum device had become the core focus for anti-Marketeers of all political persuasions who hoped that given the lack of enthusiasm for membership among the general public, a referendum was the means by which they would finally triumph. Quite apart from this, the call for a referendum on membership fitted well with the need for 'full-hearted consent', the phrase Edward Heath had included in the Conservative Party's 1970 manifesto. It also made tactical sense, since the anti-Marketeers appeared to have very little to lose in a referendum. If they won, the result would be withdrawal, '… and if they lost they would not be significantly worse off than they would have been anyway' (King, 1977:58).

That said, the ideal, so far as the Labour sceptics at least were concerned, was a policy commitment in favour of withdrawal endorsed by a general election victory. Although tactically opposed to membership on Heath's terms, Wilson had made clear he would not join the anti-membership camp and would resign if the party came out against the principle of membership (Wilson, 1979:53).[1] Ultimately, for Wilson the European issue was always one to be viewed through the prism of internal party politics, and in October 1971 over sixty-nine Labour MPs, over a third of the parliamentary party, had put their support for membership before loyalty to the party. Wilson therefore knew that a definitive anti-membership stance would force a large proportion of the men and women who gave Labour governmental capacity and electoral credibility to quit (King, 1977:59).

Equally, Wilson's commitment to a referendum was also motivated by other concerns. While it did have the great merit of allowing Labour to claim to be more democratic than the Conservatives, the main advantage so far as he was concerned was that it would allow the party to avoid responsibility for the final decision on membership. Moreover, it bought the party time, since there was no need to declare its position until the referendum campaign. By 1975 a referendum had the further advantage that it obviated the need to go to the country for a third time in fifteen months and so to jeopardise Wilson's majority of three, won in the October 1974 general election.

The commitment to a referendum offered two specific opportunities to anti-Marketeers. First, a referendum bill would need to pass through Parliament and this would provide the chance for sceptics to ensure that the rules of the referendum were fair. Since a referendum had never been held, the terms and conditions would be important in ensuring equity between pro- and anti-Marketeers and would also set a precedent. Second, the actual campaign in the country would change the arena in which the European issue was debated and decided. For the first time the electorate would be offered a choice on British membership of the EC. This was an arena which was far more difficult for governments to control, since voters did not have the same degree of party loyalty as MPs, and were not vulnerable to the pressure of party managers. The referendum therefore offered the greatest single opportunity to date to promote the anti-Market case more widely and to secure withdrawal.

In the aftermath of the referendum, opportunities for anti-Marketeers to advance their cause became considerably more scarce. With the rather modest exception of the European Parliament elections in June 1979, the European issue did not really engage the general public after June 1975 and reverted to being an elite concern certainly until Margaret Thatcher's Bruges speech of September 1988. In the parliamentary arena, the main opportunity for sceptics to campaign against closer European integration related to the issue of direct elections to the European Parliament. In this arena, it was the Labour anti-Marketeers who did most to oppose the government rather than Conservative anti-Marketeers. This was in part because Conservative sceptics wanted to re-establish their loyalty to their own party after the referendum and in part because the approaching general election limited the attraction of parliamentary disobedience. The evolving dynamics of the parliamentary balance also limited the scope for anti-Marketeer success. In particular, from early 1977, the pro-European Liberal Party supported the Labour government to give it a majority. This served to dampen down some of the Labour government's scepticism while also making it harder for anti-Marketeers to defeat the government. While sceptics' partisan loyalties had been put to one side during the referendum campaign, they resurfaced after 1975, but in the immediate aftermath of the referendum other domestic concerns such as the deteriorating economic climate and devolution rose to dominate the political agenda.

Opponents: who were they?

The main result of the reduction of the pressure of party allegiances prompted by the referendum commitment was the formation of two cross-party umbrella organisations, Britain in Europe (BIE) and the National Referendum Campaign (NRC) to campaign for a 'Yes' and a 'No' vote respectively. The founders of the National Referendum Campaign were Christopher Frere-Smith from Get Britain Out (formerly Keep Britain Out), the Conservative backbenchers Neil Marten and Richard Body, and Douglas Jay from Labour. It was formally launched on 7 January 1975 and its basic aims were to reclaim for Parliament the exclusive right to pass laws and raise taxes, to restore freedom of trade between Britain and the wider world, and to act as a co-ordinating body for its member groups (Butler and Kitzinger, 1976:99).

The principal components of the NRC were the Labour anti-Marketeers from the Common Market Safeguards Campaign, the Conservatives against the Treaty of Rome (CATOR) group,[2] and the Liberal 'No' to the Common Market Campaign. It also drew in the Plaid Cymru, Scottish National Party (SNP) and Ulster unionist campaigns. Other leading non-partisan groups operating under its banner included the British League of Rights and British Business for World Markets. It was also joined later by the strongly right-wing National Council of Common Market Associations led by a retired Air Vice-Marshal (Butler and Kitzinger, 1976:97).

Overall, the NRC formed an uncomfortable coalition since groups tended to be on the far right or the far left (Butler and Kitzinger, 1976:97). It was true that the National Front's application to join was rejected, but so too was that of Women Against the Common Market, the New Politics Movement, and others on the pretext that they were too small. Participation by anti-Market Communists was avoided by means of the expedient that only parties represented in Parliament could be admitted. NRC was also riven with personal animosities, especially between Richard Body and Christopher Frere-Smith on the one hand, and the Labour anti-Marketeers on the other. In part, this stemmed from a dispute over the failure of ACML and the Common Market Safeguards Campaign to support the costs of a bookstand at the Conservative Party conference in October 1973. It was also a result of the fact that Frere-Smith and Body had poached Ron Leighton from his post as director of the Common Market Safeguards Campaign when they founded Get Britain Out in January 1974 (Butler and Kitzinger, 1976:98).[3]

In terms of the leadership of the NRC, the dissenting Cabinet Ministers Tony Benn, Peter Shore, Barbara Castle, Michael Foot and Judith Hart were prominent on the Labour side. There was also support from Hugh Scanlon and Jack Jones, two prominent trades union leaders. The NRC faced a difficulty, however, in terms of leadership on the Conservative side, since Enoch Powell had now deserted the Conservative Party, urging a Labour vote in the elections of February and October 1974 and so deprived the NRC of a high profile Conservative leader. In the event, the Conservative leader almost by default was Neil Marten, who came from the centre of the party and was a junior minister in the government from 1962 to 1964. Marten had strong anti-Market credentials, having refused office in Heath's 1970 government, played a leading role in the 1970 Group and voted some sixty-nine times against the EC Bill. Perhaps most importantly, Marten was with Enoch Powell the sponsor of the first attempt to secure a referendum through a parliamentary amendment to the EC Bill in March 1972.

But the more general absence of Conservative anti-Marketeers was striking. In October 1971, forty-one Conservatives had defied their whip to vote against the principle of membership. Of these, only Ronald Bell, Richard Body, Neil Marten, Teddy Taylor and Robin Turton (elevated to the House of Lords as Lord Tranmire) played an active role in the NRC, with the remaining Conservative anti-Marketeers remaining silent. Other notable public figures involved in the NRC were few and far between. Those who did participate included the historian Sir Arthur Bryant; Lord Woolley, a former president of the National Farmers' Union; the journalists Paul Johnson and Peregrine Worsthorne; Patrick Neill QC; and the economists Lord Kaldor and Robert Neild (Butler and Kitzinger, 1976:100).

This was by any standards a motley assortment, and the fact that its leadership was considered second rate and radical was a major obstacle for the NRC. Indeed, according to opinion polls, the NRC leaders were amongst the unpopular politicians in Britain (Butler and Kitzinger, 1976:256). The Labour ministers were, with the exception of Jay, Shore and Castle, all to the left of the Labour Party, and Powell along with the Conservative contingent were, with the exception of Marten, all well to the right. While these politicians did manage to work together, the difficulty for the NRC was that 'the active anti-Marketeers who could be presented as symbols of reasonable moderation or of "establishment" respectability were very few in number' (Butler and Kitzinger, 1976:99–100). NRC leaders were united not just by attitude, but their image as being extremist, non-conformist politicians (H. Young, 1999:291). The situation was underscored by the contrast with the 'great and good' who were ranged against the NRC in Britain in Europe. Indeed, BIE encompassed almost all the business community, the press, and even the Anglican Church, mobilised by a young ex-Conservative MP, John Selwyn Gummer (Butler and Kitzinger, 1976:82).

Although the period after the referendum defeat saw the anti-Marketeers demoralised and their influence on the wane, they were by no means completely vanquished. The most immediate result was the breaking down of the always insecure cross-party co-operation witnessed during the referendum campaign as party loyalties reasserted themselves. Within five months the Labour Party's own Committee for Safeguards on the Common Market was re-launched, with a membership of fifty MPs including Peter Shore, Tony Benn, Barbara Castle and a number of trade unionists. The Safeguards Committee put forward anti-Market resolutions at party conferences, including a demand for another referendum in 1977. In addition, in February 1976, Labour MPs launched the Safeguard Britain Campaign to 'combat European federalism and stop progress to direct elections to the European parliament' (George, 1998:97). In the main, it was therefore notable that most mobilisation occurred inside the Labour Party and that party-based organisations and allegiances once again divided Conservative and Labour anti-Marketeers.

Arguments

In terms of the substance of the referendum debate, it should be noted that the campaign had in one sense been going on for some fourteen years, ever since Harold Macmillan had first announced in the summer of 1961 that Britain was seeking EC membership (King, 1977:115). However, there was an important difference. In the past the debate had been focused on the political elite. The language, character of the discourse and means of resolving this issue had been driven by a parliamentary dynamic. The issue now had to be addressed through a plebiscite in language and arguments accessible to all.

The eclectic nature of the sceptics ensured they could not agree on a collective approach in terms of the arguments to be deployed or the strategy to be adopted. The dilemma was that the NRC wanted all possible votes, but that the main contribution to its organisation came from the left. The Labourites wanted to campaign against the Common Market on the basis that it was the product of a capitalist conspiracy, and the Conservatives on the grounds that it was opposed to free trade and was protectionist. Get Britain Out was in some respects an anti-political body and its leadership would have preferred the campaign to have a much more 'anti-establishment' tone, but as MPs and loyal party members, Marten and Jay opposed this (Butler and Kitzinger, 1976:110).

The NRC therefore had no single message and the anti-Marketeers thought that, '... it was best to let everyone plough their own furrow and argue that EEC membership meant unemployment or loss of sovereignty or high food prices or exploitation of Scotland and Wales and any or all of them together' (Butler and Kitzinger, 1976:110). Opinion poll evidence was that shop prices were a more important issue than sovereignty. Robert Worcester of MORI reported that fifty-eight per cent of the electorate thought the cost of living the key issue (H. Young, 1999:291). Douglas Jay and Barbara Castle therefore chose to focus on the populist issues of food prices, the budget, Britain's trade deficit with the countries of the EC and other practical drawbacks of membership (Butler and Kitzinger, 1976:109 and 246). The problem here was threefold. First, anxiety about prices, above all about food prices, had been central to public unease about entry into the EC, but '... the anti-Marketeers had their case weakened by the general rise in prices and BIE spokesmen were able to argue, in a very technical way, that by 1975 the EC had caused food prices to Britain to be lower than they would otherwise have been' (Butler and Kitzinger, 1976:186). A second problem was that the Labour NRC leadership were inhibited by the fact that too much focus on inflation would reflect badly on their own government. Third and finally, though the electorate was aware of the importance of rising prices, all the indications were that it was still going to vote 'Yes'. For example, opinion polls now showed that fifty-three per cent wanted to remain in the EC on the right terms (George, 1998:89).

Other NRC leaders did, however, campaign on the issue of sovereignty and specifically the 'threat to democracy' which membership was perceived as representing (Butler and Kitzinger, 1976:50). Prominent amongst those emphasising national independence and parliamentary sovereignty were Enoch Powell, Neil Marten, Michael Foot and Peter Shore. Moreover, as George points out, sovereignty was '... a theme that was to become increasingly prominent in the speeches of the anti-Marketeers as it became obvious that they were unlikely to win the argument on the bread and butter issues that had been the subject of the re-negotiation ...' (George, 1998:89).

The motivation of other 'No' campaigners was also complicated. In Scotland the SNP regarded a Scottish 'No' vote as '... a splendid tactical device at once against Westminster and against Labour ...' (Butler and Kitzinger, 1976:151). For Plaid Cymru, on the other hand, the alliance with Labour anti-Marketeers would, it was hoped, allow them '... to make electoral inroads into the Labour fief in South Wales in the future ...' (Butler and Kitzinger, 1976:54). Yet issues of substance were also involved. Thus a key SNP argument was that Community energy policy would restrict freedom over Scottish oil; they also highlighted concerns about fisheries and becoming '... the periphery of the periphery ...' in industrial terms (Butler and Kitzinger, 1976:151). Plaid Cymru campaigned on the fear that the Common Market would swallow up Welsh identity, language and hopes of self-determination, leaving Wales on the margins of a capitalist bloc. In Northern Ireland, the Unionists opposed continued membership on grounds which included the argument that the EC represented a threat to national sovereignty, that membership was a Roman Catholic superstate and that membership would lead to pressure for unification with the south (Butler and Kitzinger, 1976:156).

A central obstacle for the anti-Marketeers was that there were few conclusive arguments one way or the other. The NRC's campaign pamphlet argued that the economic advantages promised by membership had not materialised, that the cost of living would go up, and that unemployment would worsen. However, prices were already high and these arguments were '... more in the realm of fear and speculation ...' (H. Young, 1999:291). An NRC campaign document made with great passion the argument that the Common Market 'sets out by stages to merge Britain with France, Germany and Italy and other countries into a single nation', but fundamentally the sovereignty issue was hard to promote since, by the time of the referendum, Britain had been an EC member for two-and-a-half years (H. Young, 1999:292). A full and open debate was certainly not assisted by the determination of BIE to avoid arguments about the political and federal nature of the EC. But while the anti-Marketeers like Ronald Bell repeatedly pointed to '... every sign that many politicians in Britain and very many on the continent are hell bent on political union' these arguments made little headway' (Butler and Kitzinger, 1976:187). The basic problem for the NRC was, therefore, that 'if voters did not already realise that Britain's Common Market membership involved a substantial loss of sovereignty, it was not clear how at this late date the point could be brought home to them' (Butler and Kitzinger, 1976:114).

Another dynamic working against the anti-Marketeers was the rather defeatist arguments which they deployed in support of their position. Heath made much of the counter-argument that Britain could hold its own inside the European Community, that Britain could compete in the open markets of Europe and could survive the rigours of fair competition. The anti-Marketeers could thus be portrayed as 'talking Britain down' (Butler and Kitzinger, 1976:183). The absence of an agreed or attractive alternative to membership strengthened the plausibility of this criticism of the anti-Marketeers.

Most important of all, the NRC failed to overcome the feeling that Britain was already in the EC, and that it would be risky to pull out and attempt to go it alone. The NRC had no clear alternative to offer, in part because they disagreed amongst themselves, and in part because a free trade area had already been rejected by EC governments. They therefore fell back on the formula set out in the NRC campaign pamphlet that the EC was less important than NATO, the UN and the OECD and that Norway had voted 'No' without suffering any dire consequences (Butler and Kitzinger, 1976:290–304). However, Britain had not flourished outside the Common Market and membership appeared to be one of the few means of re-capturing some of its previous economic strength. For Young, what settled the outcome was the conservatism of the electorate and fear of the unknown outside the European Community (H. Young, 1999:296). This, coupled with the desperate economic circumstances of the early 1970s, the three-day week, hyperinflation and the potential threat to jobs were the key explanations of the large referendum majority of 67.2 per cent in favour of the re-negotiated terms of membership, and a turnout of 64.5 per cent. As Sir Christopher Soames put it, '… this is no time for Britain to be considering leaving a Christmas club, let alone the Common Market …' (H. Young, 1999:289).

After the June 1975 result the intrinsic divisions between the views of the anti-Marketeers resurfaced. One group, exemplified by the actions of Neil Marten, accepted the defeat and returned to the party fold. Marten observed, 'we, the anti-Marketeers, pressed for this referendum. We had it and we've got the result. And I think we've got to accept that this is the wish of the British people' (Butler and Kitzinger, 1976:274). Some, like Peter Walker, who had founded the ACML along with John Biggs Davidson, even became pro-membership supporters following the referendum (Norton, 1978:65). A second group acknowledged the verdict, but did not fully accept it. Clive Jenkins refused to accept the decision and the *Morning Star* championed the point of view that pro-Marketeers had deceived the British people with false claims which would be exposed by the continuing realities of membership (Butler and Kitzinger, 1976:276). A third group typified by Tony Benn and Enoch Powell claimed to accept the validity of the result, but wanted to continue the arguments against continued membership. Benn remarked, 'I have just been in receipt of a big message from the British people … By an overwhelming majority the British people have voted to stay in and I am sure that everybody would want to accept that' (Butler and Kitzinger, 1976:273). However, almost immediately Benn began to campaign for withdrawal.

Amongst the second and third groups three broad sets of arguments emerged. One focused on the sovereignty issue, as highlighted principally by Powell, but also by Shore. Another argument concentrated on the failure on the electorate's part to grasp fully the issues at stake. So far as some were concerned, this was due to a conspiracy. In this vein a *Morning Star* editorial two days after the result for instance remarked that, 'millions who voted "Yes" will discover that the pro-Marketeers made false claims when they said that membership does not involve an attack on the rights of British people …' (Butler and Kitzinger, 1976:276). Enoch Powell, on the other hand, concluded that the electorate had simply not been able to understand the implications of remaining in the Common Market despite a thorough debate. But he counselled, '… they will learn. I am convinced that in this referendum, the vast majority of those voting had no notion that they were saying yes or no to Britain continuing as a nation at all' (Ritchie, 1988:4). Adherents of this school of thought drew comfort moreover from the belief that, as Powell noted in the *Daily Telegraph* four days after the result, 'our continued membership will depend on the continuing assent of Parliament' (Butler and Kitzinger, 1996:276). This opened up the medium and long-term prospect of revisiting the membership issue.

A third set of arguments focused on the nature of future integration and its impact on Britain. A variation on this theme was the increasing emphasis on a partisan critique of the EC which developed amongst Labour anti-Marketeers. In particular, the EC was seized on as a ready scapegoat for the failure of Labour's economic policies and was viewed more broadly as an impediment to the implementation of a Socialist agenda including the Alternative Economic Strategy (AES). In this way, as Chapter 5 discusses, membership of the EC remained a key issue in the broader struggle over the future shape and direction of the Labour Party.

Arena

The Labour Party's October 1974 manifesto made clear that the final decision on membership of the EC should rest with the electorate. This marked an important broadening of the debate away from the political elite, and a shift of the arena of the debate away from Westminster. However, the issue would only be put to the public once Westminster had reached agreement on the re-negotiated terms of entry and this offered an opportunity for Harold Wilson to exert some influence on the outcome.

When the re-negotiated terms were eventually put to a two-day Cabinet meeting in March 1975, Wilson won by sixteen votes to seven, with Tony Benn, Barbara Castle, Michael Foot, William Ross, Peter Shore, Peter Silkin and Eric Varley opposed. The slow shift away from opposition to membership of the EC, to a position in which a majority of the Cabinet supported the re-negotiated terms requires some comment. First, the Prime Minister took steps to ensure that his Cabinet was not filled with anti-Marketeers and the overall balance of the Cabinet was split roughly in three ways, with a third committed to membership, one third opposed and one third uncommitted but personally loyal to Wilson. The fact that pro-Europeans managed to get into the Cabinet when the majority of the party was clearly sceptic reflects both on the qualities and ability of those individuals, but also on Wilson's oft stated desire to maintain the party as a broad church and to prevent it splitting on this issue (King, 1977:81).

Second, Wilson gave the task of the re-negotiation to his Foreign Secretary, James Callaghan, the minister who had first come out in favour of re-negotiating Heath's terms but who had made clear that he regarded the issue as less important than party unity. Wilson thus handed a poisoned chalice to his leading rival: success would reflect well on both the Prime Minister and his Foreign Secretary, but failure would condemn Callaghan since he had championed the cause of re-negotiation and a referendum against those diehard anti-Marketeers who had advocated withdrawal. Callaghan was also likely to become committed to whatever terms he secured.

Third, Wilson and Callaghan played the issue of re-negotiation very close to their chests. The Cabinet was consistently excluded from discussing the negotiations that Callaghan claimed were so intensive as to preclude wider ministerial involvement (Castle, 1984:111). When Cabinet discussions did occur, Wilson insisted on focusing on individual points and avoided debate on the principle of membership.

With the Prime Minister and Foreign Secretary against them, the anti-Marketeers did not have an opportunity directly to challenge the basis on which the negotiations took place and were left fighting a guerrilla war at Cabinet committee level, placing as many obstacles in the way of their pro-European colleagues as possible.

Fourth, when the issue was put to a Cabinet vote, all but one of the uncommitted members of the Cabinet voted in favour of membership. A number of ministers previously opposed to membership were also won over, notably Fred Peart, the Agriculture Minister, along with Callaghan himself. Anti-Marketeers were reduced to suggesting that Fred Peart had been unduly influenced by his officials (Benn, 1989:165). Butler and Kitzinger argue that Callaghan was probably won over by the opportunities provided by foreign policy co-operation with other EC governments that might halt a decline to British international influence (Butler and Kitzinger, 1976:32). Harold Wilson, on the other hand, suggested that it was the terms of the re-negotiation which had changed the view of Fred Peart, John Morris, Merlyn Rees, Lord Shepherd and Reg Prentice (Wilson, 1979:103).

Fifth, the anti-Marketeers lost several crucial debates once Labour had come to power in February 1974. In May 1974, for instance, the Cabinet decided that the re-negotiation should only take place within the existing treaties. Not for the last time the anti-Marketeers' ignorance of the EC political system led them to overlook the fact that Treaty revisions would have required ratification in other countries and this would have almost certainly have increased the chances of preventing acceptance of the terms (J. Young, 1993:121). In July 1974, moreover, Wilson and Callaghan came out in support of a long re-negotiation lasting just over twelve months. This too would help the pro-membership cause since by the time of the referendum Britain would have belonged to the Community for two-and-a-half years and the electorate would by then have had an opportunity to experience membership on a day-to-day basis. Despite the warnings of anti-Marketeers '… what hit the British public was not any sudden change imposed by the Community, but the fact that Community or no Community, fanfare or no fanfare, most of British life went on much as it always had done in the past …' (Butler and Kitzinger, 1976:23). This made the challenge of securing withdrawal all the harder.

The anti-Marketeers did attempt to organise a vote against the re-negotiated terms in Parliament and won one minor concession, namely that they could vote as they wished over the terms. In reality, however, they had already set their sights on the referendum campaign as the key opportunity to defeat the government. When the parliamentary vote on whether to accept the re-negotiated terms took place on 9 April 1975, the anti-Marketeers lost by 398 to 172 (King, 1977:86). However, the Labour Party was deeply split, and in the free vote 145 voted against the terms, and 137 in favour with thirty-three abstaining (King, 1977:86). Amongst government ministers, seven members of the Cabinet voted against the terms, along with thirty-one out of sixty-two junior ministers, and there were nine abstentions (Butler and Kitzinger, 1976:53). However, the anti-Marketeers failed badly to persuade the 275 Conservative MPs to oppose the government, with only eight voting against the government and eighteen abstaining (George, 1998:92). Thus, whereas in 1971 forty-one Conservative MPs opposed their party whip, in 1975 only eight did.

The failure of the sceptics in the parliamentary vote on the re-negotiated terms is interesting, since it is unusual for an opposition party to show more disciplined support for the government's policy than the governing party. Why then was the Conservative Party unwilling to subordinate the issue of membership to the broader party struggle of defeating the Labour government? The leadership of the Conservative Party was in fact very supportive of the substance of the re-negotiations – though not the tactics – and in a rare show of bipartisanship backed the government. The failure of the Conservative sceptics to defy their own whip can in part be explained by the fact that they were chastened by the experience of the February and October 1974 general elections, when Enoch Powell advocated that Conservative voters should vote for Labour. This position deflated the willingness of Conservative anti-Marketeers to walk through the lobbies with Labour. Moreover, the defection of Powell to the Ulster Unionists had deprived Conservative anti-Marketeers of a leader in the party. There was also a feeling that the battle had by now been lost in Parliament and that the referendum offered the best opportunity to secure withdrawal.

But although the decision to hold a referendum signified the shifting of the debate on membership into the public arena, there remained considerable scope for the government to shape the way the referendum was conducted to suit its own position. In particular, as Prime Minister, Wilson could deploy three important resources. First, the exact wording of the referendum question was in his hands, as was the issue of whether the government would make a recommendation on how to vote to the electorate. Second, Wilson could decide on the timing of the referendum. Third, he could channel governmental and, to a lesser extent, party resources in support of any decision which the Cabinet took.

Throughout 1974 there was considerable debate amongst the Cabinet as to whether the government should make any recommendation on the referendum question. When it was finally agreed that Wilson should indeed go on record with a commitment to commend the terms, a corollary was that collective responsibility would be relaxed to allow the anti-Marketeers to campaign against the government's position. However, Wilson demonstrated his influence by coupling the 'agree to differ' policy with a series of guidelines announced in spring 1975 as to how government ministers were to behave to keep differences within acceptable bounds.[4] First, in Parliament, all ministers had to support the government's official position and were not allowed to be drawn into making points against it. Second, all contributors had to focus on the issues and were barred from including personal attacks or trivialisations of the argument. Third, ministers were prohibited from appearing in direct confrontation on the same platform or in the same broadcast. These rules made it considerably more difficult for Labour anti-Marketeers to recruit Labour voters to their cause, although Peter Shore proved himself a cunning exponent of the use of the despatch box to oppose government policy, while Tony Benn and Roy Jenkins did hold a head-to-head televised debate towards the end of the campaign (Goodhart, 1976:225).[5] Nevertheless, since official government policy was to support the re-negotiated terms, Wilson's measures had an important asymmetrical effect on the anti-Marketeers, limiting their freedom to campaign effectively.

The government was also able to shape the conduct of the referendum in other ways. The Referendum Bill was put before Parliament and completed its passage in May 1975 with little Conservative opposition. While it was clear that everyone had a vested interest in the referendum being seen to be fair, the resolution of four key issues affecting its conduct reflected a mixed outcome for the anti-Market camp. The first issue was whether a minimum turnout or a minimum of the total poll was required before the government could be mandated to withdraw. Here the decision that there would be no such minimum requirements worked in the sceptics' favour. The second issue was the role of money in the campaign. Britain in Europe had by May 1975 raised £1,481,583, the largest sum ever amassed for an electoral campaign, while the National Referendum Campaign had generated only £250,000. The anti-Marketeers failed to achieve an upper limit on campaign spending, but did secure a government subsidy of £125,000 each (Butler and Kitzinger, 1976:110). The third issue was what question should appear on the ballot paper. Here the anti-Marketeers were concerned that opinion polls had shown that some questions had produced pro-European majorities. Butler and Kitzinger argue that the question asked made a vast difference to the answer given, with one poll estimating that this was worth around twenty percentage points in favour of whichever position the government chose (Butler and Kitzinger, 1976:248). In the event, the question read as follows: 'The Government have announced the results of the re-negotiation of the United Kingdom's terms of membership of the European Community. Do you think that the United Kingdom should stay in the European Community (The Common Market)?' Although as a concession to the anti-Marketeers the unpopular words 'Common Market' were therefore included, the underscoring of government support for continued membership was clearly a major aid to the pro-Market cause.

The timing of the referendum was the fourth and last issue to be resolved. As the re-negotiation began in the summer of 1974, public opinion was generally negative to membership. However, these opinions were not strongly held, with most of the electorate undecided or quite volatile with no settled view, suggesting that with clear leadership opinion was essentially malleable (King, 1977:25). Moreover, to consider public opinion pro- or anti-European was to misunderstand the impact of the issue on voters. By and large they were simply not interested. As the government took an increasingly decisive stance on the re-negotiated terms from March 1975 onwards, opinion shifted in support of continued membership and remained so until eighteen months after the referendum (Jowell and Spence, 1975).[6] Wilson was keen to hold the referendum as quickly as possible once the signs were that public opinion was likely to come out in favour of membership, and it was therefore decided to hold the referendum during the first week in June at a time designed to encourage high turnout.

Wilson also made clear that since support for British membership on the re-negotiated terms was government policy, the government machine would be deployed in support of a 'Yes' vote. The anti-Marketeers reacted by trying to harness the Labour Party machine to their own position, but here too they were hampered by Wilson's influence. At a Labour Party special conference held in

April 1975, a vote opposing membership was endorsed by 3,724,000 to 1,986,000. As George argues, '… the country thus witnessed the spectacle of a Labour government recommending to the people in a referendum a line of action that it was official Labour Party policy to oppose …' (George, 1998:93). At the direction of the pro-European General Secretary, however, the NEC indicated that the party organisation would not get directly involved in the referendum. Thus despite the best efforts of the anti-Marketeers, the party leadership managed to neutralise the local Labour parties which would have given the 'No' campaign a national network of campaign offices (Butler and Kitzinger, 1977: 50).

The result was an overwhelming endorsement by nearly 2:1 for continued membership, with 17,378,581 voting 'Yes' and 8,470,073 voting 'No'. All regions except two (the Shetlands and the Western Isles) voted 'Yes' and turnout was 64.5 per cent. Post-referendum analysis suggested that voters followed their parties' lead with the most divided voters being Labour supporters, of whom over half had endorsed continued membership (George, 1998:95). The sole ray of hope for anti-Marketeers was that only 43 per cent of the electorate registered to vote had voted 'Yes', which did not give the outcome an absolute majority. On the other hand, only 20.9 per cent of the electorate had voted 'No' (Butler and Kitzinger, 1976:282).

Conclusions

The referendum offered anti-Marketeers their greatest opportunity to date to put the case for British withdrawal from the EC directly to the electorate. That they failed so dramatically to take advantage of this situation was explained by three core factors. First, the anti-Marketeers were challenging the political establishment, which could bring to bear enormous political and financial resources to support their case. Clearly, the role of Wilson, who used the language of scepticism while at the same time taking a number of steps to facilitate an endorsement of membership on the re-negotiated terms was a critical factor here. Nevertheless, the solidarity of the pro-Market Britain in Europe, its levels of professionalism and the multi-faceted nature of its campaign, which drew in all the parties and leading newspapers and enjoyed the use of Conservative Party constituency offices, made it a formidable opponent. The sincerity of anti-Marketeers was never in doubt, but the NRC's organisation was by contrast widely perceived as ramshackle and incompetent. It lacked financial resources and a professional campaign team, relying instead on political leaders to communicate key messages, many of whom were unpopular and widely distrusted.

Second, the anti-Marketeers failed to create a genuinely cross-party organisation with which to convince the whole of the electorate of their case. The problem was that the NRC alliance was essentially one between those who, as Richard Briginshaw, the founder of Forward Britain, commented, '… would not want to be seen dead in the same coffin …' (Kitzinger, 1977:242). Outside of Parliament and despite the chance of a very significant prize, the anti-Marketeers proved themselves unwilling or unable to overcome their party loyalties and hostilities.

Third, and finally, the anti-Marketeers fell prey to complacency, and saw the referendum device as an end itself, rather than as a means to an end. They exhausted themselves in fighting for a popular plebiscite without investing sufficient planning and foresight into how the referendum might be won.

The referendum defeat was undeniably a crushing blow for the anti-Marketeers. All but two parts of Britain voted 'Yes' and the margin varied within narrow limits, underlining that this was a national result. Over the longer term, however, the sceptics drew two important lessons from their failure in this period. These lessons were increasingly to inform their actions, albeit coming fully to fruition only during the 1990s. First, the sceptics concluded that the nature of their arguments needed to evolve to take into account the overwhelming wish of the electorate to remain a part of the EC, even if this wish had been expressed with hesitation and little enthusiasm. Though anti-Marketeers might prefer to highlight the deception through which a 'Yes' vote was secured, the fact was that they had been incapable of articulating their fears about the implications of EC membership for British sovereignty and economic well-being in ways which appealed to the electorate. The electorate had now spoken and it would take some time before it might be willing to look with fresh eyes at the European issue, but anti-Marketeers needed to reflect on this experience and invest intellectual capital in developing their ideas.

The second lesson was that the sceptics needed to match the effectiveness of the pro-membership camp in the field of campaigning. However well meaning, amateurism and improvisation had proved no match for the professionalism and political marketing that BIE so effectively deployed in 1975. Effective use of the media was a crucial lacuna in the NRC campaign and a key requirement for transmitting the sceptics' message. Moreover, the need for a nationwide organisation with constituency offices and a network of activists was an important supplementary aspect of a national campaign on what would remain a national issue.

Ultimately, the evidence of this period is that the party system was highly vulnerable to disloyalty over the European issue. In the parliamentary arena, disagreement on Europe had since 1971 moved outside of the structured constraints of the main party battle, with pro-Marketeers as well as anti-Marketeers showing themselves ready to break with the official stance of their parties, although not as yet willing to bring down their own governments. Wilson's tactic was to attempt to cut the Gordian knot by agreeing to move the issue into the public arena. Here the leaders of the two main parties sought to depoliticise the matter by remaining detached from the minutiae of the referendum debate. In the short-term, the referendum strategy proved successful and the anti-Marketeers were roundly defeated. Yet, despite this success for the government, and the ironic fact that party loyalties had worked to weaken the effectiveness of the anti-Marketeers' campaign, the genie of parliamentary disobedience on Europe could not be put back in the bottle. As King notes, the point remained for the longer term that Europe was now 'an article of faith' that was unlike any other policy issue in its power to move both supporters and opponents to act in unusual ways (King, 1977:51). In particular, the comment made at the end of the referendum campaign by Edward du Cann, Chairman of the Conservative 1922 Committee, to the effect that 'there is always a higher loyalty than party loyalty – loyalty to one's country, and what one honestly believes to be her best interests' (King, 1977:123), was to find an ongoing resonance with subsequent generations of sceptics.

Notes

1 Wilson claimed to have convinced Barbara Castle and Joan Lester of the seriousness of his threat, resulting in his winning an NEC vote on the issue by fourteen votes to eleven (Wilson, 1979:53).
2 Hugh Simmonds, an officer in the Beaconsfield party of Ronald Bell, founded CATOR. It focused on distributing circulars to Conservative constituency associations.
3 It was GBO in February 1974 that gave a platform for Enoch Powell's two anti-Market 'principles before party' speeches.
4 For the initial statement see *The Times*, 24 January 1975 and the more elaborate set of rules see *The Times*, 8 April 1975. For an excellent commentary on these see King, 1977:80.
5 Only one minister, Eric Heffer, was sacked for breach of these rules in the campaign.
6 Opinion polls showed almost no connection between changes in attitude towards the EC and knowledge or views about the new terms (King, 1977:93).

5 Changing attitudes to Europe, 1979–1990

Introduction

This period was bounded by the entry of Margaret Thatcher into 10 Downing Street in 1979 and her resignation on 22 November 1990. For the Conservative sceptics, the period can be clearly divided into two. Between 1979 and 1988, the Prime Minister pursued a European policy of engagement, the high point of which was the signing of the Single European Act (SEA) in February 1986. This marked a watershed of sorts for the Conservative Party. Thereafter, the Prime Minister moved to a more sceptical position, crystallising her arguments in the Bruges speech on 20 September 1988, in which she set out a Eurosceptic vision of Europe and the European Community.

In the first period, Conservative fundamentalist sceptics remained unreconciled to the leadership and yet found themselves outflanked by a Prime Minister whose public image comprised talking tough – especially over the British budgetary contribution to the EC – whilst at the same time using the language of scepticism. However, behind closed doors Margaret Thatcher made a series of compromises and concessions to secure key policy objectives. Thatcher's position was characterised by Douglas Hurd, one of her Foreign Secretaries, as 'No No Yes' (H. Young, 1998:351). According to Hurd, Thatcher thus used the vocabulary of the sceptics but ultimately acquiesced in, and at times added momentum to, further European integration. It was Thatcher's approach to Europe and the old anti-Marketeers' own lack of personal standing within the party which effectively prevented any serious resistance to a series of polices which took Britain more deeply into 'ever closer union' during this period.

In the period from 1979 until 1988, European debate was deliberately and effectively confined to the parliamentary arena. Here, the size of the Conservative majority in the House of Commons and the willingness of many backbench MPs in the Conservative Party to wait and see whether a policy of engagement could deliver results, resulted in the Single European Act passing all but unchallenged with very minor exceptions. Only a handful of fundamentalist sceptics stood out against this major development in the integration process, since their natural recruiting pool on the right wing of the Conservative Party was seriously divided. Most dry and liberal Conservatives supported Margaret Thatcher and were willing to overlook the implications for British sovereignty, so long as a pro-integration policy delivered economic policy gains, but a small minority considered British sovereignty the most pressing issue and were unwilling to compromise. The Bruges speech of 1988 set the seal on a new phase characterised by Margaret Thatcher's move from an instrumental and pragmatic position on European integration to an ideological one. She therefore shifted from initially seeing membership of the European Community as an opportunity, to a position where EC membership was perceived as a threat. During this second period, the sceptics' star began to move into the ascendant and the newly emergent phenomenon of Euroscepticism became more pronounced within the Conservative Party. The period closed in November 1990 with a leadership challenge to Margaret Thatcher from Michael Heseltine based around differences on how to handle the European issue and her replacement by John Major, a leader willing to take a more pragmatic line on Europe.

In the Labour Party the period can also be divided into two. In the first period, between 1979 and 1988, scepticism became dominant soon after the change in leadership from James Callaghan to Michael Foot and needs to be viewed as part of the general shift of the party to the left. Opposition to European integration peaked in 1983 with a manifesto commitment to negotiated withdrawal from the European Community. Thereafter, official Labour Party scepticism began to decline, though the commitment to withdrawal formally remained until 1988. Progressively, the anti-Marketeers lost control of party policy to the modernisers and the Labour Party's policy on Europe moved to a pro-integration stance as a key part of this process. In part, this was driven by the need to jettison any polices which might be considered extremist, the growing opportunities which closer European integration offered the party and trade unions and the increasing Conservative opposition to a Europe which they feared paved the way for 'Socialism through the back door'.

This chapter argues that the conventional view, that the sceptics had no influence in the period between 1979 and 1990, is rather one-dimensional. It was true that sceptics once again failed to unite across the party divide. The swing leftward of the Labour Party made co-operation with the Conservative sceptics, found mainly on the right wing of the Conservative Party, very difficult. Another problem was that in both the Labour and Conservative Parties, the ascendancy of a sceptic leader occurred at a moment in which the sceptics' direct influence on policy formation was non-existent. In the Labour Party, by 1983, almost all the key leadership positions of the Labour Party were occupied by opponents of EC membership but at a time when Labour was out of power and its influence on Britain's European policy at low ebb. In the case of the Conservative Party, Thatcher's growing scepticism emerged at a time when her dominance in the parliamentary party and her own influence on European policy was diminishing, not least because of the role of senior Cabinet ministers who wanted to maintain a pragmatic approach to European policy.

But while some of the greatest transfers of sovereignty in the integration process to date took place in this period, principally through the signature of the Single European Act, which essentially went unchallenged, to focus on their failures is to overlook the important contribution which sceptics made during this period. This contribution was essentially fivefold. First, fundamentalist sceptics prepared the ground for the European debates that followed. Despite no obvious successes, a crucial learning process did take place during this period amongst sceptics in all parties, who for a variety of reasons became better informed. Second, fundamentalist sceptics used this period to monitor Community membership for evidence to convince others both of the duplicity of the integration process, but also the federal nature of the *projet européen*. Third, even in their darkest hour – the ratification process of the Single European Act – the fundamentalists' commitment to their beliefs remained steadfast, and an important source of resilience for the future. Fourth, fundamentalist sceptics challenged the wisdom of British engagement with Europe with increased plausibility during the second part of the 1980s. Events in this period cast doubt on the most important Conservative justification for membership, that Britain could win the arguments inside the Community and that engagement offered a genuine means of compensating for the loss of a world role. When Conservative MPs felt betrayed and dissatisfied with Community developments, the hardcore of fundamentalist sceptics provided a ready made set of arguments – credible and consistently advanced – on which they could fall back. Finally, and most important of all, in this period the first key steps were taken in the movement of opponents to European integration from an anti-Market position to a Eurosceptic one. With one or two exceptions, until the Bruges speech, opposition to Europe focused on an anti-Market position. This applied both to the left, where there was a fear of the implications of membership for a Socialist economic and political agenda, and to the right, where there were objections to the protectionist and corporatist dimensions of the Common Market. From the Bruges speech onwards, a core element of the thinking of opponents to European integration comprised what might be considered Powellite arguments against a Political and Economic Union and the implications this would have for British self-government. In this way, the second period marked the start-point of a 'new era' of Euroscepticism discussed in further detail in Chapters 6 and 7.

Opportunity

In comparison with the previous period there were few set piece opportunities during the 1980s to oppose closer European integration with the important exception of the parliamentary ratification of the SEA in February 1986. However, in the first period between 1979 and 1988, anti-Marketeers within the Labour and Conservative parties never gave up the struggle. Indeed, the very nature of their cause led them into a war of attrition as they began to scrutinise every aspect of Britain's membership of the EC. Theoretically, the parliamentary procedural mechanisms created to cope with membership gave the anti-Marketeers an opportunity to attack the government's policies on Europe. Overall, however, the opportunities were few and far between. The exceptions were, first, the issue of Britain's budgetary contribution to the EC, second, the European Parliament elections of 1979, 1984 and 1989, and third, the parliamentary ratification of the Single European Act.

On the issue of British budgetary contributions, the anti-Marketeers were in the event completely overshadowed by Margaret Thatcher's robust defence of British interests and her crusade to get 'our money back'. By June 1984 her strategy of confrontation appeared to deliver results with a British rebate on Community contributions (J. Young, 1993:149; George, 1998:156–8). Although the anti-Marketeers remained confident that their arguments would ultimately prevail, the issue was ultimately a lean one in terms of providing clear and identifiable opportunities for opponents of European integration to highlight the principles at stake.

The European elections of 1979, 1984 and 1989 on the face of it offered greater scope for sceptics to make their case and win over recruits. In particular, the Euro elections of 1979 and 1984 gave Labour opponents a chance to set out an alternative approach to the pro-Europeanism of the Conservative government and they did this rather effectively – even though unsuccessfully. Even the Labour Safeguards Committee argued in 1977 that such elections provided 'the opportunity to have a public debate about the Common Market, and get support for the changes needed to bring power back to national government' (Butler and Marquand, 1981:49). However, the Safeguards Committee was thwarted by the nature and timing of the European elections. The first European elections, of 1979, were held in the aftermath of the general election and broadly reflected disillusionment with the previous Labour administration, with the Conservative Party winning just under half of the electoral vote and sixty out of the eighty-one seats (Morgan and Tame, 1996:xxvii). The 1984 European election was held in the year following another Conservative landslide victory and, once again, the issues recently debated in the general election overshadowed any serious debate about the EC. On this occasion the Conservatives won forty-five of the eighty-one seats.

The problem faced by anti-Marketeers in both parties during the 1979 and 1984 elections was principally that of convincing their own party activists that Europe was an important issue. At root, anti-Marketeers especially in the Labour Party did not want any Euro elections at all and were not in favour of taking part in them. They therefore faced a serious problem of credibility in standing for a parliament they did not wish to see work. Indeed, in a branch selection meeting one anti-Market prospective candidate was told, 'sending you to Strasbourg would be like sending Guy Fawkes to Westminster' (Butler and Marquand, 1981:58).

Second, in both the 1979 and 1984 Euro elections, the political parties did not want a full and open debate about the costs and benefits of Community membership, but essentially saw the elections through the prism of domestic party politics. The party leadership wanted to minimise party splits and maximise votes through subordinating the European issue to broader domestic party struggle. In the case of Labour, in the run-up to the first Euro election the party leadership consciously took a decision to ensure that candidates 'should be "balanced" as between pro-Marketeers and anti-Marketeers', with the list omitting 'the strongest, most vociferous, or in party terms, the most "divisive" inside the party' (Butler and Marquand, 1981:23). The 1984 election was a damp squib, in part because of the inability '… of the Labour Party to draw the Prime Minister or key Cabinet Ministers into any campaign confrontation …' (Hearl, 1989:248). Moreover, in both 1979 and 1984 the party leaderships saw electoral advantage in focusing on domestic rather than European politics.[1] It was only in 1989, as Labour moved to a more pro-integration position and Margaret Thatcher took a much harder line in promoting more sceptical policies, that some sort of choice on Europe was offered to the electorate.

The predominance of candidates who supported a policy of constructive engagement was a problem for sceptics in all parties, since this limited the practical opportunities for a full airing of an alternative and more sceptical viewpoint. For the Labour Party, the 1984 and 1989 elections took place at a time in which the party leadership was moving away from withdrawal to a policy of more active engagement. This limited both the number of Labour sceptics standing as candidates and the incentive for an actively sceptical campaign. In the Conservative Party, even in 1989 when Margaret Thatcher insisted on a sceptical manifesto, most Conservative prospective European parliamentary candidates were advocates of closer European integration and distanced themselves from the national campaign. Finally, the partisan nature of the Euro elections effectively precluded any form of cross-party collaboration without the charge of disloyalty being made at a moment when MPs were most vulnerable to the appeal to party loyalty.

The failure of the Conservative sceptics at the 1989 European elections at which Labour won forty-five of the eighty-one seats, a gain of thirteen on the 1984 result, does however merit further comment. Here the dynamics were very different from the first two European elections, since Margaret Thatcher put her personal stamp on the election and campaigned on a platform of opposing Brussels and further integration. The disappointing results were nevertheless written off by sceptics on two grounds. First, it was argued that they had been disadvantaged by the timing of the European elections in the mid-term cycle of the third consecutive Conservative term in office. Second, and for some more importantly, it was argued that the failure stemmed from a reluctance to fully embrace a wholehearted Eurosceptic agenda for fear of upsetting sitting Conservative MEPs.

The most clearcut and important opportunity for sceptics to make their case in this period came therefore when the Single European Act (SEA) was presented to Parliament in the spring of 1986. The SEA was the first formal revision of the Rome Treaty in thirty years. Not only did it remove the British government's veto through the extension of majority voting to create a Single European Market incorporating the free movement of goods, capital services and labour, it also extended the competences of the EC into new areas including foreign policy co-operation, the environment, and social policy. In addition, it enhanced the powers of the European Parliament, giving it a power of veto over Single Market legislation. The SEA hence offered a set piece opportunity, through the need for parliamentary ratification, to try to defeat the government. In the event, however, sceptics' attempts to oppose the ratification of the SEA can only be described as somewhat pathetic, with 200 absentees from the vote on the guillotine and only forty-three opponents at the third reading. It was true that the size of the government's majority and the supportive role of the Liberals and Social Democrats would always have made a government defeat difficult, but the fact further remains that there was also little attempt at cross-party collaboration by Labour and Conservative sceptics.

Opponents: who were they?

In exploring the identity of the opponents of closer European integration in the period between 1979 and 1990, two features are particularly notable. First, although initially divided between a small group of hard line opponents and a much larger group of pragmatic sceptics, there was growing if tentative convergence among Conservative sceptics after 1988. Second, there was a growing divergence among those on the left of the political spectrum, as Labour modernisers picked off the pragmatic anti-Marketeers, who were further encouraged to embrace European integration by Thatcher's trumpeting the fear of its paving the way for Socialism through the back door. By the end of the period, the Labour Party sceptics were marginalised, whilst Conservative sceptics looked and sounded as though they might in the future win the political and economic arguments on Europe. Once again, the dynamics within each of the major political parties worked to prevent those who opposed Europe transcending party loyalties to join forces.

By the start of the Conservative period in office in 1979, the Labour Party had almost completed its shift from a pragmatic sceptical position to outright opposition to the EC. Hugo Young argues that, 'Europe became part of a radical leftist catalogue that captured the party' (H. Young, 1999:475). However, this underestimates the widespread anti-integration feeling that existed within the party. The bulk of the Labour constituency parties and fifty per cent of the parliamentary party were opposed to EC membership, with a consistent sceptic majority in the party as a whole of two to one and within the constituency parties of at least three to one (Shaw, 1994:391). The election of Michael Foot to the leadership in 1980 took place against a background of three of the four candidates standing for the leadership – Michael Foot, Peter Shore, and John Silkin – opposed to membership, with Denis Healey only marginally less sceptical. The active anti-Market roles of Tony Benn on the National Executive Committee and Joan Lester as Party Chairman, were a further reflection of (and stimulus to) the extent of opposition to membership within the party. Accordingly, the October 1980 Labour Party conference voted by five million to two million votes to withdraw from the EC, a decision which led to the splitting of the party, with a number of prominent pro-Europeans such as Roy Jenkins, Bill Rodgers and Shirley Williams and nearly two dozen MPs leaving to form the new Social Democratic Party and thus further underscoring the predominance of anti-Market views. It was no surprise that the Labour Party included a manifesto commitment to withdrawal its 1983 manifesto, *The New Hope For Britain*, the high watermark of anti-Market feeling in the party.

The key Labour sceptic group was the Labour Safeguards Committee. Here, Bryan Gould MP and Ron Leighton, an anti-Marketeer since the early 1960s, remained active campaigners. The Safeguards Committee monitored developments and, on each anniversary of the 1975 referendum, produced an update on the implications of membership (Butler and Marquand, 1981:61). It sponsored fringe meetings at the annual Labour Party conference and promoted anti-Market resolutions. It also had strong links with the NEC, which, like the Shadow Cabinet, had a majority of anti-Marketeers. However, it should be noted that the strength of the Labour Safeguards Committee during this period was in many ways a direct consequence of the prior commitment to withdrawal of the major left-wing groups within the party, especially the Tribune Group, the group of MPs around Tony Benn and other left leaning groups within the party such as the Campaign for Labour Party Democracy. It was also largely thanks to these groupings, and the publications under their control, the *Tribune* and *Labour Weekly*, that the sceptics achieved the publicity they did and so managed to reach a wider Labour Party audience.

The underlying problem was that the anti-Marketeers were not particularly unified in their goals, a fact which became particularly evident after the 1983 election defeat. Bryan Gould noted that in this period unity of purpose to continue the polices against the right decreased. This was in large measure due to the pressure of personal ambitions (H. Shaw, 1994:131). One factor was that frequent electoral contests led to a scramble for party posts. A second was that the Tribune Group increasingly lost ideological coherence as it became infiltrated with careerist MPs more intent on promoting themselves than specific policy goals – especially ones which did not seem important to the electorate. When Michael Foot stepped down as leader in 1983 and Neil Kinnock was elected to replace him, the unity of Labour anti-Marketeers could be sustained no longer. The collapse of the miners' strike and the drive to devise more electorally popular polices made '… the Labour Party increasingly reliant on the leadership to win elections for it' (Heffernan and Murqusee, 1992:61). Slowly, Kinnock moved party policy from the 1983 commitment to withdrawal, to a position in 1984 of considering withdrawal, should reform of the EC fail and exit be in Britain's interest, to a position by 1989 that it would more actively engage in the Community and fight for British interests (Shaw, 1994:394). In addition, over his nine years as party leader, Neil Kinnock actively courted those MPs who were from the 'soft left' and who might be willing to embrace a pragmatic approach to Europe and to suspend – and in some cases overturn – their distrust of EC membership, in order to construct policies with more appeal to the electorate. In this way, for many, opposition to Europe was subordinated to an electoral need for a root and branch policy review.

For a variety of reasons, throughout the 1960s and 1970s the Conservative Party, on the other hand, had chosen to portray itself as 'the party of Europe'. However, by 1979 the party was becoming increasingly sceptical about the value of the EC. With the exception perhaps of Edward Heath, the Conservative leadership has taken an instrumental view of EC membership and was deeply if not yet fundamentally divided over Europe. Survey evidence in 1979 showed that forty-two per cent of Conservative voters supported withdrawal with forty-six per cent opposing withdrawal. Of the forty-six per cent who supported membership, many were only committed second hand through adherence to three beliefs. The first was that a Conservative government would be better able to play the European game through a commitment to the success of the Community and was more likely to make progress by adopting a positive attitude than by continually threatening to leave. Second, there was a hope that the EC could deliver positive objectives both in terms of domestic policy goals and at the European level. Third, this group held that a robust defence of British interests in the European Community would be electorally popular and trump the Labour Party's policy of withdrawal. Thus the existence of a pro-membership majority of the Conservative Party and its long-term sustainability was dependent on a highly instrumental and pragmatic view of EC membership: the EC had to deliver results to maintain the commitment of the party.

The division of the Conservative Party's natural pool of opponents to European integration during the period 1979 to 1988, and its unification – albeit at this stage slow, partial and very imperfect – in the second period, is central to an understanding of the growing importance of the sceptics inside the Conservative Party. The group that formally became identified as Eurosceptics at the end of the 1980s was in fact a confederacy comprising the fundamentalist sceptics who had now been joined by what Hugo Young terms the 'lurchers' – though a more accurate description is pragmatic sceptics (H. Young, 1999:387). As Chapter 3 indicated, fundamentalist sceptics had consistently argued against the dangers of European Community membership. John Biffen, Roger Moate, Teddy Taylor, Richard Body and the one time Conservative Enoch Powell had well-established records as opponents of closer European integration and, once Britain joined the EC, they became the 'Cassandras' of Community membership, forever warning of the dangers but never taken seriously. The pragmatic sceptics comprised those MPs who initially ignored the warnings of the fundamentalist sceptics and went on to back key developments such as the SEA. They were thus initially supportive of integration, but moved to a position of opposition when their hopes were frustrated. It was only with the deteriorating benefits of membership that their position began to alter. The most notable of the pragmatic sceptics were Bill Cash, Norman Tebbit and, eventually, Margaret Thatcher herself.

As Hugo Young argued, what complicated the picture was that within the two broad pragmatic and fundamentalist camps there were in fact five broad clusters of individuals, many of whose views overlapped (H. Young, 1999). First, there were those who had been irreconcilable anti-Marketeers from the start, like Richard Body – a leading supporter of Keep Britain Out in the 1960s and a veteran 'No' vote campaigner in the 1975 referendum – along with John Biffen, Roger Moate and Teddy Taylor who all voted against the 1972 EC Bill. The second group consisted of constitutionalists such as Bill Cash, James Cran, Christopher Gill and Richard Shepherd, who were concerned with the threat to sovereignty represented by the EC. Indeed, it has been commented that Shepherd's 'position sprang from an almost Cromwellian romance with the historic sovereignty of Parliament' (H. Young, 1999:387). Despite now being outside the Conservative Party, it was Enoch Powell who provided the intellectual reference points for this group. As Chapters 3 and 4 further explored, Powell argued that to focus on the potential financial or economic benefits of EC membership was to overlook the much deeper issues. For Powell the bread and butter issues of politics were only symptoms of a much wider and more important question of sovereignty (Ritchie, 1989:10). The Powellite view, which became so important after he had himself left the House of Commons, was not based on a financial calculation of advantage; it was a matter of principle.

The third cluster amongst the Conservative sceptics were the free-Marketeers or Thatcherites including Michael Spicer and Nicholas Budgen. Their opposition was rooted in a commitment to the free market and trade liberalisation, and more broadly, the achievement of Thatcherite goals. They supported membership so long as it delivered these goals, but when membership appeared to threaten these objectives, they quickly turned to a sceptical position. A sub-group was those MPs who were personally committed to Margaret Thatcher as well as to Thatcherism. They followed her own *volte face* and the removal of Thatcher from Downing Street accelerated the divergence from the official party line of many, including Michael Spicer and Teresa Gorman, who had an almost fanatical devotion to the former prime minister (Gorman, 1993:78). Hugo Young argues that this group in many instances came into politics because of Margaret Thatcher and was not willing to break with her over Europe. It was only after her removal that their scepticism came into sharper focus and 'expressing anti-Europeanism at least as strong as hers was one way of securing revenge for what the other side had done' (H. Young, 1999:384). The overlap between the No Turning Back (NTB) Group, set up in 1985 by thirteen MPs, was striking. NTB contained a number of young MPs who would become leading sceptics a decade later, including Michael Forsyth, Neil Hamilton, Alan Howorth, Peter Lilley, Michael Portillo, Edward Leigh, Francis Maude and John Redwood. The purpose of this group was to stiffen Mrs Thatcher's resolve to pursue radical policies that included a more sceptical policy on Europe (Gorman, 1993:12–13).

A fourth cluster was the unashamed patriots who believed that 'England is best'. This included Nicholas Winterton, John Carlisle, Tony Marlow, Rhodes Boyson, Bill Walker and Richard Shepherd. They formed an English populist nationalist group. Finally, a fifth group comprised the left-wingers in the party, notably Peter Walker and Peter Tapsell, both with quite long and somewhat chequered histories in terms of opposition to closer European integration. They opposed the European Community in part because they saw it as a trade cartel with a 'common' rather than a 'free' market, and preferred the more global multi-racialism of the Commonwealth. The EC promised external tariffs against the rest of the world and it was totally white, whereas Walker and Tapsell believed that Asia and Africa were the emergent powers (H. Young, 1999:375).

During the period between 1979 and 1988, these clusters lacked any unity of purpose, a fact which was most clearly underlined by their quiescence over the SEA. With the Bruges speech, however, and the shift of Margaret Thatcher to a position of scepticism which the speech epitomised, along with the growing momentum behind the idea of a European Union with a single currency, the groupings began slowly to coalesce and to form a very loose federation around the parliamentary Friends of Bruges Group. This was an offshoot from the Bruges Group, created in February 1989 by David Robertson, an Oxford undergraduate under the guidance of Lord Harris and Margaret Thatcher, to promote Mrs Thatcher's Bruges agenda and provide organisational momentum behind the ideas she had espoused (Shore, 1996:42–9). By the end of the decade, the Friends of Bruges Group could claim over 100 MPs as members and was seen by many as an embryonic party within a party. Published reports suggest that it had a turnover of £100,000 per annum with financial support from Lord Forte, Sir James Goldsmith and Lord King.

Two further features of scepticism are important here. First, the growing coalescence around the Bruges agenda marked a shift away from the domination of the sceptic ranks by the anti-Market Labour left, to a position of growing ascendancy for a rightist Eurosceptic movement. A second feature was the rapidity with which this grouping broadened out its membership to draw in disaffected journalists in the weekly and weekend editions of *The Times* and the *Telegraph*, which now increasingly devoted column space to Eurosceptic writers. It also recruited academic contributors to the debate including Oxford dons Martin Holmes and Nevil Johnson, Cambridge dons Noel Malcolm and Lord Harris, economists such as Patrick Minford at the University of Liverpool and Kenneth Minogue at the London School of Economics, and historians such as Alan Sked (who later went on to found the UK Independence Party). This lent credibility, and provided a broader support network outside Parliament. It also deepened the quality of the intellectual debate and created a receptive intellectual environment in which to advance the Eurosceptic case on a three-dimensional front.

Arguments

Within the Labour Party, from 1979 until 1984, opposition to EC membership centred around and was embedded in a broader shift to the left. Specifically, the left's adoption of what became known as the Alternative Economic Strategy (AES) in 1976 provided a set of reasons for withdrawal from the EC, since the AES's commitment to import controls, public ownership and state planning would not be permitted under Britain's membership of the EC. The AES therefore gave practical focus to more general concerns in the 1970s, that membership of the EC would prevent the Labour Party achieving its policy objectives; indeed, withdrawal from the EC was a formal commitment under the AES.

To the left-wing Labour sceptics, led above all by Tony Benn, the SEA in particular was a means of thwarting the interests of workers. It was argued that the majority voting brought in by the SEA was anti-democratic, that the EC was too focused on capitalist objectives, especially the single market, and that it would restrict the powers of governments to plan their own economies (Seyd, 1987:29). In addition, there were concerns on Labour's nationalist right wing, where veterans like Ron Leighton argued that EC membership meant the sacrifice of the British government's capacity to govern. 'Sovereignty', Leighton argued, 'is the right of the people to run their own country in their own way. It is the right to democratic parliamentary government' (Judge, 1988:455). However, these sovereignty-based arguments were very much subordinate to the instrumental critique offered by the dominant left-wing groupings.

Labour anti-market views of the EC and the process of European integration did not fundamentally change after the ratification of the SEA, but their arguments appeared less relevant as the party underwent a policy review which changed a future Labour government's policy objectives to a position more supportive of membership, based around the social dimension of closer European integration. What was also striking about this period was that whilst Labour's 1983 election manifesto called for withdrawal from the EC, the 1987 manifesto barely mentioned European policy and, indeed, included more on its policy position on the Cyprus conflict than on the EC (Forster and Wallace, 2000a). By 1989 the Labour Party had endorsed a pro-membership, pro-engagement stance. However, there remained many on its parliamentary benches and amongst the constituency activists who were unreconciled, making for a natural reluctance to challenge the Conservative government on European policy.[2] But the shift in official Labour Party policy did lead to a change of emphasis in the Labour sceptics' critique. Hitherto, instrumentally focused arguments, a critique based on fear of frustrating Labour's policy objectives, had been predominant. Now, however, the voices of fundamentalist opponents such as Peter Shore came to the fore, arguing that whatever the potential economic and social benefits of a Community which seemed increasingly to be moving in a socialist direction, membership was a threat to sovereignty and should be opposed as an article of faith.

It was this which at least theoretically offered the possibility of a more bipartisan approach to the issue of opposing Europe. After all, many Conservatives had undergone a similar transition from an instrumental to a principled argument against the EC, contending that whatever the benefits of the SEA, this could not outweigh the sacrifice in sovereignty required. In a close echo of the 1973 membership debates and the 1975 referendum, the common ground between Labour and Conservative sceptics was agreement on the government's right to govern Britain without interference. Whereas the political differences between the Conservative and Labour types of opposition to Europe had created a nearly insurmountable barrier to co-operation between the mid-1970s and late 1980s, by the late 1980s their shared concerns about the implications of European integration for British sovereignty had the potential at least to bring them together.

During the period prior to the 1988 Bruges speech, and certainly as regards the SEA, Conservative sceptics faced a set of problems. First, many Conservative sceptics – just like Margaret Thatcher – were convinced that shifting the economic basis of the EC from a protectionist customs union, to a Single European Market (SEM), and dismantling non-tariff barriers, was sufficient to justify any concessions on sovereignty (George and Sowemimo, 1996: 252). Moreover, as Jim Buller argues, the SEM would legitimise and entrench the Thatcherite project: it would provide an external force, a *deus ex machina*, for industrial modernisation, it would help address the supply side of unemployment and create growth, sound money and free markets. It would also offload responsibility onto the European arena by limiting the government's economic obligations. Finally, it would make a return to supply side interventionism impossible. These policies offered a code or set of political ideas that would be popular with the electorate and arguments which could be used to attack opponents and deflect criticism (Buller, 2000:156). Many potential sceptics were therefore carried along by the conviction with which Margaret Thatcher argued her case. What the government told them was on offer was an agreement which would deliver domestic gains as well as exporting Thatcherism to the European level. This would enable a Single Market to be created against vested interests in other member states.[3]

Second, the SEA was presented as a technical set of measures with few practical implications for national sovereignty. Subsequent sceptics like Michael Portillo and Peter Lilley claimed to have voted for the headline agreement that the government thought the SEA represented, without much concern for the detail of the treaty (H. Young, 1999:445). Another reason for the sceptics' quiescence was a packed political agenda that drew their attention away from the SEA towards other apparently more pressing issues.

In addition, after investing so much effort in negotiating the SEA, it was hard to convince other Conservatives that the SEA was in fact a poisoned chalice. To do so would have raised questions as to the principle upon which the Conservative Party had advanced itself as 'the party of Europe' and to Margaret Thatcher's personal approach. Moreover, even close examination of the treaty left many readers with the feeling that much of the content beyond that dealing with the Single Market was rather innocuous. Bill Cash chided the sceptics for undervaluing the achievements of the negotiations and overrating the dangers (H. Young, 1999:382). Even if there were dangers, the Thatcherites were confident that Margaret Thatcher would prevent any moves towards closer integration. The fundamentalist sceptics simply did not have enough credibility at this stage to carry the counter argument with any conviction against a Prime Minister like Mrs Thatcher. Their lack of standing and experience reduced their ability to command the attention of the rank and file in the parliamentary party who viewed them as zealots, incapable of recognising the value of European integration to a domestic Conservative Party programme.

Once the SEA had been ratified, however, the position of the Conservative fundamentalist sceptics strengthened as growing numbers of pragmatists joined their cause. For the fundamentalists, the malign implications were clear from the moment of Britain's entry into the EC. For the pragmatic sceptics who started from a more instrumental and less absolutist view of membership, disillusionment with the SEA was a necessary part of their conversion. Thatcherites now had a definitive benchmark against which they could demonstrate that the European integration carried with it the implications that the fundamentalist sceptics had long made clear. If Margaret Thatcher armed with the SEA could not make membership of the Community work for Britain, then the feeling amongst a growing number of Tories was that nobody could. The SEA therefore raised the stakes and changed the nature of the game.

From 1986 onwards the seeds of a more robust and increasingly coherent critique of EC membership also began to emerge. At its core was the argument that the British government had tried to work from within the EC and failed. This argument contained four key elements. The first was that the governments of other member states were insincere about creating a Single Market and through failure to implement agreed legislation – an argument popularised by the Commission's own league tables – had reneged on their Single Market responsibilities (H. Young, 1999:39). Here the growing body of sceptics pointed to important imperfections in trade which still remained, especially as regards air transport and banking and insurance. It was therefore clear that further sacrifices of sovereignty would be necessary to secure a comprehensive SEM.

Second, the Commission was perceived as having seized on harmonisation to pursue political power (Ritchie, 1989:108). The Commission was seen as an agent of federalist governments, aided and abetted by the European Court of Justice, which now became a new target of pragmatic sceptics. The cavalier use by the Commission of the Qualified Majority Voting (QMV) provisions for health and safety proposals to secure its directives against the British government's wishes, enraged many Thatcherites in the Conservative Party (Grant, 1994:86). The support of the ECJ for this and other matters in opposition to the British government underscored what the fundamentalist sceptics had said from the outset: that the ECJ was an integrationist body and used a continental code with wide ranging powers of interpretation which gave it powers well beyond those of the British courts. It was an irony lost on most Thatcherites – though not the fundamentalist sceptics – that it was the Single Market issue of open access to British fishing grounds (the Factortame case) which led the British Law Lords to overturn, for the first time, an Act of Parliament as being incompatible with Community obligations. This fed into a third strand of the critique, that as an island nation Britain was different from its continental partners in terms of both its politico-judicial system and its economic and welfare state model. This was an argument particularly popular amongst the right-wing English nationalist group. There was a feeling that the SEA and the European Community more broadly would not be Thatcherite, but was more likely to be Christian, or even worse, Social Democratic in character.

Fourth, sceptics argued that the SEA was not the end of the process, 'the apogee of Europe's trajectory', as Hugo Young calls it (H. Young, 1999:344), but added momentum to it. Within twelve months of the SEA being signed, the Delors Committee was set up to consider steps towards monetary union and the Commission with French and Belgian support proposed the Social Charter, a non-binding declaration to strengthen the social dimension of the EC. As it became clear that the SEA had added to the momentum of integration, doubt was clearly cast on the contention that Britain was winning the arguments. On 6 July 1988, Delors addressed MEPs in Strasbourg and argued that 'in ten years, eighty per cent of economic legislation, perhaps even tax and social policy, will come from the EC' (Grant, 1994:88). This gave credence to what many had begun to fear, that in the name of the Single Market Britain would lose the capacity to govern herself, with key economic decisions being taken in Brussels. The Commission had hence become self-serving and a rival power.

In short, for many Conservatives, attempts to work from within the Community appeared to have failed as it became increasingly clear that the SEA had not delivered the policy goals of the Conservative government and might even threaten them. This aggravated the incipient concerns of many on the right that if Mrs Thatcher could not secure Britain's interests then it would be impossible for anyone else to do so either. This suspicion increasingly fed into the arguments used by Thatcher and eventually culminated in the Bruges speech, the event which finally caused the emerging partnership between the fundamentalist and the Thatcherite sceptics to gel around opposition to what might be termed the Political Union agenda. The speech was accompanied by quite strident 'spinning' by the Prime

Minister's press secretary, which led to tabloid headlines that exceeded much of the content. However, the substantive points did amount to a Eurosceptic agenda that would add new and more vigorous Eurosceptics to the existing anti-Marketeers who for nearly a quarter of a century had opposed closer European integration.

In essence, the agenda set out in the Bruges speech of 20 September 1988 attacked the process of European integration, though it fell short of attacking British membership as such. It argued that the core aim of European integration should in fact be to strengthen the nation states involved in the process. It acknowledged that, on some issues, independent nation states would seek to co-operate for their own benefit, but contended that the EC should be no more than an association of states. Thus Thatcher's Bruges speech offered an essentially confederalist position that co-operation could and should leave the sovereignty of the nation state unchanged. This was an approach which in a milder form could be traced back to members of the Conservative Party in the late 1940s and 1950s, notably Leo Amery and perhaps also Anthony Eden.

In her speech, Margaret Thatcher therefore argued that 'willing and active co-operation between independent sovereign states is the best way to build a successful European Community' (Thatcher, 1996:91). To her, the process was neither inevitable nor irreversible: it was dependent on governments and their judgement as to the value of current and future agreements. This view was not anti-European, but saw the process as conditional upon an individual assessment by each government involved in the process. In terms of the type of issues on which states might co-operate, Thatcher suggested that this included the establishment of a free market and trade.

It was on the basis of these arguments that Mrs Thatcher's three main criticisms turned. First, she argued that the EC had overstepped the mark in terms of what it was; second, that something pernicious had developed in the process through which European integration was advanced; and finally, that what the EC aspired to do was inappropriate. In terms of what the EC was, Thatcher underlined that the EC was simply one of many institutions that states might choose to rely on, and that it did not have a unique or exclusive claim to any role or responsibility. To her, promotion of the exclusive role of the EC was myopic, and she argued that 'the European Community is one manifestation of European identity, but it is not the only one' (Thatcher, 1996:90). Europe furthermore was not defined by the current members of the European Community, but '... Warsaw, Prague and Budapest are also great European cities' (Thatcher, 1996:90). This position offset the charge of inconsistency since she could legitimately claim that she had always been for Europe – just a different sort of Europe. It also raised the possibility of overturning the British government's signature to the Treaty of Rome whilst still being committed to the idea of Europe integration (Ritchie, 1989:134).

Second, Mrs Thatcher argued that the Commission had advanced the process of integration by underhand methods. Her speech specifically highlighted ways in which the Commission had seized on populist issues. She also commented on the way in which the Commission had illegitimately distorted and then exploited ambiguous treaty language to advance the integrationist cause. In particular, she underlined the abuse of majority voting treaty articles for purposes other than those intended (by her government) to by-pass British opposition to particular legislative proposals.[4] She posed two specific challenges. She questioned the orthodoxy that the EC must keep developing lest it collapse, arguing that any transfer of sovereignty had to be by design and not by stealth. She also challenged the legitimacy of the use of the EC framework by others to overturn the policy choices of the British government. In a much quoted phrase she introduced a partisan dimension by arguing that 'We have not successfully rolled back the frontiers of the state in Britain only to see them re-imposed at a European level, with a European super-state exercising a new dominance from Brussels'. This was an abuse of British membership of the EC and she made much of exposing member states and the Commission who claimed the idea of Europe for themselves and used it to pursue their own institutional and national advantages. As she curtly remarked in her memoirs, 'I had by now heard about as much of the European "ideal" as I could take' (Thatcher, 1993:743). For Thatcher, the EC should limit itself to addressing present problems in a practical way; so far as the British government was concerned, moreover, its focus should be on encouraging enterprise and avoiding protectionism.

Third, Mrs Thatcher challenged what the EC might become. She simply did not accept that it should become a United States of Europe in the same way that there was a United States of America. There could be no submersion of identity, and no handing over of the core functions of the nation state.[5] For her, defence should be handled through NATO and monetary competence should remain a nation state function. This argument underscored her conviction that institutions were the servant of governments and not the other way round.

The hostile reaction from some international quarters and the tabloid headlines served to make the Bruges speech a milestone in the development of British scepticism both in terms of substance and symbolism. Mrs Thatcher herself noted she could not have predicted the furore the Bruges speech unleashed: '... stunned outrage' (Thatcher, 1993:746). The potency of the critique was not in its intellectual rigour but rather that a strand of Euroscepticism and arguments which certain members of the political elite had been making, had now moved from the margins and into the mainstream of respectable British politics (Sharpe, 1996: 306).

For most of the anti-Market Conservative sceptics, the speech was very welcome. But for some, like Enoch Powell, a crucial Rubicon had yet to be crossed. The personal divide between Powell and Thatcher was over whether having recognised the EC's failings Britain could any longer remain a member of the EC and manage her own affairs. Powell was wary of the Thatcherite argument that the EC could be stopped at a Single Market which anyway raised so many challenges as to make withdrawal immediately necessary to preserve the nation state. For Powell the nation state was prior to and more important than the market and the economic dimension simply a lever for political unification. Free trade could not be extracted from it (Ritchie, 1989:129). Where there was common ground was that the British government could and should threaten to break up the Community and so make it impossible for the Community to evolve in a federalist way or create a two tier

Europe in which Britain would be in the second free trade tier (Ritchie, 1989:132). Above all else, however, the Bruges speech connected an existing small group of the anti-Marketeers with a much larger group of pragmatic Conservative sceptics, on the basis of a set of sovereignty concerns which can be termed the Eurosceptic agenda.

Hugo Young argues that the Bruges speech 'stopped nothing happening' and that it had no 'instructive impact' (H. Young, 1999:351). However, this overlooks three landmark qualities of the speech. First, it underestimates the respectability that Mrs Thatcher lent to opposition to Europe through the speech; a normalisation, indeed legitimisation, of what had hitherto been a position perceived by many as one held by mavericks and extremists. Second, it gave rise to an organisation, the Bruges Group, that brought together a disparate collection of people who in one way or another opposed the process of European integration and EC membership. This was notwithstanding the fact that tensions did remain between Eurosceptics and anti-Marketeers, the latter regarding the former as politically naïve and as having demonstrated flawed political judgement through a misinterpretation of the European integration process (H. Young, 1999:387). Third, the speech lent momentum to scepticism by establishing an intellectual agenda for opposing European integration. It therefore usurped the credo of the anti-Marketeers as the leading and most virulent form of anti-integrationism and replaced it with Euro-scepticism – a new critique of the Political Union agenda.

Arena

The first point to make is that opposition to European integration in the period before 1988 remained an elite concern, confined to Parliament with the exception of the European Parliament elections of 1979 and 1984 when the issues managed temporarily to break out of the Westminster arena and engage the general public. The arena in which there was the major opportunity to defeat the government was Parliament when, in 1986, the Single European Act Bill was placed before the Commons. However, odds for defeating a government with a majority of 144 always looked rather long.

In this arena, the government had the resources and instruments of power to ensure that it got its own way. Party managers controlled the timing of the Bill, and could bring pressure to bear on their own backbenchers to support the government. They could also rely on the partisan instincts of those from within the Conservative ranks who opposed the SEA not to hand a success to the Labour Party, especially in the run up to a general election.

In the event, the task of managing opposition within the parliamentary Conservative Party was eased by divisions among the sceptics as to the implications of the SEA. As indicated above, certain features of the SEA in fact appealed to the pragmatists. The failure of Conservative sceptics to build a credible opposition to the policy of SEA ratification was thus in large measure due to the fact, that although the right of the party had always been reluctant Europeans, they differed with their diehard sceptical colleagues over the importance of sovereignty and the best means to achieve their policy goals (Gamble, 1998:19). To many on the right, the SEA was a visible sign that the British government was winning the arguments and this became a self-reinforcing reason to support the SEA. After all, the purpose of the SEA was the 1992 project to create a Single Market for goods, services, capital and labour. The reluctance of the free-marketeers, notably Bill Cash, Michael Spicer and Nicholas Budgen, was overcome by the principal commitment to the creation of a Single Market by 1 January 1993. For them, as for the Prime Minister, closer European integration would deliver significant benefits with very little costs. They accepted the argument that supply side economics would reduce unemployment and improve the chances of British exports. Through the deregulation of financial services the SEA would also offer the City an increase in business with one-third of the predicted rise in GDP expected to benefit the financial services sector.

Second, some sceptics failed to take action because of the role of the Prime Minister. There were a number of MPs who were personally committed to Thatcher as well as Thatcherism, and it was her personal stance rather than her arguments and assurances which were central to winning them over. Whilst one might have expected more anti-Thatcherites on the left of the party to oppose the SEA, their position was complicated by the fact that most of them were pro-Europeans. The strong opposition to Thatcher did not extend to the European issue, and only Edward Heath focused on Europe, albeit arguing that Thatcher should be even more pro-European. The left sceptic group was very small indeed, with only a handful of MPs. In the main, therefore, the left of the party differed only on how to achieve the best results inside the European Community (Morris, 1996:31).

Third, many Conservative sceptics did not vote against the government as a consequence of the size of their parliamentary majority, with Conservatives holding 397 out of 633 seats. The size of the Conservative majority, and the support of the Liberals and Social Democrats, meant that not just one, but two eventualities were required in order to bring about a government defeat in the parliamentary ratification process. It required a sizeable number of Conservative rebels not merely to abstain, but actually to walk through the lobbies with the Labour opposition. In the run up to a general election, all backbenchers were very sensitive to the need to toe the party line. Many Conservative MPs also wanted to highlight Labour divisions rather than their own. The whips had little trouble in managing the pool of potential opponents. Any act of defiance would have little effect and opposition of this nature would carry with it personal implications for promotion, with few practical chances of defeating the government anyway.

Defeating the government also required the whole of the parliamentary Labour Party to oppose the SEA, and in the event the Labour Party managers were unable to deliver their own MPs on the issue. Despite the fact that by the 1980s fifty-eight per cent of Labour voters supported withdrawal and thirty per cent supported membership, many backbench MPs were more likely to support EC membership than the rank and file. In truth, Labour's position was ambivalent. On the one hand it opposed the SEA, but at the same time, as discussed above, the Labour Party was moving towards a policy of more active engagement and the parliamentary party was therefore split. By 1986, the new Labour leader, Neil Kinnock, had started the process of distancing the party from its electorally unpopular manifesto commitment to withdrawal, and Labour struggled to avoid its own splits rather than attack the government for signing the SEA.

It was not surprising then that the process of the guillotine was managed easily. After three sessions in committee, debate was curtailed with a guillotine motion carried by 270 to 153. The final Bill was rushed through Parliament with forty-three opponents and 149 supporters. Hugo Young notes the defiance of the sceptics was both gentlemanly and orderly and, it might be added, completely ineffective (H. Young, 1999:335).

With the Bruges speech, however, a change began to be seen in the arena in which the issues were raised. The speech aired a robust and sceptical approach to European integration that changed the way in which all subsequent governments would handle the European issue. Between 1975 and 1988 the issue of European integration had been treated as an elite concern. From 1988, as Mrs Thatcher fell out with her Chancellor and Foreign Secretary and increasingly the rest of her Cabinet over EC membership and moves towards Economic and Monetary Union, she turned to more populist platforms. And whilst the Conservative parliamentary party opposed her increasingly assertive attacks, party conferences demonstrated widespread support for her stance. She therefore sought to use the 1989 European elections as a means of securing a popular mandate for a more sceptical approach to Europe and as a dress rehearsal for the general election that had to be held by spring 1992. In fact, whilst arguments previously never heard outside Westminster were widely debated for the first time, the strategy was, as has been noted, electorally unsuccessful with the Conservatives losing ten of forty-four MEPs. Nevertheless, Thatcher's interpretation was not that the policy was wrong, but that the outcome had been a product of domestic politics, with the elections operating as a mid-term opinion poll reflecting her government's declining popularity (Lawson, 1992:922; Thatcher, 1993:742–6).

Moreover, the genie was now out of the bottle and despite this temporary setback Mrs Thatcher had succeeded in galvanising the Conservative press (*Economist*, 1991:31–2). The *Daily Telegraph*, the most influential newspaper for Conservative constituency parties, now began to take a nationalist, anti-EC and pro-American editorial line. Similarly, the most influential broadsheet newspapers of the News International Group, *The Times* and *Sunday Times*, were 'encouraged' by Rupert Murdoch to adopt a strongly sceptical position on European policy. This at last marked a step change in the way in which the sceptics could get their message across and the shift was to become increasingly important in the next decade.

Conclusions

Between 1979 and 1988, the opportunities for mass participation in the European question remained few and far between and the issues at stake were essentially an elite concern. The opportunities to oppose closer integration were dominated by the broader party struggle, whether in terms of the three European elections in this period or the ratification of the Single European Act at Westminster.

The shift of the Labour Party to a hard line sceptical stance and a policy of withdrawal from the European Community coincided with the party being out of office. In this period, the opponents of closer European integration were divided, and for a variety of reasons unwilling to consider working across the party divide to unite in a common cause. Within the Labour Party the shift of pragmatic sceptics away from the fundamentalist anti-Marketeers, in the search of an electorally popular policy platform progressively watered down official Labour Party scepticism on Europe.

In the Conservative Party, the division between a small group of hard line fundamentalists and a much larger group of more pragmatic sceptics, ensured that for much of this period opposition to the government's pro-European line was muted. Margaret Thatcher's personal conversion to the sceptic cause acted as a catalyst for a re-connection of these two groups but at the expense of her continued hold on the premiership. Nevertheless, the situation had now changed markedly from 1979, not least because the scepticism which Thatcher had brought into the mainstream via the Bruges speech was qualitatively different from that of James Callaghan both in content and approach. Not only were her arguments and critique more comprehensive, but the implications for halting European integration in its tracks were far more radical. Hers was the combative and virulent Euroscepticism of a conviction politician; it was moreover the product of a convert's zeal.

Experience of membership of the EC in this eleven-year period had led to the emergence of a more coherent and, in some ways, more sophisticated critique of European integration and an emerging conventional wisdom that the cards were stacked against British national interests and that constructive engagement could never deliver results. Looking back, what is striking is the inability of the sceptics on the left and right to subordinate their partisan interest to the cause of opposing European integration. However, by the end of this period the move on both the left and right of important sceptic groupings from an instrumental to a principled critique of European Community membership apparently held out the prospect of a more constructive alliance between Labour and Conservative sceptics. The broad thrust of the Bruges critique, if not much of its anti-Socialist argumentation, struck a cord with many on the left as well as the right of the political spectrum. On the face of it, the removal of Thatcher should then have opened the way for the bipartisan convergence which had always been lacking. However, as the next chapter discusses, Thatcher was increasingly perceived by sceptics within her party as a martyr to the cause, and this was to result not in bipartisan convergence, but in the partisan endorsement of her arguments by Conservative sceptics.

Notes

1 The Labour party's 1984 Euro election manifesto comprised only ten pages of widely spaced type.

2 The report of the party's policy review group on 'Britain in the World' is published in *Meet the Challenge, Make the Change: a new agenda for Britain*, Labour Party, July 1989. See Forster and Wallace, 2000a.

3 Hansard (Commons) 1985–6, vol. 96, cols 317–21 and 326. Part of the reason why the Single Market was deliberately over-sold was the adversarial system. This encourages British governments to overlook the package deal nature for fear of attack by the opposition and concern that backbenchers might demand the use of the veto on unpalatable issues.

4 Leaks to the press suggested this criticism was implicitly directed towards the FCO who were unwilling adequately to defend British interests. David Owen corroborates this impression by arguing that the Foreign Office had taken on a campaigning role for the EC (H. Young, 1999:316).

5 Hugo Young argues that three issues were kept out of the Bruges speech: first, a strong anti-German attack in a passage on saving Europe from being united under Prussian domination; second, the argument that Britain had a justified claim to the leadership of the Community; and third, an attack on the growth of majority voting and the loss of national sovereignty (H. Young, 1999:348).

6 The struggle against Political Union, 1990–1993

Introduction

The period from the fall of Margaret Thatcher until the ratification of the Maastricht Treaty saw Euroscepticism come of age. After November 1990, Euroscepticism developed inside the Conservative Party with such dynamism that it quickly impacted on the government's pursuit of its European policy. This chapter focuses on the negotiation and ratification of the Maastricht Treaty. By the time of the Treaty's negotiation which took place between December 1990 and December 1991, there was growing unease inside the Conservative Party that EC membership was no longer delivering the type of benefits for which it had hoped. The Bruges speech had sketched out a philosophy of sorts in analysing the process of European integration and had established a practical benchmark against which to judge ongoing developments. From the outset, John Major's future and that of his government was intimately connected to his being able to demonstrate that his mildly pro-engagement European policy was capable of delivering results and that the fear of a federal Europe was misplaced. Facing two major intergovernmental conferences (IGCs), one on Political Union (IGC-PU) and the second on Economic and Monetary Union (IGC-EMU), this was a challenging proposition.

The Maastricht Treaty provided the opportunity for sceptics to oppose closer integration. However, Eurosceptics' burgeoning influence derived from the fact that the party was increasingly fractured. Between 1990 and 1993, the sceptics effectively linked the European question to the future of the party and succeeded in making it the issue on which John Major's leadership was routinely challenged. The inability of the party managers to fully control the parliamentary party or to subordinate ratification to the party struggle, offered the first real prospect since the 1975 referendum of halting European integration in its tracks. At the third reading forty-six MPs were willing to challenge the government up the point of threatening to hold the party to ransom on the issue of ratification. It was only when the government put the issue to a vote of confidence that all but one acquiesced.

This chapter develops three themes. First, it argues that the period saw sceptical groups within the Conservative Party gathering strength in two key areas. Not only did their organisational structure became better developed, but their arguments also gained an increasingly credible intellectual basis. During the ratification of the Maastricht Treaty, though not its negotiation, a hardcore of Conservative Eurosceptics was therefore ready and willing to seize the opportunity to oppose the government. Second, the chapter contends that the period of Eurosceptic disobedience lasting over fifteen months and the bitterness engendered by the government's recourse to a confidence vote, meant that the European issue in the Conservative Party would never be quite the same again. For a few it raised the issue of Europe from being one amongst many issues, to being a matter of conscience, in which loyalty to an idea was more important than loyalty to party. Through the intensity of the debates in Parliament, Eurosceptics were also able to mobilise activists outside the parliamentary arena. Thus, whilst opposition to closer European integration ended in legislative failure, it made an important contribution to a more active form of Euroscepticism. Finally, however, the chapter makes the point that despite the fact that the Bruges speech set out an intellectual agenda which should have been able to draw Labour and Conservative sceptics together, party political obstacles prevented the opponents of European integration from making common cause.

Opportunity

The origins of the Maastricht Treaty lay in the Single European Act (SEA). Agreed in December 1985, the SEA contained two commitments which led to the twin IGCs underpinning the Maastricht Treaty. First, the preamble to the SEA contained a political – though not a legal – commitment to Monetary Union. As soon as the Treaty was signed, some member state governments, with support from the Commission President Jacques Delors, pressed for a committee to be established to explore how Economic and Monetary Union might be realised. The Delors Committee, set up in 1988, submitted a report to the European Council in April 1989 and this led to the IGC–EMU with a remit to recommend changes to the treaties to create a single currency. A second commitment within the SEA was to review the foreign policy co-operation clauses five years after the Treaty came into effect. This therefore required an IGC by mid-1991 and created added pressure to open a second parallel set of treaty negotiations. Finally, the collapse of the Berlin Wall in October 1989 and the rapid re-unification of Germany led President Mitterrand and Chancellor Kohl to propose a Political Union IGC to explore how the European Community could be transformed into a European Union, with a common foreign and security policy. Agreement by the Heads of State and Government in 1990 to open two, year-long parallel treaty negotiations, one on Economic and Monetary Union and the other on Political Union provide the background to the creation of the Treaty on European Union, which took its popular name from the town of Maastricht where the European Council which agreed the treaty took place.

Ratifying the Maastricht Treaty ensured that Parliament would be able to make a direct contribution to the development of European integration. As in 1985 when the SEA was agreed, the government was obliged to make changes to domestic law to give effect to the treaty commitments. As will be explored further in this chapter, few sceptics really seized the opportunity in Parliament to oppose the government during the year-long Maastricht negotiations themselves. However, by the time of the conclusion of the Intergovernmental Conference in December 1991, concern about the implications of the treaty was spreading beyond the hard-core of committed sceptics. Three events then combined to strengthen the hand of the sceptics. First, John Major called a general election in April 1992 and, despite most predictions, won a majority of twenty-one. The small size of the majority made the government dependent on backbench Conservative Eurosceptic votes to deliver its programme and for the first time since 1973, Conservative sceptics had the ability to disrupt and ultimately defeat their own government if they voted with the opposition. Second, the Danish government held a referendum on the Maastricht Treaty on 2 June 1992, which rejected the Treaty by 48,000 votes. This was a psychological boost for the sceptics, and led to calls to abandon the ratification process in Britain altogether, since the treaty had to be ratified according to national practice in all the twelve member states. In fact, Major offered to delay the ratification process until after the Danish government had reached a decision on how to proceed, but the Danish vote remained a thorn in the side of governments throughout Europe. A third event was the suspension of sterling from the Exchange Rate Mechanism (ERM) on 16 September 1992. This damaged the economic credibility of the government but also emboldened Eurosceptics within the Conservative Party to believe that their time had come, and that the tide of European integration could be turned.

Opponents: who were they?

Three types of group were evident among the sceptics of this period. First, there were partisan groups drawing supporters from one of the two main parties; second, there were umbrella organisations which contained one or more sub-groupings; and finally, there were more general interest groups which were drawn to take a stance on the European issue because of its growing importance. In all of these three groups, an interesting feature was the way in which concern with the European issue was now shown to be leaving the confines of Westminster and mobilising involvement on a wider front.

As regards the partisan, party-based groupings, these were most prominent in the Conservative Party. The number of sceptics in the party received a dramatic boost from the downfall of Margaret Thatcher on 28 November 1990 which worked to extend their influence far and wide into the Conservative Party. Amongst her personal supporters and on the right of the party more generally, there was a prevailing feeling that Mrs Thatcher had been removed from office by her more pro-European colleagues within the Cabinet. John Wilkinson described it '… as a plot against the Lady. If the truth was known it was a plot' (Alexandre-Collier, 1998:94). It was, after all, the European issue which triggered her downfall through an unguarded but robust reply to a question which made clear that she had definitively moved from pragmatic scepticism to a position of outright hostility.[1] In part, the sceptics were therefore brought together by the desire to mobilise support for Thatcher and subsequently their preferred successor, in order to ensure the leadership remained true to Mrs Thatcher's intellectual inheritance. In this regard, a particularly strong incentive was the need to prevent the Europhiles in Cabinet from getting their way in replacing her with Michael Heseltine or Douglas Hurd.[2]

All the leadership contenders deployed the European issue as a weapon in their campaigns, with Hurd and Heseltine using it to encapsulate key differences with Margaret Thatcher. John Major's campaign team presented his policy positions in a way which underscored his Thatcherite credentials and implied he would hold a sceptical line on Europe.[3] Expectation was therefore high that although Margaret Thatcher had gone her policies would remain. The contest for the leadership was bloody and divisive, pitting the Cabinet against the backbenchers and the right of the party against the left. The conclusion of the election left the party both traumatised and deeply factionalised, with the right wing having been driven together by the need to support a successor who might continue Thatcherite policies.

Notwithstanding the efforts of Major's campaign team, uncertainty remained as to whether he would be as robust as his predecessor on Europe. After all, it was Major who as Chancellor had taken sterling into the ERM in October 1990 and during the short but intense campaign he left almost everyone he met with the impression that he supported their view on Europe – whether sceptical or pro-European. The right wing of the party therefore saw the new Prime Minister as a leader on probation, and was prepared to look to Mrs Thatcher if Major was felt to be deviating from her policies.[4] Indeed, this was an attitude she was keen to encourage, readily emphasising her own skills as a 'back seat driver' (*Economist*, 1991:29). This provided encouragement to quite a substantial number of MPs to join the parliamentary Friends of Bruges Group, which had as its express aim the need to stiffen the resolve of the government in pursuing a more sceptical stance on Europe.

For the longstanding parliamentary members of the Friends of Bruges Group, the irony of the situation was all too evident. Just at the moment when the most senior member of government had embraced a Eurosceptic creed, she had been removed. Nevertheless, within two years, over 130 Conservative backbench MPs were rumoured to be in some way associated with the group. While to a certain extent this was a reflection of the way in which it had become a haven for the dispossessed, it was also a symptom of the growing importance of the European issue and the determination of the sceptics to maintain their vigil in support of Thatcher's opposition to further steps towards European integration.

With the exception of the Friends of Bruges Group, which became quite active in the period of the Maastricht negotiations, it was however left to a new group to provide the organisational dynamism to challenge the government's European policies. The Fresh Start Group was founded by Michael Spicer, and its leading members included Bill Cash, James Cran, Christopher Gill and Roger Knapman. It had its origins in two EDMs, the first prompted by the failure of the Danish electorate to ratify the Treaty on 2 June 1992 and which called on the government to seize this opportunity to let the Maastricht Treaty fall and to begin again anew.

This EDM collected eighty-four signatures (Baker *et al.*, 1993a:166; Gorman, 1993:53). A second EDM, tabled in September 1992, welcomed sterling's withdrawal from the ERM, calling on the government to make a fresh start in economic policy as well, and attracted over sixty supporters. Following this, the membership of the Fresh Start Group quickly grew to over fifty MPs.

The Fresh Start Group's core purpose, however, was opposition to the parliamentary ratification of the Maastricht Treaty, with a secondary objective being to attempt to secure a referendum on the treaty and the issue of the single currency (Gorman, 1993:60). It was true that opponents of European integration had organised themselves with an unofficial whip in 1972 during the passage of the European Communities Bill. But what was different about the Fresh Start Group was their access to financial resources, their militancy, the organisational skills which they brought to the parliamentary battles and their method of operation. Their base at 17 Great College Street, a town house loaned by former party treasurer and funder of the Bruges Group, Lord MacAlpine, was within walking distance of Parliament and was a sufficiently effective headquarters to be dubbed 'Major's House of Horrors' (Gorman, 1993:198). Michael Spicer was the chair, and James Cran and Christopher Gill were appointed joint secretaries and unofficial whips. Throughout the ratification process the group met regularly to co-ordinate opposition and draft amendments to the three clause European Communities (Amendment) Bill. Both in appearance and to some extent reality, the group thus became a party within a party.

An indication of its organisational capacity was the fact that the group tabled over 500 amendments and proposed 100 new clauses. In addition, however, the Fresh Start Group broke the party whips' rule book on loyal dissent. They did not inform the whips of their voting intentions, and they did not simply abstain, but were willing to vote with the opposition. Their strategy was hence both premeditated and co-ordinated. Moreover it went well beyond simply opposing the government in parliamentary debates on key points, since the group also refused to support the government in procedural votes (Alderman, 1993). The group therefore opposed government guillotines and occupied parliamentary time over Maastricht, so that the government's commitment to the treaty could only come about at the cost to its legislative programme. In all, they voted against the government 985 times and abstained on some 1,515 occasions in order to thwart the Bill.

As Hugo Young suggests, this behaviour changed the way in which Tory politics was done and the rules of political conduct (H. Young, 1999:396). In particular, the Fresh Start Group broke new ground in two areas. First, through their behaviour in Parliament its members demonstrated a willingness not just to express displeasure at government policy, but to take almost all means necessary to prevent legislation from being enacted. Second, funds were raised from outside the Conservative Party to establish an independent organisation beyond its reach. Finally, the Fresh Start Group changed the organisational face of parliamentary sceptical groups, with some longstanding Conservative sceptical groupings such as the Anti-Common Market League fading into the background as Fresh Start became dominant. Until its creation, sceptics had been rather like individual fish who had been swimming in the same general direction. Fresh Start offered a sense of community and purpose, transforming the sceptics into a shoal of fish synchronising their activities with a shared objective, opposition to the ratification of the Maastricht Treaty. Thanks to the Fresh Start Group, Euroscepticism thus matured rapidly within the parliamentary Conservative Party.

Whilst organisational developments were limited during the year-long Maastricht negotiations, from early 1992 there was a also huge growth in the number of sceptical groups among Conservative Party activists. Some twenty-seven separate organisations were created in the 18 months after the December 1991 Maastricht European Council.[5] A number of Conservative backbenchers were instrumental in the foundation of such groups and, indeed, often led them. Michael Spicer ran the European Reform Group, a small group chaired by himself and Jonathan Aitken, which met regularly to discuss and debate European issues. Bill Cash with support from Sir James Goldsmith and Margaret Thatcher created the European Foundation, which published the monthly *European Journal*, again attracting complaints that it was too well organised to sit comfortably with an MP's commitment to the Conservative Party. Other groups within the broader Conservative family included the Campaign for UK Conservatism founded by Rodney Atkinson, the co-author of *Treason at Maastricht*, The League of Concerned Conservatives which organised occasional speaker meetings on right-wing themes including Europe, and Red Lion Talks, a group founded by Dr Helen Szamuely which took its name from a public house near Parliament, and met once a month to discuss European issues. In addition, Conservative Youth against a Federal Europe and Conservative Graduates were connected to Young Conservative activities and provided an indication that a generational change in attitude was now underway, with Euroscepticism the prevailing attitude amongst youth activists.

This extra-parliamentary mobilisation was a new and important sign that unease with Conservative policy was now not simply a parliamentary concern as it had been between 1975 and 1990. Political activists were now deeply disturbed by the government line and willing to mobilise in support of Eurosceptic positions in groups outside Parliament. In February 1991 the Young Conservatives publicly rejected the government's policy on Europe. This mood was further underlined by the support for sceptical speakers at the party conference in Brighton in October 1992 when Lord Tebbit led a chorus from a youthful section of the audience opposing government policy, and in Bournemouth the following year when Teresa Gorman launched her book *The Bastards* and Margaret Thatcher her memoirs, both criticising Major's European policy (Seldon, 1997:327).

Within the Labour Party, on the other hand, the Labour Common Market Safeguards Committee created in 1967, now in the new incarnation of the Labour Euro Safeguards Campaign, continued to be active. In 1990, it claimed to have just under a quarter of the parliamentary party as paid up members and still published regular newsletters. In the upper chamber Lords Bruce, Jay and Stoddart continued to be active, and in the House of Commons Tony Benn, Austin Mitchell, Peter Shore and Nigel Spearing acted as spokesmen. In the European Parliament, the MEPs Tom Megahy and Barry Seal (a former leader of the British Labour group in the Parliament) provided transnational representation (Baker and Seawright, 1998b:354). As with the Conservative Party, there was also extra-parliamentary activity in the form of the Campaign Against Euro-Federalism, a new Socialist anti-EU group with a magazine called *The Democrat*. Aside from this, however, partisan Labour groups were remarkably few and far between, in part at least because the Shadow Cabinet was moving to more a pragmatic stance on Europe and did not wish to focus on the European issue in Parliament or during any election campaign. Peter Shore of the Euro Safeguards Campaign noted that from the early 1990s it was increasingly difficult to get ambitious MPs to join for fear of damaging their careers. Indeed, the Safeguards group stopped making public its membership lists and switched to a strategy of protecting the confidentiality of members.

The second category of organisations engaged in the European issue were extra-parliamentary umbrella organisations which contained two or more groups within them. These came in two different forms, partisan and non-partisan organisations. In the main, those with partisan leanings were connected with the Conservative Party. The Conservatives Against Federal Europe (CAFE), founded and supported by Vivian Bendall and William Walker, was a leading example of a Conservative umbrella group. An example of a non-partisan umbrella organisation was the Maastricht Referendum Campaign which organised a parliamentary petition calling for a referendum on the treaty and which 'was well funded through established Tory business fundraising channels and reportedly received over £300,000 from overseas supporters'. Supporters included Tom Mackie, Jim Miller, Joe Bamford and James Goldsmith (*Sunday Times*, 1993:1).

The third category was groups with a more general focus, where the potency of the European question prompted the development of a stance on the issue. Within Parliament, the Conservative Selsdon Group, created to encourage the Heath government of 1970 to 1974 to return to neo-liberal policies, contained a number of sceptics including Norman Tebbit, Richard Body, Sir George Gardiner and Michael Brown and issued its own publication in February 1992 expressing reservations about the Maastricht Treaty. The 1992 group created by George Gardiner took a similar stance, although it did not publish any pamphlets. In addition, almost all the members of the No Turning Back group were reportedly members of the Bruges Group. As Chapter 5 noted, NTB included John Redwood, Peter Lilley, Michael Portillo, Edward Leigh, Michael Forsyth, Francis Maude, Neil Hamilton and Alan Howarth. Most were junior ministers in the first Major government of 1990 to 1992 who in time might expect to hold high office. This was an important indicator that scepticism was no longer a marginal position in the Conservative Party – or a stance for the ambitious to avoid. The contrast with Heath's administration of 1970 to 1974 was striking, since anti-Marketeers were excluded from or at best marginalised within the government. Finally, from the extreme right wing of the Party, the Monday Club – albeit by the 1990s small and quite marginalised, also showed a concern with European issues, as did the *Salisbury Review*, which used its pages to advocate sceptical positions.

Outside Parliament, the Freedom Association presided over by Norris McWhirter took a particular interest in the European issue and with the *Freedom Journal* circulated to over 6,000 members reached a wide audience. Likewise the *International Currency Review* published a pamphlet on the issue of Europe entitled *Europe in Europe: A Reply to the British Government publication 'Britain in Europe'* (Alexandre-Collier, 1998:235).

The press was an additional and central factor in giving what could now be described as the Eurosceptical movement added momentum. From the middle of 1991, and for the first time since Britain had joined the European Community, the *Daily Telegraph*, the most influential newspaper for Conservative activists, embraced a nationalist and anti-Maastricht editorial line and advanced the need for strong Anglo-Saxon ties. The most influential broadsheet newspapers of the News International Group, *The Times* and *Sunday Times*, were slightly slower in embracing a sceptical position on European policy but by the end of the Maastricht negotiations in December 1991 were fully supportive.[6] *The Times* played a small but important role in launching a campaign for a referendum on the treaty on 23 March 1993 and in promoting the referendum cause thereafter. The *Spectator*, a right-wing weekly journal, more irreverently highlighted the contrast between Major and Thatcher, disparaging Major's managerial style and making play of his intellectual inferiority.[7] It was also suspicious of the corrosive influence of a 'Europeanising' Foreign Office which placed a diplomatic dividend on the avoidance of conflict.[8] The press therefore provided a platform for sceptics to publish their views, in a medium which reached the grassroots of the Conservative Party as well as the wider public. In addition to moving the European issue out of Parliament and into public discourse, however, expression of sceptic views in the press was psychologically beneficial, providing them with the oxygen of publicity and a support network to bolster their instincts.

The role of the *Sun* newspaper, part of the Murdoch newsgroup, deserves particular mention in terms of the platform it offered to sceptical viewpoints. Routinely the level of debate and quality of analysis was of a rather low standard, but it had the largest readership of any of the newsprint media and it did a great deal to ignite a sort of popular Euroscepticism, voicing the general unease with a European integration process which few understood and which was open to easy ridicule. A prime example of this was the 'Up Yours Delors' headline of 1 November 1990, beneath which the *Sun* 'today calls on its patriotic family of readers to tell the filthy French to FROG OFF!' (Alexandre-Collier, 1998:91). This approach was important since, notwithstanding the questionable merit of its case, the *Sun* encouraged a climate of opinion in which more reflective arguments might take root.

Arguments

By the time of Margaret Thatcher's downfall in November 1990, unease with the process and direction of European integration had spread from a very small minority of committed sceptics to a much wider audience centred above all within the Conservative Party. As Chapter 5 demonstrated, there was now an emerging outer circle of MPs who felt growing disquiet concerning the value of EC membership. Some scholars argue that the specific circumstances of this period – Margaret Thatcher's downfall and Major's problems with backbenchers – should not, however, overshadow the fact that the arguments used by the sceptics were '… essentially a replay of those of the 1960s and 1970s' (Aughey 1996a:210).

Certainly, some concerns were in general similar: the rejection of European integration in favour of the image of Anglo-Saxon independence, the loss of parliamentary sovereignty and fear of centralisation. One of the most important elements in the arguments against Maastricht explicitly drew on the old Powellite contention that economic advantages could never justify the sacrifice of national sovereignty. For nearly twenty years almost all British concessions on Europe had been justified on grounds of the benefit to her economic well-being which would ensue. Accession to the EC had been based on these arguments, as too had been Margaret Thatcher's adherence to the SEA, which ended the national veto on Single Market measures. The fundamentalist sceptics had long argued that this logic placed Britain on a conveyor belt to federalism, since for two decades integration had been speeding up rather than slowing down, and these arguments now once more came into fashion (Baker *et al.*, 1994:46; Ridley,1991:160).

Indeed, many themes could be traced back to the early sceptics of the late 1940s and early 1950s: the feeling of Britain's geographical separation from the continent; Britain's distinctiveness in cultural, political and economic terms; the threat which the '*projet européen*' posed and the zero sum nature of the integration process. What had changed in regard to these familiar areas of complaint related mainly to the quality of the arguments deployed and their specificity, with a closer focus of the critique on the structures, process and output of the Community and the drivers of the integrative process. Thus, whereas with the Bruges speech the Conservative Party had been equipped with a telescope through which it could view the EC and comprehend the costs and benefits of membership, with the Maastricht Treaty Eurosceptics had an object on which they could fix, to judge just how far integration had developed.

The fall of the Berlin Wall in October 1989 and the rapid reunification of Germany the following year ignited Conservative sceptics' longstanding anxiety over the influence of Germany. For many it was never far from the surface, although the crude xenophobia expressed by Nicholas Ridley in a *Spectator* interview in which the EC was depicted as '… a German racket designed to take over the whole of Europe' was for the most part avoided. The critique offered by Bill Cash, for instance, was an attempt to more clearly articulate a reasoned assessment of German influence in the EU. Cash argued that the shape of EU institutions structurally and disproportionately benefited Germany. The German economic model as well as its employment structures were well served by attempts to construct an EU level social partnership, which was itself modelled on the German approach. The outline and structure of the European Central Bank took as its inspiration the Bundesbank model.[9] Nevertheless at cruder moments even Cash argued there was a '"Germano-Russian condominium", of which the European Union would form the western pillar' (Stephens, 1997:350).

However, there were also remarkable differences in the kinds of arguments now used by the Eurosceptics in relation to the Maastricht Treaty. First, Eurosceptics were united in their view that the Maastricht Treaty crossed a Rubicon in terms of the range and power ceded to a central authority. The IGCs had as their explicit objective the creation of Economic and Monetary Union, the scrapping of national currencies and the creation of a European (Political) Union equipped with a foreign and security policy, the possibility of a defence capability and justice and home affairs (JHA) responsibilities (policing and border controls). The stated aim of the Maastricht Treaty was to transform the European Community into a European Union. This was a far cry from the Common Market which Britain had joined (Spicer, 1992). The Eurosceptics' position was thus a rebuttal of the traditional argument of Conservative leaders that the next step was both incremental and had few significant consequences and was anyway necessary to secure British influence over future developments. 'What in the 1970s, Neil Marten claimed to be the federalist *potential* of the Common Market now appears to some to be the federalist *agenda* of the European Union of the 1990s' (Aughey, 1996a:210).

Second, whereas previous arguments had depicted the EC as alien yet distant, the sceptic case now focused on the way it impinged on and threatened every aspect of daily life. The burden of EC legislation and bureaucracy here became a particular target, with Christopher Booker playing a leading role through his column in the *Sunday Telegraph* which denounced and poured scorn on the Commission and its pernicious impact on Britain (Booker and North,1997; Ritchie 1989:108). In addition, the direct threat posed to the security, prosperity and sovereignty of the British state was given a party political resonance by the fact that these were 'matters that go to the very soul of Conservatism' (Baker *et al.*, 1994:47).

A third area in which the arguments surrounding the Maastricht Treaty differed from previous periods lay in the calls which were now made for a referendum on the issue of a single currency. This was the first point at which some members of the political elite advocated putting to the electorate the question of the kind of European structure to which they wished to belong. The charge was led by Margaret Thatcher. Where John Major sought to de-dramatize the single currency issue so that it became a matter of the calculation of technical advantage, Margaret Thatcher linked it to national independence (Morris, 1996:135). It is striking that the idea of a referendum fitted in poorly with sceptics' notion of parliamentary sovereignty. But it was the most likely means of wrecking the treaty which it looked as though the political elite would ratify.

It should further be noted that Mrs Thatcher's personal championing of the referendum cause and her own public opposition to the government's policy of ratifying the treaty with an opt-out from EMU, meant that the issue of a single currency quickly 'became a litmus test of Euroscepticism and, by implication, adherence to the old Thatcherite cause' (Seldon, 1996:430). The issue of Europe was therefore linked to the broader questions of Major's leadership and general party policy, and as Peter Morris argues, Europe became a weapon in the hands of those who opposed the leadership of John Major (Morris, 1996:133). Scepticism on the European issue appealed to a growing number of Thatcherite backbenchers, who came into Parliament under the leadership of Mrs Thatcher and more especially and somewhat paradoxically under John Major's leadership in the April 1992 general election. 'Thatcher's children' as one commentator refers to them thought John Major a traitor to the right and 'they wanted Major to fail, not least over Europe' (H. Young, 1999:396). Europe thus became a surrogate issue for opposition to Major and the government's broader social and economic programme.[10]

During the negotiations themselves, however, most Conservatives – and even some Cabinet ministers – were prepared to take the treaty on trust, and few made the effort to analyse its micro-detail. Confidence in Major as Mrs Thatcher's protégé was still predominant, and the sceptics were as yet subdued, couching their arguments in largely general terms. They therefore urged that any treaty should exclude a commitment to a '*vocation fédérale*', that the national veto should be preserved in decision making with no extension of majority voting, and that any commitments in new policy sectors such as an EU foreign and security policy, should be inter-governmental in nature and preclude interference from the EU's supranational institutions. It was also argued that Britain should not have to make institutional and decision-making concessions on the issue of an enhanced social policy since this would undermine a decade of Conservative industrial legislation and reforms, allowing the nightmare of Socialism through the backdoor to become a reality. In addition, there was opposition to any attempt to force Britain to join a single currency. The situation during the period of the negotiations was epitomised by Mrs Thatcher's own position: while favouring a referendum on the single currency issue, the former Prime Minister remained at the same time sufficiently circumspect to stop short of counselling her successor to avoid signing the treaty.

However, the mood darkened rapidly once the negotiations were concluded and Conservative MPs were able to take stock of the treaty in its final form following its signature in February 1992. This growing tide of criticism was further encouraged when in June 1992 the Danish electorate voted to reject the treaty. What was particularly striking about the Eurosceptic critique which now emerged, however, was the close attention to the detail of the treaty; such an approach was indeed to become the hallmark of Euroscepticism in the 1990s. Along with an increase in the sophistication of the arguments used, it marked a qualitative shift in the sceptical analysis of the integration process and owed much to the election on 9 April 1992 to the House of Commons of a new generation of MPs, among them Iain Duncan Smith and Walter Sweeney. This new cohort had amongst their number lawyers schooled in the *acquis communautaire*, party insiders and activists with European expertise and was in general terms the Thatcherite army Mrs Thatcher had never had whilst in power. The Eurosceptic case was now advanced on four broad fronts, focusing on the betrayal, complacency, lack of attention to detail and complicity of which the government was seen as having been guilty in signing the Treaty.

In support of their depiction of the treaty as a betrayal, the sceptics highlighted with remarkable attention to detail some of the key concessions which proved that the Maastricht Treaty had not been the triumph which the government rashly claimed to have won 'game set and match'. The weakness of the pillared structure, especially the third pillar which endorsed Commission involvement in the decision-making process and contained a commitment to revisit the issue of communautarising the pillar within five years, was depicted as little more than a stay of execution, while the agreement to hold another IGC within five years underscored the continued dynamism of the integration process. In addition, it was argued that the government's willingness (against the advice of the Foreign and Commonwealth Office) to allow the mandates of the European Parliament and the Commission to be synchronised, opened the way for the Commission to become the executive of the EU, subordinate to and appointed by the European Parliament.

The second key Eurosceptic criticism targeted the complacency of the Major government. Sceptics argued that the government had not learnt the lesson of the SEA, namely that to concede to expansive Treaty language even when the substance of an agreement looked innocuous, was to offer a powerful integrative weapon to European federalists. Most concern was focused on the ambitious language of Title III of the Treaty which opened with the declaration that 'a common foreign and security policy is hereby established' and as part and parcel of this included a commitment to '... a common defence policy which might in time lead to a common defence'. To more perceptive Eurosceptics this was yet another hostage to fortune. Walter Sweeney was prominent amongst those suggesting that despite preserving a veto on the possibility of Common Foreign and Security Policy (CFSP) leading to a common defence policy, key concessions in the development of this policy sector had been made. 'I think we are moving inevitably in that direction and the interests of Britain as a nation state are being sacrificed to some form of European ideal' (Alexandre-Collier, 1998:138).

A third strand of the Eurosceptic critique was the government's lack of attention to detail. Here the attack focused on the fact that the British opt-outs were not as water tight as the government had suggested. After all, the opt-outs allowed the other member states to use the structures and decision-making processes of the new EU, implying that at some stage in the future Britain would have to join and in doing so sign up to legislation which it had played no part in shaping (Crewe, 1996:430). There was also concern that the centrality of nation states and their ability to control the process of European integration was insufficiently safeguarded. In particular, it was argued that there had been a lack of attention to detail on the issue of majority voting, which was extended by the Treaty into nine new areas beyond those delineated in the SEA. Again, Walter Sweeney argued that 'I think the principle of Qualified Majority Voting was disastrous for our long-term prospects of remaining a nation state'.[11]

Fourth and finally, the Eurosceptics contended that the Major government was guilty of complicity in what was clearly an act of political integration with significant implications for national sovereignty. In this regard, it was argued that the drive towards Monetary Union and a single currency necessitated a single economic authority. Fiscal and monetary policy would need to be controlled by the Commission or a European Central Bank, and this would create a very powerful centre of sovereignty distinct from that of individual member states.[12] Thus in a paving debate on ratification, the Conservative backbench MP Patrick McNair-Wilson for instance argued that, 'people used to laugh at the words "loss of sovereignty" but if we cannot issue our own money, we have no control over our own destiny' (Alexandre-Collier, 1998:38). In short, the four arguments deployed by the Eurosceptics combined to portray the Maastricht Treaty as a treaty too far, and clear proof that, with or without opt-outs, Britain could no longer win the arguments by constructive engagement. The Maastricht agenda was also unambiguously committed to a political strategy of creating a European Union.

The official opposition's critique of the government's policy was by contrast striking in its absence, not least because the Labour frontbench had by now moved to a pragmatic position not dissimilar to that of the government. While essentially supportive of the treaty, however, the party did on occasion strike a posture against it for the tactical reason of wishing to cause the government maximum difficulty. The pretext for this opposition was the inclusion of the social chapter in a separate protocol of which Britain was not a signatory. As many contemporary commentators pointed out, a deeply ironic situation thus resulted, with a marriage of convenience in opposition to the treaty between Conservative Eurosceptics who rejected the Social Protocol and could never agree to its incorporation into the treaty, and a Labour Party which tactically made acceptance of the treaty conditional on that very thing.

Nevertheless, in the debates which occurred after the treaty had been signed, Labour sceptics did advance arguments that had a strong resonance with those of the Conservative sceptics. Thus Bryan Gould for example opposed European Monetary Union because it removed the government's control of monetary and fiscal policy in general. Equally, a small minority on the right including Peter Shore and Austin Mitchell remained deeply opposed to European integration and advanced arguments similar to those used by the Conservative Eurosceptics relating to sovereignty, national autonomy, and the loose drafting of key elements of the treaty.

For more left-wing Labour sceptics, however, the main problem with the treaty was that it imposed a deflationary policy that would make it impossible for a future Labour government to deliver its policy commitments on investment in public services and greater public expenditure. As the former frontbencher Denzil Davies put it, 'at the heart of the treaty lies an economic ideology which would be anathema to everything Labour has stood for. Maastricht incorporates a monetary and deflationary ideology into the domestic law of Britain' (Baker *et al.*, 1993a:151).

Part of the problem for the Labour sceptics was that they were heavily reliant for their influence on support from party heavyweights. Initially, they had such a figure in the form of Bryan Gould, John Smith's opponent in the leadership contest of 1992 and a powerful advocate of a referendum on the treaty. Gould's defeat by Smith, his resignation from the Labour frontbench in September 1992 to campaign against the Maastricht Treaty and his subsequent retirement from British politics was hence a serious blow for sceptical voices within the party. Ultimately the Labour sceptics' position remained weak since their party's flirtation with opposition to the treaty was more about the domestic party political struggle with the Conservative government, than it was to do with any genuinely held objection to its contents. This was most evident on the issue of the Social Protocol which on Labour's election to office in 1997 was immediately signed without the need for further ratification.

Arena

In the twelve-month period of the negotiations leading to the Maastricht Treaty, the government worked hard in the Westminster arena to be as inclusive as possible and so to ensure both its own unity and that of the parliamentary Conservative Party. In this regard John Major pursued a multi-faceted strategy to neutralise the sceptics within the party. The first element of this strategy comprised the involvement – and thus implication – of leading Cabinet sceptics in the negotiations, so that all were bound by collective responsibility and sceptics in the wider party deprived of leadership. It was an open secret that the Cabinet was deeply divided over the wisdom of attempting to negotiate the treaty, but Major's inclusive approach implicitly forced the sceptics within the Cabinet, notably Michael Howard, Peter Lilley, Ken Baker and, to a lesser extent Norman Lamont, to think twice about the cost of opposing government policy.

A measure of the success of this strategy was the fact that the Eurosceptics in Cabinet did prove unwilling to voice collective opposition to the treaty, and focused instead on a more subtle use of the issue to further their own particular agendas. Peter Lilley was by dint of his ministerial post and role in the foundation of the No Turning Back Group the most senior sceptic, although as Secretary of State for Industry he was only engaged in the IGC negotiations in a very limited way.[13] While disparaging about the situation behind the closed doors of the Bruges group meetings, Lilley grudgingly accepted the government's position in Cabinet and was careful not to make public the extent of his scepticism. Similarly, Michael Howard, the Secretary of State for Employment and Norman Lamont, the Chancellor, both chose to concentrate on their own departmental responsibilities rather than on the wider implications of the treaty. Thus Howard focused on the social chapter, enhanced employment legislation and the role of the Commission, while Lamont remained preoccupied with the EMU negotiations.

None of the Cabinet Eurosceptics sought support from the parliamentary party nor disseminated information on the conduct of the negotiations. The Cabinet sceptics publicly 'kept their distance from the Eurosceptics' on the backbenches who they considered maverick and unreliable (Gorman, 1993:13). Likewise, the fundamentalists considered the Cabinet ministers and the more junior ministers ultimately unwilling to place their commitment to the European issue before personal advancement in government. This failure to unite gave John Major sufficient flexibility to pick off his opponents and negotiate a treaty.

At the same time, within the parliamentary arena, government whips moved against the growing influence of sceptics within Conservative backbench committees so that the leading office holders of these committees would be supportive of government policy. Thus the whips orchestrated the ousting of the Bruges Group

Friends from the Conservative backbench European Affairs Committee, replacing Bill Cash as the committee chairman by the loyalist candidate Sir Norman Fowler (Gorman, 1993:29–35). This was followed one week later by the replacement of the Eurosceptic chairman of the Conservative Foreign Affairs Committee, Sir George Gardiner, by Cyril Townsend. Both Fowler and Townsend immediately used their access to the media to offer fulsome support for the government's negotiating stance.

In addition, the Prime Minister routinely met with sceptical MPs to brief them on developments and the major stumbling blocks, and to sketch out the government's position on key issues. He constantly and very personally reassured them that he would not sign a treaty which would undermine national sovereignty. At the same time, some of the most awkward were wooed with the promise of posts within the government. The silence of Jonathan Aitken, many other Eurosceptics thought, was bought with the promise of promotion after the next election – a view corroborated by the speed with which Aitken was promoted after the 1992 general election. Bill Cash, routinely consulted by the Prime Minister, was offered a parliamentary private secretary's post with the promise of a junior minister's post and was even asked by the Foreign Secretary to assist in the drafting of the April 1992 general election manifesto (H. Young, 1999:394). He resisted such inducements and continued to attack the government's policy.

Major also made judicious use of the government's control of the parliamentary agenda to facilitate parliamentary endorsement of his negotiating position. Whilst some point to Major's willingness to seek parliamentary approval for his negotiating stance in November 1991, two weeks prior to the Maastricht European Council as an act of courage, in many ways, however, it was also an act of deception. The motion was very weak and almost impossible to oppose unless MPs subscribed to the hard line sceptical position. Major's commitments were remarkably open-ended, carefully constructed to allow him the maximum amount of flexibility in finding a means to agree British support for the treaty. He also talked up his government's opposition to commitments that were neither in the draft treaties nor even a likely outcome. And he was vague on issues which had still to be decided. It was then little surprise that he succeeded in securing a majority of 101 in the final vote, with only six sceptical MPs opposing the motion.

In addition, ostensibly on the grounds of the need for confidentiality, treaty drafts were effectively withheld from Parliament, so MPs were obliged to take the word of ministers on face value when they spoke of the major issues, outstanding difficulties and potential final shape of the treaty. The majority of MPs readily accepted the reassuring words of ministers, in part at least in the interests of party unity. However, the sceptics were also negligent in failing to search out treaty drafts which were readily available in other European capitals and which would have confirmed many of their own suspicions. Part of the reason for this failure was the fact that Euroscepticism was still firmly rooted within a national frame of reference and there was as yet little contact with continental opponents of the Maastricht Treaty. The nationalistic flavour of Euroscepticism rendered its adherents reluctant at this stage to seek out information. This weakness was rectified once the Maastricht Treaty had been signed; as the ratification process underlined, opposition was now to become increasingly pan-European.[14]

A further element of Major's strategy was a careful focus on the imagery of any potential treaty rather than the substance; the treaty would be intergovernmental and break the 'community – one model fits all – method' of decision making (Forster, 1999). In this regard, Major also sought to outflank the sceptics by pandering to the preferences of the Conservative Party. But while the creation of a pillared structure in which CFSP and JHA were included could be portrayed as purely intergovernmental, the reality was that this was somewhat disingenuous. The power of the national veto was watered down to a right of exclusion from collective and binding decisions, while the right of governments to propose actions was now to be shared with the Commission. Moreover, the Community dynamics of decision making were anyway likely to lead to a greater role for the EU's supranational institutions, and the government acquiesced in a review of the intergovernmental pillars within five years. In a similar way, the government fought hard to remove the provocative phrase 'federal vocation', but was willing to concede the inclusion of the idea of subsidiarity, an essentially federalist concept. Thanks, however, to the concentration on symbolism, these important substantive developments went unnoticed and unremarked at the time of the negotiations.

Another related tactic which Major used to make the treaty digestible was to adopt the position that he was willing to deepen integration in areas where concessions had already been made by Mrs Thatcher in the SEA, but resistant to offering new concessions. Thus, Major was willing to allow the powers of the European Parliament (EP) to be extended in areas where majority voting had been conceded by his predecessor in the SEA, but fought a rearguard action against extending the power of the EP to new policy areas. Likewise, he was willing to align the terms of office of the European Parliament and the European Commission since the incoming Commission President had voluntarily submitted himself and the newly appointed Commissioners to a vote of confidence.

Major thus worked hard to outwit the sceptics both through his tactical use of the various parliamentary instruments at his disposal and his presentation of the treaty. The final element of his strategy in the parliamentary arena was the very explicit linkage which the government made between the successful negotiation of the treaty and the party struggle. In particular, success in the negotiations was linked to success in the general election which needed to be held by May 1992. This effectively curtailed the willingness of MPs to rebel since it would wreak, arguably, John Major's only triumph in the run up to the polls.

During the period of the negotiation of the treaty, Major's tactics proved remarkably successful and the forces of scepticism in his party remained muted. The majority of Conservative MPs were unnerved by the negotiations but not yet anti-EU. Their concerns were as yet unfocused and they were in general willing to follow where the Prime Minister might lead. Although living on borrowed time, the hope still prevailed that pragmatic engagement could deliver results and there was a willingness to allow the government to prove that this was still possible.

The ratification of the treaty, which was again played out in the parliamentary arena, was however, an entirely different matter. The rebound within the Conservative Party against the treaty and indeed against Major's tactics was remarkable, and resulted in what one group of scholars has termed, 'the parliamentary siege of Maastricht' (Baker *et al.*, 1994). This point is illustrated by the parliamentary figures for the period. The Maastricht Bill began life with a paving motion in February 1992 and took over a year to ratify – seventy parliamentary votes and sixty-one debates – and was only passed in July 1993 when the government made it a confidence issue. On the second reading on 21 May 1992, the European Communities (Amendment) Bill was passed by 336 to ninety-two, with Labour abstaining. Twenty-two Tories voted against their own government. On 6 June after the Danish referendum, the first Fresh Start EDM was tabled. The government then delayed the progress of the Bill until November 1992, when it put forward a paving motion which it won by just three votes. Twenty-six rebels voted against the government on this occasion and a further three abstained. Indeed the paving motion was only won by a promise to delay the third reading until after a positive Danish referendum vote. In March 1993, on Amendment 28 relating the selection process for the Committee of the Regions, the government lost by twenty-two votes. At the third reading in May 1993, forty-one Conservatives voted against the government with a further five abstentions. They were joined by sixty-six Labour MPs who defied their party whips to vote against the treaty rather than abstaining. Twenty-three rebels voted against the government in the second vote on the Social Protocol of 22 July 1993 leading to the largest defeat of a sitting Conservative government in the twentieth century. Thereafter, in a well-publicised vote of confidence, the government eventually achieved its wish to ratify the treaty which came into force in November 1993. The committee stage took 163 hours and over twenty-three sitting days. The Bill consumed over 210 hours of debate with 600 amendments and prompted greater disobedience in the Conservative Party than any other single issue (Mckie, 1994:136).[15]

The sceptics were empowered by a number of events. First, Major's majority dropped from 110 to twenty-one at the April 1992 general election and this gave them an opportunity to flex their muscles which had not existed since Britain joined the European Community in 1973. As Teresa Gorman made clear, '… with a majority of 100 a rebellion was futile. But with a majority of twenty Conservatives, a group of MPs can change government policy' (Gorman, 1993:36). Major faced dissenters who were willing to be unconventional in the methods which they employed to oppose the treaty. They were well organised, with their own whipping system and collective strategy centred around members of the Fresh Start Group, and ultimately willing to be tenacious in the way in which they operated. The second key development to empower the sceptics was the Danish referendum of 2 June 1992. This provided a fillip by the opportunity it apparently offered to kill off the treaty. The third key event was the dramatic ejection of sterling from the ERM in November 1992, which not only caused a serious undermining of confidence in the government's European policy, but also did much to damage Major's personal prestige and popularity. The government thus faced a rebellion which continued to gather momentum, and which was furthermore increasingly able to draw support from extra-parliamentary bodies and, above all, the media with whom the arguments against ratification had a growing resonance.

The Conservative rebels had both short- and longer-term aims. Most immediately, they hoped to delay the Bill as long as possible so that the price of government support was its broader legislative programme. In addition, they hoped to maul the treaty in such a way as to render it unacceptable to the government and the wider party. They also clung to the hope that a referendum might be held in Britain, with Teddy Taylor repeating an offer to the Prime Minister that if he committed himself to a referendum 'the rebellion would end tomorrow' (Baker *et al.*, 1994:39). In the longer term, they wanted to demonstrate just how strong and widespread sceptical opinion was in the Conservative Party. In addition, however, and in marked contrast to their isolationist approach during the negotiations, they also hoped that their opposition would inspire sceptics in other countries to bring down the treaty, first in France, and then Denmark, where referenda had been promised.

The government reacted by attempting to use a range of instruments to ensure that the Maastricht Bill was not lost to rebel action. Major continued, for instance, to be assiduous in wooing key opinion formers, and succeeded at a meeting of 29 October 1992 in winning the support of the right wing dominated 1922 Committee. A further weapon which the government continued to put to use against the sceptics was its detailed knowledge of the parliamentary party. This enabled it to identify those MPs who were vulnerable to pressure in order to win them over or at worst limit their rebellion to abstention. Attention focused in particular on the Fresh Start members who signed the June EDM. Those who did not aspire to office (and here it should be remembered that several belonged to the older generation, with one signatory aged seventy-four and six over the age of sixty) were left alone, as were the twenty-two diehards who voted against the treaty at the second reading in May. As during the negotiations, the tactics used against the remainder included inducements of office, the use of patronage of various sorts (rooms, pairing and committee memberships), and indirect constituency association pressure. In addition, there was now recourse to some rather physical man-handling during divisions. In this way, the government succeeded in picking off a number of its opponents, and the rebellion was limited to a hard core of twenty-five, with the maximum number of rebels reaching forty-six at the third reading with forty-one voting against and five abstaining.[16]

The government's hand was strengthened by the fact that it had access to legal advice which could not be easily challenged. The best example of this related to Labour's tactic of seeking to force a vote on the Social Protocol opt-out. On 20 January 1993, the Junior Foreign Minister, Tristan Garel Jones, argued that adoption of the proposed Labour amendment on this question would prevent treaty ratification. Since Eurosceptics already planned to support the amendment, Garel Jones's statement was seen as effort to avoid government defeat by winning over pro-Maastricht opposition members. However, when it became clear that this strategy would not work, the Foreign Secretary on 15 February announced new advice from the Attorney-General which made clear the amendment would not actually affect the treaty. Indeed, the use of Crown prerogative was even threatened to enact the Treaty (Baker *et al.*, 1994:59; Alderman, 1993).

In addition, thanks to its control of the parliamentary agenda, the government resorted to the ploy of postponing any vote which it thought it might lose both in committee and on the floor of the chamber. Thus following the *volte face* in its position on the implications of a Social Protocol vote, it acquiesced in accepting the Labour amendment which 'required a specific vote on the social chapter after the completion of all the Bill's stages but before it became operative or the Treaty were ratified' (Alderman, 1993:504). Again to pre-empt defeat, it further 'accepted three Labour amendments requiring ministers and the Bank of England to report to Parliament on progress towards economic union' (Alderman, 1993:503).

The government also resorted to treating the issue as one of confidence for its own parliamentary supporters, with Major making clear his intention to resign and call a general election if he were defeated. This raised the stakes in terms of the consequences of rebellion. A corollary of this was the way in which the whips worked to indicate where defeat would not affect the overall passage of the Bill, and in the event there were just two outright defeats. The first defeat, on 8 March 1993, was on Amendment 28, concerning the method by which British members of the new Committee of the Regions were to be selected. On this occasion, the scale of defeat – twenty-two votes – was more embarrassing than the issue itself, although it did mean that more time would be required for a report stage.

The second defeat was more crucial, and occurred on 22 July 1993 on the second vote of that day relating to the Social Protocol. Having managed in the first vote to defeat the Labour amendment on the need for a separate vote on the Social Protocol, the government was now defeated on its own motion to 'note' existing policy by 316 votes to 324. 'Seizing on the opportunity offered by the advice of the House of Commons Clerks that defeat on the motion would prevent the Act from coming into force and thus ratification too,' twenty-three Conservatives now voted against the government (Alderman, 1993:506). 'In the uproar following the votes the Prime Minister, reading from a prepared text, announced the tabling of a further motion linking confidence in the government to the approval of its policy on the Protocol necessary to permit ratification. Defeat, he declared, would result in a general election' (Alderman, 1993:506). The debate on this motion took place the following day with only one Conservative MP, Rupert Allason, abstaining. The Prime Minister therefore emerged the victor by forty votes. The government had thus finally succeeded in calling the sceptics' bluff, but the result was a lasting legacy of bitterness on both sides of the argument. In particular, there was a feeling amongst the Conservative Eurosceptics that the government had been forced to overreact, and that its inappropriate use of the ultimate weapon of coercion, a vote of confidence, would work to win it the battle, but them the war (Gorman, 1993:230; 232).

A key difficulty for the Conservative Eurosceptics was that to defeat the treaty they were heavily dependent on support from the Labour Party, which proved itself rather fickle for much of the passage of the Bill. Essentially, the dilemma for

Labour was that it was broadly in favour of the treaty but was attracted for tactical reasons to opposing it, since the opportunity to maximise the misery of the government was a tempting prize for a party in its fourth term in opposition. At the same time, there was a deep concern to avoid a replay of Labour's own previous internecine warfare on the European issue (Alderman, 1993). The Shadow Cabinet, now dominated by pro-integration modernisers, therefore settled on a strategy of attempting to overturn the opt-outs from the social chapter and the single currency. In particular, it deployed its so called 'ticking time bomb' amendment, calling for the government to hold a vote on subscribing to the Social Protocol before the treaty could be accepted. In this way, Labour Party managers hoped that the government would be faced with a choice of accepting the Social Protocol or abandoning the treaty, and that it would be compelled to opt for the former. The Labour leadership also decided that on the main votes the policy would be one of abstention in order to maximise Conservative differences and avoid claims that Labour was unprincipled (Alderman, 1993).

This compromise position undermined the position of Labour Eurosceptics, but despite an instruction to abstain sixty-one Labour MPs voted against the Bill on the second reading. However, the Labour sceptics' room for manoeuvre was further curtailed by the Shadow Cabinet's rejection in June 1992 of a call for a referendum on the treaty, which it feared would open old Labour wounds and was anyway designed to wreck the Bill. Attempts to overturn the parliamentary party's position at the October 1992 conference only resulted in a re-commitment to the policy that the treaty was the best that could be achieved in the circumstances. The Shadow Cabinet therefore pressed for opposing any guillotine and closure motions, but in order to maximise Conservative differences and raise the stakes, left open the question of the party's position on the third reading of the Bill.

As the distress of the government deepened, however, Labour moved to a position in January 1993 of taking no action which would help Conservative Eurosceptics destroy the Bill. Finally, on the third reading, the Shadow Cabinet again decided to abstain, ostensibly because of the Social Protocol opt-out. Notwithstanding a rebellion by sixty-six Labour MPs who voted against the government, enough had now been done to ensure the passage of the Bill. Ultimately, therefore, as Baker *et al.* argue, 'the government survived the passage of the Bill itself not because it put down its internal rebellion, but because of the support of the main opposition parties for the Bill as a whole and on certain key issues like the demand for a referendum' (Baker *et al.*, 1994:37). The irony was that Labour too had had its share of rebels on the issue, but the Labour sceptics ultimately lacked the organisation and co-ordination which characterised the Conservative sceptics. In the last resort, what was striking and as the vote of confidence made clear, was that party allegiances retained their hold, and this worked to impede the development of cross-party co-ordination amongst Eurosceptics. In this way, the potential for an alliance based on the Bruges agenda apparently on the cards at the end of the 1980s remained unfulfilled.

Conclusions

The period from the beginning of the negotiation of the Maastricht Treaty until its parliamentary ratification in July 1993 was pivotal in the development and character of modern Euroscepticism and witnessed a growing dominance within the political fight. Hitherto, the opponents of closer European integration had been divided between fundamentalist sceptics and more pragmatic opponents. However, the parliamentary ratification of the Maastricht Treaty led to a joining of these forces to oppose the treaty. Resistance to the Maastricht Treaty therefore gave opponents a much clearer sense of identity and solidarity in opposing government policy. The emerging Europeanisation of British opposition to Europe during this period is also worthy of note, and unlike the earlier anti-Marketeers, Eurosceptics began to establish links with other opposition groups within the EU.

Moreover, for the first time since 1975, throughout the ratification, opponents of the treaty drew support from well beyond Parliament. Sceptical Conservative MPs who opposed party policy turned to their constituency activists – amongst whom there was growing mobilisation – for support and to avoid de-selection for opposing government policy. In addition, a number of non-partisan groups sprung up, and the newsprint media which had turned against the Maastricht Treaty in the course of its ratification greatly boosted the credibility of the sceptic cause. Indeed, as late as 19 July 1993, the willingness of Lord Rees-Mogg to refuse to accept the failure of parliamentary battle and to take court action by petitioning for a judicial review was an indication of the new lengths to which Eurosceptics were prepared to go outside of Parliament. Eurosceptics now had a vanguard both inside and outside Parliament, and a platform from which to try to move passive sceptics to a more active position. However, the general public remained as yet uninterested in the European issue and notwithstanding the extension of opposition to Europe into the wider political arena, was in many ways still willing to sub-contract concern to others.

Ultimately, it was true that the Conservative government secured the passage of the Maastricht Bill. However, from both a Conservative and Labour perspective, this was not a cost-free exercise. From the point of view of the Conservative Party, the first legacy of the Maastricht revolt was the growing resentment amongst the rank and file of a leadership which continued to participate in a European integration process which had for many now served its purpose. Coupled with this was a growing need for a much clearer position in terms of what the party stood for in Europe than John Major had been willing to offer. At the same time, the knowledge base of Eurosceptics and the complexity of their arguments developed rapidly, leaving many observers with the feeling that the government had lost the case for closer European integration, even if it had secured the ratification of the treaty.

There also was an overwhelming feeling that the Conservative Party leadership had misused the instruments of party discipline to deliver ratification of the Treaty, ultimately forcing sceptics to choose between bringing down the government on a vote of confidence or supporting the treaty. Sceptics were not yet willing to do the former, and ultimately the government got its way, but at a heavy cost to the solidarity and cohesion of the party. After this period, and as a consequence of this heavy-handedness, the opposition to Europe of some Eurosceptics at least became an issue of conscience on which they felt increasingly justified in defying the party. Indeed, ultimately the divisions caused by John Major's handling of the European issue forced him, in June 1995, to resign as leader of the Conservative Party, to secure a new mandate to maintain the government's moderately pro-engagement position. As Chapter 7 discusses, Major succeeded in being re-elected, but failed to silence his Eurosceptic critics. The government's strategy thus came at the price of a new and more militant form of Euroscepticism. There was thus a fundamental distinction in the way opponents of European integration pursued opposition to government policy in the 1970s and the parliamentary behaviour and tactics of the Eurosceptics during the passage of the Maastricht Bill. Through external funds, Eurosceptics were better organised and resourced, and through more aggressive parliamentary tactics were willing not just to register a protest but also to vote the Bill down.

From a Labour Party perspective, it was clear that there would be no support from the Labour frontbench for a Eurosceptic position on Europe and, indeed, on the evidence of the passage of the Maastricht Bill, there was some suspicion that there had been collusion between the Labour and Conservative frontbenches to secure its passage. Despite this, around sixty MPs had been willing to disobey instructions, admittedly only to abstain on the crucial Treaty votes and had voted against the Bill. However, as the party continued further rounds of modernisation, Labour opponents of further integration would need to look beyond the party to secure their objectives.

The failure of Conservative and Labour opponents of closer European integration to unite was a significant feature of the parliamentary ratification of the Maastricht Treaty. On the face of it, opposition to the Political and Economic and Monetary Union agenda should have provided common cause around which sceptics could rally. However, in the Conservative Party, pressure to support government policy and loyalty to the party prevented many MPs who were latent sceptics from actively opposing the treaty. In the Labour Party, the pull of party loyalty, a willingness to avoid divisions on Europe and, ultimately, a recognition that without official Labour Party opposition to the ratification of the treaty, resistance would be futile, prompted many to choose not to make common cause with Tory sceptics. Thus in a speech to the Bruges Group, for instance, Peter Shore, the veteran Labour anti-Market campaigner recognised the all-party nature of the group, but felt it necessary to remind his audience: 'I am a Labour politician whose loyalties and perspectives remain firmly based in the Party of which I remain a member' (Shore, 1996:42). An additional disincentive for the dwindling band of Labour sceptics was the increasing domination of Conservative Eurosceptic thinking by a right-wing post-Thatcherite philosophy, which increasingly appropriated the arguments against the Political Union agenda and took them in a partisan direction. Overall, therefore, despite the fact that for a few MPs Europe was to become an issue of conscience, for most MPs party allegiances still came first.

Notes

1   In reply to questioning on the approaching IGCs, she made clear she 'did not want the Commission to increase its powers at the expense of the House. Mr Delors said he wanted the European Parliament to be the democratic body of the Community, he wanted the Commission to be the Executive and he wanted the Council of Ministers to be the Senate. No. No. No.' Hansard Parliamentary Debates, 30/10/90.

2   Margaret Thatcher's enforced resignation, alongside the earlier resignation of Nicholas Ridley, generated a sense of fear that Cabinet Europhiles were targeting sceptics in government. See the *Spectator* article 14 July 1990. For the fears of the sceptics see John Wilkinson quoted in Alexandre-Collier, 2000:94; Gorman, 1993:21. See also Heseltine's two 'Europe manifestos', (Heseltine, 1987; Heseltine, 1989).

3   Norman Lamont took the lead in this. It was a mark of the importance of the Friends of Bruges Group that Lamont even made a personal appearance to present John Major's credentials during the leadership campaign (Stephens, 1996:187).

4   For the doubts on the right wing of the party, see Gorman, 1993:13.

5   For a near complete list of bodies which were set up, see Tame, 1997.

6   In spring 1991 Peter Stodthart moved from Washington to London to take up his post as editor of *The Times*. He was reported to have been sympathetic to a policy of constructive engagement on European policy, but received clear instructions from Rupert Murdoch to take a strongly sceptical line.

7   Paul Johnson and Simon Heffer took the first line while Charles Moore took the second.

8   For a flavour of the antagonism towards 'the inertia, Euro-piety and Hurd instinct' of the Foreign Office see, Malcolm, 1991:6.

9   This view was all the more prescient since it was written before the final Treaty was agreed. For an analysis of the personal contribution of Bill Cash, see Chapter 10 'Europe Made Me', H.Young, 1998:389–93. For still the best analysis concerning the 'British' problem with Germany, see H. Young, 1998:390.

10   Eurosceptics did better in the election of 1992 than in either 1983 or 1987; one-third of them were returned in 1992, as against less than one-fifth of pro-Europeans (Berrington and Hague, 1998:50).

11   Interview quoted in Alexandre-Collier, 1998:138.

12   Michael Spicer, Hansard Parliamentary Debates 06/05/92.

13   One of the important dossiers was the issue of retrospective pension provision, the so-called Barber issue, in which Lilley was directly involved.

14   The activities of the European Foundation and the European Reform Group were leading examples of this.

15   Information in this section draws on data contained in Alderman, 1993; Baker *et al.*, 1993a, 1993b and 1994. These sources remain the best and most comprehensive account of the ratification process.

16   Twenty-four members of the Fresh Start Group were from the 1992 intake and only Duncan Smith and Legg voted against at second reading, and Jenkin, Sweeney and Whittingdale abstained.

7 The struggle against Monetary Union, 1992–2001

Introduction

Among the most significant developments in the history of European integration were the articles in the Maastricht Treaty on European Union which committed the member states to a series of steps to create a single currency – the Euro – by 1 January 1999.[1] The first stage, on 1 July 1990, required the removal of exchange controls and membership of the narrow band of the Exchange Rate Mechanism. The second stage, now set out in the Maastricht Treaty was to begin on 1 January 1994 with the creation of an Economic and Monetary Institute (EMI) to be based in Frankfurt, acting as an embryonic central bank. In this stage national banks were to be made independent of political control. At the end of 1996, governments had then to decide whether a majority of countries met the convergence criteria for membership of the Euro and had to agree a timetable for the Euro's introduction. If no agreement could be reached, the Euro would automatically be introduced on 1 January 1999 by those governments which met the convergence criteria. The Euro would be an irrevocable fixing of exchange rates, with the EMI transformed into a European Central Bank (ECB) responsible for the issuing of notes and coins and the setting of a single interest rate for the Euro zone (Baimbridge and Teasdale, 1997:125).

In September 1992 sterling and the lira were forced to leave the European Exchange Rate Mechanism (ERM) and the peseta was devalued by five per cent as a consequence of speculative attacks. In August the following year speculators nearly destroyed the ERM which was only saved by the widening of the bands permitting greater currency fluctuation. In the light of these developments, John Major argued that pressing on with the Maastricht commitment to create the Euro 'had all the potency of a primitive rain dance'. However it soon became clear that all the other member state governments with the exception of Denmark wanted to maintain the timetable agreed at Maastricht to create a single currency on 1 January 1997 or if this failed on 1 January 1999. On this date, therefore, eleven countries joined the Euro with Britain, Denmark, Greece and Sweden retaining their national currencies, and Greece joining in January 2001.

Once the Maastricht Treaty was ratified in July 1993, there was an almost seamless re-focusing of the opposition which had previously been targeted on the

Political Union question onto the issue of a single currency. This chapter examines the struggle to maintain the British opt-out secured at Maastricht from the withdrawal of sterling from the ERM on Wednesday 16 September 1992 until the June 2001 general election. With the June 2001 Labour election campaign committing Tony Blair to deciding within the next two years whether to recommend membership of the European single currency to the British electorate and thus to trigger a referendum on the issue, the campaign to prevent the introduction of the Euro became the key Eurosceptic battle. Indeed, this even overshadowed the negotiation and parliamentary ratification of the Amsterdam Treaty in 1997–8.

In the period up to 1997, Euroscepticism emerged as a powerful constraint on Conservative government thinking. Indeed, the influence of sceptics in Parliament brought into question the very existence of the government. Not content with severing the Party's commitment to a referendum on the issue, Eurosceptics increasingly shifted opinion on the Conservative backbenches away from Major's policy of accepting the theoretical possibility of membership but rejecting it in practice, the so-called 'negotiate and decide' policy contained in the May 1997 general election manifesto. By June 2001 the Conservative Party had adopted a manifesto pledge rejecting first, for five years, and then ten years, any decision to join the Euro. But despite the development of Euroscepticism as a predominant feature of the Conservative Party, with only 165 seats in the House of Commons and a Labour majority of 179 in the Parliament of 1997 to 2001, influence on government policy was limited. Where Eurosceptics did succeed was in securing a pledge from the Labour government that it too would hold a referendum on the Euro. The chapter argues that a process of democratisation of the European issue therefore commenced, with the public finally being actively courted by the political elite to share in the decision on whether Britain should join the Euro. This was a major Eurosceptic achievement and offered a landmark opportunity for Eurosceptics in Parliament and amongst the general public to unite in a common cause to oppose the Euro.

The chapter further argues that the referendum decision signalled a merger of the parliamentary and public arenas which governments had always preferred to keep separate, lest the issue escape from the control of the party leadership and party managers. At the same time as the broadening of the arena in which the European issue was debated, the identity of opponents of European integration further evolved during this period. In the past, prior to their current manifestation as Eurosceptics, opponents had been anti-European and then anti-Market. The question of the single currency now introduced a new cohort of sceptics typified by the New Europe campaign, which opposed the Euro, but did not want Britain to withdraw from the European Union. This injected much greater diversity into the Eurosceptic movement with some not only wishing for withdrawal, but openly advocating it, and others who simply opposed British membership of the Euro. Below the surface of their improved organisation and resources, the chapter therefore concludes that deep divisions remained in sceptics' arguments and thinking.

Opportunity

The ratification of the Maastricht Treaty offered a set piece opportunity for sceptics to oppose the integration process. The issue of the single currency was far more problematic for the sceptics since, in legal terms, it could be adopted so long as the British economy met the conditions set out in the Maastricht Treaty, including the so-called convergence criteria, and there was a positive recommendation from the British government having secured a majority in Parliament.[2] However, three factors assisted the Eurosceptics. First, the conditions leading to Economic and Monetary Union were clearly set. Stage one started on 1 July 1990 involving the completion of the Single European Market. Stage two began on 1 January 1994 and involved the creation of the EMI to administer the European Monetary System. In stage three exchange rates were irrevocably locked and a single currency was created with the EMI transformed into a European Central Bank. The dates for stage three were also clearly set out in the Maastricht Treaty.

At each of these stages specific actions were required from governments to meet the criteria for joining the single currency. Given that a key Eurosceptic argument had always been that Britain had been deceived into joining the EC by her leaders, these requirements were then an important means for the sceptics to monitor developments and flag them up to the public. For the first time since the creation of the Single European Market project (the launch of which, by 1 January 1993, was a political commitment only), Eurosceptics had legally binding targets offering clear points at which to judge steps towards a specific objective. The criteria set for Economic and Monetary Union also offered an opportunity to judge the progress of the other member states towards the single currency.[3]

The second factor which assisted the sceptics was Britain's ejection from the ERM on 16 September 1992 and the near collapse of the ERM itself in July and August 1993.[4] This was a huge boost for the sceptics who argued for a re-evaluation of government policy, and indeed it has been contended that but for sterling's ejection from the ERM, the Maastricht Treaty and the government's policies on Europe would have remained in tact (Baker *et al.*, 1993a). Suspension of Sterling from the ERM, which cost the country £4 billion of its currency reserves and inflicted lasting damage on the economic credibility of Conservative governments, was a catalyst for many, moving their position from that of tacit scepticism and acquiescence to active scepticism and a willingness to oppose the government's policy on the Euro. To meet the convergence criteria, Sterling needed to re-enter the ERM for two years, and politically (if not in law), this would require parlia-mentary approval. If a rough ride on the issue was probable in Parliament, the Eurosceptic hope was that this might dissuade the government from taking further steps towards the single currency.

The final factor from which the sceptic cause benefited was the commitment of both Labour and Conservatives to holding a referendum on the issue of the single currency. In large measure it must be said that this was an opportunity which Eurosceptic pressure had succeeded in engineering. The Eurosceptics had now learnt from previous experience that they had to seize the initiative from the government to actively prevent the adoption of the Euro. Their endeavours focused on raising the political temperature of the single currency question, and shifting the issue from the parliamentary to the public arena to ensure that consent of the electorate would be an absolute precondition for the abolition of Sterling. Both the Conservative and Labour Parties would have preferred the issue to be dealt with in the parliamentary and executive dominated arena, and not to expose it to scrutiny by the general public who were, according to opinion poll sampling, now more sceptical than most in Parliament. So vocal had Eurosceptic dissent become, however, that on 2 April 1996, after four months of preparation, John Major's administration issued a consultation paper on Europe committing itself to a referendum if a Conservative government recommended the Euro (Norton, 1998:90). Once the Conservative leadership conceded this point, it became politically impossible for the Labour Party to resist matching the pledge. This was a great prize for the Eurosceptics, but it was a means to an end and not an end in itself. Another referendum would enable the sceptics to plan, prepare and better co-ordinate opposition across arenas which all governments had worked so hard to separate. Moreover, once the principle of a referendum had been conceded, it provided an ideal opportunity for a much wider group of Eurosceptics to be mobilised.

Opponents: who were they?

Chapter 6 explored how Euroscepticism received a significant boost during the negotiation and ratification of the Maastricht Treaty, particularly on the Conservative side of the political spectrum. Those opposed to further European integration were increasing in number all the time, but what now marked out the Eurosceptics was not just their expansion both within and outside Parliament, but also their composition. In the period between 1992 and 2001, a complex and overlapping network of opponents emerged to oppose EMU. The groupings had four key characteristics: whether they were partisan or non-partisan, and whether they were anti-EMU or anti-EU.

Within the parliamentary Conservative Party, the new intake of MPs elected in 1992, including Iain Duncan Smith, Bernard Jenkin and Walter Sweeney comprised an influential group capable of challenging the government's policy. Under such influences, the Conservative parliamentary party as a whole moved to a more sceptical position during the Parliament of 1992 to 1997. In a 1997 survey, Philip Norton found a majority of Conservative MPs sceptical towards integration with some thirty-two per cent on the Eurosceptical right, twenty-four per cent party faithful with Eurosceptical leanings, twenty per cent agnostic on the issue of Europe and only twenty-five per cent on the left in some form supportive of integration (Norton, 1996:94).

In addition, a number of MPs who retired at the 1992 election provided a support network of active and respected politicians in the House of Lords. These individuals were less constrained by party discipline, in part because of the nature of party management in the House of Lords, but also because their seniority diminished the influence of the party machine. Lord Tebbit alongside Lord Lamont joined Lady Thatcher and Lord Baker to lead an influential group in the Lords that included existing sceptical Conservative peers, many of whom Thatcher had proposed. These included Lord Pearson of Rannoch (founder of Global Britain), Lord McAlpine (funder of the Bruges Group) and Lord Deedes (former editor of the *Daily Telegraph*).

Within the Conservative government of 1992–7, it quickly emerged that there were fundamental differences between Cabinet members. In July 1993 immediately after the successful vote of confidence on the ratification of the Maastricht Treaty, John Major singled out Michael Portillo, Peter Lilley and John Redwood for particular opprobrium. Major's frustration at their disloyalty was expressed to Michael Brunson, when in remarks off the record but subsequently published, the Prime Minister referred to them as 'bastards' indicating that he could not force ministers to resign for fear that they might cause even more damage on the government's backbenches (Stephens, 1997:307; Gorman, 1993:233).[5]

This group of initially three senior Cabinet members soon grew to a majority as some uncommitted ministers switched camp. Malcolm Rifkind and Gillian Shepherd, and even some pro-Europeans like Stephen Dorrell, were belatedly converted to the sceptic cause. Motivations for such a change were varied, but it took place as it became clear that most Conservative backbench MPs were moving to a hostile position (Stephens, 1997:332).[6] As the influence of Euroscepticism increased, these ministers flouted the Prime Minister's authority and Major seemed, by inclination or because of the circumstances, quite incapable of exercising any authority over them. They routinely broke the agreed Cabinet line on the single currency and many provided support for backbench MPs who were even more free to speak their mind, semi-openly campaigning against government policy in fringe meetings both at the party conference and in constituency association meetings as well as in Eurosceptical groupings. Norman Lamont, after his sacking as Chancellor in 1993, became increasingly outspoken, claiming that he had never been in favour of ERM membership and causing a storm at the Bournemouth party conference in October 1994 by being the first Eurosceptic to suggest that the possibility of withdrawal from the EU needed to be openly debated (*Sunday Times*, 1994).[7]

Major did, however, attempt to assert control in two ways. First, in June 1995 he resigned as party leader to secure a mandate to continue to lead the government without facing challenges to his leadership. This he succeeded in doing by 129 votes. Second, in November 1995 eight Conservative MPs refused to support the government in the vote on the European Community (Finance) Bill. The Bill was subject to a three line whip, making it an issue of confidence. The result was the immediate withdrawal of the whip from the eight MPs, and its restoration only after a suspension of six months. The MPs – Nicholas Budgen, Michael Cartiss, Christopher Gill, Teresa Gorman, Tony Marlow, Richard Shephard, Teddy Taylor and John Wilkinson – were joined by Richard Body who voluntarily resigned the whip in disgust at their treatment. In many respects, however, Major's actions proved to be counter-productive, since the removal of the whip freed the dissidents to actively campaign for a wide range of Eurosceptical causes including a position of ruling out the single currency indefinitely. In addition, others were encouraged by their example to challenge the leadership.

Outside Parliament, but part of the broader activist community, were a group of Young Turk Conservatives, who enjoyed still greater freedom to express their views. Within many Young Conservative and student clubs, Euroscepticism was in the ascendant. At Oxford, for instance, the Campaign for an Independent Britain was almost synonymous with the University Conservative Club and ran some of the most interesting student political activities. In the aftermath of the 1992 election victory, the issue of Europe quickly became the main bone of contention with a Prime Minster whose policies and style of leadership young activists disliked. They therefore joined forces with the parliamentary sceptics to create an inter-generational sceptical alliance of a type not seen since the 1975 referendum, willing to challenge the government from both within and outside its ranks. Their influence was underlined by the fact that over one third of Conservative parliamentary candidates issued 'personal manifestos' ruling out a single currency during the 1997 election campaign.

The Tory press comprised the third pillar on which Conservative Eurosceptic influence was built. As noted in the previous chapter, *The Sun*, *The Times*, and the *Daily Telegraph* along with the *Daily Mail* and, to a lesser extent, the *Spectator* formed an influential family of publications opposed to a single currency. Peter Stothard (editor of *The Times*), David Yelland (editor of *The Sun*) and Boris Johnson (editor of the *Spectator*), played a key part in maintaining this trend. Just as important as the editorial stance of the papers however were the contributions of individual journalists. Here, Mary Ann Sieghart (*The Times*), Simon Heffer (*Daily Mail*), Christopher Booker (the *Daily Telegraph* and *Sunday Telegraph*) and Matthew d'Ancona (*Sunday Telegraph*) waged personal campaigns against the Euro and so provided ready-made arguments for their readers.

The circulation of newspapers advocating opposition to the single currency amounted to nearly eight million, almost double that of those newspapers in favour of it, principally the *Financial Times*, the *Mirror* and the *Daily Express*. In a less cautious moment the Conservative Chancellor Ken Clarke lamented that, 'the former Conservative press is now almost without exception edited by way-out Eurosceptics …' ruefully adding, '… as way out as our more difficult people in the House of Commons' (Stephens, 1997:350). However, as Sir Paul Lever, the British Ambassador to the Federal Republic of Germany was forced to concede, Conrad Black's family of publications were not anti-European, but was vehemently anti-EU, and its proprietor was quick to prove the point in a court of law.[8] As Peter Riddell notes, not only were the Eurosceptics widely published in the press, but they also expressed themselves more passionately than pro-integration supporters and as a consequence carried greater influence. The effect of this increasing transformation from a press dominated by Euro-enthusiasts to those now opposing 'the abolition of the pound' cannot be underestimated. As Riddell suggests, 'the shift in the press during the 1990s probably had a cumulative impact in influencing public attitudes, particularly during the absence of a clear lead from politicians' (Riddell, 1998:112).

The fourth pillar of Conservative Eurosceptic influence comprised the growing number of think tanks linked to Conservative politicians, which provided intellectual support for opposition to the single currency. The European Foundation directed by Bill Cash and funded by Lady Thatcher, much to the public unease of John Major, quickly established itself as a generally serious attempt to provide informed but partisan criticism of government policy.[9] Similarly, John Redwood's Conservative 2000 Foundation was set up in the aftermath of Redwood's resignation from Cabinet and failed leadership bid of June 1995. It aimed to challenge the status quo and specifically what it perceived as the goal of creating a 'United States of Europe'. It was not especially well financed, but provided heavyweight intellectual ammunition for sceptics on a wide range of European issues (Gowland and Turner, 2000:296). Besides this, Global Britain, founded by the Conservative peer Lord Pearson of Rannoch and directed by Ian Milne, was well funded and quickly became active in promoting a more reflective analysis of the EU. The Bruges Group continued with new vigour under the part-time direction of an Oxford lecturer, Martin Holmes, and reached out to the academic community who provided more rigorous arguments for the sceptics. However, it never managed to fully articulate an alternative European vision.

As regards the Labour Party, veteran sceptics including Peter Shore (who became Lord Shore of Stepney in 1997) on the right wing and Denzil Davies, Tam Dalyell, Tony Benn, Dennis Skinner and Ken Livingstone on the left, were now joined by new faces including Frank Field, Diane Abbot and Alan Simpson. In the Upper Chamber, Lords Jay, Stoddart and Bruce continued to be active, and to these were now added a group of Labour (or former Labour) politicians such as Lord Healey and Lord Owen who specifically opposed the abolition of the pound although they were not anti-EU. The continued influence of sceptic views was demonstrated when, in March 1996, fifty Labour MPs signed a statement entitled 'Europe isn't working', which included as its headline goal a call to the Labour Party to rule out a single currency.

However, the election of Tony Blair as Labour leader in 1994, with an explicit modernising agenda, put the seal the party's adoption of a pro-engagement policy. Marginalised by the party leadership, and inhibited by the growing proximity of Labour to power, Labour sceptics felt obliged to maintain a relatively low profile. Despite some indication of passive scepticism within the party, a survey of MPs revealed that divisions over EU institutions were a matter of presentation and timing more than substance. Despite fifty-three per cent of Labour MPs agreeing that there was a paucity of debate in the party, only three per cent advocated withdrawal and only twenty per cent agreed that Britain should never permit its monetary policy to be determined by a European Central Bank (Brivati and Baker, 1998:11).[10] Thus, while traditional Labour groupings like the Euro Safeguards Campaign remained extant, the battle over European integration inside the party had by and large been lost. With a handful of exceptions, Labour sceptics fought their battles from the margins of party fora, and increasingly found that the only outlet for their views was in the new non-party groupings which now emerged.

The driving force behind these non-party groupings was the widening debate on EMU both amongst the public and the economic as well as the political elite. In August 1998, for instance, the multi-millionaire ex-Conservative MP Paul Sykes announced a nationwide multimedia Euro information campaign. This was amalgamated in January 1999 with the Referendum Movement (the successor organisation to the Referendum Party founded in 1994) to form the Democracy Movement. This new group benefited from a donation of over £200,000 from Lady Annabel Goldsmith whose son was appointed director. Similarly, the Institute of Economic Affairs published a series of pamphlets, not only on the single currency, but also on the impact of the EU more generally. TEAM, the European anti-Maastricht alliance, also continued its role in acting as an umbrella organisation for all those opposed to the Maastricht agenda.

The foremost example of the new strength of the non-partisan sceptical groupings, however, was The New Europe movement, created in March 1999. What was also distinctive about New Europe was the fact that it was explicitly pro-EU but anti-Euro. The movement attracted a high level of support from establishment figures, particularly in the House of Lords, where its cross-party character was underlined by the fact that while led by the one time Labour Foreign Secretary, Lord Owen, and including Lord Ashburton, Lord Sainsbury, Lord Healey, and Lord Shore, it was also supported by the Conservative peers Lord Prior and Lord Lawson. Convening either in party or cross-party format, these individuals met regularly to plan their attacks on the Labour government. Outside Parliament, the movement's establishment credentials were further highlighted by the involvement of Roger Bootle, former Chief Economist of the Midland Bank and HSBC, along with the journalists Christopher Smallwood and Mary Ann Sieghart, and Neil Mendoza of Forward Publishing.

The widening reach of Eurosceptic arguments against the single currency into non-partisan circles was also demonstrated by the increasing number of anti-Euro business groupings. City of London Concern Over Maastricht (COLCOM), for instance, comprised a number of leading City figures and focused on the economic implications of EMU for City of London interests. In addition, on 11 June 1998 Business for Sterling was launched, with Tim Melville Ross, Director General of the Institute of Directors, Brian Prime, Executive Director of the Federation of Small Businesses, and Sir John Banham, former Director General of the CBI, among its leading supporters.[11] A further important development was the way in which separate organisations campaigning against EMU were able to unite to provide greater focus. Thus, in October 1999, Business for Sterling and New Europe announced an initiative to work together in a new fundraising and campaigning alliance, aimed at avoiding unnecessary competition while also retaining their separate identities. In addition, although they continued to eschew links with party political organisations, they maintained constructive dialogue with allies, including the Conservative Party Chairman Archie Norman.

In the 1975 referendum, business was either silent or supportive of British entry to the Common Market. In the 1990s, however, business and other non-partisan groups added a new dimension to the Eurosceptic cause, broadening the movement and making it increasingly serious in terms of credibility and profile. At the same time, however, it is arguable that the emergence of such business groups along with New Europe also added a complication to the Eurosceptic cause by the nuanced pro-EU but anti-Euro position they adopted. One important characteristic of Business for Sterling, for instance, typical of many new Eurosceptic groupings was that it was not opposed to European integration as such, and it supported the Single Market. Notwithstanding, some concern about the inherent design weaknesses of EMU, Business for Sterling did hope the Euro might succeed for the countries that had adopted it, a position which was not necessarily shared by all Eurosceptics.

Arguments

Despite the increasing number of non-partisan sceptical groupings which emerged following the conclusion of the Maastricht Treaty, it was striking that the most fully developed arguments during this period were articulated by those on the right of the political spectrum. This was hardly surprising given the energy and resources devoted to the subject of Europe, and above all the single currency, by the right in general and the Conservative Party in particular. In addition, it was notable that in a change from earlier periods, many of the arguments now advanced were evidence-based, offering hard economic rather than softer political analysis. They also tended to have strong academic credentials, reflecting the involvement of scholars including Patrick Minford. What therefore resulted was a highly complex network of arguments and alliances, in which the various sceptical groupings subscribed to some or all of the arguments postulated, depending for instance on whether it was simply the Euro to which they objected or whether they were more in favour of re-negotiation and withdrawal.

The first key premise of the new brand of sceptical arguments was that the EU had not delivered the economic benefits which its advocates had claimed. It was argued, for instance, that the EU propped up inefficient producers at the expense of British taxpayers (Hindley and Howe, 1996), while Patrick Minford focused on the implications of an interventionist Social Charter, the flawed Common Agricultural Policy and protectionist use of anti-dumping legislation. The costs of EU regulation were also highlighted (Hindley and Howe, 1996). In all cases, the arguments were based on the view that the EU was constructed in a way that disadvantaged Britain, which in turn cast doubt on the potential benefits that might be available. A further contention was that the possibilities for Britain in finance, trade and investment in the global economy were greater outside the EU and that Britain's earnings from invisible trade and particularly investment income were more significant than the issue of EU membership (Jamieson, 1996:220). This position was strongly supported by the Conservative Paymaster General, David Heathcote-Amery, who had resigned from John Major's government in 1996 and who argued that over half of Britain's trade was with countries outside the EU (Heathcote-Amery, 1996:15).

A second argument advanced against EMU was that the goal of a single currency was based on an unachievable timetable and flawed convergence criteria (Burkitt and Baimbridge, 1996:180). A number of economists criticised the three stage process, which they believed would never be able to deliver a single currency. Walter

Eltiss, former Chief Economic Adviser to the Treasury, was for instance prominent in arguing that if the international financial community lost confidence in the project, it could destroy the Euro by speculating against the national currencies of its weakest members, a flaw which would exist until 2002. The Commission's declaration that currencies linked in EMU would legally become units of the same currency closed one loop hole, but still left open the danger of speculation against the currency in bill and bond markets, where huge gains and losses would arise if there was ever a break up of the Euro zone (Eltiss, 1999: xii–xiii).

Perceptions of the flaws in the system were reinforced by the severe strains on the ERM in September 1992 and July and August 1993, which led to the suspension of several currencies from the ERM. Indeed, Eurosceptic concerns were shared by sixty-two German economists who set out a manifesto arguing that the convergence criteria were not anti-inflationary enough for Germany, but were sufficiently restrictive to create unnecessary and potentially unmanageable tensions elsewhere in the EU. Visiting Washington in the immediate aftermath of Britain's disastrous withdrawal from the ERM on 16 September 1992, Margaret Thatcher argued that, 'if the divergence between different European economies is so great that even the ERM cannot contain them, how would they react to a single currency?' (Stephens, 1997:300).

Another argument favoured by Conservative Eurosceptics related to the practical problems of keeping the Central Bank free from political interference and the inadequacy of the mechanisms to ensure that governments kept to their commitments once a single currency was in place. On the first issue, the German and French governments were at loggerheads. Following his election as French Prime Minister in June 1997, Lionel Jospin was at the forefront of a campaign to create an economic government or council to exercise leverage over the ECB, which he felt focused too narrowly on inflation. Although the French lost this particular battle, sceptics continued to fear for the long-term independence of the Central Bank. The possibility of a shared appointment for the position of head of the newly formed ECB was for many Eurosceptics another example of 'a shabby fix that undermined the credibility of the Euro and set a dangerous precedent of political interference in the affairs of the ECB' (Gowland and Turner, 2000:362). On the issue of ensuring that the currency was as 'hard' as the Deutschmark, a Stability Pact was created to ensure that fiscal discipline was maintained in the Euro zone. The sceptics, however, argued that this system was too weak and that pressure would grow for its modification to include a commitment to growth and employment as well as targeting inflation.

A further cluster of arguments focused on challenging the economic benefits which a single currency might deliver. The Commission's contention that gains from a single currency amounted to an increase of ten per cent of GDP depended on removing currency uncertainty and exchange costs. Patrick Minford and a team of economists from Liverpool University challenged this, arguing that it was crucially dependent on a reduction in the risk premium of capital that was unlikely (Minford, 1996:152). Minford contended that economic gains would only be forthcoming where there was a much higher degree of economic integration than currently existed. Without real convergence, external shocks would have a damaging effect, making the system structurally unstable.

Sceptics also argued that Britain had an economic cycle and mix of economic and political factors which made her an unsuitable participant in EU economic and monetary policy. It was pointed out, for instance, that the British economy was sufficiently distinctive to warrant self-exclusion (Burkitt, Baimbridge and Whyman, 1996), while Eltiss argued that the British financial sector was very different from that of continental Europe, with a much more significant role for interest rates. Moreover, the fact that Britain was an oil producer in fact linked Sterling far more closely to the dollar than to the Euro. Any change to existing arrangements might handicap commerce and undermine the high tech industries that were more extensive in Britain than in other European countries. Spending was also more interest rate sensitive in Britain than in other parts of Europe, in part as a consequence of the high number of homeowners in Britain. This made interest rates a far more important means of regulating the economy in Britain than on the continent. Given the lack of coincidence of economic cycles, an interest rate for continental Europe would be wholly inappropriate for Britain (Eltiss, 1999:184–208).

The latter views found a particular resonance among the non-partisan groupings. Christopher Smallwood, the Director of New Europe, argued for example that personal holdings of financial assets in Britain, mainly of shares, meant that any change in interest rates would have four times as much impact in Britain as in the other parts of Euro zone. Since Britain's share of EU GDP was about fifteen per cent, this meant that about forty per cent of the total EU-wide impact on spending changes in the Euro interest rate would be felt in Britain (Smallwood, 2000). COLCOM pointed out that much of City scepticism was due to the volume of non-EU currency transactions handled in Britain and fears about less responsive European wide monetary policy-making. Similarly, the Institute of Directors, under the leadership of Ruth Lea, was amongst the most forthright in arguing that, '… for the foreseeable future it will not be in the economic interests of the UK to take part in a single currency'(IoD, 2000). The issue of the economic cycle remained a major point of difference between Britain and other EU member states, with the Governor of the Bank of England and other economists expressing concern both in evidence to the House of Commons and in the press (*Independent*, 1997b).[12]

But the arguments of Conservative sceptics against a single currency were never purely economic, and were also rooted in political ideas relating to sovereignty and national identity. A related theme which now resurfaced was the Powellite contention that whatever the supposed economic benefits of the single currency, these did not outweigh the political costs of the project. Principally, Conservative sceptics advanced two central arguments in this area. The first argument was that retention of control of monetary instruments was a prerequisite for maintaining the sovereign identity of the nation state. Thus it was noted, for instance, that exchange rate certainty did not compensate for the main cost of EMU, namely, the unacceptable loss of sovereignty in terms of the ability to devalue and boost competitiveness.

The second main argument relating to the sovereignty issue was that Monetary Union would lead to Fiscal Union and that this would in turn lead to Political Union. It was feared that within the strait jacket of a single currency, national governments' capacity to launch independent policies of wealth creation, employment generation and welfare improvement would be removed. Artificial federalist rules would prevent governments responding to their electorates and extremist movements would fill this unnecessary vacuum (Burkitt and Baimbridge, 1996:182). Likewise, William Hague, Major's successor as Conservative leader, suggested that EMU would lead to a banking and financial crisis like that of South East Asia or to the kind of conflict witnessed in Bosnia. Indeed, he compared membership of the single currency to being 'trapped in a burning building with no exits'. Norman Lamont was an equally strong proponent of the view that a single currency would require further integration: 'a single European currency would thus be a gigantic step towards the creation of a European government and a European state' (Lamont, 1996:100). It would also remove the ability to govern, and thus the domestic implications of a loss of sovereignty under EMU were at least as important as its effects on sovereignty in the international system.

As it became clear that EU governments were going to press ahead with the single currency, the arguments of sceptics shifted from the impossibility of a single currency and its costs to British business, to focus on the unsustainability of the project in the short to medium term. Here the critique drew on political–economic arguments that the EU would eventually be torn apart by the single currency project, as a political and economic hard core emerged and those outside at best lost influence and at worst were politically and economically disadvantaged. In addition, it was argued that the lack of real convergence would become clear when the EU experienced asymmetric shocks, and this would lead to economic and political dislocation. A further concern was that a single currency might lead to voluntary or involuntary German domination (Connolly, 1995:169).

A key problem for the sceptics was that when John Major described the commitment of the other member states to achieving a single currency within the timetable as, 'having all the potency of a primitive rain dance', he was as his former Chancellor pointed out, suffering from 'wishful thinking' (Lamont, 1996:99). Not only did Major's characterisation overlook the political will amongst the other member states in favour of the single currency, but it also underestimated the considerable flexibility which in reality existed for deciding whether member states met the convergence criteria. Indeed, as has been noted, the Maastricht Treaty provided as a backstop position a mechanism for a majority of governments to proceed in 1999 so long as they considered that they had met the convergence criteria. The British government armed with its opt-out was never in reality going to be able to wield a veto over a project which it did not want to join. Bernard Connolly, a former Commission official, went so far as to argue that the mechanisms leading to Monetary Union were always an instrument of a political project, which made it inevitable that Britain would be wrong-footed and eventually sidelined (Connolly, 1995).

On the Labour side of the political spectrum on the other hand, the first point to make is that much of the historical conflict in the party had focused on the nature and direction of national economic policy. This made the issue of the single currency particularly important (Gamble and Kelly, 2000:1–25), and does much to explain the acute sensitivity of the New Labour governments of 1997 onwards to any internal dissent on the issue. This was despite the numerical weakness of Labour sceptics, a weakness further underlined by the marked lack of academics ready to invest in their case, certainly by comparison with the Conservative camp. Nevertheless, the Labour sceptics, although marginalised, voiced a number of arguments in opposition to the single currency.

One group of opponents viewed the single currency as a reinvigoration of the capitalist tendencies of the original Common Market project. Not only would governments lose monetary policy instruments but the influence and importance of multinational capital and financial markets would be enhanced (Gamble and Kelly, 2000:12). Rooted in Keynesianism, one view of EMU was that the process of achieving economic convergence enshrined in the Maastricht Treaty's convergence criteria and the creation and maintenance of the single currency (and the penalties for non-adherence – the so-called Stability Pact) were based on *laissez faire* rather than interventionist economic principles. Governments would therefore lose the policy instruments to address low levels of investment and the ability to tackle long-term unemployment (Mitchie, 1997). It was the latter which for some Labour supporters was the purpose of Labour winning office. This view was championed by two leading trades unionists, Bill Morris of the Transport and General Workers Union (TGWU) and John Edmonds of the General and Municipal Boilermakers Union (GMB). They opposed the independence of the European Central Bank, the priority given to inflation over employment and growth and the setting of independent monetary targets. The *Guardian* broadly supported this position as did the *Observer*, arguing that monetary policy would be too restrictive for domestic policy objectives. They were therefore unsympathetic to transferring control of interest rates to a European Central Bank (Riddell, 1998:106).

The Labour Euro Safeguards Campaign offered similarly 'Old Labour' arguments. Participation in the Euro would require public expenditure to be artificially capped at the levels set by the convergence criteria in the Maastricht Treaty. This would mean substantial cuts, with the inevitable consequence being fewer resources for essential services such as health, education and training. Interest rates and monetary policy would be determined by the European Central Bank, and not by the Chancellor of the Exchequer since the exchange rate for the pound would be irrevocably fixed. In addition, according to the Maastricht Treaty, there would be no escape from the single currency, as there was from the ERM. As their publicity material highlighted, 'the case against Stage III and the single currency is not a question of arid economic theory. It is a struggle for the soul of the Labour Party'.

Another group of Labour MPs were, by contrast, suspicious of handing over monetary sovereignty without also transferring to a central European government the power to affect Social Democratic objectives. Ken Livingstone, for instance, argued that without a European level government, Social Democratic and Socialist aims would always be pushed into second place. This kind of argument hence demonstrated another difficulty which existed for Labour sceptics, who as well as being marginalised were also divided amongst themselves, not just on the nature of the integration project, but also as to its ultimate desirability.

A further set of arguments focused on the issues of accountability and representation. Where governments had ceded the power to act, but remained nationally accountable for economic welfare, any difference of priorities ran the risk of destroying the political system and particularly the ability of voters to change national governments and policies. It was, for instance, argued that EMU had to be linked to Political Union in order to allow legitimacy and accountability to be effective. Without these safeguards, EMU would be anti-democratic and in the longer term built on unviable political structures. In addition to this, it was suggested that the separation of economic and political structures and the enshrinement of deflationary macroeconomic policy would lead to competitive bidding downwards of standards of social protection and tax rates, as well as higher unemployment (Gill, 1998:15). As Gamble and Kelly remark, 'in this way it would destroy the institutions of Social Democracy' (Gamble and Kelly, 2000:20).

Another concern on the left was that whatever the inherent merits of EMU, the timing of the introduction of a single currency was inconvenient for the Labour Party and/or the EU. On the former point, it was that argued the Labour (and indeed the previous Conservative) government had found economic success through a series of alternative measures to those of EMU, which give credibility to its anti-inflation and sustainable growth policies. As one Treasury aide said, 'the position has changed from three years ago, when we thought we would need the iron discipline of the Bundesbank to lend credibility to economic policy. ... The economy is going well so the decision on whether or not we join the Euro can be taken on a much more level playing field' (*Sunday Times*, 1999a:15). The fear was that premature entry might take place at the wrong point in the economic cycle and at the wrong rate of exchange, the two major policy flaws in Britain's entry into the Exchange Rate Mechanism (Gamble and Kelly, 2000:14).

On the latter point, the argument ran that the EU had a limited amount of institutional energy and the opportunity cost of focusing on the creation of a single currency was the inability to pursue other more worthy projects. Ralf Dahrendorf was, for instance, at the forefront of suggesting that EMU was less important than the re-integration of central and eastern Europe into European institutions and that EMU might even endanger the long-term future of the EU (Dahrendorf, 1998).

The arguments on both the right and the left inevitably concentrated on the single currency issue. Reflecting their position of political influence, certainly until the 1997 general election, the arguments on the Conservative wing of the Eurosceptic family were the most fully developed and indeed dominant. At the same time, however, the proliferation of Eurosceptical groupings during this period, while reflecting the strength of Eurosceptic views, also underlined to a greater extent than ever before the variety of these views and the degree of inconsistency which they often exhibited. One sign of this was the conflicting views on Europe between Peter Shore and Ken Livingstone within the Labour Party. More important, however, was the upsurge in non-partisan groupings such as New Europe together with business groupings like Business for Sterling which were explicitly and quite consciously opposed to membership of the Euro alone, and not to the EU as such. This was markedly different from the position of some Conservative Eurosceptics who believed that if Britain could hold off joining a single currency such isolation would lead to a policy of 'progressive detachment' (Stephens, 1997:355). During the period between 1992 and 2001, such inconsistencies did not prove an obstacle to the Eurosceptic case. However, they arguably retained the potential to weaken Eurosceptic influence, since Eurosceptics lacked a clearly articulated set of unifying aims and objectives, and an alternative vision of the future.

Arena

From the moment the Conservative government secured the ratification of the Maastricht Treaty, it came under pressure from Eurosceptics within the party to rule out the theoretical prospect of joining a single currency and to guarantee a referendum on any decision to abolish the pound. As the government's majority diminished, party managers lost control of the parliamentary arena. Sceptics used every opportunity to demonstrate that their loyalty could no longer be taken for granted and that they were willing to bring the government down over its future stance on the issue of the single currency.

Initially, the government reacted to its loss of control of the parliamentary arena by neither ruling in nor out the possibility of a referendum. The official government position was that it was most unlikely that the other governments would meet the convergence criteria, and that as a consequence no decision to join a single currency would be necessary in the lifetime of the Parliament of 1992 to 1997. This did not, however, satisfy opponents of the single currency, who, scarred and galvanised by the Maastricht ratification process, were willing to press the case. As the Conservative majority continued to diminish and it became clear that other governments would press ahead with Monetary Union, the government's position became increasingly untenable. Moreover, with the approach of the deadline for the next general election, there was also a feeling, reminiscent of the last phase of Mrs Thatcher's premiership, that the only means to re-election was on a more Eurosceptic platform, opposing the abolition of the pound and making a manifesto commitment to a referendum.

Whilst continuing to eschew immediate endorsement of a referendum, Major now therefore proceeded to characterise John Smith, the Labour leader, as, 'Monsieur Oui, the poodle of Brussels', attacking Labour's commitment to ending the social policy opt-out and claiming that its desire for '… a United States of Europe made it unfit to govern' (Gower and Turner, 2000:287). This rhetorical scepticism was also taken up by other government ministers, and notably the Defence Secretary, Michael Portillo. Nevertheless, Major continued to resist making a decision on whether to join the single currency, in part because he was convinced that the government would be able to shape decisions on the single currency whether Britain was a member or not. The problem was that this policy of negotiate and decide made Major highly vulnerable to pressure from within and outside government as opposing camps jockeyed for position to try to harden the position in the short term, and to secure the future position of the party in the long term.

The emergence of the Referendum Party in November 1994 put additional pressure on Major to commit to a referendum on the issue of a single currency. With a general election looming in 1997, Sir James Goldsmith committed £20 million to create a new political party with the sole purpose of forcing a referendum on Britain's future in Europe. Its candidates would stand against any MPs who did not publicly commit themselves to a referendum not just on the single currency but also on withdrawal from the EU, with the possibility of up to 600 candidates standing. Conservative Central Office researchers calculated that this might cost the Tories up to twenty seats in marginal constituencies.[13]

One of the most sceptical Conservatives, John Redwood, by now out of the Cabinet, was involved in mediating with James Goldsmith in the spring of 1997 to explore the possibility of a compromise, and in the run-up to the election Major did indeed promise a referendum. This, however, was not a referendum on Britain's continued membership of the EU, but on the narrower issue of a single currency, and was subject to the government's having first decided the join the single currency. As Philip Stephens remarks, in this way Major '... hoped that by offering its own referendum, the government could outflank both the Referendum Party and Labour' (Stephens, 1997:338). At the same time, however, the groundswell of unease over the single currency amongst party activists and MPs, the effectiveness of the Eurosceptics – notably Howard, Lilley, Cranborne, Portillo, Forsyth and Hague – inside the Cabinet and the weakness of pro-European ministers, estimated at only four in number, made the decision almost inevitable if the Prime Minister wanted to avoid wholesale disobedience on this issue in the general election (Seldon, 1997:639). Indeed, in June 1997, the strength of Eurosceptic feeling within the Conservative Party was underlined by a vote by seventy-eight Tory MPs in favour of a referendum not on the single currency, but on Britain's continued membership of the European Union itself.[14]

The importance of the commitment to a referendum was that it symbolised the democratisation of the European question and provided evidence that it was no longer solely the province of the political elite. In order to survive, the Conservative government had been obliged to allow the issue to move from the confines of the parliamentary to the electoral arena where its influence and control was significantly diminished. Exploiting Major's small parliamentary majority, the Eurosceptics therefore secured a major victory on the issue of the Euro through disobedience in Cabinet and on the backbenches, although they were also assisted by the hardening of public opinion against the Euro. Once the Conservative Party had formally committed itself to the position of a referendum, it was only a matter of time before Labour did so. It was true that the Labour Party had no large-scale Eurosceptic contingent within its ranks to satisfy, and the Labour leadership did not wish to see the issue move to an arena it could not control. However, as Hugo Young points out, 'it feared any challenge to its populist credentials' (H. Young, 1999:487).

The crucial aspects of the new position to which both parties were now committed were that the referendum would only be held after the Cabinet decision to join the single currency, and after legislation to achieve this had been endorsed by Parliament. Moreover, the commitment to hold such a referendum was limited to the duration of the next Parliament; the wording would be simply on the lines 'should Britain take part in a single currency?' and a simple majority of those voting would be sufficient to introduce the Euro. Finally, since a referendum would take place only because the Cabinet and Parliament had decided in favour of joining the single currency, all Cabinet members would be bound by collective responsibility to support this position.

Notwithstanding that cross-party commitment to a referendum had been secured, not all Eurosceptics were pleased by the provisos with which it was surrounded. Michael Portillo, one of the most ardent opponents of a single currency (Stephens, 1997:273), held for instance that to accept a referendum was to accept that the government of the day was willing to abolish the pound, and that this would therefore given the pro-Euro campaign a significant advantage (Stephens, 1997: 342). Thus the referendum option was to Portillo very much a second best, and his preference was for a manifesto commitment never to enter the Euro. Others, like Baroness Thatcher and Lord Lamont as well as Howard, Lilley, Forsyth and Hague, were more positive and thought that a referendum was the best vehicle to rule out a single currency indefinitely.[15]

With the general election of 1997, however, a more pro-European government than any seen during the previous thirty years was elected to power, and the omens for preventing the adoption of the single currency were not propitious. The New Labour government had a majority of 179 and the Cabinet was dominated by pro-Europeans, with the sceptics – notwithstanding that they included the Chancellor, Gordon Brown – few and of a mild persuasion, more pragmatic than outright opponents. In these circumstances, the Eurosceptics, so influential under the previous administration, were temporarily thrown on the back foot. The new government signalled its intent with the rapid agreement of the Amsterdam Treaty at the European Council of June 1997. Following Labour's signature of the Social Protocol, this Treaty amongst other things now included the Social Chapter (Gowland and Turner, 2000:337). In addition, Labour quickly began to exploit its domination of the parliamentary arena to wrest back control of the European issue. On 27 October 1997, Brown made clear that whilst Britain would not be part of the first wave, the British government was in principle in support of membership of the Euro (Gowland and Turner, 2000:348). In Parliament, he therefore went on to say that, 'if, in the end a single currency is successful, and the economic case is clear and unambiguous, then the government believes Britain should be part of it'.

To judge the economic case, Brown set out five tests to define early in the 2001 Parliament whether an argument for entry could be made. These tests were whether there could be sustainable convergence between Britain and the economies of the single currency; whether there was sufficient flexibility to cope with economic change; what the effect was on investment; the impact on the financial services industry; and whether employment benefited. As Russell Holden notes, the advent of the Labour government thus marked a shift from negotiate and decide to a policy of 'prepare and join'. A key element of the Labour Party's strategy was to normalise the issue of the single currency and de-sensitise the possibility of membership, seeking to portray itself as essentially pragmatic, its attitude that of a 'constructive agnostic' letting 'the facts' speak for themselves in determining a recommendation from the government.[16] The bottom line, however, was as the House of Commons Treasury Select Committee highlighted, the five economic tests remained vague and lacking specification (Treasury Select Committee, 1998); their fulfilment would thus be a matter of political as much as economic interpretation.

Early evidence of the government's support for membership came in the form of the decision to give operational independence to the Bank of England on the basis of a mandate from the government to meet as closely as possible the inflation target of 2.5 per cent. This was a manifesto commitment, but the speed with which it took place surprised many and whilst justified on domestic grounds it did also meet one of the most important conditions for membership of the Euro. In addition, in February 1999, Brown set out a National Changeover Plan to prepare the country for entry to the Euro in the event of a positive vote in a referendum. A further feature of the plan was the encouragement given to firms and the financial markets to accept (and trade in) the Euro.

The government also solicited support from the business community and used its contact with Japanese companies (especially Honda, Matsushita and Toyota) to encourage them to press publicly for the government to make its position on the Euro clear. Accordingly, the argument was voiced that the high value of the pound was damaging sales and investment, Britain's waiting game was described as a 'headache' and Nissan and Matsushita rumbled that Britain should make its intentions clear or face 'dire consequences' (Smallwood, 2000). Similarly in August 2000, Toyota announced its decision to ask its British suppliers to quote their prices in Euros (Fildes, 2000). More generally, Brown took steps to ensure that the budget was in balance, an important acceptance of the macroeconomic basis upon which the Euro was constructed. In these ways the government worked to outflank sceptics by avoiding a political commitment while at the same time taking practical steps on the road to EMU.

However, despite these steps, the sceptics' battle to prevent Britain joining the single currency was by no means over. What differentiated this period from earlier phases was that, assisted by the activities of the party political and non-partisan sceptical campaign groups, the public was now engaged by the European issue, and in particular the question of the single currency, to a greater extent than ever before. This was a trend further encouraged by the commitment of both main parties to hold a referendum on the Euro. In addition to this, however, government policy was particularly vulnerable in the arena of public opinion due to the almost pathological concern of New Labour with electoral popularity. The problem for Labour was that the public was predominantly hostile to membership of the Euro. Thus the fear of a humiliating rejection, particularly in a referendum vote, of Blair's pro-European strategy was critical in curbing and restricting the extent of the government's positive stance on Europe. Indeed, it was instrumental in the government's selection of a strategy of stealth rather than confrontation over the issue of the Euro. It was true that on Labour's advent to power, public hostility did subside, with a three to one rejection of the single currency in November 1996 shifting to a margin of less than one to two in 1997. Initially, therefore, the government felt that it could quickly win over the general public if it could get its message across, as indeed had been the case in the 1975 referendum.[17] However, over Labour's next four years in office, it was clear that opposition was mounting, peaking at sixty per cent opposing a single currency, with thirty per cent supporting it and with ten per cent undecided.

Nevertheless, sceptics were careful not to take the views of the electorate for granted. At the same time as showing sustained opposition to the scrapping of the pound, opinion poll evidence indicated that around three out of five of the electorate did not hold very strong views on the issue and were therefore susceptible to influence. Over half of all those sampled made it clear that the key battleground was the economic arguments and the impact of the single currency on the British economy (Kellner, 1998:120).[18] The concern was therefore that 'if the conditions are right, opposition to the Euro may melt away'. Drawing on the lessons of the 1975 referendum, sceptics accordingly worked assiduously to ensure that the views of the 'No' camp would not weaken in a government dominated referendum campaign. Business for Sterling and New Europe were at the forefront of providing the economic arguments for opposing the abolition of sterling and sampling business opinion.[19] The success of this strategy was demonstrated in an ICM poll in February 2000 which showed that nearly three-quarters of Britain's businesses opposed the government's 'in principle' commitment to join the Euro.[20]

Both Business for Sterling and New Europe were also at the forefront of campaigning for the observation in the proposed referendum of the recommendations of the Neill Committee on Standards in Public Life. Produced in autumn 1998, the Neill Report recommended that neither taxpayers' money nor the government machine should be used to promote the government's side of the argument; that the government should not distribute literature, 'even purportedly factual literature' setting out or otherwise promoting its case at public expense; and that the government should give both sides of the argument in any referendum equal access to 'core funding' to mount their campaigns. In fact, however, as New Europe highlighted in November 1999, the government had already acted against the explicit advice of the Committee on Standards in Public Life by proposing to limit campaign spending in the referendum to £5 million compared with the £29 million of taxpayers' funds it had already spent on Euro preparation material (Herbert, 1999).

The sceptical press also played a leading role in maintaining the salience of the European issue in the public arena. The News International group of papers continued to argue against the Euro and to promote a 'Save the Pound' campaign. chapter, *The Sun* was prominent in fighting moves towards the Euro by stealth, particularly under its new editor David Yelland. The Prime Minister's apparent support for the Euro at the Cardiff European Council in June 1998 was, for instance, promptly followed by a front page picture of a masked Blair with the headline: 'is this the most dangerous man in Britain?' (Riddell, 1998:114). Sensitive as the government was to the climate of opinion, the position of the press did much to restrict its freedom of manoeuvre, as Blair made clear in May 2000: 'the modern media is immensely powerful. It is omnipresent. It makes decision-making often very difficult … There is just a massive and often completely factually inaccurate campaign against Europe run by a very large part of the press that literally suppresses any news that would reflect well on Europe' (Blair, 2000). Indeed, Hugo Young notes of Blair that, 'by sidelining EMU from an immediate decision, he was pre-empting a Murdoch onslaught, which he feared, might undercut his prospect of a second term' (H. Young, 1999:494).

The sceptical cause in the public arena was bolstered by the policies of the Conservative opposition. In the wake of the 1997 defeat, William Hague, the Conservative leader from 1997–2001, was keen to unite the party and ensure that frontbench policy accurately reflected the views of party activists. In October 1998, the party held a vote on what became the new policy of ruling out membership of the single currency not only for the current Parliament but also for the next ten years, and this received eighty-four per cent backing. The position became a central plank of the Conservatives' electoral strategy and in the European Parliament election of June 1999, the party gained a number of seats, bringing strong Conservative Eurosceptic representation into the EP for the first time. During the same year, Hague also launched his own 'Save the Pound' campaign, travelling throughout Britain to publicise the cause. With public opinion polls reflecting increasing hostility to the Euro and, indeed, British membership of the EU, the Conservatives were hopeful that they had found New Labour's Achilles heel. Certainly, in the context of the June 2001 election campaign the strategy was unsuccessful, leading to another landslide defeat for the Conservative Party; however, it did firm up public attitudes on the Euro.

The effect of this pressure outside as well as inside Parliament was critical. In particular, without abandoning its aim of joining the Euro, the government was forced to postpone any consideration of a referendum until early in the Parliament of 2001 to 2005. A further reflection of the government's concern was its role in August 1999 in the re-launch of Britain in Europe, a cross-party alliance designed to re-claim the European initiative from the sceptics. The aim was to try to replicate the winning strategy of 1971 to 1972 and 1975, when a generally wary and certainly volatile public was convinced to shift to a pro-integration position. On both occasions, the government of the day supported by leading opposition party politicians mounted a strong, broad-based campaign and was able to demonstrate the economic benefits of engagement with the EC. With support from Michael Heseltine, Ken Clarke and Charles Kennedy, the Britain in Europe campaign therefore claimed to 'put country above party' (*Sunday Times*, 1999a).

Government support for BIE was clearly flagged when the visit of the Executive Director to Denmark during the Danish referendum on the Euro was trailed as having semi-official status. Again, however, government inhibitions about pressing home the pro-European case with any degree of enthusiasm were well to the fore. Thus BIE explicitly advocated an active role for Britain in the process of European integration, but only quietly pressed for Britain to join the Euro. Since the latter objective was too explicit for current government policy, the strategy was instead to accuse Eurosceptics '… of being extremist little Englanders' and '… to put the

Tories on the far right and label them as extremists' (*Sunday Times*, 1999a). Ultimately, however, the rather apologetic approach taken by BIE only served to underline the extent to which Eurosceptic influence now pervaded both the public arena, and inhibited the government from daring to voice the opposing case. But in a sense it was also true that there was little new in this, since governments of all political hues had never attempted to set out for the public the issues involved in membership of the EC/EU, and this was an old habit which proved hard to break. The irony was that, although increasingly cautious, the Blair government continued to be strongly pro-European in deed if not in word, as underlined by the launch of the European defence capability initiative and its agreement of the Nice Treaty in December 2000.

Conclusions

From 1992 until 2001, Eurosceptics succeeded in seizing and creating a range of opportunities to oppose the government's policy on the Euro and in mobilising opinion against membership. Ultimately, through a breakdown in consensus within the Conservative Party, John Major was cajoled into conceding a referendum on the Euro if the government recommended entry. The Labour leadership found it difficult to resist making a similar commitment and for the first time since 1975 both major political parties accepted the need for popular consent. Importantly, too, the government was forced into a position in which a 'No' vote would support the *status quo*. The commitment of both parties to a referendum on the Euro meant that the ultimate decision over Britain's relationship with the integration project had moved out of the hands of the political elite in Parliament and into the hands of the electorate. However, this was an arena in which the government did not enjoy unrivalled authority. Indeed, precisely for this reason, wherever possible, governments had always fought to keep the European issue within the parliamentary arena. Moreover, the Neill Report on the future conduct of any referendum had now set limitations on the government's ability to shape its outcome that did not exist in 1975.

During this period the composition and characteristics of opponents of closer European integration also underwent a transformation. The period saw the forces of Euroscepticism growing both more virulent and more broadly based than at any other time since the Second World War. Moreover, much as Britain in Europe sought to portray its opponents as such, the alliance against the Euro was not extremist. Most of the Conservative Party under the new leadership of Iain Duncan Smith supported the anti-Euro policy. To this were added two new single issue political parties, the Referendum Party/Democracy Movement and the UK Independence Party, along with the majority of the press. Here, in contrast to the 1975 referendum, by the mid-1990s the number of newspapers campaigning against the Euro or supporting Eurosceptics was almost double those favouring the pro-Euro camp. This sustained a wide range of opposition groups outside Parliament including New Europe and other non-partisan bodies.

A striking feature of this period was the increasing sophistication of the arguments now deployed by the sceptics. The credibility of the sceptic case was further assisted by the support it received from leading members of the establishment, including a number of peers in the reformed House of Lords along with business leaders. Nevertheless, it was notable that the arguments advanced against the Euro were principally based on economic grounds. Facts and figures were cited in preference to more intangible and potentially more divisive political arguments. Fundamentally, the fact was that the issue of the Euro united sceptics who had quite differing views of the integration process, bringing together as it did both those who were essentially anti-EU and saw the Euro as a means to fight a much wider campaign against British membership, and those who were pro-membership but who opposed the Euro.

Over the years, Eurosceptics had always been much clearer about what they were against than what they were for, and this was a characteristic which was therefore strengthened during the 1990s. Whereas in the past, however, divisions had tended to follow the lines determined by party political allegiance, the decline in prominence of sceptics on the left of the political spectrum had now led to a changed picture. In party political terms, the scene was now dominated by the Conservative Eurosceptics, but they had been joined by large numbers of non-partisan groupings, motivated at least ostensibly by practical as opposed to political concerns.

Notes

1 The name of the single currency was decided at the Madrid European Council in December 1995.
2 The convergence criteria were contained in Article 109j and protocol six of the Treaty. They required a high degree of price stability with an average rate of inflation of not more than 1.5 per cent higher than that of the three best performing member states; a sustainable financial position, including a budget deficit of not more than three per cent of GDP and a public debt ratio not exceeding sixty per cent of GDP; currency stability, with participation in the narrow bands of ERM for two years without severe tension or devaluation; interest rate convergence, and with member states to have an average nominal long-term interest rate not more than two per cent higher than that of the three best performing member states.
3 It was German insistence that led to clear and explicit criteria (Gowland and Turner, 2000:290).
4 The currency fluctuation bands of the ERM were widened from 2.25 per cent to fifteen per cent to prevent the collapse of the system.
5 'The way people who oppose our European policy go about it is to attack me personally … You have three right-wing members of the Cabinet. What happens if they resign? Where do you think most of the poison has come from? It is coming from the dispossessed and the never possessed on the backbenches. Would you like three more of the bastards out there?' (Gorman, 1993:233).
6 Certainly, those who remained committed to a single currency did so out of a belief that despite current economic circumstances a single currency was inevitable. As a corollary, those with pragmatic instincts recognised that membership of the Euro was unlikely in the short or medium term. An incentive to move to a sceptical position was undoubtedly the standing of the Conservative Party in the opinion polls. As the party slipped to some thirty percentage points behind the Labour Party and defeat looked inevitable, the shadow of the future – the need to

win the support of sceptical backbenchers in a future party leadership campaign – was a strong incentive.

7 This greatly annoyed Bill Cash who found his launch of the European Foundation completely overshadowed by Lamont's speech.

8 For an analysis of the hostility of chapter, *The Sun* and other newspapers to the Euro and the Blair government's tactics for dealing with it see Riddell, 1998:105–16.

9 Major described this as 'treachery' and went on to publicly state that it would have been better to give the money to the Conservative Party (Seldon, 1997:651).

10 Equivalent figures for Conservative MPs were twenty-one per cent on the absence of an informed debate, twenty-six per cent advocating withdrawal; and sixty-six per cent that the ECB should not determine monetary policy.

11 Supporters in the Lords comprised an influential grouping of leading industrialists: Lord Hanson; Lord Clitheroe, Chairman, Yorkshire Bank plc; The Rt Hon Lord Marsh PC; Lord Remnant CVO, former Chairman, National Provident; Lord Sainsbury of Preston Candover KG; Lord Weinstock, Chairman Emeritus, GEC; Lord Wolfson of Sunningdale, Chairman, Great Universal Stores plc; The Rt Hon Lord Young PC, Chairman, Young Associates.

12 See, for example, Gavyn Davies's evidence to the Treasury Select Committee on 29 January and 2 April 1998 quoted in Gowland and Turner, 2000:307.

13 In the event, the Referendum Party fielded 550 candidates at the election with little noticeable effect on Conservative electoral fortunes. It won only 3.1 per cent of the vote and possibly played a role in the loss of four seats to opposition parties and the saving of another three (Curtice and Stead, 1997).

14 This was supported by Norman Lamont, Ken Baker and John Redwood and demonstrated how far the party had moved since Norman Lamont first mooted the possibility of withdrawal (Stephens, 1997:351).

15 One senior minister joked that meetings of the Cabinet's European sub-committee had by now become like a dress rehearsal for the looming leadership contest. The would-be candidates drew notes from their pockets before addressing colleagues in the manner of a public meeting (Stephens, 1997:354).

16 The phrases used in an influential CEPR report (Rupert Pennant Rea *et al.*, 1997).

17 As Tony Blair made clear in an interview in the *Guardian*, 'If we decided to make a recommendation to people, the whole dynamics of the argument would change, because the circumstances would have changed' 23 May 2000.

18 Peter Kellner reports a Eurobarometer survey that found that only one in three would put sovereignty issues ahead of greater prosperity (Kellner, 1998:123).

19 For a typical example of this, see the article in the Business section of the *Sunday Times*, 'Runaway Inflation – the Euro lesson from Ireland' by Christopher Smallwood (Smallwood, 2000:4).

20 This was the most comprehensive independent survey ever undertaken of 1,001 heads of companies and was conducted by ICM on behalf of Business for Sterling.

8 Patterns and trends in Euroscepticism

Introduction

This study has examined the ebb and flow of opposition to European integration in Britain in the period following the Second World War. In doing so, it has explored the way in which scepticism was affected by, and its influence on, the formulation of British policy towards Europe on six issues: the failed membership applications of 1961 and 1967; the passage of the EC Bill of 1970 to 1972; the referendum of June 1975; the Single European Act of 1986; the Political and Monetary Union agenda in the form of the Maastricht Treaty, and the single currency. This chapter is concerned with the patterns and trends which scepticism has displayed over this period. To this end, it focuses on four issues: the scale and nature of Labour and Conservative scepticism towards Europe; the identity of the sceptics; the themes evident in sceptical arguments; and the overall impact of opposition to European integration. The chapter concludes by reflecting on the reasons behind the changing fortunes of scepticism, and what the future holds for its adherents.

The scale and nature of Labour and Conservative scepticism

At almost all times since 1945, but especially since the mid-1960s, there was a distinct group of MPs who challenged closer supranational engagement with the continental powers: initially anti-Europeans, then anti-Marketeers and in their current guise Eurosceptics. The number of these sceptics has waxed and waned, fluctuating between approximately forty to sixty, although there has always been a greater number of passive sceptics than those MPs actively willing to oppose their party.

In the Conservative Party in the late 1950s and the 1960s, thirty to forty MPs were opposed to Macmillan's policy of entry to the EC. In the 1970s, some sixty Conservative MPs were opposed to membership, with forty-one MPs opposing the 1971 EC Bill and sixteen backbenchers willing to oppose the terms of the re-negotiation in April 1975. Between 1973 and the late 1980s, the number shrank to seven Conservative MPs who were willing to disobey the government on the ratification of the Single European Act. By the time of the Maastricht Treaty, the total had once again grown to around sixty-nine, with forty-six routinely willing to disobey the government on almost all of its European legislation and nine willing to put the issue before loyalty to the party. After 1997 at least three-quarters of the parliamentary Conservative Party embraced a form of Euroscepticism, and the party's choice of leaders along with its 1997 and 2001 general election manifestos reflected this.

In the 1960s and 1970s, almost two-thirds of the parliamentary Labour Party were opposed to EC membership and campaigned and voted against it. In votes on the re-negotiated terms of British EC membership, an indication of the strength of feeling on the European issue was the fact that seven Cabinet ministers and thirty-one out of sixty-two junior ministers were willing to oppose the government's own policy on membership. A total of 147 backbench Labour MPs voted against the terms, a number exceeding those Labour MPs who voted for their government's policy. From 1979 and for almost a decade thereafter, the anti-Marketeers flourished in the Labour Party, reducing steadily only from the late 1980s as the party modernised and transformed itself into 'New Labour'. Estimates of the level of Euroscepticism in the parliamentary party of the late 1990s suggested that around ten backbench MPs were Eurosceptical with about one-third of the parliamentary party agnostic about the value of closer integration.

The first point to make about the waxing and waning of scepticism is that with the exception of the 1964 to 1970 and the 1974 to 1979 periods, mass scepticism in political parties has been a phenomenon which has coincided with periods of opposition. Between 1961 and 1963, the Labour Party under Hugh Gaitskell's leadership adopted an anti-membership stance; while between 1979 and 1983 under Michael Foot and between 1984 and 1988 under Neil Kinnock, it was committed to withdrawal from the EC. Likewise, from 1997, the Conservative Party steadily embraced a robust sceptical position. This culminated in a policy in 1999 of negotiating a flexibility clause on closer European integration, coupled with warnings that European integration had reached its limits and a commitment to referenda on all new treaties. However, in terms of the number of sceptics and periods in which Labour was opposed to closer European integration, it, rather than the Conservative Party, can claim to have been the most sceptical major party in the half century after 1945.

The fact that the two major parties have been at their most sceptical in periods out of office is something that requires further comment. Since 1970, all parties have started their period of office more positive about European integration than when they have left office. This was true of the Heath government of 1970 to 1974, the Labour governments of 1974 to 1979, the Thatcher and Major governments of 1979 to 1997, and, perhaps more arguably, the Blair government of 1997 to 2001. In part this is a consequence of a pragmatic, instrumental view of the value of European integration. Over a government's lifetime the failure to secure British objectives and the speed and direction of European integration has eventually culminated in disillusionment. Moreover, following eviction from office, both Labour and Conservative parties have embraced more radical policies as a means of rejuvenating themselves. As part of this general trend of radicalisation, the party leaderships have embraced more sceptical polices on Europe, as was the case of the cooler approach of Margaret Thatcher when elected as leader of the

Conservative Party in 1975, the Labour Party in 1979 and the Conservative Party two decades later. Thus although in historical perspective political parties have only won office after moving to the centre ground, Europe has often been subject to the influence of the cycle of transformation and re-transformation, pitting a sceptical stance on Europe against an appetite for government. Opposition to integration has therefore been a feature of the disillusionment with pragmatism experienced by political parties in office faced with the realities of governing. Scepticism is part of the radicalisation process parties undergo out of office.

However, on three occasions whilst in office, the parliamentary parties have embraced sceptical positions. First, between 1964 and 1970 the majority of the parliamentary Labour Party opposed membership, though Wilson overturned this position by speaking the language of scepticism whilst at the same time opening discussions with EC members to see if adequate terms for British entry could be found. Second, as noted above, between 1974 and 1975, over one-third of the parliamentary Labour Party opposed the re-negotiated terms of membership. Again, Wilson managed to resist this pressure and to neutralise the anti-Market activists and dissenting cabinet ministers within the Labour Party. But whilst he was able temporarily to overcome this internal opposition, it was only through the Conservatives voting in overwhelming numbers in support of the government that parliamentary acceptance of the re-negotiated terms was secured. Indeed, on the crucial vote in April 1975, Conservative MPs voting for the Labour government exceeded Labour MPs by nearly 100.

In this regard, it is interesting to observe that pro-EC MPs have been more willing than sceptics, not merely to disobey their party, but to place loyalty to the European cause before their party. This was also true of those Labour MPs supporting the EC Bill in 1972, and was seen again in 1983 with the defection of the 'Gang of Three', later joined by Roy Jenkins and supported by nearly two dozen Labour MPs, to form the Social Democratic Party. Harold Wilson once described the commitment of Labour MPs who adhered to the EC as, 'not so much a policy as a way of life' and went on to say that they '...would, if the choice had to be made, reject the party in favour of what was to them the wider aim' (Wilson, 1979:50–1). The number of sceptics who have been prepared to go to these extremes has been considerably fewer. Only two MPs, Enoch Powell and Sir George Gardiner, have for instance gone so far as to leave the Conservative Party over Europe, the former to join the Ulster Unionists and the latter the Referendum Party – although only after being deselected by his Reigate constituency.

The third occasion on which the party of government has embraced a sceptical position was during the Major administration of 1992 to 1997. At this time, over half the Conservative Party's backbenchers supported a more sceptical line towards the European Union, including re-negotiation of the Maastricht Treaty and abandonment of the commitment to Political and Monetary Union. Through use of the whips and Major's willingness to place his own leadership on the line and to make the government's policy on Europe a question of confidence, thus pitting party loyalty against MPs' opposition to Europe, widespread rebellion was averted. Nevertheless, Major had to face a leadership contest and dissent continued resulting in eight Conservatives being deprived of the whip over Europe, and the veteran sceptic Sir Richard Body resigning it in sympathy.

Identity of the sceptics

A small group of parliamentarians on both sides of the House of Commons has a long-standing record of opposition to European integration, often sustained at the expense of promotion within their parties. At the same time, however, there have been important developments in the identity and support base of sceptics in the period after the Second World War. Moreover, despite its longevity and what is in many respects its faith-like character, scepticism lacked any founding fathers.

In the late 1940s and early 1950s most politicians were sceptical of Britain's need to join in the process of supranational European integration. In the mid-1950s, Anthony Eden and, to a lesser extent, R.A. Butler stood out as leading sceptics within the parliamentary Conservative Party, capturing the prevailing mood by arguing for intergovernmental co-operation, but nothing more (Skär, 2000). On the Labour benches Hugh Gaitskell, leader of the Labour Party between 1960 and 1963, crudely caught the imagination of sceptics with his claim 'that entering Europe could mean the end of Britain as an independent state ... It means the end of a thousand years of history' (Heffernan, 2000:383).

By the mid-1960s the mantle had passed to a new generation of anti-Marketeers within the Conservative and Labour parties. In the Conservative Party, Richard Body, Neil Marten, Teddy Taylor, Sir Derek Walker-Smith, but above all Enoch Powell had replaced Max Aitken, John Biggs-Davidson, Major Legge-Bourke and Captain Ryder as the leading anti-Marketeers. What these Conservatives shared was their non-conformity with the prevailing view within their party. Enoch Powell perhaps best exemplified this with his mix of traditional appearance, patrician style and anti-establishment views. Ultimately, however, Powell's plea for Conservative voters to support Labour at the February and October 1974 general elections and his defection to the Ulster Unionists highlighted his exceptionalism. This was less true for the Labour Party, where until the late 1980s sceptics have always been more mainstream politicians of exceptional ability, most notably Barbara Castle, Douglas Jay, and from the right of the party, Peter Shore.

After 1979, as the party languished out of power, and as scepticism dominated its thinking, the reality was that the pool of leading Labour sceptics was not renewed in any thoroughgoing way. Subsequently, as the party modernised, few new entrants were willing to stand out against official party policy on the European issue, leaving a handful of sceptics such as Tam Dalyell, Austin Mitchell and Alan Simpson. Bryan Gould, one of the few fundamentalist sceptics within the Shadow Cabinet, continued the fight against the ERM and a single currency, but left politics following his defeat in the 1992 leadership contest. The remaining Labour sceptics were thus principally of an ageing generation, many of them now elevated to the House of Lords, including Lord Stoddart, Lord Tonypandy and, from 1997, Lord Shore.

A quite different process occurred in the Conservative Party however. Triggered by the Bruges speech of 1988, and subsequently by the ratification of the Maastricht

Treaty, a new generation of sceptical MPs joined the more established Conservative anti-Marketeers, John Biffen, Sir Richard Body, Toby Jessel, Roger Moate and Teddy Taylor, all of whom had political reputations as fundamentalist sceptics and had voted against the 1971 EC Bill. On the backbenches, this new generation included Nicholas Budgen, Bill Cash, James Cran, Christopher Gill, Teresa Gorman, Toby Jessel, Sir Ivan Lawrence, Tony Marlow, Richard Shepherd, Sir Trevor Skeet, Michael Spicer, Bill Walker and Ann and Nicholas Winterton. In the government, the sceptics included Michael Howard, Peter Lilley and Michael Portillo, and the junior ministers Edward Leigh and David Davies. To this group was added new blood from the 1992 election intake, including Iain Duncan Smith, Bernard Jenkin, Roger Knapman, Barry Legg, Walter Sweeney and John Whittingdale. Thereafter, Euroscepticism became a mainstream Conservative rather than a Labour phenomenon.[1] As underlined in Chapters 6 and 7, this generational renewal of scepticism brought with it a new radicalism and a willingness to take all measures to oppose the government short of defection from the Conservative Party.

What is also notable, however, is the way in which scepticism has increasingly moved from being an elite parliamentary concern, drawing in most of the Labour Party and sixty or so anti-Marketeers from the Conservative Party, to being a phenomenon which has mobilised a much larger group of activists and indeed the wider the electorate. In 1975, the National Referendum Campaign had twelve regional offices and 350 local branches and these quickly disappeared after the referendum had taken place. Following the signature of the Maastricht Treaty, by contrast, over twenty-seven organisations emerged outside Parliament to oppose ratification and to campaign for a referendum on the Treaty, a single currency or both. This was one of the largest mobilisations of the public on a single issue since 1945. It has in turn offered an extra-parliamentary support base that Eurosceptic MPs could draw upon to sustain themselves against their parties.

Four further developments are worthy of comment. First, as noted in Chapter 7, two new political parties have come into being and have campaigned not just on a sceptical platform but also specifically on an explicit commitment to withdrawal from the EU. The Referendum Party, created in 1994 (later becoming the Democracy Movement), and the Campaign for an Independent Britain, now the UK Independence Party, were both founded on the basis of challenging the approach of the two major political parties. In particular both have highlighted their view that 'it is impossible to be in Europe but not run by Europe' (North, 1999). In the April 1997 general election over 800,000 voted for the Referendum Party and the UK Independence Party (UKIP) won 1.1 per cent of the vote in the 194 constituencies where it fielded candidates, winning two seats in the 1999 European elections with 696,000 votes (Mather, 2001:224). Analysing this success, Anthony Heath argues that the motivation of those who voted for these parties was not that of 'right-wing ideologues and was not part of a specifically right-wing revolt against the Conservatives … but was undoubtedly a result of their long-standing and specific concerns about Europe' (Heath *et al.*, 1998).

A second striking development has been the creation of autonomous external organisations and think tanks associated with sceptical parliamentarians. Initially, anti-Marketeers were reluctant to establish internal or external organisations that might be seen to rival their own political parties. The Labour Safeguards Committee and the Conservative 1970 group were both registered with the whips' offices to avoid the charge of disloyalty, and many organisations created during the 1975 referendum campaign were short-lived. In stark contrast, by 1993 the Fresh Start Group was resourced with offices in a town house close to Parliament and during the Maastricht Treaty ratification acted in a way that gave the impression of being a party within a party.

The growing involvement of the generation of sceptics who succeeded the anti-Marketeers with an organisation which they either established, led or with which they were otherwise closely associated was nevertheless more common amongst Conservative than Labour Party supporters. For example, the Bruges Group was closely associated with Margaret Thatcher, Norman Tebbit, Norman Lamont and, initially, Bill Cash. Following his failed leadership campaign in June 1995, John Redwood set up Conservative 2000 with a remit to chart a radical policy on Europe. The European Foundation created in 1994 was chaired by Bill Cash and, until 1996, funded by Sir James Goldsmith, thereafter receiving a substantial contribution from Margaret Thatcher (Seldon, 1997:651). Similarly, Global Britain was created by Lord Pearson of Rannoch (Conservative), Lord Stoddart of Swindon (Labour) and Lord Harris of High Cross (cross-bencher) and was supported by a small group of Conservative peers in the House of Lords.

A third development has been the shift of the newsprint media from a position in which almost all were supportive of British membership in 1973 and 1975 to a position in 2001 in which the majority of newspapers were far more sceptical than both John Major's and Tony Blair's governments. The Murdoch press, especially *The Times* and the *Spectator*, and Conrad Black's *Daily Telegraph* have provided a ready home for sceptics to publish their views, consistently promoting sceptical causes such as the Maastricht Referendum Campaign in their editorial columns (Crewe, 1996:433). Indeed some writers have fashioned a reputation by becoming single-issue journalists. For example, since 1992 Christopher Booker has written a weekly column in the *Sunday Telegraph*, highlighting the consequences of EU membership.

Finally, in terms of organisation, a striking feature is that British sceptics have increasingly sought to Europeanise their activities. In the late 1940s through to the early 1990s sceptics were remarkably rooted in and to the national political arena. Links with sceptical groups from other European countries were few and far between and knowledge and monitoring of the legislation of the EC and its procedures was limited. From the ratification of the Maastricht Treaty, however, sceptical leaders (though less so rank and file activists) have been active in sharing platforms and building institutional links with allies on the continent. The EP elections in June 1999 returned more sceptical MEPs from the Conservative Party with estimates of around six new MEPs wanting withdrawal from the EU (Cooper, 2000). Alongside the election of two UKIP MEPs, Nigel Farage and Geoffrey Titford, this strengthened European level contacts. So too has the creation of an international umbrella group formally linking sceptical groups together, as well as the internet which has proved an effective tool in overcoming geographical boundaries.

Themes in sceptical arguments

Three features have been evident in the arguments used by sceptics. First, the arguments used to oppose European integration have not been static, but have adapted over time in response to how the '*projet européen*' has developed. There are several strands to this. As Chapter 2 demonstrated, many Conservatives opposed EC membership in the 1950s and 1960s as a direct consequence of a prior commitment to the Empire and Commonwealth and to the trade and political value of such links – a type of negative opposition. But in the early 1970s, Enoch Powell led the way in arguing that opposition to the EC should not simply be a consequence of a prior commitment to an external alternative political and economic organisation, but was a necessary reaction to the implications of EC membership for the governance and sovereignty of Britain – what might be considered positive scepticism.

Another aspect of adaptation has been the transformation of opponents of integration from anti-Europeans and anti-Marketeers into Eurosceptics, a change that has in turn transformed the opportunities for co-operation between Conservative and Labour sceptics. In the 1960s and 1970s, a substantial amount of opposition to British membership of the EC and closer European integration was based on opposition from the left of the Labour Party to Britain's joining a capitalist club. It was argued that membership would prevent a Labour government delivering a Socialist manifesto, including nationalisation and prices and incomes control. On the right, anti-Marketeers in the Conservative Party argued that the EC was not a free trade area, but a protectionist customs union with a centralised bureaucracy and *dirigiste* interventionist polices such as the Common Agricultural Policy. Disagreements over the type of EC which was acceptable, if any, clearly limited the intellectual synergy of sceptics in the 1975 referendum campaign, a situation complicated still further by the fact that parliamentary opponents were generally drawn from the extreme left or right of the Labour and Conservative parties.[2]

However, the Bruges speech in September 1988, and more especially the negotiation of the Maastricht Treaty on European Union between December 1990 and December 1991, highlighted the sovereignty issues involved in closer integration. The Maastricht Treaty transformed the European Community into a European Union, with a single market, common foreign and security policy, justice and home affairs co-operation and a single currency. This led to the emergence of a different set of arguments highlighting the fact that continued membership of the EU required the deep exchange of sovereignty in areas previously considered core functions of the state, notably territorial control, foreign and defence policy and control of a national currency. Opposition to the Political and Economic Union agenda comprised the main distinction between anti-Market arguments and the subsequent arguments used by Eurosceptics.

Opposing the Political Union agenda might have been expected to provide a set of principles that would lead to convergence on the left and right of the political spectrum, not least because some of the arguments used in the Bruges speech could be traced back to the arguments of Powell and Shore some twenty-five years earlier. For a brief period following the downfall of Margaret Thatcher it did look as though there might be some convergence. But because of the feeling of guilt in the Conservative Party over the treatment of Thatcher and more directly because of the emergence of a right-wing intake of MPs who won seats at the 1992 election, the right-wing anti-Socialist arguments retained their hold at precisely the time Labour modernised itself and sceptics in the Labour Party became less vociferous. As a consequence of these two factors, the Political Union agenda did not really lead to a convergence.

However, in parallel with these two developments in the Conservative and Labour Parties, Eurosceptics also drew on the experience of the 1970s, increasingly understanding that they had to woo the public because governments always preferred to act pragmatically. Moreover, governments were able to shore up support for their policies through the instruments of party management in the parliamentary arena. As attention focused more and more on the public arena, opposition to the adoption of the Euro became the new rallying point, representing a sort of neutral meeting ground for opponents of closer integration. Certainly the Conservative right continued to draw on Powellite arguments and the concerns articulated in the Bruges speech. But while their arguments were certainly informed by issues of sovereignty and nationhood, opponents of the Euro were able to express their arguments in a non-partisan way, and thus attract a wider spectrum of sympathisers than simply the Conservative right.

Nevertheless, the convergence of Eurosceptic opposition around the issue of the Euro cannot be described with full accuracy as a cross-party phenomenon. Rather, the issue of the Euro and the related commitment of both parties to hold a referendum on membership of the single currency has led to a democratisation and a de-politicisation of Euroscepticism. Introduction of the Euro would affect all members of society on a day-to-day basis, and this has meant that the Euro cannot be treated as an issue only of concern to the political elite. Hence in the most recent phase of opposition to closer European integration, there has been a much wider engagement both of the public and of figures from the establishment more broadly, including business and financial leaders and academics. This has made Euroscepticism in the form of the anti-Euro campaign both much wider and also much deeper than other sceptical campaigns. However, it is not really a bipartisan phenomenon because the Labour Party members are engaged in a politically neutral way.

A second feature noticeable over time has been the steady improvement in the quality and intellectual rigour of the arguments that sceptics have deployed. In the 1950s, though less so in the 1960s, opponents to Britain's membership of the EC were often anti-Europeans. Many opposed any entanglement with Europe whatsoever, principally in the form of the supranational EC, but sometimes even in the form of intergovernmental organisations such as the OECD or the Council of Europe. In the immediate shadow of the Second World War, many were xenophobic, hating Europeans and championing British, or often more accurately English, nationalism. As Chapter 2 suggests, a number of respectable sceptics have found it difficult to resist the siren calls of populism. By the 1990s many parliamentary sceptics did not subscribe to or avoided nationalistic justifications for opposing closer European integration. Many of them went out of their way to stress that opposition to the European Union was not anti-European, not least because the EU was only one institutional manifestation of Europe. However, as Chapter 6 underlined, there has been a strong anti-German aspect interlaced into the critique of some leading sceptics, notably Nicholas Ridley and Bill Cash, as well as some newspapers.

The quality of arguments has also become more sophisticated as the nature and implications of EU membership have become more apparent. In the 1960s the critique of British membership was based upon supposition and anticipated outcomes. By the late 1980s the implications of membership were much clearer and could be directly confronted. Moreover, the technical and legalistic nature of the EU's approach to integration has required a more sophisticated understanding of its policies, laws and procedures, the *acquis communautaire*. Until the late 1980s few sceptics invested the time and intellectual energy needed to develop their knowledge of the EC. In some, though not all parts of what might now be termed the Eurosceptic movement, the levels of knowledge have significantly increased and this has changed the nature of debate by challenging the government's monopoly of interpretation and access to information. As Chapter 6 indicated, the widespread perception in the Conservative Party that Major's government attempted to deceive backbenchers into supporting the Maastricht Treaty was a major spur to this process.

Especially from 1992, serious Eurosceptic groupings have advanced important critiques of European integration and Britain's membership of the EU. Distinctive and credible arguments came from Global Britain, which produced eight fortnightly 'Eurofacts', including a leading article and data on European issues in the House of Commons and House of Lords, along with information on meetings. The European Foundation also offered some sophisticated analysis with its *European Journal*, as, with varying degrees of credibility, did at least some of the occasional papers of the Bruges group. However, many sceptical groups have chosen to launch popular campaigns that oversimplify the issues, some to the extent of straining the truth.

In reviewing sceptical arguments over the last fifty years, it is clear that they have not always been consistently held or coherently advanced. Throughout this time it remained unclear whether the sceptics' ideal was withdrawal, or whether their hopes were more modestly targeted on changing the type of EU of which Britain was a member. What is striking is that sceptics have rarely been able to articulate a clear alternative to the EU and Britain's membership of it. Recent work has attempted to address this particular weakness, but there remains a widespread feeling that there are few alternatives and that European integration is somehow inevitable (Shore, 2000). Identifying the centre of gravity of sceptical arguments is further complicated by two recent developments: the fact that political

Euroscepticism has come to be dominated by the right, and the near simultaneous proliferation of non-party political anti-Euro groups.

The impact of scepticism

So far as major legislation is concerned, the direct effect of sceptics has been quite limited and essentially the record one of failure, despite the public's move from initial disengagement to increasing anxiety about the implications of integration. The government was not prevented from securing British membership of the European Community on 1 January 1973, and sceptics failed to convince the elect-orate to vote against continued membership in the June 1975 referendum campaign. Similarly, the government successfully agreed the 1986 SEA, which abolished the national veto in nine areas covering eighty per cent of the legislative programme of the European Community, and accepted the Maastricht Treaty. This transformed the EC into a Political Union, extended competences to include foreign and security policy and justice and home affairs, and committed the EU to a single currency on 1 January 2000. The Amsterdam Treaty of 1997 was ratified with less debate than the SEA a decade earlier. The overall record of sceptics within the Conservative and Labour parties in impeding far less preventing these sweeping legislative changes is hence one of failure.

However, scepticism has had several important indirect effects. In particular, sceptics have forced successive governments to go to extreme lengths, and in so doing to break new ground, in securing the passage of European legislation. There was a high dependence on cross-party voting over the EC Bill, and again in 1975 in order to gain acceptance of the re-negotiated terms of British membership of the EC. In the 1970s, Conservative and Labour governments offered free votes when party managers calculated that they could not rely on their own supporters, and resorted to relaxing the rigid party political norms in order to deliver opposition votes. Moreover, within their own parties, party managers have been forced to cope with the European issue through exceptional means. Two Prime Ministers, Harold Wilson in 1975 and John Major in 1993 and 1995, put their leadership of their parties on the line in order to shore up support for their European policy (Wilson, 1979:106; Seldon, 1997:568). Wilson was forced to relax collective Cabinet responsibility to allow dissenting ministers to campaign against the government in the 1975 referendum. To secure support for the Maastricht Treaty in 1993 and the European Union Finance Bill of November 1995, Conservative Party managers tied the survival of Major's government to the success of the bills by making them issues of confidence.

However, the price of shoring up support in this way has been to transform the question of European integration from a troublesome and divisive issue into a matter of conscience. Indeed, the exceptional means that parties have used has created a type of martyr effect. Sceptics especially in the Conservative Party have routinely had to pay a heavy penalty for persistent adherence to their views. In 1970, John Biffen, Edward du Cann, Angus Maude, Enoch Powell and Peter Tapsell were excluded from government for not sharing Heath's views (Norton, 1978:38).

Between 1979 and 1997, committed sceptics including Jonathan Aitken, Bill Cash, James Cran, Iain Duncan Smith and Teddy Taylor were excluded from government posts. The removal of the Conservative whip from the eight backbench MPs who defied the party on the vote of confidence on the European Union Finance Bill similarly created sacrificial victims for the Eurosceptic cause to champion.[3] Interestingly, this phenomenon has been less prevalent in the Labour Party, which was for instance more tolerant of fundamentalist anti-Marketeers in the 1960s and 1970s, with Tony Benn, Barbara Castle, Michael Foot and Peter Shore reaching Cabinet rank. Indeed, even under New Labour, 'soft' Eurosceptics like Gordon Brown and Jack Straw have attained the highest-ranking Cabinet posts. However Judith Hart was left out of the 1975 Wilson government following her role in the referendum campaign, and Eric Heffer was sacked for breaching the rules Wilson set out for ministers campaigning for a 'No' vote in the 1975 referendum.

The influence of sceptics has also been felt in three further indirect ways. First, the level of open debate on Europe, whether in the public or the parliamentary arena, has been muted, only starting to develop in any meaningful way in the period following the ratification of the Maastricht Treaty. Part of the reason for this is that sceptics have been sufficiently vocal to make supporters of closer integration self-censor themselves, rendering them hesitant in engaging in a thoroughgoing debate on the costs and benefits of Britain's membership of the EC/EU. Indeed, even Edward Heath, perhaps the most pro-European of them all, was prey to this unwillingness to discuss the issues. In the 1971 White Paper, for instance, he argued that 'there is no question of any erosion of essential national sovereignty', yet the fact was that he had received information from Lord Kilmuir, the Lord Chancellor, that the issues relating to 'the surrender of sovereignty involved are serious ones … I am sure it would be a great mistake to underestimate the force of the objections to them. But these objections ought to be brought out into the open now …' (Shore, 2000:16).

Sceptics in Parliament and journalists in the sceptical newsprint share a sizeable part of the responsibility for the poor quality of exchange and the lack of interest in the European issue among the general public, who consistently rank it as of little importance in shaping their voting intentions (Baker and Seawright, 1998a:9). The resulting situation is one in which the public is relatively suggestible and ready to welcome the simplification of the argument by sceptics in the form of scare stories and tabloidisation of the issues. At the same time, it should also be said that pro-membership politicians too have been tempted down this route, often overselling Britain's membership of the EU as a panacea for British economic malaise and presenting it as an inevitable consequence of globalisation.

Second, the European issue has had a hugely disruptive effect on the Labour and Conservative Parties. Sceptics have been influential enough to destabilise political parties, even though not always powerful enough directly to affect policy. One aspect of this has been the often misleading gap seen between the rhetoric of party leaders and the reality of their actions. Harold Wilson was, for instance, always keen to give the impression that he was agnostic, winning praise from anti-Marketeers as sharing views identical with the anti-Market Gaitskell and periodically denouncing the unacceptable features of the Common Market with speeches appearing '… rejectionist in both language and intent'. But he never abandoned the British application for membership and actively supported a 'Yes' vote (Shore, 2000:69). Similarly, as Chapter 5 discussed, Margaret Thatcher negotiated and ratified the Single European Act, but was also the author of the Bruges speech. And John Major's remark that he was 'the greatest cabinet sceptic of them all' was accompanied by the negotiation and ratification of the Maastricht Treaty and the partial negotiation of the Amsterdam Treaty completed by Tony Blair in June 1997 (Seldon, 1997:340). Time and again this lack of consistency between words and actions proved to be a hostage to fortune, as sceptics in particular felt themselves to have been betrayed and voiced their bitterness with increasing openness.

Another aspect of the destabilising effect of sceptical action is that sceptics have often resorted to factionalism as a means of persuading other members of their party to support their case. Factionalism within parliamentary parties on the European issue has been a predominant feature since the 1960s. In the Labour Party, for example, the Labour Committee for Safeguards on the Common Market was founded in the early 1960s, later transforming itself into the Labour Euro Safeguards Campaign. Despite claims that loyalty is the Conservative Party's weapon, it too has been deeply factionalised (Barnes, 1994:343). The 1970 Group was the first specifically anti-Market group to be registered with the whips' office, but since then, the Friends of Bruges Group and the Fresh Start Group have become active in promoting sceptical policies on Europe. It is a consequence of the destabilising effect of the European issue in both parties that more broadly based groups on the left and right such as the Tribune Group and Selsdon and Bow Groups, have also included a sceptical stance on Europe as part of their platforms since the late 1980s. The effects of sceptical factionalism have been particularly demoralising for the Conservative Party, with sceptics accused of being a party within a party and widely perceived as a major cause of the Conservative defeat in May 1997 and a continuing source of unease amongst the electorate at the June 2001 election.

Thus in terms of the balance sheet of sceptics' impact, despite 40 years of activity, there has in fact been little direct impact on legislation. Notwithstanding this, there have been other very significant indirect effects, notably the fear sceptics have generated, limiting the willingness of governments to fully articulate the costs and benefits of membership of the EC/EU. Opposition to European integration has also had a tremendous impact on the unity of the two major political parties through factionalisation, a willingness to vote even against a three-line whip and the establishment of organisations separate from the political parties.

Although often dismissed as the sporadic and unconnected voicing of protest, these indirect effects mean that scepticism has in fact played a not insignificant role in shaping Britain's turbulent relationship with the EU. On the one hand, scepticism has been both a cause as well as a product of the poor quality of the British domestic debate on Europe, which is a key factor behind the weak foundations on which commitment to European integration is built. In addition, however, the centrality of scepticism about Europe to the cycle of pragmatism and radicalisation which parties undergo in and out of office respectively, has done much to augment the disruptive impact which the parties and working of the political system have had on the crafting and implementation of Britain's European policy.

Explaining the waxing and waning of scepticism in British politics

This book has argued that five key factors have explained the ebb and flow of scepticism about engagement with the European integration project in the half-century following the Second World War. These were the identity of the sceptics themselves, together with how they perceived the issue at stake; the opportunity to oppose the government's European policy; the arena in which opposition could occur; access to information; and finally access to resources. In general, governments have tried to limit the opportunities to oppose their policy by managing European issues within the parliamentary arena. This politicises issues by linking them to the party manifestos and to the electoral fortunes of the party. Keeping issues within Parliament also limits the access to information and the resources that are available to oppose government policy.

The ability of the government to limit the debate to the parliamentary arena has therefore been important in shaping the opportunities for influence open to opponents of British membership of the EC and closer European integration. Here, often despite small government majorities, party managers have been able to use a wide range of resources and information and above all party loyalty, to secure support for government policy. However, within the Conservative Party between 1990 and 1997, the ability of party managers to deliver backbench votes in the parliamentary arena was tested to the very limits and although they succeeded in securing the government's entire European programme, the price was widespread Euroscepticism in the Conservative Party.

Outside of Parliament the European issue has been much more difficult for governments to handle. During the period considered by this book, the key opportunity for sceptics in the non-parliamentary arena was the 1975 referendum. Part of the explanation for the failure of the anti-Marketeers in the face of this opportunity was that they were confronted by a united establishment and a press almost overwhelmingly supportive of membership. The inability of anti-Marketeers to harness the resources and information to effectively pursue a 'No' vote campaign was a significant failure.

However, over time there has been an important learning process that has taken place amongst sceptics. As the importance of the issues at stake have increased and the Rubicon of the Maastricht Treaty in particular has been crossed, opponents have tried to create their own opportunities to oppose government policy on closer integration. They have become far better resourced and have generated independent means of accessing and analysing information. By their actions they have secured a commitment to a referendum on the introduction of the Euro should its adoption become government policy. This offers a significant opportunity to draw on the lessons learnt in 1975 and redeem previous shortcomings, against a backdrop in which concern about European integration has become both democratised and de-politicised, and the basis of the sceptics' support thus strengthened.

Conclusions

For over fifty years, MPs have been willing to defy their party managers in Parliament, and to vote with the opposition on European issues. At the same time, however, for most MPs there has been an unwillingness to forsake their political party in pursuit of the European issue. Indeed, most sceptics have been willing to accept government posts and been reluctant to resign from government office when they found themselves opposing government policy. Notable exceptions were Neil Marten who refused a post in the Heath government and David Maclean who refused a Cabinet job under John Major in 1995 (Seldon, 1997:590). Teddy Taylor, a junior minister, and Jasper More, a whip, were the only MPs to resign over Europe in 1971. Similarly, even in John Major's divided government of 1992 to 1997, only John Redwood resigned his Cabinet post to fight the Prime Minister for the leadership of the Conservative Party, with David Davies and David Heathcote-Amery the only junior ministers to resign, and James Cran standing down as a PPS. Only in a handful of cases has the issue been more important than a commitment to a political party. Nonetheless, the more recent phenomenon in general and Euroscepticism in particular has often been near to an article of faith in at least four ways.

First, there does appear to be a set of core cannons or beliefs. Most sceptics share concerns about the impact of continued British membership of the European Union and all believe that British membership is no longer delivering sufficient benefits. However, there is a major difference between those who conclude that Britain should withdraw and those sceptics who argue against specific developments such as the single market and the Euro. There are also differences concerning the exact combination of arguments used, which vary between and amongst sceptics in the Labour and Conservative Parties. Second, over time, sceptics feel themselves to have suffered and sometimes to have been martyred for their beliefs, whether it be Enoch Powell, or the eight MPs who had the Conservative whip removed from them in the 1992 to 1997 Parliament or the substantial number of MPs who succumbed to voting with their party against their conscience. Third, there are a group of politicians who are considered as almost saintly in the demonstration of their moral rectitude, in both Labour and Conservative Parties, including Hugh Gaitskell, Enoch Powell and more recently Margaret Thatcher. Fourth, as Chapter 5 argued, there have been notable conversions, including Margaret Thatcher and the group of Conservative MPs in the 1980s who moved from a pragmatic to an instrumental view of Europe and who triggered the more widespread conversion of the Conservative Party in the early and mid-1990s.

However, Euroscepticism also shares some of the weaknesses of religious movements. It is prone to schism with divisions that appear almost doctrinal. Indeed, opponents of European integration have always been deeply factionalised as a movement, both between left and right, with party loyalties preventing unification of Labour and Conservative sceptics, and even within political families on the left and right. The poaching of Ron Leighton from the Safeguards to the Get Britain Out movement in 1975, and more recently the breakaway of Bill Cash from the Bruges Group, Ian Milne from the European Foundation and Alan Sked from UKIP illustrate just how divided the movement was and remains.

A core problem is that it remains unclear if opponents of closer European integration want to re-negotiate the existing terms and conditions of British membership and in essence oppose the type of EU of which Britain is a member, or whether they want withdrawal. Nor is it clear if opponents will ever be prepared or able to spell this out. Despite the broad nature of their support on the Euro, it may yet cause Eurosceptics to fail in a referendum on the issue, not least because they lack a shared alternative vision for Britain. The extent to which Eurosceptics are clear about what they oppose quite apart from what they stand for, therefore remains a weakness.

In terms of the future of Euroscepticism, a striking point is the extent to which its activists have been able to learn from and act on previous experiences. The three most important of these lessons have been the need to present a coherent, unified movement; the need to develop a set of clearly articulated arguments which the electorate can understand; and the need to recruit as leaders politicians and establishment figures who are drawn from the mainstream rather than being perceived as extremists. One mark of the sceptics' success in learning these lessons was the adoption of a Eurosceptic line as official Conservative Party policy in its 2001 election manifesto along with the subsequent selection of Iain Duncan Smith as leader. But whether Euroscepticism can now go on directly to influence policy within government, however, will crucially depend on perceptions as to the electoral appeal of Euroscepticism both within the electorate and within the Conservative Party.

Notes

1 Zaki Cooper notes that an NOP poll in September 1998 showed that fifty-eight per cent of Tory members backed the policy of holding a referendum on a single currency and eighteen per cent opposed EMU outright (Cooper, 2000).

2 There were three notable exceptions to the rule: Neil Marten and Peter Shore, both from the moderate wings of the their parties, emphasised the sovereignty rather than the anti-Market aspects of their opposition. In a different way and from the right wing of the Conservative Party, Enoch Powell championed sovereignty issues.

3 All these MPs were leading rebels against the Maastricht Treaty, with seven in the top nineteen in terms of the number of times MPs rebelled against the government during the passage of the Maastricht Bill.

Bibliography

Books

Armstrong, Keith and Bulmer, Simon (1998) *The Governance of the Single European Market*, Manchester: Manchester University Press.

Baker, David and Seawright, David, eds (1998) *Britain For and Against Europe: British Politics and the Question of European Integration*, Oxford: Clarendon Press.

Baimbridge, Timothy and Teasdale, Anthony (1997) *The Penguin Companion to the European Union*, London: Penguin.

Benn, Tony (1989) *Against the Tide: Diaries, 1973–1976*, London: Hutchinson.

Berrington, Hugh (1973) *Backbench Opinion in the House of Commons, 1945–1955*, Oxford: Pergamon Press.

Booker, Christopher and North, Richard (1997) *The Castle of Lies: Why Britain Must Get Out of Europe*, London: Duckworth, 5th impression.

Buller, Jim (2000) *National Statecraft and European Integration: the Conservative Government and the European Union, 1979–1997*, London: Pinter.

Butler, David and Marquand, David (1981) *European Elections and British Politics*, London: Longman.

Butler, David and Kitzinger, Uwe (1976) *The 1975 Referendum*, 2nd edn, London: Macmillan.

Campbell, John (1993) *Edward Heath*, London: Jonathan Cape.

Castle, Barbara (1984) *The Castle Diaries, 1964–1970*, London:Weidenfeld & Nicolson.

Connolly, Bernard (1995) *The Rotten Heart of Europe*, London: Faber and Faber.

Cosgrave, Patrick (1989) *The Lives of Enoch Powell*, London: Bodley Head.

Crossman, Richard (1991) *The Crossman Diaries*, Howard, Anthony, ed., London: Mandarin, 2nd edn.

Eltiss, Walter (1999) *Britain, Europe and EMU*, Basingstoke: Macmillan.

Forster, Anthony (1999) *Britain's Negotiation of the Maastricht Treaty*, London: Macmillan.

Gaffney, John (1996) *Political Parties and the European Union*, London: Routledge.

George, Stephen, ed (1992) *Britain and the European Community: The Politics of Semi-Detachment*, Oxford: Clarendon Press.

George, Stephen (1998) *An Awkward Partner: Britain in the European Community*, 3rd edn, Oxford: Oxford University Press.

Gorman, Teresa (1993) *The Bastards: Dirty Tricks and the Challenge of Europe*, London: Pan Books.

Grant, Charles (1994) *Inside the House that Jacques Built*, London: Nicholas Brealey.

Goodhart, Philip (1976) *Full-hearted Consent: The Story of the Referendum Campaign – and the Campaign for the Referendum*, London: Davis-Poynter.

Gowland, David and Turner, Arthur (2000) *Reluctant Europeans: Britain and European Integration, 1945–1998*, London: Longman.

Heffernan, Richard and Murqusee, Mike (1992) *Defeat from the Jaws of Victory: Inside Kinnock's Labour Party*, London: Verso.

Jay, Douglas (1980) *Change of Fortunes*, London: Hutchinson.

Kahler, Miles (1984) *Decolonisation in Britain and France: The Domestic Consequences of International Relations*, Princeton, NJ: Princeton University Press.

King, Anthony (1977) *Britain Says Yes: The 1975 Referendum on the Common Market*, Washington, DC: American Enterprise Institute for Public Policy Research.

Kitzinger, Uwe (1973) *Diplomacy and Persuasion*, London: Thames and Hudson.

Kitzinger, Uwe (1977) *Diplomacy and Persuasion: How Britain Joined the Common Market*, 2nd edn, London: Thames and Hudson.

Lawson, Nigel (1992) *The View from No. 11: Memoirs of a Tory Radical*, London: Transworld.

Lieber, Robert, J (1970) *British Politics and European Unity: Parties, Elites and Pressure Groups*, Berkeley: University of California Press.

Lord, Christopher (1993) *British Entry to the European Community under the Heath Government of 1970–1974*, Aldershot: Dartmouth.

Morgan, Kenneth O. (1984) *Labour in Power, 1945–1951*, Oxford: Clarendon Press.

Morgan, Roger and Tame, Clare (1996) *Parliaments and Parties*, Basingstoke: Macmillan.

Norton, Philip (1978) *Conservative Dissidents: Dissent Within the Parliamentary Conservative Party, 1970–1974*, London: Temple Smith.

Norton, Philip, ed. (1996) *The Conservative Party*, London: Prentice Hall.

Onslow, Sue (1997) *Backbench Debate Within the Conservative Party and Its Influence on British Foreign Policy, 1948–1957*, Basingstoke: Macmillan.

Ponting, Clive (1989) *Breach of Promise: Labour in Power 1964–1979*, London: Hamish Hamilton.

Ramsden, John (1996) *The Winds of Change: Macmillan to Heath, 1957–1975*, London: Longman.

Ridley, Nicholas (1991) *My Style of Government*, London: Hutchinson.

Ritchie, Richard, ed. (1988) *Enoch Powell on 1992*, London: Anaya.

Robins, L.J. (1979) *The Reluctant Party: Labour and the EEC, 1961–1975*, Ormskirk: G.W. and A. Hesketh.

Seldon, Anthony, ed. (1996) *How Tory Governments Fall: The Tory Party in Power Since 1783*, London: Fontana Press.

Seldon, Anthony (1997) *Major: A Political Life*, London: Weidenfeld & Nicolson.

Seyd, Patrick (1987) *The Rise and Fall of the Labour Left*, Basingstoke: Macmillan Education.

Shaw, Eric (1994) *The Labour Party Since 1979: Crisis and Transformation*, London: Routledge.

Shore, Peter (2000) *Separate Ways: The Heart of Europe*, London: Duckworth.

Spicer, Michael (1992) *A Treaty Too Far: A New Policy for Europe*, London: Fourth Estate.

Stephens, Philip (1997) *Politics and the Pound*, London: Macmillan.

Thatcher, Margaret (1993) *The Downing Street Years*, London: HarperCollins.

Wilson, Harold (1979) *Final term: The Labour Government, 1974–1976*, London: Weidenfeld & Nicolson.

Young, Hugo (1999) *This Blessed Plot: Britain and Europe from Churchill to Blair*, London: Macmillan.

Young, John W. (1993) *Britain and European Unity, 1945–1992*, Basingstoke: Macmillan.
Young, John W. (1984) *Britain, France and the Unity of Europe 1945–1951*, Leicester: Leicester University Press.
Young, S. (1973) *Terms of Entry: Britain's Negotiations with the European Community*, London: Heinemann.

Articles and chapters

Alderman, Keith (1993) 'Legislating on Maastricht', *Contemporary Record*, 7:3, 243–65.
Aspinwall, Mark (2000) 'Structuring Europe: Powersharing Institutions and British preferences on European Integration', *Political Studies*, 48:3, 415–42.
Aughey, Arthur (1996a) 'The Party and Foreign Policy', in Norton, Philip, ed., *The Conservative Party*, London: Prentice Hall, 200–12.
Aughey, Arthur (1996b) 'Philosophy and Faction', in Norton, Philip, ed., *The Conservative Party*, London: Prentice Hall, 1996, 83–94.
Baker, David, Gamble, Andrew and Ludlam, Steve (1993a) 'Whips or Scorpions? The Maastricht Vote and the Conservative Party', *Parliamentary Affairs*, 46:2, 151–66.
Baker, David, Gamble, Andrew and Ludlam, Steve (1993b) '1846…1906…1996? Conservative Splits and European Integration', *Political Quarterly*, 64:2, 420–35.
Baker, David, Gamble, Andrew and Ludlam, Steve (1994) 'The Parliamentary Siege of Maastricht 1993: Conservative Divisions and British Ratification', *Parliamentary Affairs*, 47:1, 37–59.
Baker, David and Seawright, David (1998a) 'Introduction', in Baker, David and Seawright, David, eds, *Britain For and Against Europe: British Politics and the Question of European Integration*, Oxford: Clarendon Press, 1–9.
Baker, David and Seawright, David (1998b), 'A "rosy" map of Europe? Labour Parliamentarians and European integration', in Baker, David and Seawright, David, eds, *Britain For and Against Europe: British Politics and the Question of European Integration*, Oxford: Clarendon Press, 57–87.
Barnes, John (1994) 'Ideology and factions', in Seldon, Anthony and Bell, Stuart, eds, *Conservative Century: The Conservative Party Since 1900*, Oxford: Oxford University Press, 315–45.
Barnes, John and Cockett, Richard (1994) 'The Making of Party Policy', in Seldon, Anthony and Ball, Stuart, eds, *Conservative century: the Conservative Party Since 1900*, Oxford: Oxford University Press, 347–82.
Benn, Tony (1996) 'The Common market: Loss of Self Government', in Holmes, Martin, ed., *The Eurosceptical Reader*, Basingstoke: London, 38–41.
Berrington, Hugh and Hague, Rod (1998) 'Europe, Thatcherism and Traditionalism: Opinion, Rebellion and the Maastricht Treaty in the Backbench Conservative Party, 1992–1994', *West European Politics*, 21:1, 44–60.
Bulmer, Simon (1994) 'The Governance of the European Union: A New Institutionalist Approach', *Journal of Public Policy*, 13, 351–80.
Burkitt, Mark, Baimbridge, Mark and Whyman, Mark (1996), *There is an Alternative, Britain and its Relations with the EU*, London, Campaign for an Independent Britain.
Burkitt, Mark and Baimbridge, Mark (1996) 'Britain and the European Community: Past Present … and an Unravelling Future', in Holmes, Martin, ed., *The Eurosceptical Reader*, London: Macmillan, 167–85.
Crewe, Ivor (1996) '1979–96', in Seldon, Anthony, ed., *How Tory Governments Fall: The Tory Party in Power Since 1783*, London: Fontana Press, 393–451.

Curtice, John and Stead, Michael (1997) 'Appendix 2', in Butler, David and Kavanagh, Dennis, eds, *The British General Election*, Basingstoke: Macmillan.

Daddow, Oliver J. (2002) 'Introduction: The Historiography of Wilson's Attempt to Take Britain into the EEC', in Daddow, Oliver J., ed., *Harold Wilson and European Unity: Britain's Second Application to Join the EEC*, London: Frank Cass.

Dejak, Stefano (1993) 'Labour and Europe during the Attlee governments: the image in the mirror of R.W.C. Mackay's "Europe Group", 1945–1950', in Brivati, Brian and Jones, Harriet, eds, *From Reconstruction to Integration: Britain and Europe Since 1945*, Leicester: Leicester University Press, 47–58.

Forster, Anthony (1998a) 'Britain and the Maastricht Treaty: A Critique of Liberal Inter-governmentalism', *Journal of Common Market Studies*, 36:3 September, 347–68.

Forster, Anthony (1998b) 'Britain: Still an Awkward Partner?', *Journal of European Studies*, 6:2, July–December, 41–57.

Forster, Anthony and Wallace, William (2000a) 'British Approaches to Rethinking European Order since 1989', in Niblett, Robin and Wallace, William, eds, *Rethinking European Order: West European Responses, 1989–1997*, Basingstoke: Macmillan, 124–51.

Forster, Anthony and Wallace, William (2000b) 'Common Foreign and Security Policy: the Long Road from Shadow to Substance', in Wallace, Helen and Wallace, William, eds, *Policy-Making in the European Union*, Oxford: Oxford University Press, 411–35.

Gaitskell, Hugh (1996) 'The Common Market', in Holmes, Martin, ed., *The Eurosceptical Reader*, Basingstoke: Macmillan, 13–37.

Gamble, Andrew (1998) 'The European Issue in British Politics', in Baker, David and Seawright, David, eds, *Britain For and Against Europe: British Politics and the Question of European Integration*, Oxford: Clarendon Press, 11–30.

Gamble, Andrew and Kelly, Gavin (2000) 'The British Labour Party and Monetary Union', *West European Politics*, 23:1, January, 1–25.

George, Stephen and Haythorne, Deborah (1996) 'The British Labour Party', in Gaffney, John, *Political Parties and the European Union*, London: Routledge, 110–21.

George, Stephen and Sowemimo, Mathew (1996) 'Conservative Foreign Policy towards the European Union', in Ludlam, Steve and Smith, Martin J., eds, *Contemporary British Conservatism*, Basingstoke: Macmillan, 244–63.

Gill, Stephen (1998) 'European Governance and the New Constitutionalism', *New Political Economy*, 3:1, 15–26.

Hearl, Derek (1989) 'The United Kingdom', in Lodge, Juliet, ed., *Direct Elections to the European Parliament*, Basingstoke: Macmillan, 228–49.

Heath, Anthony, Jowell, Roger, Taylor, Bridget and Thomson, Katarina (1998) *Euroscepticism and the Referendum Party*, Oxford: Centre for Research into Elections and Social Trends, Working Paper 63.

Heathcote-Amery, David (1996) *A Single European Currency: Why the United Kingdom Must Say 'No'*, London: Bruges Group, 1996.

Heffernan, Richard (2000) 'Beyond Euroscepticism? Labour and the European Union since 1945', in Brivati, Brian and Heffernan, Richard, eds, *The Labour Party: A Centenary History*, Basingstoke: Macmillan, 383–401.

Herbert, Nick (1999) Newsletter to Supporters, http://www.bfors.com/press/index.html?articleid=news/19991125z.html.

Hindley, Brian and Howe, Martin (1996) *Better Off Out?: The Benefits or Costs of EU Membership*, London, Institute of Economic Affairs, Occasional Paper 99.

Hitchens, Christopher (1993) 'Say What You Will about Harold', *London Review of Books*, 15:12, 7–9.

HM Government (1971) *The United Kingdom and the European Communities*, London: HM Stationery Office, CMND 4715.

Howe, Geoffrey (1994) *Britain and the European Community: A Twenty Year Balance Sheet*, Cambridge, Tory Reform Group, Elitian, Occasional Paper, January.

Institute of Directors (2000) *A Single European Currency: Implications for the UK Economy*, London: Institute of Directors.

Jamieson, Bill (1996) 'World's Apart', in Holmes, Martin, ed., *The Eurosceptical Reader*, Basingstoke: Macmillan, 219–60.

Jowell, Roger and Spence, Jack D. (1975) *The Grudging Europeans*, London: Social and Community Planning Research.

Judge, David (1988) 'Incomplete Sovereignty', *Parliamentary Affairs*, 41, 441–55.

Kaiser, Wolfram (1993) 'To join or not to join: the "Appeasement" policy of Britain's first application', in Brivati, Brian and Jones, Harriet, eds, *From Reconstruction to Integration: Britain and Europe Since 1945*, Leicester: Leicester University Press, 144–56.

Kellner, Peter (1998) *EMU and Public Opinion in Understanding the Euro*, London: Federal Trust, 117–28.

Larres, Klaus (1993) 'A search for order: Britain and the origins of a Western European Union, 1944–55', in Brivati, Brian, and Jones, Harriet, eds, *From Reconstruction to Integration: Britain and Europe Since 1945*, Leicester: Leicester University Press, 71–87.

Lamont, Norman (1996) 'Selsdon Group Speech, 11 October 1994', in Holmes, Martin, ed., *The Eurosceptical Reader*, Basinsgtoke: Macmillan, 97–110.

Larsen, Henrik (1997) 'British Discourses on Europe: Sovereignty Parliament, Instrumentality and the non-mythical Europe', in Jørgensen, K.E., ed., *Reflective Approaches to European Governance*, London: Routledge.

Lazer, H. (1976) 'British Populism and the Labour Party and the Common market parliamentary debate', *Political Quarterly*, 91, 259–77.

Majone, Giandominico (1993) 'The European Community Between Social Policy and Social Regulation', *Journal of Common Market Studies*, 31:2, 153–70.

Mather, Jennifer (2001) 'The United Kingdom', in Lodge, Juliet, ed., *The 1999 Elections to the European Parliament*, Basingstoke: Palgrave, 214–30.

Mckie, David (1994) 'Nightmare on Norm Street', in Margetts, Helen and Smyth, George, eds, *Turning Japanese?*, London: Lawrence and Wishart, 128–42.

Minford, Patrick (1996) 'The Price of Monetary Unification', in Holmes, Martin, ed., *The Eurosceptical Reader*, Basingstoke: Macmillan, 149–66.

Mitchie, Jonathan (1997) 'Why the left should be against EMU', in Corry, Dan and Mitchie, Jonathan, *EMU: The Left Debate*, Sheffield: PERC Policy Papers No.4.

Morris, Peter (1996) 'The British Conservative Party', in Gaffney, John, ed., *Political Parties and the European Union*, London: Routledge, 122–38.

North, Richard (1999) 'A Common Sense Solution', 6 November 1999, Bruges Group website.

Northedge, F.S. (1983) 'Britain and the EEC: Past and Present', in Jenkins, Roy, ed., *Britain and the EEC*, London: Allen and Unwin, 15–37.

Norton, Philip (1996) 'The Party in Parliament', in Norton, Philip, ed., *The Conservative Party*, London: Prentice Hall, 127–41.

Norton, Philip (1998) 'The Conservative Party', in King, Anthony, ed., *The New Labour Triumphs: Britain at the Polls*, Chatham, NJ: Chatham House Publishers, 75–112.

Pennant Rea, Rupert, *et al.* (1997) *The Ostricht and the EMU – Policy Choices Facing the UK*, London: Centre for Economic Policy Research.

Pinto-Duschinsky, Michael (1987). 'From Macmillan to Home, 1959–1964', in Hennessy, Peter and Seldon, Anthony, eds, *Ruling Performance: British Governments from Attlee to Thatcher*, Oxford: Basil Blackwell, 150–85.

Powell, Enoch (1996) 'Britain and Europe', in Holmes, Martin, ed., *The Eurosceptical Reader*, Basingstoke: Macmillan, 75–87.

Riddell, Peter (1998) 'EMU and the Press', in Duff, Andrew, ed., *Understanding the Euro*, London: Federal Trust, 105–16.

Seldon, Anthony (1996) 'Introduction: The Tory Party in Power, 1783–1996', in Seldon, Anthony, ed., *How Tory Governments Fall: The Tory Party in Power Since 1783*, London: Fontana Press, 1–22.

Sharpe, L.J. (1996) 'British scepticism and the European Union, in Holmes, Martin, ed., *The Eurosceptical Reader*, Basingstoke: Macmillan, 303–41.

Shaw, Eric (1994) 'Conflict and cohesion in the British Labour Party', in Bell, David S. and Shaw, Eric, eds, *Conflict and Cohesion in Western European Social Democratic Parties*, London: Pinter, 151–67.

Shaw, Eric (2001) 'The Wilderness years 1979–1994', in Brivati, Brian and Heffernan, Richard, eds, *The Labour Party*, Basingstoke: Macmillan, 112–42.

Shore, Peter (1996) Speech to the Bruges Group, Reform Club, 24 July in Holmes, Martin, ed., *The Eurosceptical Reader*, Basingstoke: Macmillan, 42–9.

Thatcher, Margaret (1996) 'The European Family of Nations', in Holmes, Martin, ed., *The Eurosceptical Reader*, Basingstoke: Macmillan, 88–96.

Treasury Select Committee (1998) 'The UK and Preparations for Stage Three of Economic and Monetary Union', Select Committee on Treasury Fifth Report, HMSO, London, April.

Turner, John (1996) '1951–1964', in Seldon, Anthony, ed., *How Tory Governments Fall: The Tory Party in Power Since 1783*, London: Fontana Press, 317–55.

Usherwood, Simon (2001) 'Opposition to the European Union in the UK: The dilemma of public opinion and party management', paper delivered at the 51st PSA Conference, 10–12 April, Manchester.

Wilks, Stuart (1996) 'Britain and Europe: An Awkward Partner or an Awkward State?', *Politics*, 16:3, 159–67.

Wrigley, Chris (1993) '"Now You See It, Now You Don't", Harold Wilson and Labour's Foreign Policy 1964–1970', in Coopey, Richard, Fielding, Steven and Tiratsoo, Nick, eds, *The Wilson Governments*, London: Pinter, 123–35.

Young, John W. (1993) 'Britain and the EEC, 1956–1973: an overview', in Brivati, Brian and Jones, Harriet, eds, *From Reconstruction to Integration: Britain and Europe Since 1945*, Leicester: Leicester University Press, 103–13.

Theses

Alexandre-Collier, Agnès (1998) 'L' "Euroscepticisme" Au Sein du Parti Conservateur Brittanique 1992–1997', Paris: PhD thesis, Institut d'Etudes Politiques de Paris.

Cooper, Zaki (2000) 'Civil War in the Conservative Party: Conflict, divisions and splits over Europe: the demise of the conservative Party, 1992–2000', Cambridge: MPhil.

Rose, Richard (1950) 'The Relationship between Socialist Principles and British Labour foreign policy, 1945–1951', Oxford: DPhil.

Skär, Sylke (2000) 'The British Conservative Party and European Supranational Integration: 1948–1955', Oxford: DPhil.

Newspaper articles

Brivati, Brian and Baker, David (1998) 'The History of the Blues', *The Times Higher Education Supplement*, 11 December, 11–12.

Dahrendorf, Ralph (1998) 'Disunited by a Common Currency', the *New Statesman*, 20 February.

Daily Telegraph (2001) 'I was wrong to attack Telegraph, says envoy', 24 March.

Economist (1991) 'Watch with Mother', 21 March, 29.

Economist (1991) 'Against the Current', 8 June, 31–2.

Fildes, Christopher (2000) 'Pay me in real money, please and I'll pay you in euros', *Daily Telegraph*, 14 August.

Guardian (1975) 'On the curious political affiliations and trend thrown up by the voting', 11 April.

Guardian (2000) 'Liberalism c'est Moi', 23 May.

Independent (1997b) Business Section, 15 September.

Smallwood, Christopher (2000) 'Runaway inflation – the euro lesson from Ireland', the *Sunday Times*, 20 August.

Sunday Times (1993) 'Revealed: who funds Euro-rebels', 18 July.

Sunday Times (1994) 'Lamont is right: Britain may face last exit from Brussels',16 October.

Sunday Times (1999a) 'Battle for Britain', 17 October.

Index

FINAL EVENTS

BOOKS BY NICK REDFERN

SCIENCE FICTION SECRETS
THERE'S SOMETHING IN THE WOODS
ON THE TRAIL OF THE SAUCER SPIES
A COVERT AGENDA
THE FBI FILES
COSMIC CRASHES
STRANGE SECRETS
THREE MEN SEEKING MONSTERS
BODY SNATCHERS IN THE DESERT
MAN-MONKEY
CELEBRITY SECRETS
MEMOIRS OF A MONSTER HUNTER
CONTACTEES
MONSTERS OF TEXAS

FINAL EVENTS
AND THE SECRET GOVERNMENT GROUP
ON DEMONIC UFOS AND THE AFTERLIFE

NICK REDFERN

ANOMALIST BOOKS
SAN ANTONIO * NEW YORK

An Original Publication of Anomalist Books

Final Events *and the Secret Government Group on Demonic UFOs and the Afterlife*
Copyright © 2010 by Nick Redfern
ISBN: 1933665483

Cover image by Crystal Hollis

Book design by Seale Studios

For information, go to anomalistbooks.com, or write to:
Anomalist Books, 5150 Broadway #108, San Antonio, TX 78209

CONTENTS

INTRODUCTION

Monday, November 25, 1991, was a typically cold winter's day in Lincoln, Nebraska. Yet the biting weather was the very last thing on the mind of Ray Boeche, an Anglican priest who served as the Rector of the Celebration Anglican Church in Lincoln for nearly a decade. Boeche was also the founder and former director of the Fortean Research Center, a former Nebraska State Director for the Mutual UFO Network, and the recipient of a B.A. from Peru State College and a Th.M. degree from St. Mark's School of Divinity. With a mixture of both mounting excitement and very understandable trepidation, Boeche was headed for a clandestine, lunchtime encounter of a truly extraordinary kind at the city's Cornhusker Hotel. He was about to sit down with two Department of Defense physicists who would reveal to him what they claimed was the dark and disturbing truth at the heart of the UFO mystery.

I learned of Boeche's intriguing experience a number of years ago, then spoke with him about it in 2006, and ultimately conducted an extensive interview with him in 2007. He told me: "I found it interesting because they had contacted me at work; and I have no idea how they tracked me down there. But, they wanted to know if we could get together and have lunch to discuss something important. I met them for a brief period of time on that first meeting, and then they said: 'We'd like to get together and have a longer conversation.' I arranged a time and it was quite a lengthy discussion, probably three and a half hours. And that's how it all came about.

"After both meetings, when I was able to verify that the men held the degrees they claimed to hold, and were apparently who they claimed to be, I was intrigued and excited at the possibility of having stumbled on a more or less untouched area which could be researched. But I was also cautious in terms of 'why me?'"

And thus it was that Boeche was plunged headlong into a strange and surreal world of classified Department of Defense projects, secret meetings and follow-up dialogues with *Deep Throat*-style sources, and stories of very disturbing encounters with what were described to him as NHEs, or Non-Human Entities, which many within the UFO research community believe are aliens, but that certain elements of the DoD believe are nothing less than the deceptive minions of Satan. The story told to Boeche is both provocative and startling, as are its implications, if they are genuine, of course.

At the beginning, Boeche was apprehensive and curious. "I had no way of knowing before our face-to-face meeting if there was any legitimacy to this at all," he told me. "I wasn't given any information at all before our meeting, just the indication that they were involved in areas of research I would find interesting, and that they had some concerns they wished to discuss with me.

"Both men were physicists. I'd guess they were probably in their early-to-mid fifties, and they were in a real moral dilemma. Both of them were Christians, and were working on a Department of Defense project that involved trying to contact the NHEs. In fact, this was described to me as an 'obsessive effort.' And part of this effort was to try and control the NHEs and use their powers in military weapons applications and in intelligence areas, such as remote-viewing and psychotronic weapons.

"They came to believe that the NHEs were not extraterrestrial at all; they believed they were some sort of demonic entities. And that regardless of how benevolent or beneficial any of the contact they had with these entities *seemed* to be, it always ended up being tainted, for lack of a better term, with something that ultimately turned out to be bad. There was ultimately *nothing* positive from the interaction with the

NHE entities. They felt it really fell more under the category of some vast spiritual deception instead of UFOs and aliens. In the course of the whole discussion, it was clear that they really viewed this as having a demonic origin that was there to simply try and confuse the issue in terms of who they were, what they wanted, and what the source of the ultimate truth is. If you extrapolate from their take that these are demons in the biblical sense of the word, then what they would be doing here is trying to create a spiritual deception to fool as many people as possible."

As to how elements of the DoD were engaging the NHEs in some form of contact, Boeche was given a truly strange and alarming story. "From what they told me, it seemed like someone had invoked something and it opened a doorway to let these things in. That's certainly the impression they gave me. I was never able to get an exact point of origin of these sorts of experiments, or of their involvement, and when they got started. But I did get the impression that because of what they knew and the information that they presented, they had been involved for at least several years, even if the project had gone on for much longer. They were concerned that they had undertaken this initially with the best of intentions, but then as things developed they saw a very negative side to it that wasn't apparent earlier. So, that's what leads me to think they had a relatively lengthy involvement."

The story became even more complex when the reasoning behind, and the goals of, the project were revealed to Boeche: "Most of it was related to psychotronic weaponry and remote viewing, and even deaths by what were supposed to be psychic methods." Certainly, the NHEs, it was deduced by those attached to the DoD project, possessed extraordinary, and lethal, mental powers. And, as a result, deeper plans were initiated, using nothing less than ancient rites and black rituals, to actually try and contact the NHEs with two specific—some might say utterly crackpot—goals in mind: (1) controlling them and (2) exploiting their extraordinary mental powers in the form of devastating weaponry.

While contact was apparently wholly successful, as were the attempts to use the mental powers of the NHEs, Boeche said the two physicists believed that those in the DoD working on this project were being utterly deceived and lulled into a false sense of security. They thought that "the project personnel were allowed to assume they had somehow technologically mastered the ability to do what the NHEs could do: remote-viewing and psychotronics. But, in actuality, it was these entities doing it all the time, or allowing it to happen, for purposes that suited their deception. With both psychotronic weapons and remote-viewing, I was told that the DoD had not really mastered a technology to do that at all; they were allowed by the NHEs to *think* that this is what they had done. But the NHEs were *always* the causal factor."

At this point in the meeting, the two scientists provided Boeche with disturbing evidence of not just the power of the NHEs, but also the way in which any and all NHE-related work "ultimately turned out to be bad." Boeche elaborated: "They showed me a dozen photos of three different people—four photos of each person, who had apparently been killed by these experiments. These were all post-mortem photographs, taken in-situ, after the experiments. The areas shown in all of the photographs were like a dentist's chair or a barber's chairs, and the bodies were still in those positions, sitting in the chairs. Still there, with EEG and EKG leads coming off of them. They were all wired. It was a very clinical setting, and there was no indication of who they were. It was a very disturbing sort of thing. And I'm thinking in the back of my mind: if these are real, who would they have gotten for these experiments? Were they volunteers? Were they some sort of prisoners? I have no idea. Were they American? Were they foreign? There was no way to tell."

Boeche was, however, allowed to take notes pertaining to the controversial photographs. One of the victims was a white male, age 25-to-30, who had been killed by a "remotely induced" cardiac arrest. The second was a white female, somewhere between the ages of 20 and 25, whose death was due to a "remotely transmitted head trauma" that resulted in "crushing of the right anterior portion of the skull." The third victim was a white male—probably in his 30s—killed by "...remotely controlled suffocation. The deaths and heart attacks were allowed to happen because it served the NHEs goals, the deception that they were aliens trying to help us and give us this advanced technology."

Thereafter, the meeting was terminated. Boeche did manage to engage his two contacts in conversation on other occasions, once more in person, and also by both telephone and letter. The conversations always followed broadly similar ground: namely, that the Human Race was being deceived into believing that it was receiving visitations from aliens, when in reality demonic forces were secretly squaring up for Armageddon and the final countdown. And, the DoD's overwhelmingly reckless dabbling into occult-driven areas to try and make a bizarre-but-futile pact of some sort with these same forces was inevitably, and only, destined to make things much, much worse for each and every one of us.

Of course, the two key questions in this strange affair are: why was Ray Boeche, specifically, chosen by certain elements of the DoD? And was the story his sources supplied truthful, ingenious fakery, or a swirling mixture of the two?

"The impression was that it was to test the waters, that's what they told me. They had read some of my stuff, and they knew that I'd become a pastor and that I had a Christian viewpoint from which I could examine these things. And they were concerned morally and ethically that they had allowed them-

5

selves to be duped into doing this research, and it had taken such a turn. My concern was always that: why come to me? Who am I? I can't do anything for you. I'm happy to evaluate it as best I can, but if you have this concern, why not go to a Christian leader with a lot more clout and public visibility than I've got? But that was their reason: they were aware of the research I had done on a lot of things, that I could approach it from a Christian viewpoint, and that it was more of a moral dilemma for them. They wanted the information out there. But, to me, I have to think: is any of this accurate? On one hand, is this a way to throw disinformation out? But, on the other hand, I think that even if they wanted to just spread disinformation, they could have done it with someone a lot more influential than me."

With respect to his own views, as well as those of the two DoD physicists, Boeche added: "As a pastor and someone who's trained as a theologian, I can't come to any other conclusion than there is some sort of spiritual deception going on here. In so many of these kinds of alien contacts, the entities involved make a denial of Christianity; anytime the spiritual issues are addressed, there is always some sort of denial of the validity of Christianity and the validity of the Bible. And I find it interesting that these percipients are told that Jesus was a great guy, but you just misunderstood him. They say: he wasn't really God's son. You just don't quite get it. But you never hear them say that about Buddha, or Krishna, or Mohammed. It always seems to come down to some sort of denial of Christianity. The percipients, whether you consider them contactees or abductees are engaged by the NHEs in spiritual discussions—but it's always one-sided.

"I would have a lot less suspicion of the potential of the demonic nature of these things if they were to say: 'You guys are *all* screwed up; *all* of your spiritual leaders had some good ideas, but none of them really got it. It's a big mess.' But it seems to be so specifically pointed at the Judeo-Christian tradition. It certainly seems to me like it's the two genuine forces squaring up against each other.

Anglican Priest Ray Boeche

"This is a thorny thing to dissect because, as a Christian, I believe scripture is explicit in its implications that there are definitely demonic influences at work in the world generally. These entities do want to deceive us. I'm hesitant to paint with too broad a brush and say that everything can be attributed to them. I think there are too many theologians, Christians, who want to see a demon behind every rock. But I think the demonic world is real. One of its principle goals is to deceive us. Does that negate the existence of some sort of extraterrestrial intelligence? I don't think so. I think, though, that the extraterrestrial hypothesis is too simple an explanation. Too many cases go so far beyond that."

Boeche concluded: "A valid way to distract people is the two camps: the E.T. believers and the skeptics, while the real story is buried. The more distractions you can make, the easier it is to keep people from hitting on what's actually important. That's what so confusing about the whole thing. I've been involved in this since 1965 and this is the most bizarre stuff I've ever run across. I didn't know what to make of it then and I don't know what to make of it now."(1)

Neither did I. But I was determined to find out.

I

THE QUEST BEGINS

In the several years that have now passed since I first approached Ray Boeche on this subject, I have taken up the gauntlet and have dug deep into the central theme of his revelations—something that very quickly led me into a rabbit-hole-like maze populated by shadowy informants, scared old men in possession of horrifying, decades-old secrets, and illuminating-yet-bizarre classified documentation. The long and winding story I have uncovered is both unsettling and unnerving—in equal, awful measures. At its cold heart lies a bleak and disturbing scenario to explain the UFO presence in our world that, for many years, has been firmly and secretly embraced as nothing but the literal truth by a group of American government, military, and intelligence personnel. Collectively, they call themselves the Collins Elite. Yet, for all of their military-swagger, ingrained machismo, and bravado, the Collins Elite live in a perpetual state of overwhelming apprehension, fear, and absolute dread.

That state of mind is driven by the clandestine activities of what the group perceives to be hostile and ominous intruders from a realm of existence far different than the one we inhabit. Those intruders assure us they are our friends and allies, but according to the Collins Elite, they most certainly are not. They claim to have our best interests at heart, but in reality, says the group, the exact opposite is the case. And, above all else, they earnestly want to us to embrace the idea that they are extraterrestrial visitors from far-away star-systems. For the Collins Elite, that is the biggest, blackest, and boldest deception of all.

In essence, the Collins Elite utterly refute and reject any and all notions that extraterrestrials have ever visited planet Earth or have abducted human beings for purposes relative to medical examination, scientific study, and hybridization—a scenario that many UFO researchers strongly assert is taking place. Instead, the conclusion of the group is that we have in our midst a cold-hearted and sinister intelligence of demonic origins that masquerades as alien, whose presence in our world threatens each and every one of us, and that consigns all of us to, perhaps quite literally, a living Hell.

Put very simply, the Collins Elite has a fear, a suspicion, and ultimately a solid acceptance that we, the Human Race, are being subtly, yet brilliantly, steered away from the teachings of religion. The group believes we are being encouraged to accept and embrace Satan himself—albeit in the deceptive guise of an advanced alien entity—as our savior, shortly before the countdown to Armageddon begins and time finally runs out. And the Collins Elite concludes that we are regularly and routinely farmed by an incredibly ancient life-form of poorly-understood proportions and fog-shrouded origins that harvests human souls upon death, for purposes both nightmarish and nefarious.

It is a story that is deeply and directly linked with the so-called alien abduction phenomenon that so dominates the field of UFOlogy, with the diminutive and black-eyed Grays of UFO lore and popular culture, with eschatology and the end of all things, and with the way in which human beings have since time immemorial allegedly been molded, manipulated, controlled, and ultimately digested with utterly cold, clinical, and ruthless finality. In short and simplistic terms, the Grays are hungry for our souls—voraciously and, perhaps, insanely so, too. Not only that but they apparently hate us on a scale that is nearly unimaginable.

Unsurprisingly, there is a realization on the part of some of those who have comprised the Collins Elite over the course of nearly sixty years that such a monumentally horrific story cannot easily, if at all, be told to the world at large for one, simple reason: they do not know *how* to tell such a horrific story without the revelation resulting in the possible, and irreversible, collapse of society.

Indeed, *some* of those who have been exposed to this particularly unsettling theory, who have embraced it, and who now accept it as complete and utter reality, conclude that openly revealing the perceived truth cannot serve *any* useful purpose at all—due to their somewhat-resigned conclusion that the otherworldly intelligence is near-unstoppable in its horrifying agenda, and wholly incapable of listening to, or possibly even comprehending, any form of rhyme, reason, plea, or logic of a specifically human nature.

On the other hand, however, and as will later become graphically apparent, several senior figures within the Collins Elite have been vigorously pushing for widespread disclosure to the general public and the media of the terrifying theory they accept as the literal truth. Deep dissent within the ranks, then, is also a central facet of the story that follows. And the Collins Elite are not alone in holding opinions about the nature of the non-human, devilish entities they conclude are among us, and how matters should be handled with respect to informing the public or otherwise; far from it, in fact.

To the overwhelming fury, consternation, and concern of the Collins Elite, there are others within the multifaceted, secret world of officialdom who have concluded that the best approach may be to try and engage these intruders from the outer edge in some form of unholy Faustian pact. While they realize this approach is one that gambles recklessly with our very existence, they also see it as an approach that may buy the Human Race some vitally-needed time, that may allow us to combat and halt the onslaught, and that might even give us the knowledge to understand and exploit the technology that the unearthly force utilizes against us—a technology that appears to be a strange, magical brew comprised of truly advanced science, ancient alchemy, and archaic rite and ritual.

In other words, this story does not just tell of a brilliantly executed, satanic deception. No, it also tells of a secret conflict—perhaps even an outright *battle* would be far more accurate—between various factions of the intelligence community and the military as they collectively struggle to comprehend and cope with the stark and mind-numbing knowledge and realization that the people of Earth are a slave race to techno-demons and hate-filled fallen angels.

Yet, for all of their power, the Collins Elite—and just about all those officials in the United States whose views accord with those of the group—await the future with overwhelming dread. They fear *everyone's* last breath. For, in their minds at least, when that day arrives, they believe the dream is over and the nightmarish, final events well and truly begin in earnest. And they conclude it is all the fault of two near-legendary characters within the world of the occult who succeeded in unleashing upon us what might accurately be termed a veritable army of demons. What follows is their terrible, and terrifying, story.

With that said, it is important to note that the accounts, beliefs, theories and conclusions that I uncovered are strictly those of the people who have been willing to have them publicized. As the author of this book, I am only the messenger for those who adhere to the message. In view of this, it is perhaps wise and apposite for me to cite the words of Sir Walter Scott: "I cannot tell how the truth may be; I say the tale as 'twas said to me."(1)

2

SYMPATHY FOR THE DEVIL

To fully understand and appreciate the complex nature, make-up, history, and origins of the darkness that elements of the government believe surrounds us, we have to first turn our attentions to one of the most notorious characters of the late 19th and early-to-mid 20th centuries, the absolute grand-master of the occult himself, Aleister Crowley. Born in 1875, in Leamington, England, Crowley was the son of a rich brewer and was raised in a strict Christian household. Indeed, Crowley's father, Edward, was also a preacher in a sect known as the Plymouth Brethren.

In 1881 the Crowley family moved to Redhill, Surrey, and the young Aleister was sent to an evangelist school. Although it was his intention to become a chemist, Crowley soon became interested in religious studies and then developed a deep passion for alchemy and magic. In 1898, that interest led him to the Hermetic Order of the Golden Dawn, a magical order founded in Great Britain during the late 19th century that practiced theurgy and spiritual development; it was one of the largest single influences on 20th century Western occultism. Crowley then moved in with a man named Alan Bennett, a member of the Golden Dawn, and under his guidance began to personally experiment with ritual magic. Inheriting a considerable fortune from his father, Crowley lived life to its absolute fullest and wildest in London, Paris, and Mexico –where he quickly became a 33rd Degree Mason. (1)

Then, in 1900, he returned to England and at the age of twenty-five headed to Scotland, where he purchased Boleskine

House, located on the shores of the famous Loch Ness, the site of what is probably the world's most well-known, alleged lake-monster. Interestingly, Crowley's actions, which included black masses and wild orgies, led to some highly disturbing phenomena. He described, for example, how the spirits he had supposedly succeeded in summoning at the mysterious and murky loch got perilously out of hand, causing one housemaid to flee in terror and a workman to go utterly insane. Crowley also insinuated that he was indirectly responsible for a local butcher accidentally severing an artery and bleeding to death, after he, Crowley, had allegedly written the names of certain demons on a bill from the butcher's shop. (2)

From January to March 1918, Crowley received a series of visions via his "Scarlet Woman," one Roddie Minor; this is the infamous Amalantrah Working. Throughout his strange and turbulent life, Crowley had a number of these Scarlet Women, all of whom essentially acted as channels or vessels for the transfer of messages perceived to be of angelic and/or demonic origin. But Crowley was interested in more than mere messages; it was his deep desire to invite, or to invoke, the entities behind the messages into our world and to engage them on a one-to-one basis. Crowley was certainly no fool and he was fully aware of the potentially hazardous and disastrous implications that might very well result from his planned door-opening activities. This did not, however, in any way dissuade him from enthusiastically pressing ahead. And, it seems, he succeeded beyond his wildest dreams—or nightmares, maybe.

It was during the Amalantrah Working, which included the ingestion of hashish and mescaline to achieve an altered state of consciousness, that Crowley made contact with an interdimensional entity known as Lam, a large-headed figure that could have quite easily passed for a close relative of the enigmatic being that stares eerily forth from the cover of *Communion*, Whitley Strieber's alien abduction book published

Aleister Crowley's "Lam"

in 1987. Crowley preferred not to identify Lam as a literal extraterrestrial, however. Rather, he opted for the term "Enochian entity," which took its inspiration from the so-called "Enochian Call," a Cabalistic language devised by 17th century Elizabethan magician, Dr. John Dee. Interestingly, Dee and his "scryer," one Edward Kelly, had their very own strange experiences with—as they termed them—"little men" who moved around "in a little fiery cloud," a proto-UFO, perhaps. (3)

Today, there are researchers who have carefully studied the life and work of Crowley and who believe that he succeeded in tapping into the very same twilight realm that is home to the so-called alien "Grays" who practically dominate the modern era of UFOlogy and who feature heavily within the alien abduction-based works of the likes of Budd Hopkins, the late Dr. John Mack, and historian David Jacobs. And, it is worth noting, countless abductees only recall their encounters with these black-eyed, gray entities after they have been hypnotically regressed, in other words, when they are in an altered form of consciousness. Yet again, then, we see that trance-like states—not at all unlike those generated during the Amalantrah Working—are very often the triggering factors that succeed in granting access to the world of these strange, unearthly intelligences.

So Crowley certainly created the scene and set the wheels in motion for what was to follow. The ultimate culprit, however, was someone who dared to go where even Crowley feared to tread.

The time is shortly after 5:00 p.m. on the afternoon of Tuesday, June 17, 1952. The location is a large and imposing pre-war mansion on South Orange Grove Avenue in Pasadena, California. And complete and utter carnage and chaos is currently reigning supreme. Within the deep bowels of the old house, a laboratory packed with all manner of chemicals and scientific gadgetry is enveloped in flames. The Hell-like inferno is borne out of two terrifying explosions of fulminate of mercury, the rumbling and reverberating echoes of which can still be heard at least a mile away, and which cause the neighbors to run screaming onto the streets, petrified that an all-destructive Third World War has just begun. And, in a curious and cosmic way, just maybe it has.

Lying on the floor of the laboratory is a man whose body has been horribly mutilated as a result of the awesome power of the explosion and the inferno. A sickening, bleak hole dominates what is left of the man's lower-jaw. The bones of his left arm are violently broken, and both of his legs are completely shattered. Half of his right arm is missing, and the remainder is a tangle of exposed muscle, sinew, and bloodied bone. The man's life is ebbing away fast—and what is left of his mind knows it, too. A wild and careering ride in an ambulance is undertaken to try and save the man from the icy clutches of that grimmest of all reapers, but it is to no avail. He expires at 5:45 p.m. at Pasadena's Huntington Memorial Hospital. (4)

Some people insisted, in hushed tones, that the man got everything he deserved—and then some. After all, for years he had been working to summon up unholy entities from some vile netherworld and may very well have succeeded in doing so, too. There were even rumors that the man had attempted to bargain with the Devil (yes, *the* Devil), as a means to further his power and influence, and to ensure for himself a position alongside the fork-tailed and horned one for the battle of Armageddon. And, at one point, the man had even loudly pro-

Aleister Crowley

claimed himself to be nothing less than the Antichrist.

This story is made all the more incredible by virtue of the fact that the man at the center of this event was no mere fantasist, mentally-deranged dreamer, or wannabe Satanist. Rather, without this man—whose life ended so violently and terribly on that long-gone day in 1952—the world would be very different one today. Without him, neither John Glenn nor Gordon Cooper would have likely ventured into space. Without him, Neil Armstrong would probably never have uttered those immortal, famous words of July 1969, when he took his first, tentative steps on the surface of the Moon. In short, without this man there might well have never been a U.S. space-program, no NASA, no *Apollo* missions, and no space shuttle. In his own way, and in his short-but-packed lifetime, the man did not just change history or influence the present day, he arguably played an integral role in creating both.

That man, whose life was so violently taken at the age of only 37, was Jack Parsons, a solid devotee of Aleister Crowley and a brilliant-yet-maverick rocket-scientist who was—as many within the corridors of power utterly believe, at least—responsible for opening an ancient and mighty doorway that ushered in the UFO phenomenon in all its diabolical might and power in the summer of 1947. It was Parsons' tremendous ego, they also believe, that led him to assume he could actually take on those soulless entities who were brilliantly, yet utterly cold-heartedly, manipulating both him and the UFO phenomenon for their own evil needs and desires.

Of course, Parsons was catastrophically wrong in his beliefs and assumptions. He quite literally came crashing down in flames and paid the ultimate price—his soul. (5)

3

"BE CAREFUL; THEY BITE"

At his birth in 1914, Jack Parsons was given the memorable and unusual name of Marvel Whiteside Parsons and had a truly extraordinary life. An undoubted genius, he indirectly led NASA to send the *Apollo* astronauts to the Moon in 1969. Moreover, the Aerojet Corporation—which Parsons personally founded—today produces solid-fuel rocket boosters for the Space Shuttle that are based on Parsons' very own, decades-old innovations. For his accomplishments, a large crater on the far side of the Moon was named in his honor, and each and every year, on Halloween no less, NASA's Jet Propulsion Laboratory holds an open-house memorial, replete with mannequins of Jack Parsons and his early JPL cohorts known as "Nativity Day." And, within the aerospace community, there is a long-standing joke that JPL actually stands for "Jack Parsons Laboratory" or "Jack Parsons Lives."(1)

In fact, however, this man Parsons, who was so revered and honored by very senior figures within the U.S. space-program, was an admitted occultist, a follower of Aleister Crowley, and someone who topped even Crowley himself by engaging in bestiality with the family dog and sexual relations with his own mother, perhaps at the same time, no less. Moreover, before each rocket test, Parsons would undertake a ritual to try and invoke the Greek god, Pan. (2)

It was perhaps inevitable that his path would eventually cross with that of Aleister Crowley. In 1942, after the two had become acquainted as a result of their like-minds and pursuits, Crowley chose Parsons to lead the Agape Lodge of the

Thelemic Ordo Templi Orientis (O.T.O.) in California, after Crowley expelled one Wilfred Smith from the position. The devoted Parsons eagerly practiced Aleister Crowley's Thelemic Rituals, the goal of which was the creation of a new breed of human being that, if the ritual proved successful, would lead to the destruction of Christianity. Meanwhile, during the same time frame, and within the confines of his Pasadena mansion—dubbed "The Parsonage"—the darkly handsome Parsons held parties for those friends and colleagues in the field of science fiction. Indeed, writers Robert Heinlein, Jack Williamson, Anthony Boucher, and Ray Bradbury were all regular visitors to Parsons' home. (3)

Moving on, much of Parsons'—and the JPL's—initial rocket research in this period was undertaken at the appropriately-named Devil's Gate Dam in Los Angeles. Interestingly, the JPL was itself established at this very locale in 1930 by the California Institute of Technology. The dam had been constructed a decade earlier by engineers from the Los Angeles County Flood Control District and took its title from Devil's Gate Gorge, a rocky out-cropping that eerily resembles a demonic face. (4) And just as Parsons was busy working at the gate of the Devil himself, so to speak, another figure in early U.S. rocket research, Robert Goddard, was making important advances in this same, burgeoning arena. Goddard had a long-standing link to the New Mexico town of Roswell, no less, and had heard a good deal about Parsons.

Robert Hutchings Goddard, a child of the late 19th century, developed a fascination for outer space and rocketry at the age of 16, after he enthusiastically devoured H.G. Wells' classic science-fiction novel, *The War of the Worlds*. Goddard's first big break came in 1919, when the Smithsonian Institution published his revolutionary work, *A Method of Reaching Extreme*

Altitudes, which extensively detailed his mathematical theories of rocket flight, his experiments with solid-fuel rockets, and the possibilities he saw of extensively exploring the Earth's upper-atmosphere—and, one day, far beyond, too. Goddard also had the memorable distinction of launching the world's first liquid-fueled rocket, specifically in Auburn, Massachusetts, on March 16, 1926. Today, the site is a national historic landmark known as the Goddard Rocket Launching Site.

Due to his successes, and with some very welcome financial support, in 1930 Goddard elected to move his base of operations to Roswell, New Mexico, where he worked with a team of technicians in near-isolation and overwhelming secrecy—and succeeded in launching more than 30 rockets of a truly innovative and revolutionary design. In the summer of 1936, a close friend and colleague of Parsons—Frank J. Malina, who held the distinction of being the first director of the JPL—traveled to Roswell to meet with Goddard. Malina found that Goddard held his research cards very close to his chest and displayed clear and astute concerns that others might try and capitalize on his research—people such as Parsons, for example, should Goddard reveal a tad too much.

But, in the larger scheme of things, it didn't really matter at all. Goddard was diagnosed with throat cancer in 1945 and died in August of that year in Baltimore, Maryland. By that time, Malina's own rocket research had outgrown its original facility, and his tests were soon moved to the White Sands Missile Range, New Mexico. (5)

The players and the places were coming together.

A figure from the science-fiction community who came to know Parsons in this same period was none other than L. Ron Hubbard of Church of Scientology fame. And it was in front of Hubbard that Parsons engaged in his Babalon rituals—with which Hubbard quickly became fascinated and near obsessed. And, in turn, the Jack Parsons of the mid-1940s was favorably impressed by L. Ron Hubbard's personal interest in, and support of, the ways of Aleister Crowley. Parsons penned a letter to the Great Beast that, in part, said: "I deduced that [Hubbard] is in direct touch with some higher intelligence. He is the most Thelemic person I have ever met and is in complete accord with our own principles."

In the wake of this glowing statement, Hubbard moved in to live with Parsons, was brought into Crowley's Ordo Templi Orientis, and soon had his eyes set on Parsons' girlfriend, a 19-year-old named Sara Northrup. In early 1946, Parsons and Hubbard began an extensive, magical ritual that has become known as the Babalon Working, the ultimate goal of which was to try and manifest an elemental entity in much the same way that Crowley had succeeded in doing with the very alien-looking Lam several decades earlier. Parsons was overwhelmingly convinced that the complicated ritual had worked when, approximately two weeks later, a beautiful woman, a certain Marjorie Elizabeth Cameron, came upon the scene.

On February 26, 1946, a very pleased and infinitely proud Parsons told Crowley: "I have my elemental!" Two months later, Parsons, Cameron, and Hubbard tackled the next stage of the Babalon Working, the aim of which, this time, was to attempt to summon up a "moonchild" just as had been portrayed within the pages of Crowley's novel of the same name. Things did not quite go according to plan, however. Northrup was growing tired of Parsons' obvious fascination with Cameron, and she soon left him for Hubbard. The pair promptly absconded with around $10,000 of Parsons' money and vanished. The story is that a furious Parsons finally found Northrup and Hubbard out at sea and quickly cast a spell upon the pair. In the direct wake of Parsons' dark incantation, rumor has it that Hubbard and Northrup came perilously close to drowning as a near-cataclysmic storm surfaced seemingly out of nowhere.

Suggestions have been made that Hubbard's primary reason for getting close to Parsons was that he, Hubbard, was actually taking part in a secret mission for the official world, one that was carefully designed to bring to an end Parsons' dark rituals and to save Northrup from the seductive aura of Crowley's disciple. This theory—as intriguing as it is—has not, thus far, been confirmed. Crowley, meanwhile, looked on utterly appalled and considered Hubbard to be nothing more than a "stupid lout" who made off with Parsons' dollars and his girlfriend, in what he, Crowley, succinctly called an "ordinary confidence trick."(6)

Regardless of the precise nature, intent, and outcome of the strange relationship between Parsons and Hubbard, many students of Parsons' work believed that the portal of entry that Crowley opened in 1918—when he successfully invoked Lam—may have been further enlarged by Parsons and Hubbard in the 1940s with the commencement of the Babalon Working, which resulted in something wicked coming this way. Perhaps those same students were correct, as soon after Parsons' occult actions reached their tipping point, pilot Kenneth Arnold had that historic UFO encounter over Mt. Rainier, Washington, followed a little more than a week later by the legendary flying saucer crash outside of Roswell, New Mexico.

At about 3:00 p.m. on June 24, 1947, pilot Kenneth Arnold was searching for an aircraft that had reportedly slammed into the southwest side of Mt. Rainier, a peak on Washington State's sprawling Cascade Mountains. "I hadn't flown more than two or three minutes on my course when a bright flash reflected on my airplane," said Arnold. "It startled me as I thought I was too close to some other aircraft. I looked every place in the sky and couldn't find where the reflection had come from until I looked to the left and the north of Mt. Rainier, where I observed a chain of nine peculiar looking aircraft flying from north to south at approximately 9,500 feet elevation and going, seemingly, in a definite direction of about 170 degrees."

Arnold added that the mysterious craft were closing in rapidly on Mt. Rainier, and admitted to being mystified by their unusual design. "I thought it was very peculiar that I couldn't find their tails," he said, "but assumed they were some type of jet plane. The more I observed these objects, the more upset I became, as I am accustomed and familiar with most all objects flying whether I am close to the ground or at higher altitudes. The chain of these saucer-like objects [was] at least five miles long. I felt confident after I would land there would be some explanation of what I saw [sic]."(7)

Just days after his encounter, Arnold said that he had been contacted by a Texas-based preacher who warned him that flying saucers were "harbingers of doomsday" and that he was readying his flock for "the end of the world." Perhaps the preacher knew more than some might be willing to give him credit for. Interestingly, conspiracy researcher John Judge stated—in an interview on KPFK Radio, Los Angeles on August 12, 1989—that Kenneth Arnold and Jack Parsons were flying partners, although, admittedly, this extraordinary claim has not been confirmed. (8)

No concrete explanation for Arnold's experience ever did surface, but as the United States became an ever-increasing magnet for flying saucers throughout the middle of 1947, the military quickly swung into action, astutely realizing that securing an answer to the puzzle was vital. As a result, investigations were initiated and became solidified under the banner of an official operation termed Project Sign. In 1948, Sign was elbowed-out of the picture by Project Grudge, which, in turn, eventually gave way to Project Blue Book—the Air Force's most well-known UFO investigative program, which continued until 1969 when it finally closed both its doors and its files. The Air Force conceded that of the 12,618 reports that had been studied between 1947 and 1969, 701 appeared to defy rational investigation. However, the higher echelons of the military were keen to stress that they had never come across even a single shred of evidence suggesting that extraterrestrials had been—or were still—visiting the Earth. And the Air Force insisted that if it had had more data, they would have surely solved the outstanding 701 reports, too. (9)

It was only a little more than a week after Kenneth Arnold's experience that something unusual plunged to earth in the deserts of Lincoln County, New Mexico, not far from the now-infamous town of Roswell. The event has been the subject of dozens of books, official studies undertaken by both the General Accounting Office and the U.S. Air Force, a plethora of television documentaries, a movie, and considerable media scrutiny.

The admittedly-weird affair has left in its wake a near-mountain of theories to explain the event, including a weather balloon, a "Mogul Balloon" secretly utilized to monitor for Soviet atomic-bomb tests, an extraterrestrial spacecraft, some dark and dubious high-altitude-exposure experiments using Japanese prisoners-of-war, some sort of atomic mishap, the crash of a V-2 rocket with shaved monkeys on-board, and an accident involving an early "Flying-Wing"-style aircraft, secretly built by transplanted German scientists who had relocated to the United States following the end of the Second World War. (10)

Whatever the exact nature of the device, it certainly seemed to have been extraordinary. Jesse A. Marcel, the intelligence officer for the 509th Bomb Group at Roswell Army Air Field in 1947, who saw, handled, and collected some of the remains of the object at the crash-site itself, the Foster Ranch, said: "I saw a lot of wreckage but no complete machine. It had disintegrated before it hit the ground. The wreckage was scattered over an area about three quarters of a mile long and several hundred feet wide. I was pretty well acquainted with most everything that was in the air at that time, both ours and foreign. I was also acquainted with virtually every type of weather-observation or radar-tracking device being used by either the civilians or the military. What is was we didn't know. We just picked up the fragments. [It] could not be bent or broken…or even dented by a sixteen-pound sledgehammer. [It was] almost weightless…like a metal with plastic properties."(11)

The Roswell event was born and the era of the flying saucer had firmly been ushered in—in quite spectacular style, we might add. And, as author and researcher Adam Gorightly, who has carefully studied the lives and work of Crowley and Parsons, rightly observed: "After the Babalon Working, UFO sightings began to be reported en masse, as if a Devil's Floodgate had been opened, and into the earth realm flew powers and demons from beyond, much like an H.P. Lovecraft tale, unleashed upon an unsuspecting human populace. And, if we're talking about the negative aspects, just like any shamanic journey, if you're not prepared for it properly, then it's a slippery slope you're playing with. Crowley said about the Enochian entities: 'Be careful; they bite.'"(12)

4

THE PARSONS FILES

When I spoke with Ray Boeche the first time, he told me that he was happy to discuss the nature of the meetings with his clandestine, Department of Defense sources, as well as the specifics of their extraordinary revelations. There were, however, a couple of things that Boeche asked me not to publish, and those related to his speculation concerning the circumstances under which the shadowy pair initially found him and contacted him. I fully understood Boeche's concerns on this matter when he explained them to me, and I abided by his wish that certain parts of his story should remain firmly outside of the public domain. To take my investigation to its ultimate level, however, I felt that I had to pursue every lead and source—one of which was a retired intelligence operative named Ralph Summers, who led me to a certain Air Force base in Nebraska, where knowledge of the demonic theory for the UFO puzzle seemed to be curiously prevalent. (1)

I telephoned the base, and after being transferred from office to office over the course of what was probably six or seven minutes, I finally reached a representative of the Air Force Office of Special Investigations (AFOSI). Without naming Boeche, or even alluding to him in any way, I elected to do something I had never done before: I placed all my cards on the table upfront and explained that, as an author and journalist, I was chasing down a story suggesting that some U.S. officials believed that the UFO phenomenon could be explained in demonic terms.

The painfully brief silence that followed was eventually

broken by a series of questions.

"Is this a story you intend publishing?" It was.

"Do you have a publisher, yet?" Maybe, I think.

"I see, sir. Well, that's all very interesting, but it is way off anything we do." Okay. The call was terminated. It was time to try another approach. Or, rather, it *would* have been time to try another approach, had I not received a highly enigmatic telephone call three days later—from Offutt Air Force Base, which is located in Sarpy County, Nebraska.

"Mr. Redfern, I understand you want to meet with someone from the Collins Elite,"said the elderly-sounding female voice at the other end of the line.

"Meet with the what?" I replied, genuinely puzzled. For a moment or two there was silence.

"The Collins Elite," said the woman in slow, quiet and deliberate tones.

"I have no idea what that is," I replied truthfully.

"The Devil, UFOs, the story; *the* story," were the seven unforgettable words that rang around my head for days afterwards.

"Okay," I said, "that *is* a story I'm chasing down."

"*We* know that and *they* know that," was her reply, accompanied by a slight laugh. Whether or not "*they*" was a reference to Satan's hordes or to the mysterious Collins Elite, I did not know. I was told, however, to "expect a call" from someone who, in turn, would put me in touch with a "Mr. Duke" who "can help you." The game was afoot, as a certain famous, fictional detective was so fond of saying. (2)

The call came through and, eleven days later, I found myself driving to Albuquerque, New Mexico, where I was to meet the mysterious Mr. Duke. Little did I know it at the time, but I was about to come face-to-face with someone who had for years been a senior member of the Collins Elite—a highly covert group buried deeply within the U.S. intelligence community whose involvement in the issues of demonology and UFOs I would soon come to know very well. Of course, a million thoughts and questions were running through my head. Was I being set-up? Was I about to be swamped with disinformation—as some had suggested was the case while I was researching and writing *Body Snatchers in the Desert*, my controversial book on the 1947 Roswell affair? And why me, anyway? Was I being watched, or monitored, as a result of my contacts with Ray Boeche? Just about anything was possible, I reasoned. And I was just about prepared for anything, too.

"Got me through Boeche's people, did you?" Richard Duke asked me when we met, and with a knowing smile on his face.

"I suppose so, in a roundabout way," I replied, guessing that he probably already knew the answer to the question before I even offered it.

"Good, good," he added, while staring out the window of his favorite Mexican restaurant—our planned point of rendezvous. Duke was 86 years old when I met him, and I learned that he was the last surviving member of the original Collins Elite. His physical health reflected his advanced age, but his mind was still razor sharp, having been carefully honed and nurtured by his years in the Central Intelligence Agency (CIA). After asking Duke if that was his real name, to which I got the enigmatic, smile-accompanied reply of "This week it is," I sat back, ate enchiladas, drank a couple of frozen margaritas, and listened very carefully to the whistleblower words of this secret-filled old soul, all of which were focused upon secret investigations of Jack Parsons by U.S. Intelligence, the issue of Parsons' loyalty to the United States, his links to the government of Israel, and his relationship to Aleister Crowley.

Richard Duke told me that without this series of investigations there never would have been a Collins Elite, or an understanding and appreciation of the demonic nature of the UFO presence. I asked Duke what he meant and he explained that Parsons' activities brought him to the keen attention of U.S. officials very early on. But there was more to the story, much more than anyone outside of government could ever have suspected. Some of those tasked with secretly investigating the man and his actions in the late 1940s and early 1950s, Duke explained, became caught in a web of fascination that led them to dig ever-deeper into his world, his beliefs, his dealings with Aleister Crowley and L. Ron Hubbard, and even his possible role in generating the flying saucer wave of the late-1940s.

Duke brought with him to the meeting a veritable Aladdin's Cave of official documentation on Parsons that originated with the Air Force, FBI, Army, and several other U.S. agencies, offices, and departments. He assured me—several times—that it had all been officially released under the terms of the Freedom of Information Act. I had my doubts this was true of several pages I was shown, as they bore all the telltale signs of being aged and fading originals, rather than declassified, modern-day photocopies. But regardless of whether or not each and every page really was in the public domain, or if some of it was still subject to U.S. national security laws that perhaps even Duke himself was openly violating, he directed me to the most important and relevant pages—and these told a fascinating story. (3)

On November 2, 1950, a California-based special-agent of the FBI prepared a report on the actions of Jack Parsons that stated in part: "Subject, on September 15, 1950 removed certain documents pertaining to jet propulsion motors and rocket propellants without authority from Hughes Aircraft Company, Culver City, California; his place of employment [and which had been his place of employment since May 8, 1949]."

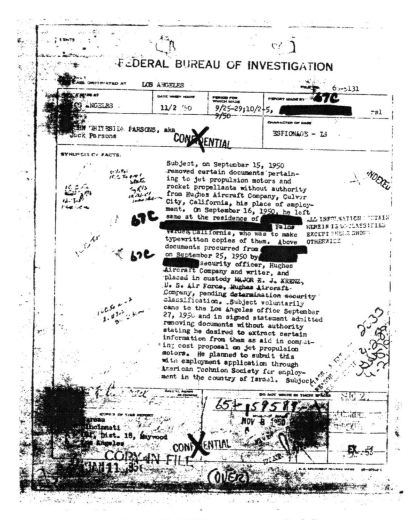

A formerly-classified FBI document on Jack Parsons

On September 25, after the documents in question had been retrieved by the authorities, they were duly handed over to a Air Force Major E.J. Krenz, after which, the FBI recorded: "[Parsons] voluntarily came to the Los Angeles office, September 27, 1950 and in [a] signed statement admitted removing documents without authority stating he desired to extract certain information from them as aid in computing [the] cost proposal on jet propulsion motors. He planned to submit this with [an] employment application through American Technion Society for employment in the country of Israel."

Twenty-four-hours later, an FBI agent, whose name has been carefully excised from the available documents, "displayed the document and papers to John T. Berdner, Air Provost Marshal, U.S. Army, who advised that it would be necessary for him to forward copies of them to the Chief of the Security and Policy Division, Intelligence Department, Headquarters, Air Materiel Command, Wright Field, Dayton, Ohio, where the documents would be examined for the purpose of determining whether or not they contained classified or non-classified information."

As a result of the brewing trouble surrounding Parsons, he was fired from Hughes Aircraft on that very day and Hughes' security personnel hastily advised the military that, at the very least, the documents should be classified Confidential. Then the next morning Parsons prepared a written statement for the FBI, the Army, and Air Materiel Command in which he conceded: "I now realize that I was wrong in taking this material from the Hughes Aircraft Plant."

Whether his apology was genuine or it was simply a groveling attempt to try and avoid serious problems with the authorities and charges that he was secretly engaged in espionage operations for Israel, Parsons certainly obfuscated the facts and played down his ongoing involvement in matters of an occult nature. When interviewed by the FBI on September 28, he said that he had "severed all relations" with the dark world that had so dominated his earlier years, and "...described himself as being an 'individualist,'" according to the interviewing special-agent in his report.

Significantly, files pertaining to Parsons' theft of the papers from Hughes Aircraft reveal that, several years earlier, he had worked with some notable bodies, including the Government's Office of Scientific Research and Development, the National Defense Research Council, and the Northrop Aircraft Company. Meanwhile, as several FBI offices across the state of California tried to determine—with help from the military— if Parsons was acting as an Israeli spy or if his actions were just plain reckless and stupid, the Cincinnati FBI Office entered into a period of liaison with the Air Force's Office of Special Investigations to "ascertain the facts" concerning Air Force knowledge of Parsons' activities.

A Major Sam Bruno of the USAF advised the FBI that the Air Force did have files on Parsons, including some that related to his relationship with Aleister Crowley, one of which, dated May 17, 1948, stated: "A religious cult, believed to advocate sexual perversion, was organized at subject's home at 1003 South Orange Grove Avenue, Pasadena, California, which has been reported subversive..."

The same documentation referred to USAF and FBI knowledge of the Church of Thelema, explaining in typically-humorless tones that "this cult broadly hinted at free love," that there had been "several complaints of 'strange goings on at this home,'" and that an unnamed source had described the church as "a gathering place of perverts." The military's records also noted that in 1943, Parsons was interviewed by the FBI and "stated that the Church of Thelema was a lodge and fraternity as well as a church, and that they studied philosophy as well as religion and attempted to inform themselves concerning all types and kinds of religion."

Parsons admitted that the church was based on the teachings of Crowley (who, rather amusingly, an obviously under-informed FBI special agent described merely as "an internationally known poet"!), and added that "...the organization was sometimes referred to as Crowleyism or Crowleyites."

A less-than-impressed Air Force advised the equally un-impressed FBI that: "...women of loose morals were involved and...the story of Parsons' activities had become fairly common knowledge among scientists in the Pasadena area."

Then, on November 14, 1950, Major Frank J. Austin, Jr., of the Ordnance Liaison Office at the Redstone Arsenal, determined that most of the documents from Hughes Aircraft should be classified as Confidential—with four remaining unclassified. It's eye opening that on the very same day, Major Donald Detwiler, of AFOSI, admitted in a letter to the FBI that on March 7, 1949, the Industrial Employment Review Board had authorized Parsons "access to military information through Top Secret." That Parsons had been highly cavalier with Confidential files and papers was a serious matter in itself. But that Parsons—occultist, literal mother-fucker, and alleged door-opener extraordinaire—had been granted a Top Secret clearance, which covered the work of the Army, Navy, and Air Force in relation to rocketry, was seen as being utterly beyond the pale.

As a result, on January 9, 1952, Parsons was informed by one J. Mason, the Chairman of the Industrial Employment Review Board, that:

The board has decided as of 7 January 1952 to revoke the clearance granted you through top secret of 7 March 1949, and to withdraw access by you to Department of Defense classified information and/or material. The foregoing and all the evidence in the case file, when considered with the duties and responsibilities of any position in which you may be engaged with Department of Defense classified contract work, indicate that you might voluntarily or involuntarily act against the security interest of the United States and constitute a danger to the national security. (4)

Parsons' security clearance may have been revoked, but the government was very far from finished with him. Actually, matters had barely begun.

5

THE COMING OF THE COLLINS ELITE

Richard Duke informed me that these investigations of Parsons—involving the FBI, Hughes Aircraft, and the intelligence arms of the Army, Air Force and Navy—exposed many of those "on the projects" to "his other world," namely the one that revolved around Aleister Crowley and L. Ron Hubbard.

"Some of the people, those names, the military names, you'll see in those Freedom of Information files on Parsons were people I got to know," Duke told me. "There was a bit of a secret envy around Parsons, with his gals and dames, as we called them then, and Thelema. It was risqué and something of a lure. But, the thing that connected everyone was we were all on the investigation of Parsons taking the papers from Hughes. But, for all his wrongs he was a fascinating man, but very troubled."

What the currently available FBI, Air Force, and Army files on Parsons specifically do *not* tell us, said Duke, are two things. First was that when the Air Materiel Command got involved with the Israeli connection to Parsons' world, "we learned this wasn't the first time they'd been speaking with Parsons. [Major Sam] Bruno himself told us they had a meeting with Parsons after [the Kenneth] Arnold [sighting]. And, there were tales of Parsons being linked into this, into Arnold."

When I asked for clarification on this particular point, Duke said that someone had undertaken some "special digging" and found out that Parsons and Arnold had a limited degree of personal contact as a result of their having mutual acquaintances. According to Duke, it went as follows: Parsons was friends with Hubbard. Hubbard wrote science fiction. He most certainly did; his celebrated story "Fear" was published as a novella in the July 1940 issue of *Unknown Fantasy Fiction*, which was edited by John W. Campbell, who was also the editor of *Astounding Science Fiction*, and Hubbard's 1980 novel *Battlefield Earth* was made into a mega-bucks movie starring actor and Scientologist John Travolta in 2000. Hubbard was well known to Raymond Palmer, the editor of the wildly popular science-fiction magazine, *Amazing Stories*. And, Palmer was friends with Arnold and helped write, and even published, Arnold's book *The Coming of the Saucers*. (1)

This was, Duke said, "enough for someone in Bruno's office to see that Parsons, who was thought of as a sorcerer, knew the man who saw the disks in 1947 and started it [sic]."

The second thing that the available FOIA material on Parsons does not tell us, Duke explained, is that the Air Force "also had reports on Parsons knowing [Robert] Goddard out at Roswell. We all knew something happened at Roswell with the crash in '47 that wasn't a weather balloon. We *knew* that; grapevine things, rumors you hear. But, there were some of those guys in OSI who said it had to mean something that Jackie-boy was linked with Arnold and with people like Goddard at Roswell."

Given that Parsons had loudly proclaimed UFOs would ultimately "play a part in converting the world to Crowleyanity," this makes the official interest in Parsons' activities of a flying- and saucer-shaped variety all the more understandable. The next phase was very simple, but of deep significance, said Duke: "They [the AFOSI] planned a meeting with Parsons and asked him—this was sometime in '48, I think—if, with his things with Crowley and Hubbard and trying to bring in equivalent things like the Crowley Lam [sic], there was something he wanted to tell them about what he knew on all this."

According to Duke, since Parsons still possessed a security

clearance at that time, engaging him in debate on matters of a somewhat sensitive nature was not seen as being problematic, providing he towed the proverbial line. And, when confronted and pressed for answers, a somewhat uncomfortable Parsons conceded that there probably *was* a connection, that the UFO wave of 1947 probably *was* linked with his door-opening actions, and that it was *not* down to chance that he knew Arnold, or that he had a tangential link to the town of Roswell. Of course, whether this was merely a case of Parsons carefully massaging his own ego, or the absolute truth, was a matter of some debate among officials.

"This was all just threads," stressed Duke. "The Air Force knew they had something with all this, but they weren't really sure what." As a result, Duke further expanded, a small project—"probably just two or three [people]"—was established at Wright-Patterson that made subtle and secret approaches to experts within the fields of demonology, ancient religions, and occult practices who could hopefully provide some answers with respect to what it was that Parsons might have set in motion, wittingly or not, and which the military was now struggling to comprehend.

And they were successful, asserted Duke, in that copious amounts of background data were obtained on the work of Crowley, as well as on Parsons himself, some of which came from Britain: "They had used [Crowley] at some point with intelligence, and shared it with us."

That Crowley *did* have links with British Intelligence is not in doubt—although the extent of that connection is a matter of *much* controversy. Former intelligence officer W. Adam Mandelbaum recorded: "…in the post-World War I years, up until the early years of World War II, Crowley did in some capacity or other serve the needs of British Intelligence, working for MI5… Given the political fallout that would have resulted from making this involvement public, it should be no surprise

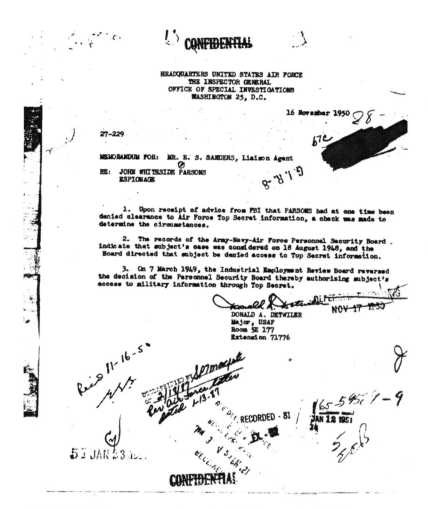

A 1950 USAF document confirms that Jack Parsons had Top Secret access

that there is a paucity of documentation concerning Crowley's intelligence efforts."(2)

So it was that "pages and pages" of material on Parsons was secured by the staff at Wright-Field. Even in those early stages, claimed Duke, the picture that came together was both bleak and disturbing. It had been noted with concern, Duke explained, that Charles Taze Russell—a prominent early 20th century Christian Restorationist minister from Pittsburgh, Pennsylvania, and the founder of what is now known as the Bible Student movement, from which the Jehovah's Witnesses emerged—had once made a prediction that the countdown to the end of the world would begin on October 2, 1914, and that this date would initiate the surfacing of the Antichrist and the harlot, Babylon the Great. (3)

John Carter, a biographer of Jack Parsons, noted: "It is ironic that John Parsons, who would later attempt to incarnate Babylon and who would also sign an oath stating that he was the Antichrist, was born the very day of Russell's eschatological event." For the U.S. military, this was most certainly not a good sign at all. (4)

Duke added: "By the time the Israeli spy-thing thing with Parsons was going on, Wright [-Patterson] had gotten a heck of a lot of information—background information—on Parsons, and what he was doing with Crowley and Hubbard. They also had a lot of interviews with priests, archaeologists—anyone, really, who might explain something about what Parsons was doing, and how all the things tied in with the flying disks. But, then, when Parsons died, what happens now [that] Parsons is gone? Is it all over? Will the disks all be gone? No more sightings? Or, was this a start? The man who'd let [the flying saucers] in wasn't around to shut it down, even if he'd wanted to. Everyone was apprehensive something big was going to come quickly."

And something big most certainly *did* occur: the Collins Elite was formed, a truly historic event that is unsurprisingly forever etched in the memory of Richard Duke. "What happened," Duke recalled, "was that we got a pleasant invite. Fifteen or sixteen of us [were] flown to the Pentagon and where an offer was made; which was probably no more than about a week after Parsons got killed, maybe a bit longer, but not much. The Air Force was having problems with the UFO project [Blue Book], and a lot of these reports were [similar to] ghost [reports]: they couldn't catch them, fading away, vanishing from radar, but not attacking us. So, they kind of puzzled the Air Force on how to handle it, which is why, eventually, they gave up on it. The UFOs didn't act like an aggressor—not a military aggressor, anyways, and just came and went, they thought.

"We were asked—this was people like me, a couple of G-2 [Army Intelligence] boys, two fellows from Naval Intelligence, several of the Air Force fellows in on the early Parsons thing at Wright, and a few more—if we would look at running an op to continue where the old Parsons project stopped. We were ready for it because of the interest that had come with watching [Parsons]—but a bit amazed the Pentagon was ready to fund what was, really, a study on if the disks had devil beginnings.

"And this is exactly why it was all kept so secret in the beginning. Everyone—particular the Pentagon boys—knew the hammer was going to come down on all this if Congress found out good U.S. dollars were being used to pay for [a study of] demonology and flying saucers. Maybe a little more mundane than you might want to hear. But that really *was* the first reason for the secrecy with us: not a big conspiracy about what we were doing, but a lot of anger and probably a hell of a lot of ridicule that would come tumbling out if anyone else found out.

"We all got an offer to relocate, with our families, to the D.C. area. The funding, we were told, was going to start coming through in a few months, after everyone was settled in D.C. The money and resources wasn't [sic] going to come exactly *to* us, but *onto* us through the [CIA's] Directorate of Plans [which was created a few months later, on August 1, 1952] to keep it all out of everyone's eyes—Congress. This wasn't really the Directorate's area at all though. It was more along the approach of flowing the money through them to us, a group no one would think to look at to find us.

"The important thing for you to understand is this was *not* like an official Blue Book, with a known name where even the press boys and the people knew of it, or some of it. It was a group of us who understood a lot about Parsons and the disk theories, and who, as a real group, didn't really exist. So, provided we did the work, interviewed as many people as we could, and looked at the links of the theory, everyone was happy, and no one outside would ever know. No one was ever saying we definitely had the answers here; they just didn't want to risk not looking at all the theories for the disks and not missing anything. We even got to name the group, as it wasn't coming off a list of available names or something like that."

And as for name the Collins Elite, Duke said: "One of our people who was brought in some time in the early part of the Parsons thing was a man who was a Quaker, from a little place in New York called Collins. He wasn't supporting Devil worship but knew a lot on it and had written a paper sometime. So we got him involved. He had a relative in the old OSS [Office of Strategic Services] who put him in touch with us. He was very interested in the Parsons story and on what the Air Force was trying to find out, and helped out a lot on some ends about alternative thinking. And we had a good relationship with him—those of us who were still stuck on what Parsons was doing.

"He was excited, I suppose, [that] he was being asked questions by the Air Force about what Parsons' work might mean and how we should interpret it. He hung around after, and we continued these debates about Parsons outside of work. [No] security or intelligence issues were discussed with people like this, of course. We really just wanted answers from them: advice and insight. There was no need, or permission, to tell them any of the deeper background.

"Our Quaker friend told us Collins was a little place where it was said everyone used to work making cheese. But, here he was helping the suits and the military on figuring out Parsons. So, we joked with him that because he was one of the few people who wasn't in cheese, he was the 'elite of Collins' and that kind of stuck and got used."

Collins is located in Erie County, New York, and was settled in 1808 by, predominantly, Quakers. And for such a small locale—today its population is barely 7,000—at one time the town *did* boast of being home to no less than ten factories involved in cheese-production. (5)

"So, we picked on the old joke about the Quaker, and it led to Collins Elite as an informal name we chose. And that's how we got started, and what we used to identify us, and for when we were speaking with NSA and the Company [meaning the CIA] and all those people. But Parsons is definitely what began it for us. He died and we got moving."(6)

The Collins Elite was born. And I had just spent a fascinating couple of hours speaking with a man who had been in on it from the very start, and who was now—almost certainly with some degree of official, or quasi-official, sanction, I carefully reasoned—spilling his guts on what was without a doubt the most extraordinary story to ever cross my path. And Duke was not finished yet. Not by a long shot. Two days later, I had my second meeting with this cosmic informant.

6

1952: Invasion

In the wake of Jack Parsons' violent death, according to Richard Duke, the people who became the Collins Elite viewed his terrible and bloody passing through highly suspicious and very worried eyes. Some Collins Elite members perceived Parsons' death as the somewhat appropriate and inevitable fulfillment of a pact that he had recklessly forged with the beings from beyond—a pact that ended with his demise after he succeeded in opening yet another portal through which even more nightmarish visitors might soon be manifesting en masse. And, just as was the case in the summer of 1947 following Parsons' successfully completion of the Babalon Working, there most certainly was a sudden upsurge in UFO activity across the United States—the likes of which had never, ever been seen before—in the weeks after the man's death.

"We can argue whether there's a connection or if it's a coincidence, but the timing was frightening," stated Duke, flatly. (1)

On both July 19 and 20, 1952, there were repeated sightings of unknown aerial objects in the Washington, D.C., airspace, something that, on July 24, led USAF Major General John A. Samford to state in a Secret memorandum for the attention of the Deputy Chief of Staff, Operations:

We are interested in these reports in that we must always on the alert for any threat or indication of a threat to the United States. We cannot ignore these reports but the mild hysteria subsequent to publicity given this subject causes an influx of reports which since the 19th of July has almost saturated our

'Emergency' procedures.

The situation really escalated after weekend of July 26-27. A two-page USAF document, prepared only days later, related the facts:

This incident involved unidentified targets observed on the radar scopes at the Air Route Traffic Control Center and the tower, both at Washington National Airport, and the Approach Control Radar at Andrews Air Force Base. In addition, visual observations were reported to Andrews and Bolling AFB and to ARTC Center, the latter by pilots of commercial aircraft and one CAA aircraft...

Varying numbers (up to 12 simultaneously) of u/i targets on ARTC radar scope. Termed by CAA personnel as "generally solid returns", similar to a/c except slower. Mr. Bill Schreve, flying a/c NC-12 reported at 2246 EDT that he had visually spotted 5 objects giving off a light glow ranging from orange to white; his altitude at time was 2,200'. Some commercial pilots reported visuals ranging from "cigarette glow" to a "light"...

ARTC crew commented that, as compared with u/i returns picked up in early hours of 20 July 52, these returns appeared to be more haphazard in their actions, i.e. they did not follow a/c around nor did they cross scope consistently on same general heading. Some commented that the returns appeared to be from objects "capable of dropping out of the pattern at will". Also that returns had "creeping appearance". One member of crew commented that one object to which F-94 was vectored just "disappeared from Scope" shortly after F-94 started pursuing. All crew members emphatic that most u/i returns have been picked up from time to time over the past few months but never before had they appeared in such quantities over such a prolonged period and with such definition as was experienced on the nights of 19/20 and 26/27 July 1952.

Although the portions extracted from this report speak for themselves, let us now examine an official transcript of a conversation, dated July 26, between staff at Washington National Airport and personnel from Andrews Air Force Base at the time of the sightings:

Wash: Andrews Tower, do you read? Did you have an airplane in sight west-northwest or east of your airport eastbound?
Andr: No, but we just got a call from the Center. We're looking for it.
Wash: We've got a big target showing up on our scope. He's just coming in on the west edge of your airport—the northwest edge of it eastbound. He'll be passing right through the northern portion of your field on an east heading. He's about a quarter of a mile from the northwest runway—right over the edge of your runway now.
Andr: This is Andrews. Our radar tracking says he's got a big fat target out here northwest of Andrews. He says he's got two more south of the field.
Wash: Yes, well the Center has about four or five around the Andrews Range Station. The Center is working a National Airlines—the Center is working him and vectoring him around his target. He went around Andrews. He saw one of them—looks like a meteor...went by him...or something. He said he's got one about three miles off his right wing right now. There are so many targets around here it is hard to tell as they are not moving very fast.

Within a matter of hours of hearing of the events of July 26-27, FBI Director J. Edgar Hoover instructed N.W. Philcox, the FBI's Air Force liaison representative, to determine what had taken place and to ascertain the Air Force's opinions on the UFO subject as a whole. On July 29, Philcox made arrangements through the office of the Director of Air Intelligence, Major General John A. Samford, to meet with Commander Randall Boyd of the Current Intelligence Branch, Estimates Division, Air Intelligence, regarding "the present status of Air Intelligence research into the numerous reports regarding flying saucers and flying discs."

Although the Air Force was publicly playing down the possibility that UFOs were anything truly extraordinary, Philcox was advised that "at the present time the Air Force has failed to arrive at any satisfactory conclusion in its research regarding numerous reports of flying saucers and flying discs sighted throughout the United States."

Philcox was further informed that Air Intelligence had set up at Wright-Patterson Air Force Base, Ohio, the Air Technical Intelligence Center, which had been established in part for the purpose of "coordinating, correlating and making research into all reports regarding flying saucers and flying discs."

As Philcox listened very carefully to what Boyd had to say on the matter, he noted that the Air Force had placed their UFO reports into three definable categories. In the first instance there were those sightings "which are reported by citizens who claim they have seen flying saucers from the ground. These sightings vary in description, color and speeds. Very little credence is given to these sightings inasmuch as in most instances they are believed to be imaginative or some explainable object which actually crossed through the sky."

Philcox then learned that the second category of encounters proved to be of greater significance:

Sightings reported by commercial or military pilots. These sightings are considered more credible by the Air Force inasmuch as commercial or military pilots are experienced in the air and are not expected to see objects which are entirely imaginative. In each of these instances, the individual who reports the sightings is thoroughly interviewed by a representative of Air Intelligence so that a complete description of the object can be obtained.

The third category of encounters, Boyd advised Philcox, were those where, in addition to a visual sighting by a pilot, there was corroboration either from a ground-based source or by radar. Philcox wrote to Hoover: "Commander Boyd advised that this latter classification constitutes two or three per cent of the total number of sightings, but that they are the most credible reports received and are difficult to explain."

"In these instances," Philcox was told, "there is no doubt that these individuals reporting the sightings actually did see something in the sky." And to demonstrate that Boyd was well acquainted with the UFO issue on a worldwide scale, he confided in Philcox that "sightings have also recently been reported as far distant as Acapulco, Mexico, Korea and French Morocco… the sightings reported in the last classification have never been satisfactorily explained."

The commander then came out with a true bombshell, as Philcox noted in his report on the meeting: "[Boyd] advised that it is not entirely impossible that the objects may possibly be ships from another planet such as Mars."(2)

In other words, in the direct wake of the Washington, D.C., encounters of July 1952—those the Collins Elite concluded were connected to the activities of Jack Parsons that resulted in his death only weeks earlier—the idea that UFOs had extraterrestrial origins was becoming accepted, or was at least being treated as a serious possibility, by senior personnel within the U.S. military. To the concern and consternation of the Collins Elite, Duke related, the unholy deception that Parsons helped to initiate in 1947, and that he continued to embrace and encourage until his death in 1952, seemed to be working all too disturbingly well.

7

Occult Space-Brothers

When the terrifying realization hit home that Jack Parsons was actually onto something very big and incredibly ominous, one of the first things that struck those who held the distinction of becoming the first incarnation of the Collins Elite, Richard Duke explained to me, was that many of the Crowley and Parsons experiences occurred while the men were in altered states of mind. As a result, a tentative conclusion—albeit a not wholly understood or fully appreciated conclusion—was reached by Duke and his colleagues to the effect that successfully accessing the world of the UFO intelligences, and understanding both their true point of origin and their actual intent, was perhaps far more likely to be achieved by opening the mind to radically new experiences and twilight realms than by vigilantly scanning the skies via radar and fighter-planes.

Duke told me that attempts were made to determine how, and under what specific circumstances, the human mind could be taught to skillfully penetrate the veils of secrecy and stealth under which the UFO intelligences were apparently operating. If blasting flying saucers out of the sky was not going to work as a viable option, they reasoned with a fair degree of logic and common sense, then perhaps invading their space and territory remotely, perhaps even via astral-form, might provide the much-sought-after answers. Thus began a deep and lengthy study of how such actions might very well be successfully achieved.

This weird saga encompassed government agents, official secrets, and revolutionary powers of the mind, and had its ori-

George Van Tassel's famous Integratron

gins in the early 1950s with the controversial UFO contactees George Van Tassel, George Adamski, and George Hunt Williamson—all of whom, said Duke, the Collins Elite came to believe were being visited by occult entities rather than by extraterrestrials.

Let us start with Van Tassel, who asserted that his life was radically altered when, late one night in 1951, alien entities seemingly deemed him worthy of an interstellar visit. By Van Tassel's own admission, he was laying on the desert floor outside of Landers, California that night ("meditating" as he described it), when his astral form was transferred to a huge flying saucer that was orbiting the Earth. There he met with a select body of extraterrestrials who referred to themselves as the Council of Seven Lights and who warned Van Tassel of humankind's wicked and self-destructive ways. (1)

One of those people who had the near-unique opportunity

of seeing Van Tassel meditating and initiating contact with aliens via astral projection and the powers of the mind was Reverend Robert Short, who is without doubt one of the very last-surviving members of the original contactee movement that so dominated the UFO scene back in the 1950s.

One night in 1952 Short felt eerily directed to drive to California from his home in Arizona in search of Van Tassel. Today, Reverend Short believes that disembodied alien voices specifically directed him to Van Tassel's home at Giant Rock, California, so that the two of them could meet. And, in a truly memorable situation, on arriving at the Van Tassel abode, Short was invited by Mrs. Van Tassel to sit in on one of her husband's attempts to contact his purported alien friends—an offer that Short enthusiastically accepted without question. Short says that on that night both he and Van Tassel were blessed with messages from extraterrestrials—messages warning of atomic warfare and advising one and all to live in peace and harmony –all after the pair had allowed themselves to enter distinctly altered states of consciousness. And, indeed, Van Tassel was—and Short still is—very open about the fact that meditation is a vital aspect of alien communication. (2)

Meditation is essentially a mental discipline by which one achieves a state beyond the reflexive, thinking mind and in which deep states of relaxation and/or awareness dominate. It is also a vital component of countless religions, including Buddhism, Islam, Christianity, Judaism, and Hinduism. When the groundwork was completed, Reverend Short explained: "... George Van Tassel began to speak. But then something even stranger happened. Momentarily, his voice changed... became deeper, a monotone. Whoever was speaking through him now introduced himself as some space being!" (3)

This process is known as channelling—a highly altered state of awareness in which the person enters a trance-like state and plays host to a specific entity, which may be an angel, a demon, an extraterrestrial, or a dead relative who then proceeds to speak through them, very often in extremely distorted tones and while giving the listener words of wisdom, spiritual comfort, or—as the Collins Elite came to believe—nothing but vile deceit.

As a result of his alleged August 1953 encounter, Van Tassel compiled the first issue of what he titled *The Proceedings of the College of Universal Wisdom*, a small journal that served as a mouthpiece not only for Van Tassel but for his supposed cosmic friends, as well. In the first issue, one of Van Tassel's alleged alien contacts, Desca of the Fourth Density, urged his followers (whose number would very quickly reach four figures) to "remove the binding chains of limit on your minds, throw out the barriers of fear [and] dissipate the selfishness of individual desire to attain physical and material things."

In the edition of the *Proceedings* dated December 1, 1953, Van Tassel stated that, less than a month previously, orders came from Ashtar, "the Commandant of Space Station Schare," to contact the office of Air Force Intelligence at Wright-Patterson Air Force Base, Dayton, Ohio. Van Tassel then passed on Astar's message to the Air Force: "The present destructive plans formulated for offensive and defensive war are known to us in their entirety…the present trend toward destructive war will not be interfered with by us, unless the condition warrants our interference in order to secure this solar system. This is a friendly warning."(4)

Were Van Tassel's contacts really of alien origin? Were they the strange rants of a deranged mind? Or were they possibly a part of a sophisticated Communist-inspired intelligence operation designed to disrupt the internal security of the United States? This third possibility was definitely of concern to a Yucca Valley resident who on August 5, 1954, wrote to the FBI suggesting that Van Tassel be investigated to determine if he was working as a communist infiltrator.

Giant Rock, California, scene of George Van Tassel's encounters

Very concerned that Van Tassel was either a witting or an unwitting player in an ingenious, but subversive, Soviet plot, the FBI sought to ascertain the full picture. On November 13, 1954, two Special Agents of the Los Angeles FBI office met with Van Tassel at his Giant Rock home. In a memorandum to FBI Director J. Edgar Hoover dated November 16, 1954, the agents wrote:

Relative to spacemen and space craft, Van Tassel declared that a year ago last August, while sleeping out of doors with his wife in the Giant Rock area, and at about 2.00 a.m. he was awakened by a man from space. This individual spoke English and was dressed in a gray one-piece suit similar to a sweat suit in that it did not have any buttons, pockets, and noticeable seams. This person, according to Van Tassel, invited him to inspect a spacecraft or flying saucer, which had landed on Giant Rock airstrip. Van Tassel claimed the craft was bell shaped resembling a saucer. He further described the ship as approximately 35 feet in diameter and is now known as the scout type craft. Aboard this craft was located three other male individuals wearing the same type of dress and identical in every respect with earth people.

Van Tassel claims that the three individuals aboard the craft were mutes in that they could not talk. He claimed they conversed through thought transfers, and also operated the flight of the craft through thought control. He stated that the spokesman for the group claimed he could talk because he was trained by his family to speak. The spokesman stated that earthmen are using too much metal in their everyday work and are fouling up radio frequencies and thought transfers because of this over use of metal. According to Van Tassel, these individuals came from Venus and are by no means hostile nor do they intend to harm this country or inhabitants in any manner. He declared they did not carry weapons, and the spacecraft was not armed. He mentioned that a field of force was located around the spacecraft which would prohibit anything known to earth men to penetrate. Van Tassel claims this craft departed from the earth after 20 minutes and has not been taken back since.

Van Tassel added that "through thought transfers with space men," he had been able to ascertain that a third world war seemed imminent and was very likely to be "large" and "destructive;" that much of this correlated directly with certain biblical passages; that the war would not be "universal;" and that the "space people are peace loving and under no circumstances would enter or provoke a war."(5)

George Adamski told a similar story. Born in Poland in 1891, Adamski had the distinction of being the most supported, celebrated, and ridiculed of those who claimed direct contact with human-like extraterrestrials in the 1950s. The controversy largely began on November 20, 1952, when Adamski claimed that he witnessed, along with six other people, the landing of a UFO in the Californian desert and then made contact with its pilot, one Orthon of the planet Venus. FBI documentation of

1953 on Adamski's claimed encounter with the extraterrestrial Orthon states:

At a point ten and two-tenths miles from Desert Center on the road to Parker and Needles, Arizona, Adamski made contact with a space craft and had talked to a space man. Adamski stated that he, [deleted] and his wife Mary had been out in the desert and that he and the persons with him had seen the craft come down to the earth. Adamski stated that a small stairway in the bottom of the craft, which appeared to be a round disc, opened and a space man came down the steps. Adamski stated he believed there were other space men in the ship because the ship appeared translucent and could see the shadows of the space men. (6)

The alien that confronted Adamski was "over five feet in height, having long hair like a woman's and garbed in a suit similar to the space suits or web suits worn by the US Air Force men." And like George Van Tassel, Adamski related to the FBI and OSI agents that he conversed with the being thorugh sign language but felt that his mind was being "read." This story was greatly expanded upon in a 1953 book entitled *Flying Saucers Have Landed* that Adamski wrote with an Irish aristocrat named Desmond Leslie. Richard Duke told me that the Collins Elite quickly became concerned by the working relationship that existed between Adamski and Leslie, and for one very stark and eye-opening reason: Desmond Leslie had a long and rich link to the world of the occult, including Aleister Crowley himself. (7)

Leslie's father, Sir Shane, who was a second cousin to British Prime Minister Winston Churchill, was a truly colorful character who caused a sensation by converting to Roman Catholicism and the Nationalist cause. In addition, he spent part of his early years in Russia, where he became friends with Leo Tolstoy, before traveling across Europe. It was during these travels that Sir Shane became obsessed with the world of the supernatural, which led him to carefully collect stories for his *Ghost Book*, published in 1955. Sir Shane's closest friends at this time included the acclaimed paranormal novelist M.R. James and the eccentric Lord Tredegar, who dabbled in the black arts, under the influence of Aleister Crowley's teachings, at his country estate in Wales. (8)

So Desmond Leslie was, in reality, someone who had been firmly exposed to the occult and the teachings of Crowley. Just like Jack Parsons, in fact.

As for George Hunt Williamson, also known as Michael d'Obrenovic and as Brother Philip, Williamson became fascinated by the occult world as a teenager, and ultimately became a leading, albeit relatively brief, figure in the contactee movement. In early 1951, Williamson was summarily ejected from the University of Arizona on the grounds of poor scholarship. But having been deeply moved by William Dudley Pelley's 1950 book *Star Guests*, he went on to assist in the production of the organization's monthly journal, *Valor*.

At the time, Pelley had been recently released from prison after serving eight years for his wartime opposition to the government and to the policies of President Roosevelt. The leader of a fascist body called the Silver Shirts, Pelley, like Williamson, was hypnotized by occult matters and compiled massive volumes of material on contact with allegedly higher forms of intelligence. Pelley became a major influence on the life of Williamson, who ultimately combined his fascination with the occult and flying saucers by trying to contact extra-terrestrial-intelligences with the help of a home-made Ouija board and channelling. Commenting on the subject of Williamson's reported channelling of extraterrestrials, researcher Sean Devney stated: "When Williamson started to channel, it was something truly inexplicable. [He] would begin speaking in several different voices, one right after the other."

In 1954, Williamson published his own saucer-dominated volume, *The Saucers Speak*, which focused upon his well-publicized attempts to contact extraterrestrials via short-wave radio and Ouija boards. Actar of Mercury, Adu of Hatonn in Andromeda, Agfa Affa of Uranus, Ankar-22 of Jupiter, and Artok of Pluto were just some of the many purported extraterrestrials with whom Williamson claimed interaction. Then, in the latter part of the 1950s, Williamson changed his name, drafted a wholly fictitious academic and family background to accompany his latest identity, and essentially disappeared. He died in 1986, largely forgotten by the UFO research community that had briefly welcomed him into the fold in the 1950s. The Collins Elite never forgot him, however. (9)

In order to understand how and why the beliefs of the Collins Elite came to fruition, it is important to keep in mind the point that Adamski, Williamson, and Van Tassel had made claims that their presumed-alien visitors communicated with them by telepathy, ESP, and Ouija boards. And it is equally important to note that—as FBI records declassified under the terms of the Freedom of Information Act demonstrate—the trio was investigated by the FBI to determine if they had Communist leanings, or were knowingly or unknowingly spreading propaganda on behalf of the Soviet Union.

Richard Duke said that as far back as 1948, the FBI began to receive reports and stories very similar to those of Adamski, Williamson, and Van Tassel—that human-like aliens were among us, that they were communists, and that their means and modus-operandi of contact seemed to utilize the occult, as well as advanced science. Duke further stated that certain elements within the FBI came to a startling, albeit tentative, conclusion: that the claimed encounters with Communist extraterrestrials had nothing to do with visitors from other worlds but were instead the outcome of Soviet mind control and "brain-to-brain contact" projects, in which U.S. citizens were being "implanted with thoughts" by Russian "mind-soldiers" that led the contactees to think they were having real-life experiences with aliens who wanted to tell us how wonderful communism was.

Duke explained that the experiences were initially believed to be "stage-managed, psychological warfare" and were simply the effects of highly sophisticated "mind-management and manipulation" by the Russians on unwitting citizens, who may very well have believed precisely what they were saying. Moreover, Duke claimed that the FBI believed the Russians had apparently acquired "the skills to do this" from Nazi scientists captured at the end of the Second World War; they had been working to perfect the utilization of such "mind phenomena" for Adolf Hitler, who was indeed known for his deep interest in the occult.

Duke maintained that this theory came to fruition in 1952, specifically after cleared FBI agents had attended "two of seven or eight" lectures that had been held in the Pentagon that year on the utilization of ESP for psychological warfare purposes. That such lectures held in the Pentagon did occur, and that U.S. Intelligence was aware of Hitler's interest in such matters, is not in any doubt. In 1977, in a document titled "Parapsychology in Intelligence," Kenneth A. Kress, an engineer with the CIA's Office of Technical Services, wrote: "Anecdotal reports of extrasensory perception (ESP) capabilities have reached U.S. national security agencies at least since World War II, when Hitler was said to rely on astrologers and seers. Suggestions for military applications of ESP continued to be received after World War II. For example, in 1952 the Department of Defense was lectured on the possible usefulness of extrasensory perception in psychological warfare."(10)

Duke said that one of the 1952 Pentagon lectures, and at least two follow-up seminars in 1953, focused their attentions upon the claims of the contactees as they related to "receiving messages from what some people on the inside still thought probably *were* outer space-people."

It was during these lectures, said Duke, that a *new* theory began to emerge to explain the truth behind the contactee puzzle—and it was a theory that finally led to a complete discarding of the notion that the Soviets were somehow involved and the development of one that was more in-keeping with the views of the Collins Elite involving a demonic presence, and how it was all tied in with flying saucers. And, in view of this, said Duke, the Collins Elite decided that the only viable alternative available to them was to delve yet further into the murky and controversial realms of altered states and ESP and see what might potentially be uncovered, regardless of the outcome.

Richard Duke told me that from late 1952 to the middle of 1953, there were a couple of people within the Collins Elite who *still* adhered to the idea that literal extraterrestrials were among us. But as time progressed, and as yet more and more data came to the fore, the group came to a consensus that the mind-to-mind communications reported by the contactees were actually the devilishly cunning work of entities of far stranger origins than anything outer space could ever hope to send our way. These entities were highly deceptive and were telling the contactees precisely what they wanted to hear: namely, that flying saucers were extraterrestrial and benign. (11)

8

UFOs, Crowley, & Ouija

There is no doubt that there were elements within the U.S. Government focused upon the investigation of ESP, Ouija, and the paranormal in the early 1950s. Dr. Nelson Pacheco—who served in the USAF for 21 years and retired in 1987 as a lieutenant colonel—and USAF radio-intercept analyst Tommy Blann stated in their book *Unmasking the Enemy* that: "The CIA began infiltrating séances and occult gatherings during the 50s... A memo dated April 9, 1953, refers to a domestic—and therefore illegal—operation that required the planting of a very specialized observer at a séance in order to obtain a broad surveillance of all individuals attending the meetings."(1)

Similarly, Andrija Puharich, an American of Yugoslavian descent who began to investigate ESP in 1947 at a laboratory he founded at Glen Cove, Maine, stated that during August 1952 he had been contacted at his Glen Cove laboratory by a representative of the U.S. Army who wished to speak with him about his research into ESP: "A friend of mine, an army colonel, who was Chief of the Research Section of the Office of the Chief of Psychological Warfare, had dropped in to say hello. He expressed a rather normal sort of curiosity about my investigations of extrasensory perception and was quite interested in a device which we had been developing in order to increase the power of extrasensory perception. The colonel then surprised me by saying that if we found any positive results to be sure to let him know, as the Army was definitely not disinterested in this kind of work."

Puharich continued: "It was November 1952 before the

statistical analysis of the telepathy experiment was completed. The results showed that extrasensory perception was increased in the Faraday Cage device by a healthy margin over those scores obtained under ordinary room conditions. My enthusiasm led me to send the results to my colonel friend in the Army. He invited me to give a report on this work at the Pentagon. On November 24, 1952, I made such a report before a meeting of the Research Branch of the Office of the Chief of Psychological Warfare. As far as I could tell at the time my report evoked little interest in this group."(2)

According to Richard Duke, however—whose work with the Collins Elite had, on occasion, brought him into direct contact with the Army's psychological warfare division—the presumed lack of interest in Puharich's work on the part of the military was a "slight" ruse. In reality, the Collins Elite, as well as elements within the Army and the CIA who were sympathetic to the views of the group and who would soon become active members, had a deep interest in the subject and in trying to determine if the use of ESP, and even Ouija boards, could help resolve and understand the nature of the flying saucer presence. And Duke's claims are made all the more significant by the fact that in February 1954, the CIA published a 27-page document titled "A History of Ouija and Intelligence Applications" that demonstrated the agency was trying to determine if Ouija boards might be useful tools in the hall-of-mirrors world of espionage. (3)

The first undisputed use of what were once known as "talking boards" was borne out of the Modern Spiritualist Movement in the United States midway through the 19th century. Methods of divination that existed at the time utilized a variety of ways to spell out messages, including swinging a pendulum over a plate, that had letters carefully positioned around the edge, or by using a table to indicate letters drawn on the floor. Very often, a small wooden tablet supported on casters and known as a planchette was used.

Businessmen Elijah Bond and Charles Kennard had the bright idea to patent a planchette sold with a board on which the alphabet was printed. The patentees filed for patent protection on May 28, 1890, and the very first Ouija board came into being. In 1901, an employee of Kennard named William Fuld took over the production and began the marketing of his own boards under the name of Ouija—which continues to this very day, under Parker Brothers, to whom the business was sold in 1966. (4)

It may not be without significance that, just like contactee George Hunt Williamson, Aleister Crowley was a user of Ouija boards. Jane Wolfe, who lived with Crowley at his infamous Abbey of Thelema, also used the Ouija board. In fact, she credited some of her greatest spiritual communications to the specific use of the device. Crowley also discussed the effectiveness of the Ouija board with another of his students, Charles Stansfeld Jones—otherwise known as Frater Achad—who was an occultist and a ceremonial magician. In 1917, Achad experimented with the board as a means to summon angels, as opposed to elementals. (5)

The fact that both Crowley and Williamson were users of the board, said Duke, and that George Adamski's co-author on *Flying Saucers Have Landed*, Desmond Leslie, was absolutely steeped in the teachings of Crowley, led "those final few" of the Collins Elite who still had their doubts to firmly embrace the idea that the contactee movement was of an occult nature rather than of extraterrestrial origins. In this regard, it's worth noting the words of long-time researcher and author, Brad Steiger: "Very often UFO contactees are, by their admission, individuals who have become disillusioned with the existing religious institutions."(6)

9

THE MAINE EVENTS

In late 1953, Richard Duke told me, word reached the Collins Elite that the FBI had uncovered details of a group of Jack Parsons devotees who had been dabbling in matters occult in the Maine town of Yarmouth. Though there was apparently nothing illegal about such dabbling, taking into consideration the FBI's interest in cult-based activity and its potential effect on easily-influenced and impressionable minds, J. Edgar Hoover's finest did not ignore the situation—and, given the Parsons link, neither did the Collins Elite. Instead, they carefully monitored the activities of the group, which was described in the FBI files as "very much following those attributed to British Satanist Alistair [sic] Crowley."(1)

It was routine, Duke explained, for the Collins Elite to "stay on top" of whoever might be trying to follow in the footsteps of Jack Parsons. Notably, only months later, accounts of a UFO and occult nature began to surface from Eliot, Maine, which is situated approximately only an hour's drive from Yarmouth. These events led the Collins Elite to believe that someone had been attempting to prise open doors similar to those that Parsons had practically kicked down a number of years before. And, Duke added, it all revolved around a woman named Frances Swan—a housewife from Eliot who claimed, since May 27, 1954, startling contact with extraterrestrial intelligences via automatic-writing, which the website bible-knowledge.com describes as: "...a tool in the occult to make contact with real live demonic spirits." The site adds: "As with the Ouija board, automatic writing is also extremely dangerous and it will give full legal rights in the spiritual realm for demons to be able to attack you if you try to engage with it."

It transpires that Swan had been indirectly brought to the attention of the FBI—and unknowingly to her, to the Collins Elite—by retired Rear Admiral Herbert Bain Knowles, who happened to be Swan's next-door neighbour and, rather eerily and coincidentally (or not), later became a board director with NICAP, the National Investigations Committee on Aerial Phenomena, which was formed in 1956. Knowles helped Swan to pen –and personally endorse—a letter sent to Maine Senator Margaret Chase Smith. From there, the letter was forwarded to the Secretary of Defense, whose office then circulated it to the FBI, Navy, Army, Air Force, and finally the CIA, who in turn forwarded it the Collins Elite. (2)

That someone who was said to be producing automatic writing derived from alien intelligences just happened to live next door to Knowles was eventually viewed by the Collins Elite—perhaps quite understandably—as evidence that demonic forces were trying to get their claws and teeth into someone who would become a significant player in NICAP, and to deceive them into fully endorsing the alien hypothesis to explain the UFO presence on Earth. And indeed, history has demonstrated, that under the leadership of Major Donald H. Keyhoe, Marine Corps (Ret.), NICAP was practically obsessed with the "interplanetary" theory for the UFO phenomenon.

According to Swan, however, it was definitely aliens she was engaging, as the FBI noted in its files, which were shared with the Collins Elite, after FBI agents conducted an interview with Swan at her Maine home. "It was seen much better for Hoover's people to speak with her," said Richard Duke. "It kept us still way under radar; [which was] how we wanted it."

FBI records reported:

...Mrs. Swan stated that there were two spaceships from which she had been receiving messages. They were described as 150 miles wide, 200 miles in length, and 100 miles in depth...these ships are designated as M-4 and L-11 and they also contain mother ships which measure approximately 150 to 200 feet in length... there were approximately 5,000 of these mother ships..."Affa" is the Manager of the Commander of the ship M-4 which is from the planet Uranus and "Ponnar" is the Manager or the Commander of the ship L-11 which is from the planet Hatann...

These contacts with "Affa" and "Ponnar" were for the purpose of protecting our own earth from destruction caused by the explosion of the atomic bomb, hydrogen bomb, and wars of various kinds which they, "Affa" and "Ponnar", say disrupt the magnetic field of force which surrounds the earth..."Affa" and "Ponnar" are presently working the area of the Pacific Ocean repairing "fault lines" which are in danger of breaking. (3)

As is almost always the case with messages received via automatic writing, they did not live up to their initial promise. The mysterious Affa had assured Swan that he would appear in person for officials from the Office of Naval Intelligence, or would make contact by other means, on a particular date in the summer of 1954. He did not. Nor did Affa's prediction to Swan come true that: "...this earth is really going to end as stated in the Holy Bible around 1956." All attempts by ONI personnel to contact Affa via telepathy, in the company of Swan, also failed. (4)

"What we saw that as meaning," said Duke, with some significance, "was some attempt to smear the Bible with these alien forecasts that didn't happen." But the weird goings-on in Maine, and the contacts of Frances Swan, were not over.

Richard Duke told me that one of the things the Collins Elite noted immediately with respect to Frances Swan was that she

Documentation on Andrija Puharich provided by the Collins Elite

lived only approximately 130 miles from the Glen Cove, Maine home of Andrija Puharich, and roughly halfway between the two was Yarmouth, where activity that would have made both Crowley and Parsons infinitely proud and pleased was reportedly underway. In other words, it seemed that all along one particular stretch of Maine there was activity, and there were people, that had caught the attention of the Collins Elite in some fashion or another. As a result, the group continued to secretly follow the work and the proclamations of Frances Swan, as well as the research of Puharich, in the years that followed. For example, official documentation provided to me by Richard Duke reads as follows:

On 3 September 1957, Dr. M. K. Savely, Chief, Aero Medical Division, Air Force Office of Scientific Research, was interviewed in his office concerning [Puharich] and stated in substance: His only contact with [Puharich] was for about 2 days in August 1957 when he (Savely) and Mr. William J. Frye, Professor, Electrical Engineering, University of Illinois, visited [Puharich] in Glen Cove, Maine. [Puharich] directs from one to fourteen employees consisting of Peter Hurkos who was born in the Netherlands; Morey Bernstein who wrote *The Return of Bridie Murphy* [correct title: *The Search for Bridey Murphy*]; and others who act as domestic help. Dr. Savely was told by [Puharich] that the Round Table Foundation operates on contributions which average from $24 to $60,000 per year. Two of the Contributors and Backers are Representative Bolton of Ohio and Mr. W.K. Belk, department store owner from North Carolina. [Puharich] uses various electronic equipment and drugs in his experiments and appears to be dedicated to the study of the science of transmitting messages from one person to another through mental telepathy. [Puharich] graduated from Northwestern University in 1948 and served his internship at Permento Hospital somewhere in California. [Puharich] served in the Army Medical Corps in 1951-1953 at the Army Chemical Center, Edgewood, Maryland. Mr. Savely feels that [Puharich's] work is worthwhile and that [Puharich] could do some good in this field. Source knows nothing of a derogatory nature or anything concerning [Puharich's] political feelings or affiliations. (5)

And Puharich himself was able to add more data regarding apparent official interest in his activities in 1957: "On September 12, 1957, a military friend of mine phoned from Washington with rather startling news. He said that he had been talking to some colleagues about our research in Maine and two officials had expressed an interest in visiting the laboratory. He told me that one of the men, a busy general, had picked a date to come to Maine. The date was September 27, 1957."(6)

But the planned visit was canceled, according to Puharich. Richard Duke, however, maintained that the meeting *did* take place, and that the "busy general" in question was an associate of the Collins Elite. Duke says that it was merely rescheduled and "went black because of the UFO thing and the Parsons theories." No one wanted to admit—and have Congress, the media and the public know—that they were digging into controversies suggesting a link between UFOs, demonology and altered-states of mind. Notably, of Dr. Savely of the Air Force's Aero Medical Division, and who had spoken with Puharich, Duke said: "He knew of our work. Wasn't a believer, but was open to it." But the most startling development in the Maine mysteries was still to come.

According to a classified report prepared by Project Blue Book's Major Robert Friend —which Air Force consultant J. Allen Hynek showed astronomer and computer scientist Jacques Vallee—a secret meeting was held on July 9, 1959 at a CIA office in Washington under the direction of Arthur Lundahl of the CIA's National Photographic Interpretation Center. Present at the meeting was a representative of the Office of Naval Intelligence, and seven CIA officers—three of whom, Richard Duke maintained, were attached to the Collins Elite. Three days prior to the July 9 meeting, a Naval Intelligence officer, one Commander Larsen, discussed with Lundahl the failed Frances Swan/Naval Intelligence contact experiment of the summer of 1954. Larsen was encouraged to repeat the experiment, which involved him "going into a trance," Friend later told writer and filmmaker Robert Emenegger. This time it was successful: a flying saucer suddenly appeared on the scene.

According to an official report on this incident, what was seen in 1959 was an aerial craft described as being "round with the perimeter brighter than the center." But when checks were made with radar operatives in Washington, "for some unknown reason radar return from the direction in which the ship was supposedly seen had blocked out at the time of the sighting."

The report also noted that, "The Navy indicates that through these contacts Mrs. Swan has been able to answer technical questions beyond the level of her education or background."(7) The Collins Elite were not only fascinated but also rather bothered by the fact that some intelligence officials were now being influenced by the saucer people to such an extent that they, too, were being seduced into entering altered states to contact what might just as well have been demons as extraterrestrials.

10

THE MONTGOMERY AFFAIR

Richard Duke's very last task with the Collins Elite was to make careful and clandestine contact with a woman named Ruth Montgomery in January 1960; it lasted approximately three weeks. Montgomery, a self-described Christian psychic in the tradition of Jeane Dixon and Edgar Cayce, was a Dixon biographer and someone who believed her mission on Earth was to educate the public on her belief in life after death. She was the founder of the Association for Past Life Research and Therapy and claimed the many books she wrote were channeled via automatic writing received from spirit-guides. Montgomery, who died in 2001, is also credited with popularizing the walk-in theory, which states that a person's soul can depart a hurt or anguished body and be replaced with a new soul that takes over the body. Or, a possession, the demonic-believer would certainly say. And they certainly have said so. (1)

Of Montgomery's specific theories and beliefs, David Allen Lewis and Robert Shreckhise reported: "If the walk-ins are not evolved, ascended beings [as Montgomery believed them to be], who are they? They are demons disguised as 'not perfected souls.' Their purpose is to possess individuals and to prepare the human race for the paradigm shift and the revelation of the Antichrist."(2)

"You should not read too much into the fact that we contacted Montgomery," Duke told me: "Like with a lot of these people, we wanted to hear what they had to say, their views and ideas. She was stubborn and worried at first about getting the visit from me and 'getting a call from the government,' as she put it; or words like that. But, [she] was then quite into speaking when I told her we were looking into things with UFOs, souls and Parsons. She had a lot to say, and we had a bit of cordial back-and-forwards on ideas about UFOs, ESP, and the whole shebang."

Duke approached Montgomery in good faith and revealed "what I was cleared to and what was okay to [say]." He admitted, however, that: "Probably I overstepped it a bit in trying to get her help, telling her about the mind experiments, the trances in Maine, that type of affair." He certainly did. Not long afterwards, Montgomery spilled the beans of Duke's supposedly clandestine chat with an article entitled "Spying By Mind-Reading" published in the *New York Journal American,* a well-known newspaper, on June 14, 1960. (3)

This revelation led J. Edgar Hoover to ask "Is there anything to this?" in a memo sent to three of the FBI's most respected figures: Clyde Tolson, who had been the FBI's associate director; Alan Belmont, who held the position of Assistant Director of the Domestic Intelligence Division of the FBI; and Cartha DeLoach, who in 1948 became the liaison point between the FBI and the CIA. Forty-eight-hours later Belmont prepared a reply for Hoover's attention. It stated:

The *New York Journal American* on 6-14-60 carried a column by Ruth Montgomery *Spying by Mind-Reading!* in which she stated the Army Intelligence Service was conducting research experiments in mental telepathy. She speculated that the ultimate achievement would be to develop a method whereby U.S. spies could "receive" thoughts of plotters in the Kremlin. The Director asked, "Is there anything to this?" Lieutenant Colonel Lee Martin, Chief of Investigations, Assistant Chief of Staff for Intelligence, advised liaison agent [Deleted] that the Army is conducting no such project as described in the article. (4)

But did this mean that no such research had ever been

initiated by the military? Richard Duke had clearly indicated otherwise to Ruth Montgomery. And, when faced with inquiries, Lt. Col. Martin admitted to the FBI that the military's denial to the Montgomery article might actually not be entirely accurate. Hoover was told:

He [Lt. Col. Martin] did state that the U.S. Air Force had a contract in 1958 and 1959 with the Bureau of Social Science Research, Washington, D.C., which did research in the many phases of mental problems raised by the Korean War, with particular emphasis on brainwashing. This research did incidentally include mental telepathy or extra sensory perception; however, the results were inconclusive.

Our Laboratory experts advised that informed scientific opinion at the present time is that there is no basis in science for the validity of extra sensory perception as described in this article. It is true, of course, there are some areas and activities of the human mind which have not been explored or completely understood by psychologists for the purpose of explaining these little-understood functions of the mind. (5)

Belmont, having reviewed additional FBI files on "mental phenomena," added:

In 1957, one William Foos, Richmond, Virginia, claimed that he could teach blind persons to see through the use of extra sensory perception. He claimed he could teach people to read a paper which was covered or to see through a wall. Recognizing the value of such activity to our counterespionage work, we thoroughly checked the claim and had to conclude that his alleged powers had no scientific basis. Other Government agencies such as Veterans Association, Central Intelligence Agency and Assistant Chief of Staff for Intelligence also checked on Foos and were highly skeptical of his work. (6)

Despite official denials that the military was actively working on any ESP-based operations, Ruth Montgomery had not made mere vague observations about the Army, but—according to Richard Duke—had utterly "compromised the few pieces of data I told to her and, no doubt, used that to find out more from anyone else on the inside she might have been talking to. And there probably *were* a few more of them—not just me."

Stressing that "top intelligence agents" were involved in the classified operation, Montgomery added: "The Army Intelligence Service is beginning to delve into an unknown reach of the mind which—should it eventually prove successful—could make spying the least hazardous branch of defense... The project receives expert guidance within the department, but many of the officers have become so fascinated by the possibility [of ESP] that they have formed groups, outside of office hours, to try reading each other's minds."(7)

Richard Duke explained to me that Montgomery's references to "many...officers" having "formed groups" to research the subject matter of her article represented "the very first time we were almost caught by the press." He added, concisely and still uncomfortably to this day: "It didn't go down too well."

For Duke, however, Montgomery's revelations didn't really matter in the larger scheme of things. He resigned from the Collins Elite in January 1961, not because of the Montgomery fiasco, but because: "The more we went ahead, the more I got a feeling the flying disk beings were watching me. My wife got sick; then I got sick. Problems and more problems; bad luck and [bad] health for months. I knew exactly what it was. I wasn't a Parsons supporter, but I felt I'd dug into it too far, to where I'd gotten too exposed and gotten affected by them, the... well whatever they were... demons, devils. So, I explained myself to the rest of the group. They understood and I left, done, and walked out. And I got well, my wife got well. I still believe it all, what we did and came to [believe]. But I don't dabble anymore."(8)

Richard Duke was out of the picture, but there was a

new—or, at least, a newly identified—development in the UFO world that was soon to task the Collins Elite.

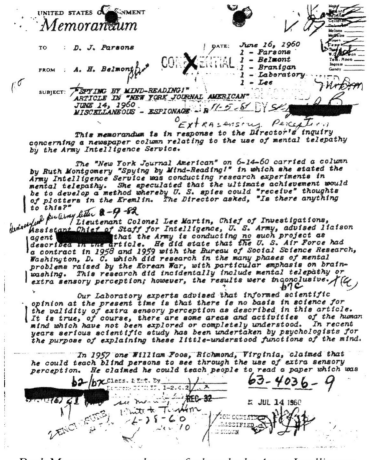

Ruth Montgomery on the use of telepathy by Army Intelligence

11

THE ARRIVAL OF THE KIDNAPPERS

Any meaningful attempt to try and accurately determine when the first so-called alien abduction of a human being took place is inevitably going to be a very difficult task. But since Richard Duke advised me, in my final conversation with him, that this is one of the primary aspects of the UFO mystery that is absolutely central to developing an understanding of the beliefs and conclusions of the Collins Elite, it is towards the heart of the abduction controversy that our journey must now head. Contrary to what many researchers and investigators within the ufological arena have either assumed, presumed, or accepted as the gospel truth—namely, that government agencies are wholly uninterested in the abduction phenomenon—the reality of the situation is very different indeed.

Most researchers and students of the UFO phenomenon would probably concede that the phenomenon that has today become popularly known as alien abduction was relatively unknown until sometime after September 19, 1961. On that night, Betty and Barney Hill, a married couple from New Hampshire, were driving home from vacationing in Canada when they were allegedly subjected to a terrifying experience. Despite viewing some form of unusual aerial object in the night sky and what appeared to be living entities that could be seen through the craft's portals, until their arrival back home, the Hill's had very little indication that there was actually far more to the encounter than they realized. It later transpired, however, that approximately two-hours of time could not be accounted for. After some months of emotional distress, sleepless nights, and strange dreams pertaining to encounters with unusual, otherworldly beings, the couple finally sought assistance from Benjamin Simon, a Boston-based psychiatrist and neurologist. Subjected to time-regression hypnosis, both Betty and Barney recalled what had taken place during that missing 120 minutes or so. Significantly, they provided very close accounts of encounters with apparent alien creatures that took the pair on board some form of alien vehicle and subjected them to a series of physical examinations—a number of which were highly distressing and intrusive in nature. The experience of the Hill's later became the subject of John Fuller's now-classic book, *The Interrupted Journey* and a 1975 movie of the same name. (1)

By far the most commonly reported creatures present during alien abduction cases are those that have become popularly known as the Grays. Typically, the Grays are short in stature, around three-to-four-feet in height; they have gray-white skin, hence the name; and their bodies are usually described as being thin to the point of near-emaciation at times. Certainly the most striking and memorable features of the Grays are their heads: they are hairless and overly large in proportion to their bodies with their ears, nose, and mouth being vestigial at best. Their eyes, on the other hand, are black, huge, almond-like in shape, and hypnotic in nature. And since that fateful 1961 night, when Betty and Barney Hill unwittingly added a whole new dimension to the UFO controversy, literally thousands of people from all across the globe have reported close encounters with the Grays and their distinctly motley ilk. And, this did not go unnoticed by the Collins Elite, Richard Duke told me.

As Duke left the Collins Elite at the dawn of the 1960s, he admitted to me that his knowledge of the group's investigations of the abduction controversy was "not as detailed as I'd like it to be." Whether or not this was true, I never found out. But, Duke did refer me to another Collins Elite member—a still serving member who went by the name of Robert Manners and whose background was as murky and clandestine as Duke's. Of course, I was not a fool, and I realized that if Duke, as a former member of the Collins Elite, had access to one of its present-day members, then he might not be as "retired" as he claimed to be.

I met with Robert Manners at a restaurant near the Johnson Space Center, Texas in June 2007, and after he grilled me for fifteen or twenty minutes about my research, my interviews with Ray Boeche, my phone-conversation with a representative of Offutt Air Force Base, and much more, Manners advised me that I would do well to "look at the Air Force's files on the Hill story: that's what got us started with the abductions."

"By 'us' you mean the Collins Elite, right?" I asked Manners.

"I do," he replied. And so that's precisely what I did.

I should note that when I met Manners, he was barely 50 years of age—maybe slightly less. In other words, he could not have played any sort of role in the Collins Elite of the 1960s. That he had so much knowledge of those long-gone years, however, suggested that someone had granted him access to the older files of the group—and probably permission to discuss them with me, too.

On the day after the Hill's encounter, Betty telephoned the 100th Bomb Wing, Strategic Air Command, at Pease Air Force Base, to report the details of her and Barney's experience—at least, those parts of the event that they could consciously recall. Of this telephone exchange, Stanton Friedman and Kathleen Marden wrote: "Barney omitted his observation of the humanoid figures that communicated with him through a double row of windows, fearing that he might be thought a 'crackpot.'

A USAF document on the Betty and Barney Hill "alien abduction" case

Later that day, Major Paul W. Henderson phoned the Hills and questioned both of them extensively. According to Betty, he seemed very interested in the wing-like structures that telescoped out from each side of the pancake shaped craft and the red lights on their tips."

Of this aspect of the affair, Betty herself wrote: "Major Henderson asked to speak with Barney, who was hesitating about talking on the phone. But, once he was on the phone, he was giving more information than I had. Later, Barney said he had done this, for Major Henderson did not seem to express any surprise or disbelief."

Betty then added something that may have a bearing on the clandestine interest shown in the case by the Collins Elite: *"Later, Major Henderson called back and asked if we would be willing to be put through to somewhere else, and have our calls monitored. We agreed to this. One call was transferred to another place and today we do not know with whom we were talking"* (emphasis mine). (2)

The following day, Major Henderson told Betty and Barney that he had spent the previous night burning the midnight-oil, while preparing an official report on the encounter of the Hill's, which reads as follows:

...on the night of 19-20 Sept between 20/0001 and 20/0100 Mr. and Mrs. Hill were travelling south on Route near Lincoln, N.H., when they observed, through the windshield of their car, a strange object in the sky. They noticed it because of its shape and the intensity of its lighting as compared to the stars in the sky. The weather and the sky were clear at the time...

They continued to observe the object from their moving car for a few minutes then stopped. After stopping the car they used binoculars at times. They report that the object was traveling north very fast. They report it changed directions rather abruptly and then headed South. Shortly thereafter it stopped and hovered in the air. There was no sound evident up to this time. Both observers used the binoculars at this point. While hovering, objects began to appear from the body of the "object" which they described as looking like wings which made a V shape when extended. The "wings" had red lights on the tips. At this point they observed it to appear to swoop down in the general direction of their auto. The object continued to descend until it appeared to be only a matter of "hundreds of feet" above their car.

At this point they decided to get out of that area, and fast. Mr. Hill was driving and Mrs. Hill watched the object by sticking her head out the window. It departed in a generally North westerly direction but Mrs. Hill was prevented from observing its full departure by her position in the car. They report that while the object was above them after it had "swooped down" they heard a series of short loud "buzzes."

They continued on their trip and when they arrived in the vicinity of Ashland, N.H., about 30 miles from Lincoln, they again heard the 'buzzing' sound of the 'object'; however, they did not see it at this time.

Mrs. Hill reported the flight pattern of the "object" to be erratic, changed directions rapidly, that during its flight it ascended and descended numerous times very rapidly. Its flight was described as jerky and not smooth.

Mr. Hill is a Civil Service employee in the Boston Post Office and doesn't possess any technical or scientific training. Neither does his wife.

During a later conversation with Mr. Hill, he volunteered the observation that he did not originally intend to report this incident but in as much as he & his wife did in fact see this occurrence he decided to report it. He says that on looking back he feels that the whole thing is incredible and he feels somewhat foolish—he just can not [sic] believe that such a thing could or did happen. He says, on the other hand, that they both saw what they reported and this fact gives it some degree of reality.

Information contained herein was collected by means of telephone conversations between the observers and the preparing individual. The reliability of the observer cannot be judged and while his apparent honesty and seriousness appears to be valid it cannot be judged at this time. (3)

In the wake of the experience of Betty and Barney Hill, said Robert Manners as we sat and ate crab-cakes, the Collins Elite began to take a very careful look at UFO cases that (A) involved a degree of "vehicle interference;" (B) were reported by women (and chiefly *young* women); and (C) that occurred late at night or in the early hours of the morning. Interestingly, the details of several such cases that had occurred within the confines of the British Isles in the early-to-mid 1960s were sent, in March 1967, to senior personnel within the U.S. Defense Intelligence Agency by the British Ministry of Defense (MoD), and were subsequently forwarded on to the Collins Elite.

The files had actually been declassified into the public domain by the MoD in the 1990s. It was not, however, until 2007 that the DIA's—and, by default, the Collins Elite's—own copies surfaced outside official circles. Declassified DIA memoranda now reveal that the MoD duly and dutifully scoured its files and was apparently happy to help its transatlantic cousin, although there is no indication that the MoD, which history has shown was hardly enamored by the UFO issue, had any real inkling of what the DIA or the Collins Elite were looking for in the reports. Moreover, there is no evidence to suggest that the DIA reciprocated—even in the slightest. The MoD forwarded the documentation to the DIA via a little-known department housed within the MoD: the Defense Intelligence Agency Liaison office. Referred to as both DIAL London and DIALL, the department was established in 1964 under the control of the DIA and functions to represent the interests of the DIA to the British Defense Intelligence Staff.

The earliest report was contained in a now-declassified British Royal Air Force Police document of 1962, written by Sergeant C.J. Perry, who outlined the facts relative to the late-night experience of a man named Ronald Wildman:

At Aylesbury on 16th February 1962, at 1530 hrs, I visited the Civil Police and requested information on an alleged "Flying Saucer" incident. I was afforded every facility by the Civil Police authorities and although no official report had been made, details of the incident were recorded in the Station Occurrence book.

The details are as follows: Mr. Wildman of Luton, a car collection driver, was travelling along the Aston Clinton road at about 0330 hrs, on 9th February 1962 when he came upon an object like a hovercraft flying approximately 30 feet above the road surface. As he approached he was travelling at 40 mph but an unknown force slowed him down to 20 mph over a distance of 400 yrd [sic], then the object suddenly flew off.

He described the object as being about 40 feet wide, oval in shape with a number of small portholes around the bottom edge. It emitted a fluorescent glow but was otherwise not illuminated.

Mr. Wildman reported the incident to a police patrol who notified the Duty Sergeant, Sergeant Schofield. A radio patrol car was dispatched to the area but no further trace of the "Flying Saucer" was seen. It was the opinion of the local police that the report by Mr. Wildman was perfectly genuine and the experience was not a figment of imagination. They saw that he was obviously shaken. I spoke to Sergeant Schofield and one of the Constables to whom the incident was reported. Both were convinced that Mr. Wildman was genuinely upset by his experience.

There ends the report, but most assuredly not the encounters, nor the official interest on the part of the MoD, the DIA—and the Collins Elite. (4)

12

LATE NIGHT LIAISONS

On the evening of August 30, 1962, the world was about to change drastically for a teenager named Anne Henson when she was plunged into a late-night UFO/bedroom encounter of the sort that the Collins Elite was beginning to focus on and understand. When I tracked her down, Henson told me about the incident: "At the time that this happened, I lived on a dairy farm and was still at school; I was sixteen at the time. I actually moved back here with my family some years ago and we run a nursery business now. It was the middle of the night and something must have woken me up because I sat up in my bed and I could see through the window what looked like a round ball of light in the sky; my room over-looked the Brendon Hills. It seemed to change color from red to green to yellow and I could see a circle with rays of light coming from it.

"At first I thought it was a star, but it wasn't static. Then I thought that it must be a helicopter or something like that, but there was absolutely no sound from it. Well, it then began moving backwards and forwards and went from left to right. I was very intrigued by it because it was making fairly rapid movements. But it was the colors of the lights that attracted me first; they were nice bright colors. It would come towards me quite quickly and appeared to increase in size, and then reversed and moved sideways at a middle speed. But it always returned to its original position just above the hills.

"Over an hour or so, the light gradually receded until it was just like a pin-prick of light. Well, I went to sleep, but the next night I wondered if it might be there again—and it was.

This happened on a few occasions and I got quite used to seeing it when it was a clear night.

"To be honest, I got quite friendly with it, really. I didn't feel threatened by it, because although it came close to our farm, it didn't come *that* close. Now, when I'd seen it a few times, I decided that I would get a compass and graph paper and try to track where it was coming from because this was intriguing me. I thought, this is a bit different."

It was what happened when Henson approached officials that really set wheels in motion: "After I saw the light for a few times and tracked the movements of it, I contacted [Royal Air Force] Chivenor. I told them what I'd seen and then I got a letter saying that my sighting was being looked at. Then this chap turned up at the house.

"It was an evening when he arrived for the first time, and he pulled up in this old black car; and when he came in the house he was wearing a black suit and tie. I would imagine that he was in his late thirties and I was most disappointed that he wasn't wearing a uniform. He announced himself as a Royal Air Force official and, of course, I took it as such. To me, he was an authority, put it like that. He actually came to visit me on several occasions. I assumed he was from RAF Chivenor; he didn't actually say so. I was a bit over-awed that somebody was actually coming to see me.

"Altogether," Henson explained, "he came on three nights. On the first night he came up to my bedroom and we sat there waiting for the clouds to clear. Unfortunately, that night and the next night he came, we couldn't see anything. So, he said that he would have to come back again. Now, on the third night, he saw it."

Did he have any opinion as to what the phenomenon was?

"No, none at all, he was just concentrating on looking at it. But he was very cagey. He wasn't very friendly, but he wasn't nasty either. But on this night he took some photos of the light.

He didn't seem very surprised by what he saw. It was all very, very low-key, which I suppose is the way to play it if it was something unusual. If he'd have got excited, I'd have got excited. He then left and he took his camera and took my compass drawings and notes—and I never got them back. But before going he said that nobody else would believe what I'd seen and there was no point in me talking about it at school. At that age, you don't want to be laughed at—and my family had laughed at me, anyway."

Henson was puzzled about her bizarre experience: "I thought originally that it was some military object, but then the Ministry of Defense said it was a planet, although that didn't explain the way it moved. Now, it all hinges on whether or not you believe in UFOs. I can't see why there shouldn't be life on other planets. And if there is, why shouldn't they come here to have a look at us?"

Anne Henson's case is a classic Man in Black encounter. It started with the sighting of a strange object and was followed by a visit from a dark-suited authority figure who warned her not to talk about what she had seen, and who confiscated her compass drawings and notes that displayed the movements of the phenomenon she had observed. But Henson's account differs in one striking aspect to many other Men in Black accounts that remain unverifiable. The official files on her experience that were forwarded onto the Collins Elite have now been officially declassified and they identify her mysterious, black-garbed visitor as an employee of the British Royal Air Force's elite Provost and Security Services—the equivalent of the United States' Air Force Office of Special Investigations (AFOSI).

That an organization of this caliber would take a keen interest in the subject of UFOs is intriguing to say the least. The Confidential report on Anne Henson's encounter that was prepared by Sergeant S.W. Scott of the P&SS's Special Investigation Section, a copy of which, according to Robert Manners, ended up in the hands of the Collins Elite, states:

MISS ANNE HENSON, aged 16, said that on 30th August, 1962 between 10.30 p.m. and 10.55 p.m. she opened the window of her room which faces N.N.E. and saw a diminishing star-like object with what appeared to be red and green colored flames coming from it. It was slightly larger than the average star and appeared to be round. After about 21/2 minutes it became very small and she could only see it with the aid of binoculars. She was quite sure that it was not the navigation lights of an aircraft because she had seen these many times and could recognize them immediately.

She did not look for it again until 17th October 1962, when she saw the object again which was partially obscured by fog. With the aid of binoculars she compared the object with several stars and noticed that the stars were silvery white whereas the object was red and green. Near to and above the object she noticed another exactly similar but smaller object. She noticed a difference in the color of the original object which was now emitting green and orange flames in the same way as before.

MRS. C. HENSON, mother of ANNE HENSON, said that she had seen the object described by her daughter. She could offer no explanation as to the identity of the object but was of the opinion that it was not a star. She declined to make a written statement.

A visit was made on 1st November, 1962 when the sky was clear and all stars visible. MISS HENSON, however, said that the object was not in view on this particular night. Observations were maintained for one hour but nothing was seen. MISS HENSON was asked to continue her observations and on the next occasion on which she saw the object or objects to compile a diagram showing its position in relation to the stars. This she agreed to do.

On 28th November, 1962, the next available opportunity, [the witnesses address] was again visited. However, although observations were maintained for 2 hours the sky remained obscured and nothing was seen. MISS HENSON was interviewed and said that she had seen the objects again on two occasions and although she had compiled a diagram she had omitted to note the date. She said that she would again watch for the objects noting times and dates and compile another diagram which she will forward by post to this Headquarters.

MISS HENSON reports unidentified aerial phenomena and provides a diagram showing their position in relation to stars. The objects have not been seen by the Investigator who cannot therefore give an opinion as to their identity. It is considered that MISS HENSON is a reasonable person, although at 16 years of age girls are inclined to be over-imaginative. However, MISS HENSON is supported by her mother, a person of about 50 years of age, who seems quite sincere. The matter should be brought to the notice of [the] Department at Air Ministry set up to investigate such phenomena.

Sergeant Scott's report was ultimately dispatched to an Air Intelligence office that concluded Anne Henson had simply misperceived a celestial body, such as a star or a planet, an explanation with which Henson vehemently disagrees. (1)

Another case that involved the three central issues that seemingly so worried the Collins Elite—the presence of a young woman, a degree of vehicle interference, and an encounter that had occurred at night—was personally investigated by Corporal R.A. Rickwood of the P&SS Special Investigation Section in 1966. In a painstakingly detailed report to his superiors, Corporal Rickwood stated:

On 10th November 1966 a telephone message was received from Flight Lieutenant Williams, RAF Shawbury, reporting that a Mrs. Foulkes of White House Cottage, Great Ness, Shrewsbury, had complained that her daughter had been frightened by an object in the sky while she had been driving along the A5 road near

Great Ness at 2355 hours on 8th November 1966. This object had emitted brilliant lights and radiation beams. On arriving home her daughter had been in a distressed condition and she had discovered marks on the car, which she considered were burn marks.

On 14th November 1966, Miss Diane Foulkes, aged 22 years, a typist employed in Shrewsbury was seen at her home in the presence of her parents. She stated that she had received a letter dated 11th November 1966 from RAF Shawbury signed by a Flight Lieutenant Penny informing her that no service aircraft had been flying in that area at the time of the incident. She was now satisfied that the incident was in no way connected with the Royal Air Force or the Armed Forces. She then went on to relate her experiences connected with this enquiry.

There had been two similar incidents. The first occurred two years ago in November 1964, when she had been driving from Shrewsbury to her home along the A5 road. This was at about 0200 hours as she neared the Montford Bridge over the River Severn. Approximately midway between Shrewsbury and Great Ness a brightly lit circular object appeared in the sky above her car. She had been frightened and had accelerated along the road. The object had kept pace with her remaining at the same height until she arrived home. She had told her mother and father who also watched the object. She described the object as an especially bright light in the sky which remained stationary due west from their home for about half an hour. It had then rapidly diminished in size and they assumed it had accelerated away from them. No sound was heard from the object. The light was yellow in color and became red as it diminished.

The second incident occurred on the 8th November 1966 at 2355 hours and again while she was returning from Shrewsbury on the same road. The object had again appeared at Montford Bridge but this time it was much lower in the sky and on the north side of the road. On this occasion she could see rays of light shooting from the object which had again appeared to keep station with her car until she arrived home.

At one time during the journey the object traveled near her and the rays seemed to come towards the right hand side of her car. She felt a bump against that side as if they had struck it. At this moment she felt as if she had received an electric shock and had felt a severe pain in her neck. The left-hand side headlight of the car also went out. This made her extremely frightened. When she got home she felt very ill and had complained to her parents. The object again remained stationary in the sky north of her home and had not been seen by her parents. They had noticed it for a short time before going inside her home. There had been no sign of the object on the following morning.

Miss Foulkes' parents confirmed seeing an object in the sky on both occasions as described by their daughter and agreed with her descriptions of these. Miss Foulkes further stated that she believed that the objects could be associated with a Mr. Griffin who lived in the area and who is reputed to have made contact with these objects and actually entered one and met one of the occupants. He is also alleged to make his contacts with them at Montford Bridge.

The local civil police had no information or reports of sightings of objects in the sky. There is no evidence to associate the incidents complained of with the Royal Air Force and the complainant Miss Foulkes is now satisfied that the incidents are unexplainable and are in no way connected with the Armed Forces.

That, in essence, is the report. The witness had reported some stunning experiences: "the rays of shooting light" that enveloped her car; the electric shock-like pain that surged through her neck as the vehicle was bathed in the beam of light; the loss of power from the car's headlights (something that is reported time and again in alien abduction-type encounters); and the potentially worrying fact that the experience had left the witness "very ill."

Perhaps the most significant factor, however, was the reference of the Provost and Security Services to a "Mr. Griffin" who had reputedly "made contact with these objects and actually entered one and met the occupants." Although additional data on the elusive and mysterious Mr. Griffin has yet to surface (if such even exists, of course), the fact is that someone, somewhere within the Collins Elite had displayed a deep interest in—and, almost certainly, gravely concern about—late-night UFO encounters involving young women and malfunctioning cars. (2) As Robert Manners conceded, by the early-to-mid 1960s, Collins Elite personnel had begun to see a pattern emerging—and, it did not appear to be a positive one, either. The dark agenda of the demonic ones was becoming ever clearer—and more widespread.

One curious matter should be mentioned before we move on. Betty and Barney Hill, who near-singlehandedly ushered in the era of alien abductions, lived—as Canadian researcher Grant Cameron correctly worded it—"just down the road" from NICAP Board Director Admiral Herbert B. Knowles and automatic-writer Francis Swan. (3) The Hill's even lunched with Knowles and his wife, Helen, in the 1960s. The Collins Elite believed Swan was specifically chosen by demonic forces who carefully anticipated she would contact Knowles about her encounters, which she believed had alien origins, thus deceiving Knowles, and eventually NICAP, about what was really afoot, namely a Trojan Horse-like demonic invasion. In a near-identical fashion, Robert Manners opined that Betty and Barney were similarly selected because of their *very* close physical proximity to Knowles, who would surely interpret their encounter in a UFO context—and that, again, would help to further sow seeds of erroneous belief in aliens within the UFO research movement and steer people away from the demonic truth of the matter.

Despite living near Swan and Knowles, the Hills never actually personally crossed paths with Swan. But about Swan, Betty Hill wrote: "A few miles from Portsmouth [New Hampshire, where the Hill's lived] is a woman who claims she is in contact with the occupants of UFOs, through automatic writing. Almost daily she sits and receives messages. Although she and I share some of the same friends, we have never met. She refuses to meet me, for she believes that Barney and I are the wrong ones—the evil ones, the ones of wrong vibrations…"(4)

I3

THE BLACK SORCERER

"During the late 1960s, the CIA experimented with mediums in an attempt to contact and possibly debrief dead CIA agents. These attempts, according to Victor Marchetti, a former high-ranking CIA official, were part of a larger effort to harness psychic powers for various intelligence-related missions that included utilizing clairvoyants to divine the intentions of the Kremlin leadership," wrote Dr. Nelson Pacheco and Tommy Blann in their book *Unmasking the Enemy*. (1)

It was also as a result of this series of CIA experiments with mediums, Robert Manners told me, that a shocking and terrifying discovery was made, a discovery that supported the beliefs and theories of the Collins Elite, and which also saw their operational abilities and scope increased. Manners pointed out that it is critical to be aware of the time frame of this new development: within the shadowy world of espionage, very strange things of a truly occult-like and demonic nature were pressing ahead during the late 1960s and early 1970s. And to understand and appreciate the precise nature of the matter, Manners said, it's necessary to delve into the world of Dr. Sidney Gottleib.

A product of New York's Bronx, Gottleib obtained a Ph.D. in chemistry from the California Institute of Technology and a Master's degree in speech therapy. Then in 1951 he was offered the position as head of the Chemical Division of the CIA's Technical Services Staff (TSS), a job that focused to a great extent on two issues: the development of lethal poisons for use in clandestine assassination operations, and understanding, harnessing, and manipulating the human brain—mind-control, in other words. It was Gottleib's work in these fields that led him to become known within the U.S. Intelligence community as the "Black Sorcerer." It proved to be a very apt title indeed.

In April 1953, Gottlieb began coordinating the work of the CIA's MKULTRA project, which was activated on the orders of the CIA Director Allen Dulles. Gottlieb routinely administered LSD, as well as a variety of other psychoactive drugs to unwitting subjects as he sought to develop "techniques that would crush the human psyche to the point that it would admit anything."

In March 1960, under the Cuban Project, a CIA plan approved by President Eisenhower and overseen by the CIA's Directorate for Plans, Richard M. Bissell, Gottlieb suggested spraying Fidel Castro's television studio with LSD and saturating Castro's shoes with thallium so that his beard would fall out. Gottlieb also hatched schemes to assassinate Castro that would have made the character "Q," from the James Bond novels and movies proud, including the use of a poisoned cigar, a poisoned wetsuit, an exploding conch shell, and a poisonous fountain pen. History has shown, of course, that all the attempts failed and Castro had just about as many lives as a cat—if not more.

But Gottlieb was not finished with assassination attempts. He also worked on a project to have Iraq's General Abdul Karim Qassim's handkerchief contaminated with botulinum, and he played a role in the CIA's attempt to assassinate Prime Minister Patrice Lumumba of the Congo. In the summer of 1960, Gottlieb himself secretly transported certain "toxic biological materials" to the CIA's field-station in the Congo. As fate would have it, however, a military coup deposed the Prime Minister before agents were able to unleash the deadly virus. (2)

Almost a decade later, Gottleib began delving into far darker areas.

Dr. Donald Ewen Cameron

In 1969, Robert Manners revealed to me, a unit of scientists attached to the CIA's Office of Research and Development dared to follow the path the TSS had taken a decade-and-a-half earlier in the field of mind control. But the scientists had other, far more controversial plans, several of which involved trying to invade, understand, and harness demonic powers as tools of espionage.

To ensure that the project stood some chance of achieving its unusual aims, Gottleib approached Richard Helms—the CIA director from 1966 to 1973—and secured a $150,000 grant for the new project, which became known as Operation Often. The curiously named study took its title from the fact that Gottleib was well known for reminding his colleagues that: "...*often* we are very close to our goals then we pull back" and "...*often* we forget that the only scientific way forward is to learn from the past."(3)

Investigative writer Gordon Thomas said: "Operation Often's roots could be traced back to the research Dr. [Donald Ewen] Cameron had approved in trying to establish links between eye coloring, soil conditions and mental illness." Thomas also noted that when he was given access to Cameron's research and notes after Cameron's death in 1967, Gottleib was struck by the fact that "Dr. Cameron could have been on the verge of a breakthrough in exploring the paranormal. Operation Often was intended to take over the unfinished work, and go beyond—to explore the world of black magic and the supernatural." And, thus, the stage was set for the next act in the U.S. Government's involvement in, and understanding of, what they perceived to be the true nature of the UFO presence on the Earth. (4)

But who exactly was Dr. Cameron? A Scottish-American psychiatrist from Scotland's Bridge of Allan who graduated from the University of Glasgow in 1924, he later moved to Albany, New York, and—like the Black Sorcerer himself, Dr. Sidney Gottleib—became involved in the controversial *MKULTRA*. After being recruited by the CIA, Cameron commuted to Montreal, Canada, every week, where he worked at the Allan Memorial Institute of the McGill University, and was paid $69,000 from 1957 to 1964 to secretly undertake experimentation on specific behalf of MKULTRA. It is not surprising, therefore, that Gottleib picked up some of the strands of Cameron's work after his death in 1967. (5)

As Operation Often progressed, the project began to immerse itself in distinctly uncharted waters, and the staff ultimately spent more time mingling with fairground fortune-tellers, palmists, clairvoyants, demonologists, and mediums than they did with fellow Agency personnel. By May 1971, the operation even had three astrologers on the payroll—each of whom were paid the tidy sum of $350 per week plus expenses—to regularly review copies of newly published magazines and newspapers in the hope that they might be "psychically alerted" to something of a defense or intelligence nature. And things got even more controversial.

In April 1972, in an effort to understand more about demonology and to ascertain if the subject held any meaningful intelligence applications, two Operation Often operatives clandestinely approached the monsignor in charge of exorcisms for New York's Catholic diocese. He quickly sent them packing, utterly refusing to get involved in the project in any manner. The relationship between Operation Often and the Collins Elite was very different, however. (6)

Two years before, on January 31, 1970, a man attached to

the Collins Elite, who Robert Manners described only as "Mr. Manza," visited the offices of Operation Often. It appears from what Manners' said, however, that the Collins Elite had heard of Operation Often's very early work in the field of espionage and the occult, and wished to determine if some sort of liaison might prove profitable and significant for both parties. (7)

The date of the meeting certainly seems to have been significant as this occurred just six weeks after the U.S. Air Force closed its publicly acknowledged UFO investigative operation, Project Blue Book, on December 17, 1969. However, UFO investigator Brad Sparks has said that the last day of Blue Book activity was actually January 30, 1970, just one day before Mr. Manza's little visit. (8)

That the Collins Elite apparently took steps to take their quest for the truth about UFOs to a new level just 24 hours after Project Blue Book finally shut down may not be entirely coincidental. Perhaps—although this is admittedly speculation on my part—those within the corridors of power viewed the closing of Blue Book as just the right time to increase the workload of UFO research bodies, like the Collins Elite, that were still overwhelmingly free of public, congressional, and media attention and scrutiny. If Blue Book had laid to rest— or, more correctly, had *tried* to lay to rest—any notion that the Air Force was hiding fantastic secrets about extraterrestrial visitations and alien encounters, then maybe it was time for the Collins Elite to become the new sheriff in town, one whose agenda was very different than Blue Book's.

As an aside, also in 1969, the U.S. Government Printing Office issued a publication compiled by the Library of Congress for the Air Force Office of Scientific Research, which was titled *UFOs and Related Subjects: An Annotated Bibliography*. In preparing the work, the senior bibliographer, Lynn E. Catoe, dug deeply into thousands of UFO articles and books. In the 400-page document, she stated: "A large part of the available

UFO literature is closely linked with mysticism and the meta-physical. It deals with subjects like mental telepathy, automatic writing and invisible entities as well as phenomena like poltergeist (ghost) manifestations and possession. Many of the UFO reports now being published in the popular press recount alleged incidents that are strikingly similar to demonic possession and psychic phenomena."(9)

No doubt, members of the Collins Elite nodded gravely at that revelation.

14

Soul Factories

The story Robert Manners related, of a group of Operation Often personnel who met on the afternoon of January 31, 1970 with Mr. Manza of the Collins Elite, is the stuff of nightmares. As the operation's personnel listened carefully and intently, Manza related that some seven months earlier, the Collins Elite had been in contact with a man named Paul Garratt, a housepainter, who had recently come to their attention after he was involved in a near-fatal and horrific car crash on a stretch of highway outside of San Francisco, California. After a fast-paced ambulance drive, his heart briefly stopped beating in the hospital to which he was taken; fortunately, he was resuscitated and ultimately made a successful and complete recovery. While in his practically deceased state, however, Garratt underwent a bizarre and frightening so-called near-death experience, which he briefly discussed in a letter to his local newspaper, after his return to full health.

It was this communication to the press, in which Garratt described seeing numerous UFOs in some hellish realm while the doctors worked frantically to kick-start his heart, that led a representative of the Collins Elite to tactfully approach Garratt—albeit under somewhat deliberately misleading circumstances. Garratt was reportedly given a cover story that the people interested in his case were actually U.S. Army psychologists, working on a project attached to the University of South Carolina, to understand and alleviate mental trauma in military personnel who had been exposed to the horrors of warfare in Vietnam, and who were specifically being plagued

Herrad von Landsberg's 12th Century rendition of Hell

by horrific dreams, as Garratt most certainly was after his experience. One of the central aspects of the project, Garratt was falsely told, focused on the study of soldiers whose dreams—just like Garratt's—involved graphic visions of Hell.

97

Perhaps feeling that a discussion might actually also alleviate some of the night-time stress that he had been experienc-
ing, Garratt agreed to spend a couple of days at the University
of South Carolina where—Manners explained—a consultant
to the Collins Elite had an office that would serve as a suitable
location for an in-depth interview and medical study of Garratt to be undertaken. It is also worth noting—and it may be of
some relevance—that personnel from Operation Often, under
the guise of a bogus outfit called the Scientific Engineering Institute, funded a course in sorcery at the very same University
of South Carolina in the early 1970s. (1)

As for near death experiences, or NDE's, as they have become known, they generally refer to a broad range of personal
experiences reported by people who have either been on the
verge of death, or who have indeed briefly passed away before
being resuscitated, and which can encompass multiple strange
sensations including detachment from the body; feelings of
levitation; extreme fear; overwhelming serenity, security, or
warmth; the experience of absolute dissolution; and the presence of a brightly-lit tunnel, which some people interpret as
a deity itself, or that others perceive as a gateway or pathway
through which a person ultimately enters into the mysterious
realm of the afterlife. (2)

Garratt also experienced this ubiquitous tunnel of bright
light, but he was suddenly and violently hauled from its com-
forting glow and enveloping warmth into a far darker and
much colder dimension. Garratt told the doctor who was consulting for the Collins Elite that he felt himself falling at high-
speed—which, with hindsight, later made him wonder if he
was actually descending into the very pits of Hell itself. But, if
his final destination *was* Hell, then it was certainly not a Hell
like that described in the pages of the Bible or traditionally
portrayed in Christian teachings.

As the doctor listened carefully and took copious notes,

and as both a microphone and a hidden-camera recorded his every word, Garratt said that he was confronted by a never-ending, utterly flat, light blue, sandy landscape that was dominated by a writhing mass of an untold number of naked human beings, screaming in what sounded like torturous agony. Above them he saw a purple sky filled with hundreds of flying saucer-like objects that pulsed and throbbed, almost as if they were living, breathing entities in their own right. The objects busily raced back and forth across the skyline in a fashion that Garratt likened to seemingly metallic soldier-ants or worker-bees performing never-ending, vitally important tasks.

Garratt never felt the calmness and tranquility that others who have experienced NDEs have reported. Quite the opposite, in fact; his mind—or his disembodied life-force, perhaps—was in utter turmoil as he watched the flying saucer-like craft suddenly slow down their movements to an eventual standstill high above the mass of people below, and then bathed each and every one of them in a green, sickly glow. What happened next was even worse, Garratt told the doctor: small balls of light seemed to fly from the bodies of the people into the green glow. These small balls were then "sucked up into the flying saucers."

At that point, an eerie and deafening silence overcame the huge mass of people, who duly rose to their feet as one and collectively stumbled and shuffled in the hundreds of thousands across the barren landscape—like in a George Romero zombie movie—towards a large black-hole that had now materialized in the distance. Suddenly, Garratt felt disorientated and the next thing he knew he was groggily coming to his senses in a hospital bed. Thanks to the work of the doctors, he firmly believed, he had been spared the wrath of the Grim Reaper and the Devil himself.

Garratt admitted to the doctor at the University of South Carolina that he was not a particularly religious man, but he *had* come to a terrifying conclusion about his experience: either it had all been a horrible and vivid nightmare provoked by his subconscious as he neared death, or he had briefly visited the gateway to Hell itself, a place where living-machines matching the descriptions of flying saucers literally harvested human souls—those countless balls of light that he saw exiting the bodies of the huge throng, which he also concluded were being utilized to fuel those piloting the craft. Then, after the reaping was over, the now soulless and zombie-like multitude took its inevitable, stumbling steps that led towards the bleak and foreboding dark hole that had appeared in the distance, and finally on to the road to Hell.

Garratt confided in the doctor—without realizing, of course, that all of the Collins Elite would eventually hear the minutiae of the conversation, too—that on his first night back at home after being released from the hospital, he awoke in the early hours of the morning to briefly see standing by the side of the bed what he described as a large-eyed "goblin." Of course, today, we might very well conclude that Garratt's goblin was one of the so-called Grays who so dominate the world of UFO research and popular-culture, too. But that was not all: four days later, the Garratt family experienced what sounded very much like poltergeist activity in their home. And, on one occasion while watching television a few weeks later, his daughter suddenly lapsed into a trance-like state and began briefly screaming in an unknown tongue, before falling into a brief, but deep, sleep.

Manners explained to me that Garratt had an interesting theory regarding all of these post-NDE experiences. He felt that while he was in his NDE state, he had "seen things" he shouldn't have and that they had followed him back. Garratt further said that, in his opinion, the entities responsible for all the activity are limited in their actions in our plane of existence unless they are invited, although he is not really sure why. As we will see later, the extent to which we allow—or, conversely, we do *not* allow—these beings into our lives has a major bearing upon their ability to interact with us, or to adversely affect, manipulate, and control us.

It is worth noting that Garratt's story sounds not unlike the scenario detailed in Cecil Michael's self-published work of 1955, the sensationally titled *Round Trip to Hell in a Flying Saucer*, about which researcher Gareth J. Medway said: "Following a sighting of a mysterious flying disc over Bakersfield, California, in August 1952, Michael wrote that two men in old-fashioned garments started materializing in his automobile repair shop. Then one day, about the end of that year, he found himself going on a trip aboard a saucer… The craft went off into space, eventually arriving at a bleak red planet with a lake of fire into which coffins were cast, the dead bodies inside them then coming to life and burning in agony. He was afraid that he would be trapped there permanently, but apparently he was saved by a vision of Christ that appeared in a beam of white light, and returned to earth. The trip seemed to have taken four days, but only four hours had passed. Here the scientific trappings are kept to the minimum, the main narrative being a familiar mystical one, the Vision of Inferno. It would be interesting to know Michael's religious background." It would, indeed. (3)

And as a further aside, one Colonel Edward Strieber, USAF, the uncle of famous abductee Whitley Strieber, told the author of *Communion* that in the late 1940s the Air Force had undertaken a secret study that concluded that the ability of the otherworldly entities to interact with us in our world depended on the extent to which we believed in them and accepted them—or not. This sounds *very* similar to the opinions of Paul Garratt as described to me by Robert Manners. (4)

When Mr. Manza was done with briefing the staff of the CIA's Operation Often on the strange story of Paul Garratt, said Manners, he—Manza—asked if the two groups might join forces and share their data. After all, even though one was focused upon alternative means of engaging in overseas espionage and the other was searching for the truth about UFOs, both had at their core of their work the domain of the occult and the supernatural. Operation Often personnel saw nothing inherently wrong with this at all, and so the two outfits agreed to a mutual sharing of material when circumstances suggested that to do so might prove to be mutually profitable. (5)

The most significant and extraordinary development in this agreement came to pass midway through 1972.

15

The Sorceress and the Spies

In April 1972, a pair of Operation Often employees secretly approached a woman named Sybil Leek—a noted witch and a prodigious author who owned a friendly pet crow with the memorable moniker of Mr. Hotfoot Jackson—in order to gain a deeper understanding of black magic, and to determine how it could be used, if at all, to penetrate the most guarded secrets of nations potentially hostile to the United States, such as Russia and China.

A sorceress, astrologer, psychic, and author of more than 60 books who came from the village of Normacot in Stoke-on-Trent, England, and who was born during the latter stages of the First World War, Leek had the distinction—if that is the correct word to use—of being dubbed "Britain's most famous witch" by the BBC.

Leek's immediate family all played integral roles in encouraging her to follow the craft of times past. Certainly, she learned much from her father about nature, about the secret lives of animals, and about the magical power of herbs. Leek also engaged at length with her father on matters of eastern philosophies. In addition, Leek's grandmother taught her astrology and did so by decorating biscuits and cakes with astrological symbols and then asking the young Sybil to put them in order and describe to her what each symbol meant.

Leek only had three years of conventional schooling; her family chose to educate her at home, but her grandmother focused on esoteric training, something that covered such matters as the psychic arts and divination. Of equal significance and interest is that Leek's family played host to some very well known figures, including H. G. Wells, who would go on long walks with the girl and her father, discussing all matter of things metaphysical and esoteric.

Another famous friend of the family was Aleister Crowley, who was a regular visitor to the family home, and who used to pass the time by reading his poetry to the young Sybil; she first met the Great Beast when she was barely nine years of age. In fact, it was Crowley himself who actively encouraged Leek to begin writing. As a result, she became a devoted poetess and published her first book, a slim volume of her own poetry, while still a teenager.

Shortly thereafter, Leek's path crossed with that of a prominent concert pianist who went on to become her music-teacher and who she married when she was just sixteen. He died two years later, however, and Leek, stricken with grief, moved into her grandmother's house to live. Later, she was sent by her grandmother to a French coven, based at Gorge du Loup (which translates as Wolf Canyon) in the hills above the city of Nice, to replace a distant relative of hers as High Priestess. Eventually Leek returned to England and stayed for a while with an acquaintance in Lyndhurst, in the New Forest, but soon found the lifestyle there tiresome and decided to run away—quite literally into the woods.

Leek quickly became friends with the Romany Gypsy folk who lived in the forest, and learned much from them about ancient folklore, and even more on the practical and magical use of herbs. She went on to live with the Gypsies for approximately one year and attended rituals with the Horsa Coven in the New Forest, of which she was High Priestess for a short time as well as a member of the Nine Covens Council.

When she was 20, Sybil returned to her family, who had now moved to the edge of the New Forest. She then opened three antique shops: one in Ringwood, one in Somerset, and one in Burley, where she moved to live. However, her open attitude about being a witch caused problems. As media interest grew, Leek found herself constantly pestered by news reporters and tourists who traveled to Burley and turned up on her doorstep, both day and night. She even had to resort to employing the use of decoys in order to leave the village to attend secret coven meetings, for fear of being pursued by news hungry, media cameramen. Although the village itself thrived on the extra tourism and visitors, some people were not at all pleased by the additional traffic and noise that resulted. As a result, Leek's landlord eventually asked her to move out. But a new development in her life was right around the corner.

In April 1964, an American publishing house asked Leek to speak in the United States about her new antiques-based book *A Shop in the High Street*. As a result, she was invited to appear on "To Tell the Truth," a television show in the U.S. Leek enthusiastically accepted the offer and flew to New York where she was duly mobbed by journalists. While there, Hans Holzer, a parapsychologist, invited her to join him as he investigated haunted houses and psychic phenomena. Following this successful pairing, Leek and Holzer went on to take part in numerous television and radio shows together.

Instead of returning to England, Leek elected to remain in the United States. She moved to Los Angeles where she met Dr. Israel Regardie, an authority on Kabbalah and ritual magic, and the two spent much time together discussing and practicing the Golden Dawn rituals of Crowley.

Strong in defense of her beliefs, Leek sometimes differed with, and even quarreled with, other witches. For example, she disapproved of nudity in rituals, which is considered to be an absolute requirement in some traditions, and was strongly against the use of drugs. Her cursing also put her at odds with many other witches. And she was one of the first of modern-day witches to take up environmental causes.

When approached by Operation Often, Leek was thrilled and happy to help. She related all she could about sorcery, black-magic, the number of witches and warlocks active in the United States, where the most active covens could be found, and much more. As to why Leek was specifically chosen by Operation Often, it may very well have had something to do with the fact that during the Second World War, she was secretly recruited by elements of the British Government to provide phony horoscopes to the astrology-obsessed Nazis. In other words, Leek had already been exposed to the clandestine operations, had seemingly proved her worth to British authorities, and thirty years later was still perceived as being a valuable and profitable asset. (1)

What has remained largely unknown until now—outside of official circles, at least—is that, according to Robert Manners, during the second or third meeting with Operation Often staff, Leek, quite out of the blue, expressed her firm opinion that the flying saucer mystery was probably somehow linked to the occult. Of course, this rang loud bells with the men from Operation Often, and the Collins Elite was duly informed. On several occasions during the summer of 1972, members of the group flew to Leek's home to meet with her and to learn whatever they could about the darkness they saw closing in all around them.

For a relatively intense-but-brief period midway through 1972, Manners claimed, Leek was consulted by the Collins Elite, who asked for her help and advice regarding how they might best utilize her skills as they sought to better understand with what it was they were dealing. Of course, admitted Manners, there were some within the Collins Elite who were overwhelmingly appalled by the idea of consulting with a woman to whom Aleister Crowley read his poetry, and who was a self-admitted, practicing witch. None of this, however, prevented the Collins Elite from pressing ahead. Sometimes, the group realized, Faustian pacts were an essential but unfortunate part of the learning process. And, as will become clear later, the forging of such pacts was only destined to continue.

Certainly the most significant development came in September 1972, said Manners, when, surrounded at her home by eager-but-apprehensive players in both Operation Often and the Collins Elite, Leek entered a trance-like state, and reportedly channeled a demonic entity that described itself as Caxuulikom—a venomous, spiteful and overwhelmingly evil and negative being whose origins could be traced back to ancient Babylon, and who outrageously mocked those present, laughed and spat in their frightened faces, and bragged in a literally hysterical and maniacal fashion about the way in which the world was being fooled into believing that aliens were among us, when, in reality, the forces of the Prince of Darkness himself were readying and steadying themselves for the final confrontation with the powers of good. Not only that, asserted Manners, but Caxuulikom informed those present that the Earth was a farm and nothing else, that energy derived from the souls of the Human Race and indeed from every living creature on the planet was being harvested as a means to feed the minions of Satan, and that the E.T. motif was merely the latest ingenious ruse under which such actions were being secretly undertaken.

Of course, some might argue—as several members of the Collins Elite certainly *did* argue, admitted Manners—that Leek, who had reportedly been briefed on the unsettling saga of Paul Garratt, was merely parroting precisely what those present wanted to hear and was duly picking up a significant paycheck in the process. Why would the purported Caxuulikom even reveal the dark truth of the satanic deception in the first place, when presumably overwhelming secrecy was absolutely paramount in ensuring that the deception ran smoothly? Leek had an answer to that question, said Manners. Insane ego had briefly and recklessly triumphed over cold logic, and Caxuulikom's absolute hatred of the Human Race had led him, her, or it, to overstep the mark and reveal a significant part of the unholy agenda.

From that moment on, the world of the Collins Elite was forever changed, Manners revealed. Whereas in the 1950s and 1960s the group certainly believed that the UFO puzzle had paranormal, supernatural, and occult origins and was overwhelmingly negative in both nature and intent, as a new decade got underway, some members of the Collins Elite were forced to take their conclusions to horrifying, new levels, namely that we, the Human Race, are cattle and that the terrible entities of the underworld masquerading as extraterrestrials are the farmers—demonic farmers, no less. And that the awful feeding frenzy that has been going on since humankind has existed is focused upon the digestion of that most significant-yet-mysterious element of our very being: the human soul.

It was no wonder that I never saw Robert Manners smile. (2)

16

DEMONS, SOULS, AND FALLEN ANGELS

In the summer of 2007, after digging further into data that Ray Boeche had given me several months earlier, and after cultivating additional sources allied with Boeche's informants, I had the opportunity to conduct a face-to-face interview with a now-retired university professor who was for a while attached to the Department of Theology at Notre Dame. "Two government people" had consulted him on some of the central themes of this book in September 1972. The initial consultation occurred at the professor's place of work, and the reasoning behind the consultation was simple, but disturbing, too.

The two men identified themselves as employees of the Department of Defense, said they were "very knowing" of his work, and represented a group who believed that the many tales of extraterrestrial visitations that had surfaced since the 1940s were actually evidence of the presence of satanic forces engaging in worldwide deceit, and who had two key goals in mind: to encourage and entice the Human Race to follow their dark ways, and to ensnare the souls of one and all for reasons that not even the Bible touched upon, but that were apparently related to the ingestion of the human life-force in some not-exactly-understood fashion.

Having been "slightly more than gently nudged not to speak on this" with colleagues, the media, friends, and family, the professor was asked if he would be willing to prepare a detailed report for the group on his knowledge of, and extensive research into, three specific issues: the nature of the human-soul, the concept and agenda of demons, and the role played by fallen-angels with respect to deception as described in the Bible. He agreed and was given a telephone number where he could always reach the pair. Six weeks later or so, his report completed, the professor placed his call, and the two men duly came back again. They thanked him for his time, and having handed over his paper, which ran to around 130 pages, he received a "very nice" payment for his efforts, courtesy of Uncle Sam. Given the clandestine nature of the experience, the professor somewhat wryly titled the document "To Whom It May Concern."

Before the two men left, they asked him if he would be willing to speak on the subject of his paper "at the Pentagon, or some such place." Nothing ultimately ever came of this offer, however, even though the professor was both quite agreeable and open to the idea of presenting a lecture on the nature of his report.

We may never be able to say for certain whether the professor's two visitors were representatives of the Collins Elite; for reasons unknown, Robert Manners declined to comment on this story—even though he conceded that "it sounds like us."

And now, onto the crux of the professor's report. The word "soul" is derived from a combination of the Old English word, *sáwol*, the Gothic *saiwala*, the German *sêula*, the Saxon *sêola*, and the Norse *sála*. Suggestions have been made that all of these words have a connection to the word "sea," which has led to speculation that the early Germanic peoples believed that souls of the dead resided in the deepest parts of the world's oceans. Notably, the Ancient Greeks used the same word for "alive" as they did for "ensouled," suggesting that the soul and the state of living are synonymous and conceptually linked. So much for the word and its origins, but how, exactly, can the soul be defined?(1)

In many teachings, the soul is classed as a definitively spiritual or everlasting part of a living entity, but one that may, or can, exist separate to the body itself, and where consciousness and personality can be found. But, not everyone is in agreement about the actual nature of the soul, its relationship to the body, or its ultimate purpose—if it even has one. Before addressing religious beliefs on such matters, let us first briefly look at the philosophical arguments that have been raised and posited on this controversial matter.

Erwin Rohde, a classic German scholar of the late 19th and early 20th centuries, wrote that the early pre-Pythagorean belief was that the soul had no life when it departed from the body, and that it simply descended into Hades with no hope at all of ever returning to a physical body. Plato, drawing upon the teachings of Socrates, concluded that the soul was the very essence of a person, an incorporeal "eternal occupant" who was central to dictating our behavior as individuals. He was also an adherent of the theory that the soul could be reborn into subsequent bodies. (2)

Aristotle, meanwhile, defined the soul as being the definitive core or essence of a living entity, but believed that the soul of a living being is defined by its activity. Even to this day, there is a wealth of debate regarding Aristotle's views on the immortality of the human soul. In his treatise *De Anima* (which translates as *On the Soul*), Aristotle made it very clear that he was an adherent of the theory that the intellective part of the soul is eternal and is separable from its physical form. In Aristotle's mind, however, it was not entirely clear to what extent the soul can be considered individual. For example, he expressed his belief that after death the soul "does not remember," a point of view and a conclusion in sync with the beliefs and teachings of the ancient Greeks. (3)

Taking the lead from the work of Aristotle, the Persian Muslim philosopher-physicians, Avicenna and Ibn al-Nafis, developed their own, sometimes conflicting, theories on how the soul can be accurately defined. Avicenna concluded that the immortality of the soul is a consequence of its nature, rather than the result of actions it wishes to fulfill or is required to fulfill. He generally supported Aristotle's theorizing that the soul originates from within the heart. (4)

Conversely, Ibn al-Nafis discarded this theory, suggested that the soul "is related to the entirety and not to one or a few organs," and finally came around to believing that the soul "is related primarily neither to the spirit nor to any organ, but rather to the entire matter whose temperament is prepared to receive that soul." He defined the soul as nothing other than "what a human indicates by saying 'I.'"(5)

St. Thomas Aquinas accepted that the soul was most definitely not corporeal. Therefore, he concluded, it had an operation separate from the body and had the ability to subsist without the body. Furthermore, he believed, that since the rational soul of human beings was subsistent and not made up of matter and form, it could not be destroyed in any natural process. (6)

But it is the Christian belief system that influenced the Collins Elite's views on the soul more than any other. The conventional, Christian viewpoint on the soul is derived from the words written in both the Old Testament and the New Testament. For its part, the Old Testament contains the following statements, which are seen as being central to the debate: "Then shall the dust return to the earth as it was: and the spirit shall return unto God who gave it (which can be found in Ecclesiastes 12:7);" and "...the Lord God formed man [of] the dust of the ground, and breathed into his nostrils the breath of life; and man became a living soul (that is detailed in Genesis 2:7)." Similarly, in the New Testament, specifically in 1 Corinthians 15:45, a statement from Paul the Apostle states: "And so it is written, the first man Adam was made a living soul; the last Adam [was made] a quickening spirit."(7)

For most Christians, the soul is seen as an ontological reality that is distinct from, yet also inextricably tied to, the physical form. Its particular characteristics are described in moral, spiritual, and philosophical terms. When people die, most Christians accept, their souls will be fairly judged by God, and a determination will be made regarding whether they spend all eternity in a blissful Heaven or in a nightmarish Hell. Throughout all branches of Christianity, there is a teaching that Jesus has a crucial role to perform in the process of salvation. But the specifics of that role, as well as the part played by individual persons or ecclesiastical rituals and relationships, are matters of wide diversity in Christian teaching, theological speculation, and popular practice.

Certainly, many Christians agree that if a person has not repented of their sins, and consistently fails to do so during the course of their life on Earth, he or she will be Hell-bound and will suffer eternal separation from God. There are also variations on this theme—one being that the souls of those who fail to repent will be totally obliterated, rather than being condemned to everlasting suffering. And some Christians completely reject the idea of an immortal soul. Citing the reference to the "resurrection of the body," they consider the soul to be the life force, but one which ends in death and that may only be restored in the resurrection. This argument was commented upon by Theologian Frederick Buechner in his 1973 book *Whistling in the Dark*: "...we go to our graves as dead as a doornail and are given our lives back again by God (i.e., resurrected) just as we were given them by God in the first place."(8)

Philosopher and theologian Augustine, who was also one of western Christianity's most influential early thinkers, described the soul as being "a special substance, endowed with reason, adapted to rule the body."(9)

And, Richard Swinburne, a Christian philosopher of religion at Oxford University, wrote that: "...it is a frequent criticism of substance dualism that dualists cannot say what souls are.... Souls are immaterial subjects of mental properties. They have sensations and thoughts, desires and beliefs, and perform intentional actions. Souls are essential parts of human beings..."(10)

As for the Catholic Church, it defines the soul as "the innermost aspect of humans; that which is of greatest value in them, that by which they are most especially in God's image: 'soul' signifies the spiritual principle in humans. The doctrine of the faith affirms that the spiritual and immortal soul is created immediately by God." At the very moment of death, the soul travels to Purgatory, Heaven, or Hell, with Purgatory being a place of atonement for sins that one goes through to pay the temporal punishment for post-baptismal sins that have not been atoned for during one's existence on Earth. (11)

Eastern Orthodox and Oriental Orthodox views are somewhat similar to those of the Roman Catholic faith, although they *do* differ in some of the specifics. Orthodox Christians, for example, believe that after death the soul is judged individually by God, and is then sent to either Abraham's Bosom (a temporary paradise) or to Hell, which they believe to be a place of specifically temporary torture. Come the day of the final judgment, however, they believe that God will assess each and every person that has ever lived, and those deemed righteous will go to Heaven, where they will experience a state of permanent paradise, while the damned will be subjected to the Lake of Fire, a condition of never-ending torture. Regardless of the differences of opinion that exist concerning what the human soul is, is not, or may be, of one thing Christianity is certain: that when we finally exit this plane of existence, the soul is at the mercy of an incredibly powerful higher-being, namely, God. (12)

But, for all their firmly held beliefs in the Christian word, the Collins Elite were unable to completely banish the nagging suspicion that religion and history did not tell the *whole* story. They could not close their minds to the notion that terrible entities from beyond—demons and fallen-angels, specifically— were playing a part in a gargantuan "mission" to "derail the train to Heaven," as one member of the Collins Elite memorably worded it in a document titled "How to Address Salvation & Fakery," which, Robert Manners told me, was circulated in the group in 1974. The role of the entities, they by now largely fully accepted—even if conventional Christian teaching did not—was to assist in the capture and utilization by even stranger, hellish beings of an admittedly poorly-defined energy extracted from human souls.

And speaking of demons and fallen-angels... within the domain of ancient near-eastern religions, as well as in the Abrahamic traditions—which includes ancient and medieval Christian demonology—a demon may be classified as an "unclean spirit," one who can possess an individual, who often requires an invitation or at least a willingness to engage it, and who generally needs an exorcism to successfully banish it from its unfortunate host. Western occultism and Renaissance magic, which flourished out of a combination of pagan Greco-Roman, Jewish, and Christian tradition, teach that a demon is considered to be a spiritual entity that may be both conjured and controlled—albeit only to a degree, and for a limited period of time. Demonic entities, or demon-like entities, play roles in a number of religions, but since the beliefs and conclusions of the Collins Elite came to be dictated and molded specifically by following a Christian perspective on such matters, it is with strict respect to biblical teachings that we must, by necessity, focus our attention. (13)

At various times throughout Christian history, attempts have been made to classify these particularly hostile beings according to a number of proposed demonic hierarchies. In contemporary Christianity, demons are generally considered to be angels who fell from grace by rebelling against God. This, however, is not consistent with historical Christianity or Judaism, which teaches that demons, or evil spirits, are the result of sexual relationships between fallen angels and human women. When these hybrids—the Nephilim, as they became known— died, they left behind disembodied spirits who "roam the earth in search of rest," as the Book of Luke describes it. (14)

The story of the Nephilim is chronicled more fully in the Book of Enoch, which connects the origin of the Nephilim with fallen angels: "And it came to pass when the children of men had multiplied that in those days were born unto them beautiful and comely daughters. And the angels, the children of the heaven, saw and lusted after them, and said to one another: 'Come, let us choose us wives from among the children of men and beget us children.' And Semjaza, who was their leader, said unto them: 'I fear ye will not indeed agree to do this deed, and I alone shall have to pay the penalty of a great sin.' And they all answered him and said: 'Let us all swear an oath, and all bind ourselves by mutual imprecations not to abandon this plan but to do this thing.' Then sware they all together and bound themselves by mutual imprecations upon it. And they were in all two hundred; who descended in the days of Jared on the summit of Mount Hermon, and they called it Mount Hermon, because they had sworn and bound themselves by mutual imprecations upon it..." (15)

Genesis, Chapter 6 verses 1 through 4, also mentions the Nephilim: "Now it came about, when men began to multiply on the face of the land, and daughters were born to them, that the sons of God saw that the daughters of men were beautiful; and they took wives for themselves, whomever they chose. Then the Lord said, 'My Spirit shall not strive with man forever, for he is indeed flesh; nevertheless his days shall be one hundred and twenty years.' The Nephilim were on the earth in those days, and also afterward, when the sons of God came in to the daughters of men, and they bore children to them. Those were the mighty men who were of old, men of renown."(16)

According to these texts, the fallen angels who begat the Nephilim were cast into Tartarus/Gehenna, a place of "total darkness." However, the Book of Jubilees states that God granted ten percent of the disembodied spirits of the Nephilim permission to remain after the great flood, in the form of demons, to try and lead the Human Race astray, up until the final judgment. The Book of Jubilees also states that ridding the Earth of the Nephilim was one of God's purposes behind the flooding of the Earth in Noah's time. The biblical reference to Noah being "perfect in his generations" may, some biblical students believe, have referred to his having a clean, Nephilim-free bloodline. (17)

In the Gospel of Mark, Jesus is described as casting out numerous demonic entities from people affected by a whole variety of ailments. Moreover, the power of Jesus is shown to be far superior to that of the demons over the beings that they inhabit. For example, the Bible says that in addition to casting out demons, Jesus can forbid them from returning to plague their victims. On the other hand, in the Book of Acts, a group of Judaistic exorcists known as the Sons of Sceva attempt to cast out a very powerful demon without believing in the words and teachings of Jesus, and ultimately they fail with utterly disastrous results. (18)

In terms of their supernatural abilities, demons are said to exhibit such powers as psychokinesis, levitation, divination, possession, seduction, ESP, and telepathy. In addition, they are said to have the ability to bind and make contracts, control the elements, and manipulate the animal kingdom. Moreover, they regularly use variants and combinations of these powers to harass, demoralize, confuse, make sick, and disorient the targets of their assaults, or the person who has chosen to become a willing subject of the demon. Christianity teaches its followers that all of these attacks, as well as their effect or scope, can be nullified by God. (19)

Many theologians agree that demons acted first as succubae to collect sperm from men and then as incubi to deposit the sperm into a woman, with the intention of creating some form of progeny on Earth; this comes into play with the story of the Nephilim. Many theologians also agree that the demon is an icy and cold entity, meaning that sperm taken from a man and rendered near-frozen may lack generative qualities. St. Thomas Aquinas, an Italian priest of the Roman Catholic Church, and St. Albertus Magnus, a Dominican friar and bishop of the Middle Ages who achieved fame for his comprehensive knowledge of, and advocacy for, the peaceful co-existence of science and religion, wrote that demons *do* act in this particular way but *can* successfully impregnate women. (20)

Peter Paludanus, a French theologian and archbishop, and Martin of Arles, a Spanish doctor of theology who died in 1521, went a step further and supported the idea that demons can take sperm from dead men and impregnate women, while other demonologists concluded that demons have the ability to extract semen from the dying, and that the recently-deceased should be buried as soon as possible to avoid violation of their corpses. (21)

As the Collins Elite came to learn, while digging further into the controversy surrounding "alien abductions" that was largely still simmering in the background in 1972 but would reach absolute boiling point in the years and decades that followed, the abilities exhibited by our purported extraterrestrial visitors are eerily similar to those that demons are said to confidently command, including levitation, ESP, and psychokinesis. And, of course, tales of demons taking human sperm and eggs as part of a truly sinister and unholy program centuries ago, are nearly identical to 20th and 21st century stories of purported alien interaction with the Human Race.

Moving still further into the domain of fallen-angels, for the majority of Christian denominations, a fallen angel is one who has been exiled or banished from Heaven by God. Very often the act of banishment is a punishment for disobeying or rebelling against the word of God. Without a doubt, the most widely recognized and infamous fallen angel of all is Lucifer, a name frequently given to Satan within Christian circles. The specific use of this term stems from Isaiah 14:3-20, which tells of an individual who is given the name of "Day Star" or "Morning Star" (or, in Latin, "Lucifer"), and means "fallen from heaven." (22)

The Morning Star is, of course, the planet Venus—the place, many of the contactees of the 1950s were repeatedly assured, their cosmic visitors originated. Cunningly saying they arrived from the Morning Star is practically akin to saying they came from Lucifer. The fallen angels, it seems, are not without a darkly warped sense of humor when it comes to spreading their particularly unique and vicious brand of deceit. (23)

According to the Catechism of the Catholic Church, angels were all created as goodly beings, yet some turned their backs on the positive road and subsequently chose to tread a far darker path. Moreover, fallen angels aren't required to have faith at all; as angels, they already have knowledge of all-things celestial. Thus, their rebellion against God constituted an unforgivable sin, rather than an actual denial on their part of his existence or his powers. The Book of Revelation, which opens with the words "The revelation of Jesus Christ, which God gave him to show to his servants what must soon take place," tells of a war in Heaven and of how a percentage of the angels fell from grace. It must be noted that the Book of Revelation is seen by many to consist principally of eschatological visions, future events, and biblical prophecies they believe are destined to come true. (24)

It continues: "Now war arose in heaven, Michael and his

angels fighting against the dragon. And the dragon and his angels fought back, but he was defeated, and there was no longer any place for them in heaven. And the great dragon was thrown down, that ancient serpent, who is called the Devil and Satan, the deceiver of the whole world—he was thrown down to the earth, and his angels were thrown down with him."(25)

This image, of a war in Heaven at the end of time, became added to the story of the fall of Satan at the beginning of time, and included not only Satan himself but other angels as well, hence the term "the dragon and his angels." The number of angels involved was said to be a third of the total number, a figure deduced by the fact that *Revelation 12:4* tells of the dragon's tail casting a third of the stars of heaven down to the earth before war erupts. (26)

Leonard R.N. Ashley, a professor of English at Brooklyn College of the City University of New York, and the author of many books, including *The Complete Book of Magic and Witchcraft*, says that in 1273, Pope John XXI, then Bishop of Tusculum, estimated that the total number of angels who sided with Lucifer's revolt against God numbered 133,306,668, which would suggest that they were fighting against a force of 266,613,336 angels who elected to remain loyal to God. (27) The sheer, overwhelming number of entities that *might* be working to subvert the people of Earth, via manipulation of the alien motif, provoked utter consternation within the ranks of the Collins Elite, admitted Robert Manners, and even though he claimed not to be familiar with these figures from the Notre Dame professor, he spurred them on yet further to find a way to defeat the forces of evil, once and for all.

As 1972 turned to 1973, we see the shadowy presence of the Collins Elite skillfully maneuvering and weaving within the unsettling world of the demonic UFO.

17

"I DREAMED THAT I WAS DEAD IN BED"

One of the most notable UFO encounters ever recorded occurred shortly after 11p.m. on October 18, 1973. That the prime witnesses were serving members of the U.S. Army Reserve only added to the credibility of the report. Having departed from Port Columbus, Ohio, their UH-1H helicopter was headed for its home base at Cleveland Hopkins Airport. Aboard were Captain Lawrence J. Coyne; Sergeant John Healey, the flight-medic; First Lieutenant Arrigo Jezzi, a chemical engineer; and a computer technician, Sergeant Robert Yanacsek. All seemed normal as the crew climbed into the air and kept the helicopter at a steady 2,500 feet altitude.

But approximately ten miles from Mansfield, they noticed a "single red light" to the west that was moving slowly in a southerly direction. Initially they thought the object might be an F-100 aircraft operating out of Mansfield. Nevertheless, Coyne advised Yanacsek to "keep an eye on it." These were wise words, as suddenly the unidentified light changed its course and began to head directly for them. Captain Coyne immediately swung into action, putting the helicopter into an emergency descent, dropping 500 feet per minute. Equally alarming was the fact that radio contact with Mansfield Tower could no longer be established, and both UHF and VHF frequencies were utterly dead, too.

When it seemed that a fatal collision was all but imminent, the red light came to a halt, hovering menacingly in front of the helicopter and its startled crew. At that close proximity to the object, Captain Coyne and his team were able to deter-

DISPOSITION FORM

For use of this form, see AR 340-15; the proponent agency is The Adjutant General's Office.

RENCE OR OFFICE SYMBOL	SUBJECT
	Near Midair Collision with UFO Report

	FROM Flight Operations Off	DATE 23 Nov 73	CMT 1
Commander	USAR Flight Facility		
83D USARCOM	Cleveland Hopkins Airport		
ATTN: AHRCCG	Cleveland, Ohio 44135		
Columbus Support Facility			
Columbus, Ohio 43215			

1. On 18 October 1973 at 2305 hours in the vicinity of Mansfield, Ohio, Army Helicopter 68-15444 assigned to Cleveland USARFFAC encountered a near midair collision with a unidentified flying object. Four crewmembers assigned to the Cleveland USARFFAC for flying proficiency were on AFTP status when this incident occurred. The flight crew assigned was CPT Lawrence J. Coyne, Pilot in Command, 1LT Arrigo Jezzi, Copilot, SSG Robert Yanacsek, Crew Chief, SSG John Healey, Flight Medic. All the above personnel are members of the 316th MED DET(HEL AMB), a tenant reserve unit of the Cleveland USARFFAC.

2. The reported incident happened as follows: Army Helicopter 68-15444 was returning from Columbus, Ohio to Cleveland, Ohio and at 2305 hours east, south east of Mansfield Airport in the vicinity of Mansfield, Ohio while flying at an altitude of 2500 feet and on a heading of 030 degrees, SSG Yanacsek observed a red light on the east horizon, 90 degrees to the flight path of the helicopter. Approximately 30 seconds later, SSG Yanacsek indicated the object was converging on the helicopter at the same altitude at a airspeed in excess of 600 knots and on a midair collision heading. Cpt Coyne observed the converging object, took over the controls of the aircraft and initiated a power descent from 2500 feet to 1700 feet to avoid impact with the object. A radio call was initiated to Mansfield Tower who acknowledged the helicopter and was asked by CPT Coyne if there were any high performance aircraft flying in the vicinity of Mansfield Airport however there was no response received from the tower. The crew expected impact from the object instead, the object was observed to hesitate momentarily over the helicopter and then slowly continued on a westerly course accelerating at a high rate of speed, clear west of Mansfield Airport then turn 45 degree heading to the Northwest. Cpt Coyne indicated the altimeter read a 1000 fpm climb and read 3500 feet with the collective in the full down position. The aircraft was returned to 2500 feet by CPT Coyne and flown back to Cleveland, Ohio. The flight plan was closed and the FAA Flight Service Station notified of the incident. The FSS told CPT Coyne to report the incident to the FAA GADO office a Cleveland Hopkins Airport MR. Porter, 83d USARCOM was notified of the incident at 1530 hours on 19 Oct 73.

3. This report has been read and attested to by the crewmembers of the aircraft with signatures acknowledgeing this report.

[signatures]

FORM 2496 — REPLACES DD FORM 96, EXISTING SUPPLIES OF WHICH WILL BE ISSUED AND USED UNTIL 1 FEB 63 UNLESS SOONER EXHAUSTED. U.S. GPO: 1973-473-893 P.O. 1

An official report on the UFO-helicopter encounter of 1973

mine that this was no mere light in the sky. Coyne, Healey, and Yanacsek agreed that the object before them was a large, gray-colored, cigar-shaped vehicle, which they described as being somewhat "domed," and with "a suggestion of windows."

They could now see that the red light was coming from the bow section of the object.

Then without warning, a green "pyramid shaped" shaft of light emanated from the object, passed over the nose of the helicopter, swung up through the windshield, and entered the tinted, upper window panels. Suddenly the interior of the helicopter was bathed in an eerie green light. A handful of seconds later the object shot off toward Lake Erie. But the danger was still not over. To the crew's concern, the altimeter showed an altitude of 3,500 feet and a climbing ascent of 1,000 feet per minute, even though the stick was still geared for descent. The helicopter reached a height of 3,800 feet before Captain Coyne was able to safely and finally regain control of the helicopter. Shortly thereafter, all radio frequencies returned to normal and Coyne proceeded on to Cleveland Hopkins Airport without further problems.

Columbus, Ohio-based UFO investigators William E. Jones and Warren Nicholson succeeded in locating a group of five people who saw the strange object near the Charles Mill Reservoir, as they were driving south from Mansfield to their rural home at the time of the helicopter's encounter. They described it, variously, as being "like a blimp." "as big as a school bus," and "sort of pear-shaped." They also caught sight of the green light that had enveloped the UH-1H: "It was like rays coming down. The helicopter, the trees, the road, the car—everything turned green."

While the UFO skeptic Philip J. Klass opined at the time that the crew had been spooked by nothing more mysterious than a "fireball of the Orinoid meteor shower," this was never proved, and an in-depth study undertaken by investigator Jennie Zeidman for the Center for UFO Studies summarily ruled out any conventional aircraft as being responsible. Zeidman concisely and accurately concluded: "The case has maintained its high 'strangeness-credibility' rating after extended investigation and analysis."

On several occasions in the immediate aftermath of their encounter, Captain Coyne received telephone calls from people identifying themselves as representatives of the Department of the Army, Surgeon General's Office, asking if he, Coyne, had experienced any "unusual dreams" subsequent to the UFO incident. As it happened, not long before the Army's call, Coyne had undergone a very vivid out-of-body-experience.

Sgt. John Healey also reported being called about the incident and its aftermath. "As time would go by," said Healey, "the Pentagon would call us up and ask us: 'Well, has this incident happened to you since the occurrence?' And in two of the instances that I recall, what they questioned me, was, number one: have I ever dreamed of body separation? And I have. I dreamed that I was dead in bed and that my spirit or whatever, was floating, looking down at me lying dead in bed. And the other thing was had I ever dreamed of anything spherical in shape; which definitely had not occurred to me."(1)

That the Army's Surgeon General's Office was interested in both out-of-body experiences and the nature of death and the after-life in the early-to-mid 1970s is not in doubt. For example, a September 1975 document titled "Soviet and Czechoslovakian Parapsychology Research" that had been prepared for the Defense Intelligence Agency by the SGO's Medical Intelligence and Information Agency contains a section titled Out-of-the-body Phenomena that focuses on the research of Sheila Ostrander and Lynn Schroeder who "reported that the Soviets were studying out-of-the-body phenomena in Yogis."(2)

Ostrander, a Canadian, and Schroeder, an American, were the authors of the classic 1971 book, *Psychic Discoveries behind the Iron Curtain*. In June 1968, the pair was invited to attend an international conference on ESP in Moscow. The invite had come from Edward Naumov, a leading figure at the time in

Soviet psi research. With the late 1960s seeing the emergence of a more relaxed atmosphere of discussion in such controversial areas of research in the Soviet Union, Ostrander and Schroeder began contacting Soviet scientists and researchers in an effort to understand the scale of investigations being undertaken behind the Iron Curtain. This ultimately led to the publication of their book. (3)

Interestingly, an Army document entitled "Soviet and Czechoslovakian Parapsychology Research" also displays interest in the issue of unusual, and somewhat unsettling, occurrences reported at the moment of death within the animal kingdom. Referring to the work of Russian scientist Pavel Naumov, the document states:

Naumov conducted animal bio-communication studies between a submerged Soviet Navy submarine and a shore research station: these tests involved a mother rabbit and her newborn litter and occurred around 1956. According to Naumov, Soviet scientists placed the baby rabbits aboard the submarine. They kept the mother rabbit in a laboratory on shore where they implanted electrodes in her brain. When the submarine was submerged, assistants killed the rabbits one by one. At each precise moment of death, the mother rabbit's brain produced detectable and recordable reactions. As late as 1970 the precise protocol and results of this test described by Naumov were believed to be classified. (4)

I was informed by Robert Manners in 2008 that a document titled "The UFO Arrival Problem, Out-of-the-Body Experiences & the Soviet Parapsychology Phenomenon," written in 1972 by a former, senior employee of the U.S. Army's Surgeon General's Office who later became an unpaid and unofficial consultant on medical matters to the Collins Elite, focuses heavily on the work of Ostrander and Schroeder, alien abductions, and Judgment Day. Manners also advised me that this document had a profound effect on the thoughts and beliefs of certain Collins Elite members in the mid-to-late 1970s when reports of alien abduction began to increase across the United States.

Written in the man's free time and shared with interested, like-minded colleagues in the Collins Elite, the Army, and the Defense Intelligence Agency, the original edition of the document is now housed in a private library in Austin, Texas, according to Manners. But my repeated attempts to secure copies of this document from the DIA, the Army, and the Austin-based individual who stubbornly holds onto the original have regrettably proved to be unsuccessful at this time. (5)

But the Army was not alone in assisting—or being influenced by—the beliefs of the Collins Elite.

18

OUT-OF-BODY ABDUCTIONS

Intriguing witness testimony demonstrates that just as the U.S. Army's Surgeon General's Office was secretly investigating the connection between UFOs, out-of-body-experiences, and the afterlife—and sharing its findings with the Collins Elite—elements of the U.S. Air Force were clandestinely doing precisely the same. According to Robert Manners, seven members of the Collins Elite held positions of some significance with the Air Force's Office of Special Investigations in the early-to-mid 1970s. One wonders if they could have been involved in the following story.

I encountered Tammy Stone *prior* to speaking with Ray Boeche, Robert Manners, and Richard Duke. But it was only *after* speaking with this trio that I realized Stone's story had a major bearing on the nature and existence of the Collins Elite, as her claims seemed to be vindicated, at least in part, by Deep Throats in the Collins Elite.

Stone claimed that, at the age of 24, in early March 1973, she underwent an alien abduction experience while living near Waco, Texas. More significantly, Stone was later plunged into a strange and surreal world involving government agents and their surveillance of both her and her immediate family. More than 30 years after these traumatic events, Stone is relatively comfortable about discussing her truly out-of-this-world encounter. She has learned to come to terms with the events in question—despite their admittedly disturbing and graphic nature.

The story begins as Stone completed her late-night shift as

DST-1810S-387-75
September 1975

PART IV

OUT-OF-THE-BODY PHENOMENA

SECTION 1 - REMOTE VIEWING

Remote viewing refers to the ability of some individuals to project themselves mentally to remote or inaccessible locations and observe and report on details of terrain, structures, and other salient features. This ability is also referred to as astral or mental projection. It differs from telepathy in that the percipient does not piece together information bits to form an image, but rather, has a vivid sense of leaving his body and personally observing the target area in toto.

Remote viewing has been investigated in the US at Stanford Research Institute (SRI), Menlo Park, California. Psychically gifted subjects were tested for the ability by presenting them with map coordinates randomly selected on a double blind basis. The subjects were required to respond immediately with a description of the target area and were tested both with and without feedback as to their accuracy. According to the SRI report on this study, there were at least some categories of information in which the results exceeded any possible statistical bounds of coincidental correlation and precluded acquisition of data by known means.

(C) SRI reports of remote viewing research have not been publicized, but other SRI research on the psychic abilities of an Israeli (Uri Geller) and a British (Ingo Swann) subject has been widely cited in the US news media. Geller has been quoted many times on his avowed ability to transport himself mentally to any place of his choosing. Soviet parapsychologists are aware of Geller's claims (he has, in fact, been invited to the Soviet Union for tests) and continuing US interest in this phenomenon, nevertheless they have reported very little similar research of their own.

53

Part of a 1975 Defense Intelligence Agency file on out-of-body experiences

a waitress in a diner situated approximately 30 miles outside of Waco. It was at around 2:00 a.m. and she was driving towards the lights of the city and back to her small apartment. Within 15 minutes, while on a lonely stretch of road, Stone began to "feel strange; like I had been drugged or was in a dream." She added: "My ears hurt and everything I could hear, like the car's engine, all sounded muffled."

Stone's light-headedness and dizziness quickly turned into a violent form of vertigo, accompanied by a spell of acute nausea. Despite feeling seriously ill, Stone continued on her way home. Alas, fate had very different plans in store for her. Quite out of the blue, a bright glow enveloped the car, its headlights and engines completely failed, and sharp and intense pains surged through Stone's body. Fighting the nausea and vertigo that was now threatening to completely overwhelm her, she brought her vehicle to a screeching halt on the shoulder of the road.

To her right in a cow-pasture, Stone saw a "pale-pink dome; a small object" a couple of hundred feet away. She watched, terrified, as two small, humanoid creatures exited the object and proceeded to head directly for her. Although groggy and fighting a near-overwhelming urge to vomit, she attempted to open the door and make a run for it. To her horror, however, as the beings came closer (in a "jerky-walking" fashion), she began to feel even more drowsy and disoriented; her arms and legs became weak and, ultimately, completely unresponsive. The next thing she recalled, it was dawn, the sun was beginning to rise and she was sitting in the front passenger seat of her car.

Feeling both scared and confused, Stone jumped into the driver's seat and quickly headed back to her apartment, where she took a long, cleansing (both mentally and physically) bath and subsequently fell into a deep sleep. She didn't wake up until after 9:00 p.m. Stone elected not to tell anyone of the high-strangeness that had occurred, and, in any case, aside from having a fragmentary recollection of seeing the strange object in the field and the two figures that approached her, she had no real recollection of much of substance anyway. Over the next several nights, however, she experienced a series of vivid and disturbing dreams that appeared to fill in at least *some* of the missing pieces of that strange encounter.

"The dreams never changed at all," Stone said. She always saw the figures heading for her vehicle. As they got ever closer, she could see that both were around five feet in height and possessed "thin faces and cheeks." Both were attired in light blue, one-piece "uniforms" and wore tight-fitting caps on their heads. In the dreams, she could only sit in the car—overwhelmed, she concluded, by a mixture of awe and fear—as one of the figures opened the driver's door. As the two entities then dragged her out of the vehicle, several more appeared and they proceeded to carry her by the ankles and wrists to the craft. Stone's next memory was of being completely stripped of her clothing and laid out on a cold hard table with five or six "similar people or things" all standing around her.

Stone recalled that some sort of cold, metallic device, "like a lead-colored tube," was inserted into her vagina. Although there was no direct pain associated with the procedure, there *was* a feeling of discomfort and burning, which lasted until the device was removed several minutes later. A similar, smaller device was then placed in her right nostril and again removed after a few minutes. Again, there was a feeling of heat. As all of this distressing activity was occurring, says Stone, "a small machine hovered over me like a big eye, and made a humming noise that made me feel *very* sick."

Her next memory was of being dressed, then carried back to the car and placed in the passenger seat. Strangely, she also had a vague recollection of seeing a man in a military uniform who was sitting in the driver's seat and looking at her with an intense-yet-scared look on his face. "The military," she said, "always have that tough image, you know? Like in all those recruitment commercials on TV; they don't smile. But I have never seen a soldier look so scared—like he was gripping the wheel, and having a panic-attack and couldn't breathe." At that point, the dream always ended.

But the strange events in Tammy Stone's life were not over. Over the next three to four weeks, she was plagued by apocalyptical dreams and nightmares. They graphically depicted a near future Earth that had been reduced to ruins from a combination of localized atomic exchanges, pollution, over-population and subsequent starvation, and the ravages of a disturbing, manufactured lethal virus that had laid waste much of the Middle East and was now spiraling out of control and spreading at an alarming rate across the rest of the planet. Judgment Day, Armageddon, the end of all things, and a disturbing afterlife in which "several types" of Gray-like entities fed—vampire-style—on human souls dominated Stone's every sleeping moment. Said Stone: "Several times I was *in* the dreams, like I was flying over the planet watching it all; but not in my body."

Weeks later, she received a knock at the door of her apartment at midday. When she opened the door a man dressed in a brown suit stood before her. "He could have passed for a marine," she said, "a built, big guy; very short hair." The man claimed he was doing a "survey" for the local police department on car crime in the area, and flashed what appeared to be a police identity card at her that, Stone explained, "looked real, but back then I was real quiet and I should have asked to see it again, close up, but didn't."

She felt uncomfortable with the situation and declined to let him in, preferring instead to just keep the door open a few inches, with her on one side and the man on the other. He fired off a whole barrage of questions. "Have you been the victim of car crime in the last month?" "How long have you owned your car?" "Are you concerned about being kidnapped from your car?" This last question completely unnerved an already-anxious Stone and she slammed the door shut in the man's face.

"I'm calling the police," she said. She assumed the man made a hasty exit from the apartment complex. But strange visitors were to become a common sight at Stone's home. On three occasions during the next month, two other people called on her. "They were military men," she revealed, "but not in their uniforms. They were real friendly with me and identified who they were and where they were from: the Kirtland Air Force [Base, which is situated in New Mexico]."

According to Stone, one of the men admitted that her previous visitor had been "with us" but that he had "gone way over the top." The pair deeply apologized for his actions, an apology that Stone accepted. And, then there came a true bombshell: the men knew intimate details of Stone's abduction experience and inquired if they could discuss it with her. She agreed.

"They were real friendly and okay with me, and made me feel real fine about talking with them," she said. The Air Force visitors told her things that were both startling and disturbing. Over the course of the previous two decades, she was quietly informed, sporadic reports had reached officials that suggested human beings across the entire planet had been "kidnapped" by otherworldly entities for purposes suspected, but never entirely proved. They added, however, that in 1971 such kidnappings had begun to increase at truly alarming rates, and particularly so in Texas, Arizona, New Mexico, Colorado, and Nevada. Stone noted that "They never mentioned the word abductions like you hear today—just kidnappings."

The men stressed that if she cooperated in answering their questions, she would be helping to resolve an issue that was of profound national security concern to the U.S. military and government. "I said yes," she told me. "What else should I have done?" With her consent obtained, the pair reeled off a number of truly strange questions. Since the kidnapping had she felt the urge to become vegetarian? Was she, before or since the apparent UFO encounter, an adherent of Buddhist teachings? Did she, prior to her experience, believe in life after death, and had her views on the subject changed since the encounter on that lonely stretch of road? And most disturbing of all: was she of the opinion that after death we would all be judged by a higher power?

Stone told the two Air Force men about her nightmares. They expressed deep concern and confided in her that a number of other kidnapped citizens had been discreetly approached "by the project" and had told *very* similar apocalyptic stories. The visitors also guardedly informed her that some of the personnel at Kirtland Air Force Base who were working on this surveillance operation of abductees were convinced that the kidnappings were the work of flesh-and-blood aliens. Others, however, had concluded that the "aliens" were deceptive, demonic beings whose origin was somehow connected with the realm of the dead and the afterlife, and that the creatures derived sustenance from the human souls. This was, of course, the belief held by many members of the Collins Elite since at least the late 1960s and early 1970s.

Stone also learned that senior figures within the U.S. intelligence community were convinced that these creatures were manipulating and infiltrating human society. Some within the military even speculated that the creatures were kidnapping and "programming" people for specific, future tasks that would be undertaken at the behest of the Antichrist, and that the ultimate intent was to bring on Armageddon "but hiding it behind UFOs," added Stone. Various personnel based at Kirtland Air Force Base had concluded that this would allow the beings to then "harvest" and feast upon the souls of the billions of people who would be annihilated in the nuclear holocaust. Of most concern to Stone to this day is that the Air Force men advised her that the creatures had kidnapped certain people within the American political arena, and that "after their return" they would speak "about the apocalypse, the end of the world, and why we needed to attack Russia quickly, while we had the chance." Apparently some within the Air Force believed that the ultimate aim of these "aliens" was to deliberately try and engineer an all-destructive Third World War. And when the carnage was over, an immense "soul-feeding" would begin in earnest. Although this was merely a theory, it greatly upset Stone.

The two men also asked Stone—"I was never ordered, only asked real nice"—if she would be willing to undergo a thorough physical examination at Kirtland. She said yes, and met the men at her home on two more occasions. Again, they asked about her dreams, her thoughts on life-after-death, and—somewhat puzzlingly—her views on life-after-death in the animal kingdom. Ultimately, the physical examination never occurred and, after the last meeting, Stone never heard from them again.

But the story was not quite over. On their final visit to her apartment, one of the men, she recalled, brought with him a fruit pie that he said he had purchased at a local store, "as a gift for me." She expanded: "I was kind of flattered that a military man would do this for little old me, you know? Like, well, who am I?" Interestingly, the man was very keen that she should eat some of the pie, but was not keen that he and his colleague should do the same. Since the pie "looked so darn good," she heartily ate a plateful.

After the two Air Force operatives departed, Stone explained, a strange feeling came over her—a combination of euphoria, recklessness, and an overriding sense of invulnerability. For reasons that even to this day she cannot adequately explain, Stone picked up her car keys and left home. Within a short time she was on the highway but had absolutely no idea where she was going. After only a few more minutes, the out-of-this-world feelings seemed to overwhelm her and became even more disturbing. She had to fight to overcome an overwhelming urge to push the accelerator to the floor and "cross the highway" into the path of nothing less than an oncoming truck. And on three other occasions within the space of mere minutes, that same deadly urge flooded her mind, and on each occasion she successfully fought against it.

Stone did not know what to think about this admittedly curious development in the story, but she speculated that her Air Force interviewers had "drugged the pie" and possibly even hypnotized her as a means of inducing suicide. She now wonders if by then she had become "too much of a risk if I had talked to anyone."

Someone was definitely out to get her. She recalled: "My mom got a call later that day saying I'd been in an accident, which freaked her out. I hadn't, but I would have done, I think, if I'd not fought against it. Why they wanted to speak with my momma and tell her that, I don't know. I hadn't told anyone either about what nearly happened on the highway, so how did someone know that if it had turned out worse, I might *really* have had an accident on that day, just like they told [my mother]?" (1)

The FBI has declassified a document that may have a direct bearing on this affair. According to the document, on March 9, 1973—only three days after Tammy Stone's experience—a Sergeant Stigliano of the USAF's Recruiting Office at Waco informed the San Antonio FBI Office that an individual, not identified in declassified FBI memoranda, had contacted the night shift supervisor at a Waco-based newspaper and had "inquired regarding any information [the newspaper] could be able to furnish him concerning any unidentified flying objects observed in the Waco, Texas, area."

Sergeant Stigliano wrote that the individual had identified himself as a captain in the U.S. Air Force and had in his possession a folder marked Top Secret that contained photographs of various military installations. "No specific information concerning these photos could be provided by Sergeant Stigliano," reported the FBI at San Antonio, adding: "The individual did not act in any strange manner, and did not attempt to obtain anything other than information from the newspaper. Sergeant Stigliano advised that this information was being furnished to the proper authorities only for information purposes as they do not suspect any unlawful activity."(2)

Could the unknown "captain in the U.S. Air Force" have been one of Stone's mysterious visitors?

But still the story was not over. Two months later, an equally strange event occurred, again in Texas. According to UFO researcher and author Greg Bishop, who has investigated the case, "The main participant in that case was named Judy Doraty, and she had been driving back from a bingo game on May 23 of that year outside Houston, Texas, with her daughter, mother, sister, and brother-in-law." Suddenly, everyone in the car witnessed "a bright light in the sky" that seemed to be pacing them. On their return home, the light was still with them and, ominously, moved in closer. The family, as well as a group who came running out of the Doraty house, was shocked to see a huge disk-shaped object with rows of windows float silently over the property and across an adjacent field. It soon shot off straight up into the sky, going from "very, very big to very, very little in a matter of seconds," Doraty recalled.

Greg Bishop noted: "She had been having nightmares and unrelenting stress since the experience, something that no one else in her family seemed to be suffering. The other passengers remembered that she had stopped the car and gotten out to look at the enigmatic light as it approached them. On March 13, 1980, [alien abduction researcher Dr. Leo] Sprinkle put Doraty in a relaxed state and brought her back to the point where she was standing next to her vehicle."

Doraty's own words described a nightmarish scenario: "[There's] like a spotlight shining down on the back of my car. And it's like it had substance to it. I can see an animal being taken up in this. I can see it squirming and trying to get free.

And it's like it's being sucked up. I can't tell what the animal is. It's a small animal."

Bishop uncovered a sensational story: "Doraty remembered that she was not taken on the craft she observed, but said that when she was outside, she experienced some sort of bi-location and was present on the craft and standing by the car at the same time. The 'small animal' turned out to be a very young calf, which was dissected on the craft with quick precision. The carcass was dropped back on the ground. With some difficulty, she also recalled seeing her daughter being examined. She got back into her car and drove home, the craft now a distant blob of light following them at a distance all the way home, where it then swooped down not fifty feet from the ground while the amazed Doraty family watched. After zipping away, it hung in the sky like a bright star long enough for everyone to go inside and return several times to see if it was still there."

Consider, too, the following. On May 5, 1980, Myrna Hansen was driving to her Eagle's Nest, New Mexico, home from a trip to Oklahoma with her young son. Hansen suddenly found herself in a nightmarish world. Under hypnosis she recalled a classic alien abduction in which she was taken on board a UFO, undressed, and subjected to a physical examination. While on board, she also witnessed a "struggling cow sucked up into its underside in some sort of 'tractor beam.'" More controversially, Hansen stated that after the abduction, she had been taken to an underground base, had seen "body parts" floating in vats, and felt that some sort of "device" had been implanted in her body so that the aliens could monitor and control her thoughts.

When details of Hansen's description of the underground base were relayed to Kirtland Air Force Base security, they immediately recognized that Hansen was describing a fortified section of one of its facilities: the Manzano Weapons Storage Complex, which, at the time, was the largest underground repository of nuclear weapons in the Western world. The U.S. Air Force seriously addressed the possibility that Hansen's abduction experience had occurred in an altered state of consciousness.

Greg Bishop learned that in 1980 Hansen was placed "under hypnosis with an Air Force psychologist" and described in great detail one specific facility at Manzano. One Air Force officer, Richard C. Doty, later recalled: "She even knew what the elevator looked like."

Said Bishop: "Myrna Hansen could have been an 'accidental remote viewer' when in an altered state induced by her experience, whether by aliens or through other means more close to home. Unhooked from normal consciousness, she 'knew' that she would later be questioned by the Air Force, and the fact that she was near such a secret installation could have caused her to lock on to it. Admittedly, this scenario is far-fetched, but Doty and his AFOSI associates couldn't come up with anything better. Eventually, they were satisfied that this was a one-time event, and that she hadn't been able to see or sense anything else of concern."(3)

Maybe so, but Myrna Hansen's experience is important and instructive for two key reasons: (A) as with the Tammy Stone case, Hansen's story confirms official interest in alien abductees by personnel at Kirtland Air Force Base, New Mexico decades ago; and (B) it parallels the experiences of both Stone and Judy Doraty, in the sense that both women underwent abduction experiences in which some part of them—the soul or life-force, it might reasonably be suggested—was somehow deliberately detached from the physical body and transported to another location, possibly to the interior of what we might perceive as a UFO from another world—or that others might view as a vessel of hungry, manipulative demons.

19

PROJECT ABDUCTION

During the course of our several discussions, Robert Manners referred to a certain "Dr. Mandor" who "might be willing to help on the abductions." And when Manners felt he had told me as much as he reasonably could—or, as I suspected, as far as those pulling his strings were *allowing* him to go—he duly arranged for me to meet with Mandor, who was without doubt the creepiest individual I have ever personally encountered. Elderly, wizened, sickly, and oily, Mandor invited me to his rundown home in 2009—an abode filled to the brim with carvings and paintings of Djinns, those ancient, supernatural, sentient beings who, according to the *Qur'an*, are made of "smokeless fire" and who may exhibit either benevolent or malevolent characteristics. Infinitely paranoid and deeply disturbing, this odd character—who bore a passing resemblance to Henry Kissinger and who was, I was advised, the only non-American ever to be invited into the Collins Elite—had apparently been at the forefront of a Collins Elite sub-project in the early 1980s that was looking into a very unusual aspect of the abduction conundrum.

In the early 1980s, the doctor told me as I sat on his filthy couch, the Collins Elite continued to undertake its clandestine study of select abductees across the United States, largely by occasional, personal visits to the homes of those who had undergone encounters and who it was felt could be trusted not to talk about their visits. This low-key surveillance included sporadic telephone monitoring and letter interception, and—*very* occasionally—even keeping stealthy watch outside of people's houses in the dead of night for any evidence of visible, unholy visitation.

Mandor said that it became apparent that more and more abductees were seemingly describing a secret surveillance program of their activities by military personnel. In these cases, the witnesses all appeared to be talking about truly extensive and highly advanced surveillance, including harassment from low-flying, black unmarked helicopters, interrogation by senior military personnel, and—most controversially of all—kidnappings, in which the abductees were taken to vast, underground installations where they claimed to have seen black-eyed, diminutive aliens and human military personnel working together on a dizzying array of out-of-this-world projects. (1)

Many abductees have indeed claimed to be under surveillance by the U.S. military.

Betty Andreasson, an abductee whose experiences have been chronicled in detail by researcher and author Raymond Fowler, has for years reportedly been the subject of official monitoring by what sounds like—initially, at least—the work of some covert arm of government, the military or the intelligence community. For example, in early 1980, when UFO investigator Larry Fawcett was working as the chief investigator for Ray Fowler on the book *The Andreasson Affair: Phase Two*, mysterious, unmarked helicopters plagued both Betty and her husband, Bob Luca.

According to Fawcett and his writing partner, Barry Greenwood: "They reported that their home was over flown numerous times by black, unmarked helicopters of the Huey UH-1H type and that these helicopters would fly over their homes at altitudes as low as 100 feet. The Luca's described these helicopters as being black in color, with no identifiable marking on them. They noticed that the windows were tinted black also, so that no one could see inside. During many of the over flights, Bob was able to take close to 200 photos of the helicopters."

On May 8, 1982, Bob Luca sent a letter to the Army's Office of the Adjutant General demanding an answer as to why he and Betty were apparently being subjected to such low-level and repeated visitations by the mystery helicopters. The only response came from the Army's Adjutant General, Major General John F. Gore, who said that: "It is difficult to determine what particular aircraft is involved or the owning unit."(2)

Abductee Debbie Jordan, who has reported longstanding alien abduction experiences with an apparent genetic link, has also been harassed and monitored by the unidentified helicopters and their equally-unidentified pilots: "These...could be seen almost daily around our houses. They are so obvious about their flights it's almost comical. On occasions too numerous to even remember, they have hovered around my house, above my house, and above me for several minutes at a time, not trying to hide themselves or the fact that they are watching us.

"Even when I am outside and obviously watching back, it doesn't seem to bother them. They just sit there in midair, about sixty to ninety feet above the ground, whirling and watching. They are completely without identification and are always low enough so that I could easily see the pilot, if the windshield were clear glass. But the windshield is smoky black, with a finish that makes it impossible to see who's inside."(3)

Melinda Leslie has detailed classic abductions undertaken by aliens since 1993, as well as follow-up abductions secretly carried out by elements of the U.S. military. As an example, she says that in November 1993, she was kidnapped and drugged by two men dressed in camouflage who took her to an unknown military facility. There, she was interrogated by a red-haired officer who was not only interested in her alien abduction experiences, but also in any data that she could supply on the technology of the aliens.

"What have they asked you?" the officer demanding to know. "Tell me about their technology. Tell me about the drive system, the drive mechanism. You tell me about what they told you to do. What did they ask you to do? Tell me, tell me, tell me. You know you are not theirs; you are ours." After the interrogation, says Leslie, she was taken by military personnel to a hangar where she saw large, unmarked helicopters, before being released. (4)

Casey Turner, the husband of the late abductee Dr. Karla Turner, stated that on one occasion he was drugged and transported to an underground installation and subjected to an in-depth interrogation by military personnel. Also, according to Casey Turner, there were a number of other people there, all equally drugged and primed for interrogation. Turner added: "They are all sitting there, sort of in a daze...I keep getting the feeling that there's a military officer who's real angry... I'm not cooperating and they're real perplexed...I get the feeling they want to know, maybe they're trying to find out what it is we know..." (5)

UFO investigator and author Greg Bishop has an interesting account to relate concerning Dr. Karla Turner: "Mail tampering is the darling of clinical paranoids, but nearly every piece of mail that the late researcher/abductee Karla Turner sent to [my] PO Box looked like it had been tampered with or opened. Since this is easy to do without having to be obvious, we figured someone was interested in her work enough to make it clear that she was being monitored. She took to putting a piece of transparent tape over the flap and writing 'sealed by sender' on it. Karla pretty much took it for granted after awhile, and suggested I do likewise."(6)

These cases seem to demonstrate that there are officials interested in unexplained alien abduction incidents and they must belong to a gigantic organization with an unlimited budget, resources, and operations. There is, however, another aspect to the phenomenon—one that is in some ways even more controversial than the extraterrestrial angle and the surveillance of abductees by the military. There are those who conclude that alien abductions actually have nothing to do with the activities of *real* aliens but are solely the result of clandestine work undertaken by the U.S. military. According to this scenario, the military uses the alien abduction motif as a carefully camouflaged cover to allow for the testing of new technologies, mind-controlling drugs, and sophisticated hypnotic techniques on unwitting citizens.

A perfect example is the case of Alison, a now-41-year-old woman from Arizona, who lives on a ranch not too far from the town of Sedona. From the age of 27 to 31, Alison says she was subjected to at least five abductions that bore all the hallmarks of alien kidnappings. On each occasion, she was in her living room reading or watching television when her two pet dogs, Lucy and Summer, began pacing around the room and whimpering. At that point, things always became a blur and Alison later found herself several hours later in a different part of the house. Grogginess, a pounding headache, and a dry mouth were staples of the experience.

For days after the weird encounters, she dreamed of the moment when things began to go awry, which always resulted in a complete loss of electricity inside the house, a deep humming noise emanating from outside the large living room window, and powerful and intensely bright lights enveloping the room. In her semiconscious state, Alison saw small shadowy figures scuttling around the room who carried her outside onto a small craft where she was subjected to a gynecological examination and some form of nasal probing. She was then returned to another part of the house and the aliens left. It was only after the aliens had departed that the intense humming noise ceased.

During what Alison believes was the fifth abduction, however, something even weirder took place. The mysterious humming sound abruptly came to a halt only a few seconds after her allegedly cosmic visitors entered the room. At that point, Alison recalled—not in a later dream, on this occasion, but in real time—she began to slowly regain her senses and the feeling of disorientation eased and then completely vanished. *And so did the aliens*. In their place was not a group of frail-looking, black-eyed extraterrestrials, but a number of rather large and burly men in what looked like black, combat fatigues.

According to Alison, one of the men screamed into a microphone: "What happened?" The men backed away slowly and, as Alison began to regain her senses, one of them held his hand up "as if to say 'stay where you are,'" and uttered the word "sorry" in her direction, in a rather awkward fashion. Alison made her way to the window in plenty of time to see the men jump into an unmarked black helicopter. At a height of several hundred feet, a powerful lamp was turned on that that lit up the night-sky around her secluded property. So much for a genuine spaceship.

Today, Alison firmly believes that a combination of subliminal hypnosis, mind-altering technologies, and perhaps even non-lethal weaponry designed to temporarily disable her nervous system and bodily movement, made her *think* she was an alien abductee. In reality, however, she was merely a guinea pig for the testing of sophisticated weaponry designed to affect and manipulate both mind and body to an incredible degree. (7)

If so, there may indeed be several reasons for the apparent secret surveillance of abductees by military forces. Researcher Helmut Lammer certainly seems to think so: "...one group may be interested in advanced mind- and behavior-control experiments...these experiments are similar to the experiments reported by survivors of the MKULTRA mind-control programs... A second group seems to be interested in biological or genetic research...a third group seems to be a military task force...This group appears to be interested in the UFO/alien abduction phenomenon for information gathering purposes... It seems to us that the leaders of this military task force believe that some alien abductions are real and that they have national security implications. If this is the case, it would be likely that the second group would work together, sharing their interest in genetic studies and their findings from alleged alien abductees."(7)

So by the late summer of 1982, said Mandor, the Collins Elite—which had come to believe it was the only arm of the official world that was secretly watching the abductees, in an effort to try and gain a more complete picture of how the perceived demonic agenda was progressing—began making waves within government. Its members, quite reasonably, sought to determine why some other group had access to military helicopters, underground installations, and much more, while their project had no access to such near-unlimited resources. The answer to their inquiry proved to be quite shocking.

20

REAGAN'S DOOMSDAY WHITE HOUSE

It has been widely reported within UFO research circles that on June 27, 1982, President Ronald Reagan made an intriguingly worded statement to one of the true giants of the Hollywood movie industry, Steven Spielberg. On that day, a select screening had been arranged for Reagan and his wife Nancy of Spielberg's soon-to-be-blockbuster production of *E.T.: The Extraterrestrial*. White House documentation now in the public domain shows that the Reagan's were movie devotees. Over the course of his two terms in office, Reagan eagerly watched close to 400 movies in the White House Theater, including nearly all of the *Star Trek* movies and, two days before the viewing of *E.T.*, Spielberg's *Poltergeist*.

The screening of *E.T.* was a significant event. With the president, Nancy Reagan, and Spielberg was a guest list of 35 people, including Supreme Court Justice Sandra Day. White House papers show that following a banquet in the Red Room, the group headed to the theater, and awaited the 8:22 p.m. screening. *E.T.* left a deep impression on the Reagans: "Nancy Reagan was crying towards the end, and the President looked like a ten-year-old-kid," Spielberg said later. But the controversy had hardly begun.

According to ufological rumor, when the movie was over, the president said to Spielberg, in distinctly hushed tones: "You know: there aren't six people in this room who know how true this really is."(1)

Dr. Mandor informed me that Reagan had a personal UFO encounter in 1974, and that this experience, along with his subsequent interest in the phenomenon and a classified briefing on UFOs he received from the National Security Council the day after viewing *E.T.* led the White House to conduct a secret study in 1982 into the national security implications of the alleged large-scale kidnapping of American citizens by forces unknown—alien abductions, in other words.

Mandor said that several authorities were apparently tasked with preparing detailed reports for Reagan, for Chief of Staff James Baker, and for Deputy Chief of Staff Michael K. Deaver—the three of whom were collectively known in official circles as "The Troika," a Russian word meaning "threesome." One of those authorities was the Collins Elite, which submitted an extensive paper that detailed for Reagan and his staff the whole demonic/fallen-angel theory and the way in which they had been surreptitiously looking at the subject for some years. They warned of the importance of not being seduced by the satanic deception.

Personnel attached to the CIA's science-and-technology division delivered a second report to Reagan. This report outlined all available data in favor of some form of vast, extraterrestrial operation with a "genetic agenda" at its heart, and which drew heavily upon the content of Budd Hopkins' book, *Missing Time*, John Fuller's account of the Betty and Barney Hill saga of 1961, *The Interrupted Journey*, and Ralph and Judy Blum's book *Beyond Earth*. (2) The third report was prepared by an Air Force psychologist who argued that alien abductions were purely the work of the human subconscious and sleep disorders, as well as issues related to cultural beliefs and folklore.

The publication of Hopkins' *Missing Time* was a major turning point within the field of alien abduction and detailed a number of cases Hopkins investigated himself. Hopkins put forward suggested that at least one extraterrestrial race might be routinely abducting human beings. His later work—including the 1987 book *Intruders*—revealed that the aliens were secretly taking people as part of a huge and covert genetic operation, the goal of which was, and still is, the production of a half-human, half-hybrid race. But why would aliens even need to undertake such actions? The Grays were said to be on a catastrophic evolutionary and genetic decline, and the only thing that can possibly halt the steady and unrelenting march towards oblivion and the extinction of their ancient species is an injection of fresh human blood. (3)

One person who may have been told details of the very official project that incorporated a study of Hopkins' work and which implicated the Reagan White House—just as Dr. Mandor had claimed—was long-time and respected UFO researcher Brian Parks, who told me: "What I had heard was that some kind of study was done at some time in the early-to-mid '80s, and it involved a study of *Missing Time*. It was mentioned that it was used in an official study, but they had come back very skeptically about it. I was told this by Bill Moore [the co-author with Charles Berlitz of the book, *The Roswell Incident*] directly and this was coming from his insider sources. It was connected to the Reagan White House. And it sounded to me like it was something official—not informal. It's probably not unlike the remote-viewing thing where they took pains to keep it very in-house. Not just because of the classification of it, but because they were concerned about the exposure. I know that when that program got out, they had critics in the military and intelligence community who, on one hand were very skeptical, and on the other side of the debate who were Christian Fundamentalists types who didn't want the government involved in psychic phenomenon because that was devil stuff and we shouldn't play with it."(4)

According to Dr. Mandor, the one theory that fascinated

Reagan most was what the Collins Elite had presented, probably because of Reagan's fascination with "End Times" belief systems and ideologies. Such doomsday beliefs proliferated in Reagan's White House. The subject had long fascinated Reagan. When the retired Hollywood actor became President with his finger seemingly poised precariously above the red-button of the most powerful nuclear arsenal on the planet, he brought with him a notable collection of books to stock the shelves of the White House library. Those books included the *Scofield Reference* Bible, first published in 1909, which predicted the end of the world resulting from future events beginning in Beirut, Lebanon. Gordon Thomas said of this book: "Its gospel of impending apocalypse was preached daily by the President's favorite evangelists, Jerry Falwell, Pat Robertson and James Swaggart." Another book cherished by Reagan was Hal Lindsay's *The Late Great Planet Earth*, which also predicted Armageddon from a military confrontation in Lebanon. And then there is the Reagans' involvement in the world of astrology, which many Christians believe to be yet another aspect of satanic deception and seduction. (5)

Joan Quigley is an astrologer who provided astrological information to the Reagan White House in the 1980s. She was called upon by First Lady Nancy Reagan in 1981, after John Hinckley's attempted assassination of the president on March 30 of that year, and stayed on as the White House astrologer in secret until being publicly "outed" in 1988 by ousted Chief-of-Staff Donald Regan. After the attempt on her husband's life, Nancy had apparently grown concerned and inquired of Quigley if she could have foreseen and possibly prevented, the assassination attempt.

"Yes," replied Quigley, had she been looking, she *would* have known. As a result, Mrs. Reagan hired Quigley to provide astrological advice on a regular basis. Explaining why she turned to Quigley, Nancy Reagan later wrote: "Very few people can understand what it's like to have your husband shot at and almost die, and then have him exposed all the time to enormous crowds, tens of thousands of people, any one of whom might be a lunatic with a gun... I was doing everything I could think of to protect my husband and keep him alive."

Quigley later wrote a book about her experiences, titled *What Does Joan Say?* in which she stated: "Not since the days of the Roman emperors—and never in the history of the United States Presidency—has an astrologer played such a significant role in the nation's affairs of State."

After Donald Regan took over as chief of President Reagan's staff in 1985, he was quietly informed by Reagan-aide Michael Deaver of Quigley's influence on the president and his wife. Regan, who frequently quarreled with Nancy Reagan, resigned in 1987 after the Iran-Contra affair and amid mixed reviews of his job performance. After his White House career was over, Regan revealed to the nation, in the pages of his autobiography *For the Record* that Nancy Reagan consulted Quigley, which some commentators interpreted as a form of revenge for being ousted from his position in the president's administration. After the leak, the media swarmed Quigley, though she rarely gave advice to the Reagans again. Of the entire incident, Mrs. Reagan later said: "Nobody was hurt by it—except, possibly, me."(6)

When the Reagan administration agreed to further increase the black-budget and scope of the work of the Collins Elite, Dr. Mandor told me, the Collins Elite were finally able to undertake an in-depth study of the one issue they found particularly vexing and mysterious, namely, the identity of the top secret group within the military that seemed to be responsible

President Ronald Reagan

for the surveillance of countless abductees like Betty Andreasson, Melinda Leslie, Dr. Karla Turner and her husband, and Debbie Jordan. But their extensive investigation was for naught. They found no evidence of the existence of such a group—none at all. Countless checks throughout the entire U.S. military failed to identify any potential players in such a project. There was just no data to support the claims of deep surveillance of abductees by military helicopters. The Collins Elite concluded that the stories of clandestine groups with outlandish budgets, of quick-reaction military units commandeering vast squadrons of black-helicopters to spy on abductees, and of massive underground installations that were home to joint alien-human operations had no basis in reality whatsoever—at least, no basis in *our* reality.

Having pounded on just about every door within government, the military, and the intelligence world –all without any success—the Collins Elite came to a jaw-dropping realization: that the mysterious black helicopters, the equally-mysterious military interrogators, and most certainly the vast alien-human underground-labs must be hallucinations, sophisticated imagery generated by demons and fallen-angels and projected into the minds of the abductees while they slept. These hallucinations were meant to reinforce the deception that the UFO presence was extraterrestrial and that the government secretly knew this. But it was all a fantastic mirage. Alien abductions, the Collins Elite concluded, had no basis—*at all*—in physical reality. They were *solely* illusions of the mind, albeit illusions generated and controlled by string-pulling demons.

The idea that the fallen-ones might well possess abilities to allow them to deceive the human-mind on a truly intricate and fantastic scale has not gone by unnoticed by those who hold deep, Christian beliefs and who have official backgrounds. In their book *Unmasking the Enemy*, Dr. Nelson Pacheco—a former Principal Scientist with the Supreme Headquarters, Allied Powers, Europe (SHAPE), Technical Center—and Tommy Blann, a now-retired USAF employee, state: "...we propose that the 'reality' behind the UFO phenomenon... is due to a manifestation of non-human preternatural consciousness—for the purpose of deception—that can interact with our physical environment and with our human consciousness to produce visual, physical, and psychological effects. The artificial construct created by this consciousness mimics our three-dimensional objects and systems and even our religious imagery—the purpose being to slowly condition our minds through subtle deception to accept a false belief, while undermining our rational thought processes and our human spirit."(7)

Nicole Malone, author of *The Bible, Physics, and the Abilities of Fallen Angels*, comes to much the same conclusion. She explained: "It is important to note that sometimes fallen angels do cause abductees to see 'humans' during the apparition; however, these are not real humans, but instead are part of the vision caused by the fallen angel... In many cases in which fallen angels cause visions of humans, the humans are military personnel, and advanced technology appears to be present. These kinds of abductions are called 'Milabs,' for 'military abductions.' Except in rare cases of actual government investigation of abductions and interviews with abductees [which is the precise path followed by the Collins Elite], these Milabs are caused by fallen angels, and are just one variety of abduction experiences... The entire experience, like other mental attack visions, is a vision, including the military personnel and advanced technology the person sees. Remember, these experiences are real to the bodily senses, and the perception of time passage seems normal to the abductee during the experience."(8)

Reality, the Collins Elite concluded, is most certainly not what it seems.

21

WHISTLE BLOWING

In May 1994, two-and-a-half years after the initial contact with his clandestine Department of Defense sources, Ray Boeche telephoned UFO researcher and author Linda Howe with some intriguing news. During one of the subsequent conversations with the shadowy pair, Boeche happened to reference Howe's book *Glimpses of Other Realities, Volume 1: Facts & Eyewitnesses*. Said Howe: "The two men asked [Boeche] if they could read *Glimpses*... Boeche called me to explain the situation and to ask if I had any objections to his giving the intelligence agents my book. I told him: 'Not only give them the book, ask them if they will write in the margins whatever comments they have about what is correct and incorrect. That would be a safe way for them to communicate and for us to learn something.' In June [1994], Boeche called again and said I would be getting a package in the mail. He said the contents would be a floppy disc in a sealed envelope handed to him by the two agents. Ray said the men did not want to write in the book, but were replying on the computer disc with comments about the content in *Glimpses*..." (1)

The text reads:

Dear Ms. Howe: Your book is an excellent, thought-provoking work. Overall many salient points are covered quite well. Following are some random notes for your consideration. Study David Bohm's *Wholeness and the Implicate Order*. Much insight into the mechanics of the NHEs (non-human entities) can be gained from study of his ideas. He is on target with his concepts, and our program is attempting, unfortunately to exploit them.

Perhaps a better description might be that the mechanics of the

NHEs ability to interact with our physical reality is what Bohm's work details, and the contact with the NHEs has occurred, and will continue to occur, regardless of our understanding of the mechanism of the contact. Our misguided program directors cling to the false belief that we can control or manipulate the NHEs, when in actuality, the reverse is occurring—we are the ones being manipulated and deceived.

Cellular changes in plants from within genuine crop circle formations are due to the same sort of energy release/exposure as that used in the so-called 'negative healing' experimentation. Once again, [the] forces being utilized by NHEs, to interact with us in a bizarre, confusing manner, designed to divert us and draw our attention from the true purpose of their actions: manipulation and deceit.

The penultimate diversion in this whole area is the mutilation of thousands of animals. The NHEs, with the ability to work unseen (read invisibly), and to create incisions and excise tissue in manners which seem humanly impossible (because they are) and to either remain totally undetected, or to create the illusion of extraterrestrial beings (the apparent UFO/phantom helicopter sightings, and concomitant occupant sightings often associated with the events), provide an extremely effective smoke screen. People are now busy chasing secret government projects, satanic cults, and UFOs, while the actual perpetrating agents go unsuspected.

Regarding the phantom helicopters, while many are direct NHE "productions" (craft is not an appropriate term as they do not need to travel via a propulsion device), many are related to our program, especially regarding running checks and surveillance on mutilation sites and so-called abduction victims.

The comment left on your telephone answering machine referenced on Page 194 (*Glimpses*, Vol. 1) may very well have been made by someone within the government hierarchy who has been convincingly fed the false ET scenario propagated as disinformation by those who are in charge of the NHE projects. Many variations of this exist, and all who are privy to a particular variation are convinced they have "the answer." With our society as it is now, the core truth of the situation is such that the public really could not handle it.

The ultimate diversionary tactic to this point (and diversions will begin to increase in frequency, degree of strangeness, and in a more overt fashion, visible to greater numbers of observers) is the UFO abduction scenario. The concept of these events, real though they are, being the result of extraterrestrial beings is a masterful piece of disinformation to divert attention away from the real source of the NHEs. Our information as to the true nature of these events does not negate the possibility of extraterrestrial life. But the causal source of the UFO and UFO abduction phenomena is not extraterrestrial.

The so-called Roswell crash of 1947 did indeed occur and debris of a non-earthly type was found, as were non-human bodies. Although in our position we cannot speak with authority, we believe that there is a basis in truth for Bob Lazar's story of government-held "craft." However, the origin is not extraterrestrial.

The NHEs being dealt with in our psi (mind control) weapons development, and who are apparently allowing themselves to be used, for a time, are neither benevolent nor neutral. It was our feeling that very few could understand or accept this. That is the reason we approached our mutual friend (Ray Boeche).

His theological training, his acceptance of orthodox Christian thought, and his obvious abilities as an astute researcher, seemed to indicate to us that we might effectively communicate our concerns through him, and still maintain our positions, which would enable us to accurately monitor the ongoing work. He has made some blunt statements which run counter to the positions of his peers, and has been roundly criticized by many for his position, but we desperately hope that at least some are listening.

Your comments and thoughts (in *Glimpses of Other Realities*) concerning ancient civilizations and their contacts with the NHEs need to be considered in light of the bigger picture of the deception of mankind as a whole. If this grand deception is taking the course it seems to be, then it makes complete sense to analyze the false gods of ancient civilizations in light of the current level of deception.

It is only logical that given their non-human, other-dimensional nature, the NHEs would be able to foresee the need to establish a foundational base, the facts of which could be slightly twisted, or distorted, by the fog of antiquity and forgotten cultural distinctiveness, to seemingly establish themselves as the bringers of all good things to humanity.

Explore [Jacques] Vallee's *Passport to Magonia* again, for

more close parallels between the 'faerie' manifestation of the NHEs, and current events. Dr. Vallee was so close to the truth of the situation, with the exception that the ultimate manipulators are not human.

You have created a remarkable piece of work which helps to begin to point to the final truth behind the phenomena. Our mutual friend could be most helpful to you in explaining details of the deception. We, on our part, will be happy to answer specific questions you may wish to put to us. You must understand, however, that some things simply can't be discussed.

Please transmit your questions and or concerns via our friend. We believe you can understand our need for discretion, and the wisdom of limiting the number of direct contacts we make.

We applaud your efforts, and we look forward to your next volume. You are a very bright and obviously courageous woman who seems to remember the maxim, "You shall know the Truth, and the Truth shall make you free." With our sincerest best wishes. (2)

Did Ray Boeche's sources confide in him and Linda Howe genuine data? Or was the pair subjected to nothing but outright lies designed to muddy the already murky waters of everything ufological? And what light might David Bohm's work shed on the matter?

In *Wholeness and the Implicate Order*, which Ray Boeche's sources urged UFO researcher Linda Howe to read, Bohm said that: "In the enfolded [or implicate] order, space and time are no longer the dominant factors determining the relationships of dependence or independence of different elements. Rather, an entirely different sort of basic connection of elements is possible, from which our ordinary notions of space and time…are abstracted as forms derived from the deeper order."(3)

Or, as researcher Mike Good concisely put it, Bohm's research suggests that "…other levels of reality are only a matter of a shift in relative frequencies."(4) Perhaps, the Collins Elite concluded, those same levels of reality include Heaven and Hell.

22

ANCIENT KNOWLEDGE

Ray Boeche's Department of Defense whistleblowers carefully advised that in addition to seeking out the work of the undoubtedly brilliant David Bohm, a number of other publications should be considered of vital importance to anyone who wanted to truly understand the demonic nature of the UFO presence that certain military, government, and intelligence community members had come to recognize. Those titles were Reginald C. Thompson's *Devils and Evil Spirits of Babylonia*; Edward Langton's *Essentials of Demonology*; John Deacon and John Walker's 1601 work, *Dialogical Discourses of Spirits and Devils*; Merrill F. Unger's *Biblical Demonology*; Emil Schneweis' *Angels and Demons According to Lactantius*—as well as the studies of C. Fred Dickason, Dr. Neil T. Anderson, and the late observer of all-things demonic, Dr. Kurt Koch. A careful study of these works reveals an accord with the thinking behind the work of the Collins Elite.

Let us begin with Reginald C. Thompson. A British archaeologist, Thompson was a renowned explorer, having excavated at Nineveh, a bustling metropolis in ancient Assyria, and one described in the Bible's Book of Jonah as a "great city." Today, little more than ruins, Nineveh lies on the eastern bank of the Tigris, in what is the Mosul region of Iraq. Thompson also sought out the elusive secrets of Carchemish, a city of the Mitanni and Hittite empires located on the frontier between Turkey and Syria; in 605 BC, Carchemish was the site of a historic battle that saw the Babylonian army of Nebuchadnezzar II defeat the Egyptian forces of Pharaoh Necho II.

In delving into the culture, beliefs, myths, and legends of ancient Babylonia, Thompson uncovered some very disturbing data—all of which was published in 1903 in *Devils and Evil Spirits of Babylonia*. As Thompson demonstrated, the people of Babylonia were plagued, tortured, and tormented by a whole range of predatory entities, including goblins, ghosts, ghouls, and vampires who invaded people's bedrooms and their dreams after the sun had set. (1)

Thompson was not alone in highlighting the beliefs, superstitions, and fears of the inhabitants of ancient Babylonia. A Franciscan monk at the age of 19 and a committed atheist before he reached 30, Joseph McCabe was a founding member of Britain's Rationalist Press Association and the author of more than two hundred books. One of the key foundations to Babylonian belief, he noted, was their extreme vagueness about life after death, although they did believe that "the mental part of a man" continued on after physical demise, albeit in some poorly defined fashion. This was the oldest and mostly deeply ingrained of their religious beliefs. But, he elaborated, there was one thing the Babylonians knew for certain: that the dead passed into a dark, dim cave under the earth, Arabu, or the House of Arabu. McCabe also revealed that the Babylonians dreaded this lower world. Their priests avoided mention of it. They felt that the dead were soured by their gloomy prison underground and would harm the living. This was one of the primitive roots of their belief in malignant spirits, and it leads us on to the next basis of Babylonian character—namely, the belief that the gods allowed legions of devils to torment the sinner in his or her physical life on Earth.

McCabe stated that there were countless numbers of devilish entities in Babylonia, which the priests organized into classes and orders for the purpose of exorcism. They lurked by day in dark places, old ruins, and groves, or in the desert, and at night set out to torture humanity. And most dreaded of all were the "night spirits," Lilu and his wife Lilitu.

McCabe asked: "Did a maid show the symptoms of anemia? Obviously Lilu or Lilitu had been busy at night with her body. Did a man or woman have an erotic dream leaving him or her excited and unsatisfied? It was Ardat Lili [the offspring of Lilu and Lilitu]. Even 'the evil wind, the terrible wind that sets one's hair on end' had its demon. Pictorially they were represented as ferocious beings of animal head and human body: the prototypes of our devil's disciples. Some were so powerful that they were next to gods."(2)

In Babylonian lore both Lilu and Lilitu were "regarded as dangerous" to both pregnant women and newborn babies. The ubiquitous and emotionless Grays of today's UFO lore seem to be forever obsessed with the nature of human reproduction and babies. Ardat Lili, meanwhile, was seen as a spirit that firmly epitomized both sexual dysfunction and night terrors. And many of these ancient demons, it should be noted, were associated with sightings of owls, which feature in countless alien abduction-style stories of modern day ufology, too. (3)

Similarly, *Communion* author Whitley Strieber has stated that the first memory he had after an encounter with unknown entities on December 26, 1985 was that he had seen an owl. (4) Strieber also noted that his sister had a strange story about an owl: "Sometime in the early sixties she was driving between Kerrville and Comfort, Texas, well after midnight. She was terrified to see a huge light sail down and cross the road ahead of her. A few minutes later an owl flew in front of the car. I have to wonder if that is not a screen memory, but my sister has no sense that it is."(5)

Consider, too, the 1992 story of Doug and his wife Sandy, as related to Whitley and Anne Strieber by Doug's friend, Rick. It sounds very much like an encounter with a benevolent, perhaps even angelic, entity trying to issue dire warnings about the darkness and deception threatening to engulf the Human species. According to Rick: "Doug related this incredible story about something that happened while taking a drive with [his wife] Sandy in Hawaii. On a remote road somewhere on the Big Island, he and his wife had a missing time event. Doug was able to remember much, if not all, of what took place. He said that he saw a white owl fly in front of his car, almost grazing the windshield. He stopped the car and got out and instead of a white owl, he saw some sort of luminous human being standing alongside the road. As he gazed at this individual, messages began to be communicated directly into his mind in the form of images. They warned of a coming global catastrophe."(6)

Then there is the experience of Quinn, a married mother of two, a "proud grandparent" from Ontario, Canada, and a member of Budd Hopkins' Intruders Foundation. Quinn has experienced a lifetime of UFO-related experiences that began at the age of seven or eight, during which she was plagued by unexplained nosebleeds. Interestingly, Quinn reported a strange encounter that followed a UFO event in 1995; it focused upon the sighting of an owl in the middle of the road while driving through the Rocky Mountains. All of those in the car, including both her spouse and son, saw the bird, which was described as being no less than four-feet in height. Quinn later expressed her opinion that: "Personally, I don't think it was an owl; but that is what my mind remembers. That's what my son and spouse remember too."(7)

And, as a footnote: Roman mythology tells of the Strix or Striga, usually described as a nocturnal and predatory bird of ill omen that viciously fed upon human flesh in vampire-like fashion. Its name was derived from the Greek term for owl. A particularly notable story tells of how one night, as a newborn, the legendary King Procas of Alba Longa—an ancient city of Latium, which was destroyed by the Romans in the 7th century BC—was savagely attacked by a group of such creatures who callously crept up on him while he slept in his cradle. (8)

So in ancient Babylon, Rome, and modern day America we have people who have reported encounters with unearthly creatures who (A) were perceived as being threatening to newborn babies and/or had an obsessive interest in human reproduction; (B) manifested in people's bedrooms while they slept at night and subjected them to distressing procedures that practically bordered upon rape; and (C) were all associated with sightings of owls, leads to the near-inescapable, and truly extraordinary, conclusion that, despite the time-span of several thousand years, they are all inextricably linked in both origin and intent.

From the studies of the late Dr. Merrill F. Unger, who was mentioned by Ray Boeche's DoD confidantes, we learn some equally provocative data. Unger earned his A.B. and PhD degrees at John's Hopkins University and his Th.M and Th.D degrees at Dallas Theological Seminary. He then taught for a year at Gordon College, and for the next 19 years he was a Professor of Old Testament Studies at Dallas Theological Seminary. The author of more than forty books, Unger penned a number of provocative studies on the world and workings of the demon, including his 1945 title *Biblical Demonology*. Within its pages, Unger espoused his firm conviction that while it was impossible for a firm believer in Jesus Christ to become demon-possessed, it *was* possible for believers to "choose sin," or at the very least, to "yield to it" and find themselves exposed to demonic power and influence, as apparently happened to certain elements inside the Department of Defense. (9)

In 1971, Unger's *Demons in the World Today* demonstrated that some of his earlier beliefs had changed, or had been modified, such as that a committed believer in Christianity could not be possessed. As he noted: "For many years the late chancellor of Wheaton College, Dr. V. Raymond Edman, taught that a Christian under certain circumstances could be invaded by demon powers. His first-hand experience with crude demonism, as a result of missionary labors in Ecuador in his earlier years, gave Dr. Edman an understanding of the subject of demonism not possessed by purely theoretical Bible interpreters."

Within *Demons in the World Today*, Unger gave just such an example of how a person of the Christian faith could fall under a demonic spell: "Believers can be hindered, bound, and oppressed by Satan and even indwelt by one or more demons, who may derange the mind and afflict the body. One woman, who excelled in the gift of intercessory prayer, was nevertheless constantly the center of a disturbance because of lack of tact and wisdom, due apparently to some alien spirit indwelling her. The writer remembers well the occasion of a prayer meeting when this woman was delivered from this evil spirit, as she and a group of us were on our knees in intercession. All of a sudden, as she quietly prayed, the demon in her gave an unearthly yell that could be heard for a block and came out of her, frightening the group almost out of their wits. After falling into an unconscious state for a minute or two, the woman regained consciousness and rose to her feet, joyfully confident that she had been set free from an evil power."(10)

Six years later, in 1977, came *What Demons Can Do to Saints*. In it, Unger stated: "Clinical evidence abounds that a Christian can be demon-possessed as a carry-over from pre-conversion days, or can fall under Satan's power after conversion and become progressively demonized, even seriously. If such a person blatantly lives in scandalous sin, subscribes to and embraces heresy, engages in occultism, or gives himself to rebellion and lawlessness against God's Word and will, he may expect a demon invasion in his life."(11)

Of course, this statement from Unger very closely parallels both the fears and the concerns expressed by certain people in the Department of Defense—namely, that the precise act of engaging in occultism that Unger was soberly warning about had indeed opened a doorway through which demonic entities, disguised as extraterrestrials, had succeeded in gaining entry to our world. Little wonder, therefore, that from their perspective, Ray Boeche's informants were very keen to see Unger's work understood and acted upon.

Next up are the studies of the late Dr. Kurt Koch, a German theologian and author. In 1970, Koch said: "...in my forty years of Christian work... I have personally come across thousands of cases in which it was the contact with occultism that was the root cause of the problem, and the oppression that was the direct result of this contact." Koch's words perhaps more than anyone else's led to the overriding concern demonstrated by Boeche's two whistleblowers.

Koch believed that occult activities could inevitably lead the participant down an extremely rocky and disastrous path towards mental illness, emotional disturbances, "blasphemous thoughts," destructive urges," "fits of mania," "conscious atheism," and worse: "The family histories and the end result of... occult workers are, in many cases known to me, so tragic that we can no longer speak in terms of coincidence... In many instances we see suicide, fatal accidents, psychoses, or horrible death-bed scenes." Koch also asserted that anyone following an occult path would almost surely encounter "puzzling phenomena in their environment"—an absolute staple ingredient in the lives of many so-called alien-abductees. (12)

John Keel, author of *The Mothman Prophecies,* made some very similar observations in 1975. Commenting on the experiences of UFO witnesses in general, Keel said: "Many, I found, suffered certain medical symptoms such as temporary amnesia, severe headaches, muscular spasms, excessive thirst and other effects, all of which have been observed throughout history in religious miracles, demonology, occult phenomena, and contacts with fairies. All of these manifestations clearly share a common source or cause."

Keel realized that contact with the NHEs revolved around deception and resulted in an utterly negative outcome for the participant: "One hundred years from now the phenomenon may be playing some new game with us. The whole interplanetary bag may be forgotten. But…isolated individuals on lonely back roads will still be getting caught in sudden beams of energy from the sky, then shuck their families, quit their jobs, and rocket into notoriety or plunge into the hell of insanity and bankruptcy."(13)

Dr. John Warwick Montgomery, editor of *Demon Possession*, also wrote of the connection between demonic forces and negative backlash. In his Principalities and Powers, he wrote: "There is a definite correlation between negative occult activity and madness. European psychiatrist L. Szondi has shown a high correlation between involvement in spiritualism and occultism on the one hand, and schizophrenia on the other. Kurt Koch's detailed case studies have confirmed this judgment. Being a genuine Christian believer is no guarantee of exemption from the consequences of sorcery and black magic... The tragedy of most sorcery, invocation of demons, and related practices is that those who carry on these activities refuse to face the fact that they always turn out for the worst. What is received through this Faustian pact never satisfies and *one pays with one's soul in the end anyway*" (emphasis mine). (14)

Neil T. Anderson, a former aerospace engineer on NASA's Apollo program of the 1960s and a Professor of Practical Theology at Talbot Theological Seminary, also apparently influenced the mindset of Boeche's clandestine DoD informants.

In his book, *Victory Over the Darkness*, Anderson recalled an incident that many people who believe they have undergone an alien abduction will instantly be able to relate to, even if they are unsettled by its potential non-extraterrestrial implications: "I was prepared to speak in chapel on the topic of deliverance and evangelism, in which I would expose some of the strategies of Satan in these areas. Early that morning I rose and showered before my wife and children were awake. When I stepped out of the shower I found several strange symbols traced on the fogged-up mirror. I didn't do it, and Joanne, Heidi, and Karl were still asleep; they hadn't done it either. I wiped the markings off the mirror, suspicious that someone was flinging darts at me to dissuade me from my chapel message. I went down to eat breakfast alone, and as I was sitting in the kitchen, suddenly I felt a slight pain on my hand that made me flinch. I looked down and saw what appeared to be two little bite-marks on my hand.

"'Is that your best shot?' I said aloud to the powers of darkness attacking me. 'Do you think symbols on the mirror and a little bite are going to keep me from giving my message in chapel today? Get out of here.' The nuisance left and my message in chapel went off without a hitch."(15)

Compare Anderson's account with that of Dr. Karla Turner, the alien abductee, who reported a strange experience the morning after a night of bizarre UFO-related activity in her and her husband's home—which included hearing "unusual sounds," "a distinct knocking," and seemingly disembodied voices, all of which can be considered perfect examples of the "puzzling phenomena in their environment" that Dr. Kurt Koch carefully warned would undoubtedly afflict those touched by the icy hand of a demon. After consulting with abductee researcher Barbara Bartholic, and explaining the strange events of the previous night, Turner carefully noted: "[Bartholic] urged us to check our bodies, to look for any unusual scars or marks, and we did so. That was when I discovered two things: a pair of small puncture wounds about a quarter of an inch apart on my inner left wrist, and three solid white circles on my lower left abdomen... The puncture marks looked as if they could have been made by two hypodermic needles, and they were still fresh, still scabbed..."(16)

Reports of strange markings on the skin proliferate in both demonology and alien abduction lore. While Anderson attributed the strange marks on his skin to the "powers of darkness," Turner's blamed her alien visitors. But if elements of the Collins Elite, the U.S. Government, the military, the intelligence community and Ray Boeche's sources are correct in their beliefs, then both Anderson and Turner may be, somewhat paradoxically, right.

Ray Boeche's Department of Defense sources also suggested a detailed and careful reading and digestion of Emil Schneweis' *Angels and Demons according to Lactantius*. Lactantius was an early Christian author who was born around 240 AD in North Africa, taught rhetoric in various cities of the Roman Empire, and ultimately ended up in Constantinople. It was Lactantius' belief that demons could initiate encounters with a false "divine" as a specific means of deception to capture the souls of human beings. And Edward Langton's *Essentials of Demonology* devoted space to a discussion of the incubi, which has long been linked to abductions of the extraterrestrial kind. (17)

Taken as a whole, the texts mentioned by Boeche's informants suggest that deceptive demons, whose unholy existence and actions can be traced back at least as far as ancient Babylonia and Rome, are manipulating the Human Race for dark and sinister purposes having to do with the human soul. And they have done so for thousands of years under various guises—the most recent one being that of benevolent extraterrestrials from far-off star systems.

23

Trojan Horses in the Desert

On March 11, 1998, a historic two-volume document was printed and made available to all the members of the Collins Elite, photocopied extracts from which Robert Manners gave me when we first met. It was titled *The Collins Report, Deception and UFOs: What we Believe and Why*. Volume II is comprised of three specific entries: Case Studies and Profiles, Interviews, and Notes. The extracts I have come from the 367-page Volume I; it outlines the thoughts, deep-seated worries, and attitudes of the Collins Elite relating to the belief that the UFO presence on our world is wholly deceptive in nature and of purely occult origins. Its chapter titles alone clearly demonstrate their concerns: 1. UFOs and Accepted Wisdom: Believers and Skeptics; 2. The Validity of the Deception Scenario: What it is and Why it Works; 3. The History of Deception; 4. The Messengers of Deception; 5. The New Mexico Crashes: Trojans; 6. The Contactee: A Lesson in Learning; 7. Missing Time 1961-1996; 8. Infiltration: Then and Now; and 9. Future Scenarios Leading to a Conclusion.

If genuine, the extracts from *The Collins Report* shed profound light on issues that are clearly deeply controversial and infinitely disturbing. Given the fact that the Collins Elite is not, and never has been, by definition an official agency of the government, military, or intelligence community, and therefore to a degree operates outside of official control and conventional legislation, *The Collins Report* may not itself be strictly considered as a classified publication and its release may not, therefore, be in violation of U.S. national security laws. But since the document refers to apparently classified documentation this issue is very murky, particularly so when one tries to understand, decipher, and interpret the complex laws that relate to the deliberate leaking of documentation—official, quasi-official, or an odd combination of both—from within the winding and dark corridors of power.

That said, certainly the most notable entry in the available material has a major bearing the Roswell events of the summer of 1947. In an introduction to a chapter titled "The New Mexico Crashes—Trojans" the unknown author of the report states:

This writer assumes Collins Elite awareness of STAC Reports (I to XI) that describe the fall, collection, analysis and present whereabouts of unusual fabrics, foils, parchments, chemical residuals and biological material found at four locations at Lincoln County, New Mexico between 3 and 13 July 1947.

This is a curious statement. Nowhere does it make any explicit mention of the recovery by the U.S. military of a crashed, intact or semi-intact, alien spacecraft and/or alien bodies outside of Roswell, as the story is usually told. Rather, the reference to recovered "unusual fabrics, foils, parchments, chemical residuals and biological material" creates in the mind's eye the scenario of the military retrieving a tangled mass of various items, intermingled with an undetermined degree of unusual bodily materials, but not specifically extraterrestrial corpses and an advanced alien vehicle. In a similar fashion, the odd-yet-specific referral to a "fall" of various materials, as opposed to a literal crash or crash-landing, practically provokes imagery of a vast amount of sundry unidentified items raining down from the skies in a situation akin to some bizarre, otherworldly snow-storm. Why this may be the case will become clear shortly.

The Collins Report continues:

This writer assumes critical independent and prior readings by Collins Elite of *The Roswell Incident* (Berlitz - - Moore, 1980); *The UFO Crash at Roswell* (Randle - - Schmitt, 1991); *The Truth About the UFO Crash at Roswell* (Randle - - Schmitt, 1994); *The Day After Roswell* (Corso - - Birnes, 1997); *Crash at Corona* (Friedman - - Berliner, 1992); *The Roswell Report: Fact vs. Fiction in the New Mexico Desert* (Weaver - - USAF, 1994); *The Roswell Report: Case Closed* (McAndrew - - USAF, 1997); *The Roswell UFO Crash* (Korff, 1997); *Results of a Search for Records Concerning the 1947 Crash Near Roswell, New Mexico* (General Accounting Office, 1995); *The Real Roswell Crashed-Saucer Coverup* (Klass, 1997); *A Hoaxing from the Skies?* (Kendall - - S&T - - Central Intelligence Agency, 1972); *Parsons, von Karman and Goddard: A Door Unlocked* (Cub Elite - - Defense Intelligence Agency, 1971); and *New Mexico Origins: Parsons, Hubbard and Babalon Working* (Monroe - - Formula Br. - - Collins Elite, 1988).

Most readers of this book will awareness of many if not all of these published books and the Air Force and General Accounting Office reports on Roswell. But few, if anyone outside of official channels, will have previously heard of the 1971 document, *Parsons, von Karman and Goddard: A Door Unlocked*; *A Hoaxing from the Skies?* and *New Mexico Origins: Parsons, Hubbard and Babalon Working* of 1988. If such reports do exist and this aspect of the story is not disinformation, then some classified documents remain far from public access and perhaps, even, equally far away from conventional, governmental oversight. Even though these documents have yet to see the public light of day, in their own way, their very titles alone offer us more than a few clues about Jack Parsons, Robert Goddard, L. Ron Hubbard, their roles in the UFO controversy, the deceptive nature of the flying saucer mystery in general, and of the Roswell affair in particular.

The document continues:

This writer assumes as per round-table dinner at *Loftus Boat* on 23 May 1997 that all theorizing, hypothesizing and attempts to form conclusions as presented in publications cited in paragraph 2, page 196 of this REPORT continue to remain unacceptable to Collins Elite.

Despite my best efforts, I have been unable to discover what the *Loftus Boat* is or was.

The next segment of the document reads:

This writer regretfully informs Collins Elite that attempts to convince S&T at PTC of viability of sharing with Collins Elite the completed NORTH files on NM discoveries of 1947 are not successful. S&T at PTC are aware of our briefing from STAC on their files but are reluctant to share NORTH material due to security issues that developed from the Nebraska debacle.

We may not know to whom, or to what, "PTC" refers, however, in all probability "S&T" is a reference to "Science and Technology," a common abbreviation within the U.S. intelligence community. No answer is currently forthcoming on what may be meant by the "NORTH files on NM discoveries of 1947" beyond the likelihood that "NM" is an abbreviation of "New Mexico" and that this is, given the specific year cited, somehow connected to the Roswell affair. One suspects that the aside to "the Nebraska debacle" and its "security issues" refers to the whistle-blowing that went on inside the Lincoln, Nebraska's Cornsucker Hotel in November 1991, when Ray Boeche's informants seemingly decided to break their oaths of secrecy in an attempt warn him of the ominous and devilish darkness they believed was fast descending upon the Human Race.

Moving on in the document:

STAC remain committed to advancement to media and population of both Mogul and extra-terra scenarios for NM fallings and discoveries and are troubled by Collins Elite wishing to advance THE THEORY to media and population.

This writer privately engaged STAC Markale in conversation on 17 June 1997 and provided him with amended copy of *New Mexico Origins: Parsons, Hubbard and Babalon Working* (Monroe - - Formula Br. - - Collins Elite, 1988; amended 14 June 1996). Markale remains convinced that if placed into public forum knowledge of THE THEORY will irreversibly and negatively affect global social order.

This writer privately explained to Markale that Collins Elite initiatives prepared to ensure a reasonably acceptable transition of the perceived true nature of the Lincoln County discoveries to public and media, as well as a reasonable long-term acceptance of THE THEORY can still proceed with limited social disorder if handled correctly.

Markale is not convinced and speaks for the STAC membership. Presently STAC-5 is privately sympathetic to the position of Collins Elite; he reiterates the position of CANDLE of 4 May 1991 that STAC is now "in too deep" with its attempts to reverse-control the situation and prevent enemy infiltration and deception beyond present levels.

This writer sees that disagreement on our part with STAC is unlikely to inflame situation beyond present levels due to STAC's genuine sympathy with difficulties created for everyone by recent developments.

STAC-5 informs this writer STAC totally rejects notion that Collins Elite's *Learning the Way* paper that theorizes radically indoctrinating population with belief and faith - - and revelation to media and population of true nature of Lincoln County discoveries - - can halt enemy infiltration.

These six paragraphs suggest that all sides realized that trying to inform the general public and the media of what the Collins Elite and others concluded was the disturbing truth behind the UFO phenomenon was no easy feat at all. And that for some of those in the know, the best approach was to do or say absolutely nothing whatsoever beyond either burying their heads in the sand or continuing to keep people busy following such diversionary pathways as crashed UFOs and military spy-balloons. Just about anything, in other words, to keep inquiring minds as far away as possible from matters demonic. Others, it seems, were intent in 1998 on campaigning for a planet-wide revelation of what they saw as the truth as a means to ensure our survival when finally faced with the nightmarish menace in all its might.

Of course, much of this discussion appears to have been hypothetical in nature. In other words, there does not seem to be any evidence, in 1998 at least, of an all-powerful New World Order-type entity secretly waiting in the wings and ready to take control of the people of Earth and mold their beliefs—or non-beliefs—relative to the teachings and beliefs of Christianity. But matters may very well have kicked up a slight notch or more in the twelve years that have passed since *The Collins Report* was published, as we will see shortly.

Precisely who the enigmatic Mr. Markale may be remains unknown.

The document continues:

This writer remains greatly troubled by STAC decision to continue its relationship with contractors Jamison and Wylie who—according to STAC-5—are still convinced that the "PARSONS TECHNIQUE" can assist in holding off deception, infiltration and final invasion.

This writer adheres to Collins Elite conclusions based on a reading of the original STAC Reports (1 to XI) that any attempt to follow the path of Parsons will only result in a catastrophe of the type warned about in *Parsons, von Karman and Goddard: A Door Unlocked* (Cub Elite - - Defense Intelligence Agency, 1971).

STAC-5 understands this but consistently feels the need to reiterate that situation has gone too far for STAC to back down. STAC-5 also informs that WPAFB sources have had some success using the "PARSONS TECHNIQUE" in achieving spontaneous brief laboratory manifestation of materials very similar to two of those that "fell" at Lincoln County, NM in 1947.

STAC-5 is of opinion that if long-term manifestation and stability of materials can be achieved and precise originating point of materials can be determined then this will assist NASA-TZER mission to answer the critical questions posed in our 1991 briefing to STAC, *Entry Points -- And How Do We Keep Them Closed?* **(1)**

Although the identity of "Jamison and Wylie" has yet to be determined, and the term "NASA-TZER" remains a distinct puzzle, this material is perhaps the most important one to come our way, for the following reason. The reference to personnel stationed at WPAFB—which can only mean Wright-Patterson Air Force Base, Dayton, Ohio—having achieved "spontaneous, brief, laboratory manifestation of materials very similar to two of those that 'fell' at Lincoln County, NM in 1947," accords very well with something that Ray Boeche's sources told him, namely, that the unusual debris found in 1947 did not result from the crash or aerial explosion of an alien spacecraft. Rather, it may have been cosmically and alchemically weaved in realms far away, then carefully and deliberately dropped on the desert floor at the Foster Ranch. (1)

Boeche's own recollections of his whistleblower meetings add much weight to the Roswell scenario as detailed in *The Collins Report*. He told me: "I was never told how they knew, but the guys knew that there was wreckage of non-earthly origin at Roswell. And I remember asking them specifically in a later conversation: 'How do you know this? And how does it happen that a demonic force can also interact physically?' Their response was to me was: 'You're a pastor; you've studied theology. Go back to the Bible and look.'"

And, that is precisely what Boeche did. Said Boeche: "That

set me on months of research as I tried to piece this together in my own mind. Scripture refers to Satan as the prince of this world and the prince of the powers of the air. I deduced that there could be a precedent, a logical precedent based on scripture that demonic forces can in some ways influence the physical world.

"So, given that that's the case, could they create something? Could they somehow pluck matter from somewhere else—a different planet, a different galaxy that was so different from Earth that it's going to be something recognized as not coming from here? Could they manufacture or create a physical object or wreckage—deliberately—to make us fall into the trap of believing that something extraterrestrial had fallen from outer space? A staged crash to make us fall into the deception that they are extraterrestrials? That was the scientists' conclusion.

"One of the things that made me believe there could be some sort of physical interaction is the mention of the Nephilim in Genesis in the Bible. Whatever these other worldly beings were—angels, fallen angels—they were able to interact physically and create some sort of progeny here on earth. More prosaic interpretations of the passages regarding the Nephilim—that they were simply 'mighty men,' for instance—are accepted by most scholars, but I don't see overwhelming evidence to completely eliminate the possibility that they were of a spiritual or supernatural nature."

And Boeche's informants also had comments to make about Jack Parsons that seem to dovetail with the data linking Parsons with Roswell, and with the strange experimentation going on at Wright-Patterson AFB, as outlined within the pages of *The Collins Report*: "[My DoD sources said that] Parsons was the start of it all. They said that was the genesis of this. Was this a doorway that was opened by Parsons to allow these demonic entities in? Or did Parsons give someone else the idea that maybe someone in the government should look into this? That was one of their big concerns: that in order to try and accomplish some sort of military advantage, demonic things—masquerading as aliens—had been contacted and forces had been unleashed that were not going to be able to be controlled for very long; or, at least, were not going to be able to be bent to the will of whoever started this project. Satanic rituals, ritual magic and even human sacrifice were all mentioned as being linked with the project. They were convinced the work had to stop."(2)

As incredible as it sounds, the startling conclusion we can reach from studying the extracts of *The Collins Report* and the words of Ray Boeche and his informants is that demonic alchemists carefully created the Roswell debris in a far-off realm or on an equally far-off world. Then, they cunningly and carefully planted it in the wilds of New Mexico, Trojan-Horse-style, knowing that it would soon be found and interpreted as something of an anomalous, otherworldly nature. And more than fifty years later, personnel at Wright-Patterson Air Force Base had achieved some measure of success in conjuring up very similar materials—albeit briefly, under wildly unpredictable means, and from who knows exactly where—via the door-opening teachings of Jack Parsons, hence the Collins Elite's use of the term "the Parsons technique." In other words, the personnel at Wright-Patterson AFB cited in *The Collins Report* may very well have been the same ones who had foolishly entered into a pact with the forces of Satan to—as Ray Boeche's sources worded it—"accomplish some sort of military advantage."

The final section of the currently available pages of *The Collins Report* states:

Until final outcome of STAC, NASA-TZER and WPAFB research in this area is known this writer recommends that Collins Elite continues to focus attention on planned disclosure to

The New Mexico Crashes: Trojans

Introduction -

This writer assumes Collins Elite deep familiarity with multiple circumstances and theorizing that centers on the discovery-recovery of unusual fabrics, foils, chemical residuals and biological materials at four locations at Lincoln County, NM, on 3 to 13 July 1947.

This writer assumes critical independent and prior readings by Collins Elite of *The Roswell Incident* (Berlitz - - Moore, 1980); *The UFO Crash at Roswell* (Randle - - Schmitt, 1994); *The Roswell Report* (Weaver - - HQ USAF, 1994); *The Truth About the UFO Crash at Roswell* (Randle - - Schmitt, 1995); *The Day After Roswell* (Corso - - Birnes, 1997); *Crash at Corona* (Friedman - - Berliner, 1992); *The Roswell Report: Fact vs. Fiction in the New Mexico Desert* (Weaver - - HQ USAF, 1994); *The Roswell Report : Case Closed* (McAndrew - - HQ USAF, 1997); *The Roswell UFO Crash* (Korff, 1997); *Results of a Search for Records Concerning the 1947 Crash Near Roswell, New Mexico* (General Accounting Office, 1995); *The Real Roswell Crashed-Saucer Coverup* (Klass, 1997); *A Hoaxing in our Skies?* (Kendall - - S&T - - Central Intelligence Agency, 1972); *Parsons, von Karman and Goddard: A Door Unlocked* (Cub Elite - - Defense Intelligence Agency, 1971); and *New Mexico Origins: Parsons, Hubbard and Babalon Working* (Monroe - - Formula Br. - - Collins Elite, 1988).

This writer assumes as per round-table dinner at Loftus Boat on 23rd May 1998 that all theorizing, hypothesizing and attempts to form conclusions as presented in publications cited in paragraph 2 of this contained chapter remain inadequate as of this day of writing, 17 August 1998.

This writer informs Collins Elite that attempts to convince S&T at PTC of viability of sharing with Collins Elite the STAC file on NM events of 1947 are not successful. STAC remain committed to advancement of both Mogul and extra-terra nature of NM recoveries and are concerned by Collins Elite wishing to advance THE THEORY into media and public domain.

This writer engaged in discussion with STAC Markale on 17 June 1998 and provided him with copy of *New Mexico Origins: Parsons, Hubbard and Babalon Working* (Monroe - - Formula Br. - - Collins Elite, 1988). Markale remains concerned that if placed into a public forum it may adversely damage both public morale and social order.

This writer explained to Markale that Collins Elite initiatives to ensure a smooth and acceptable transition to public and media and acceptance of same can still proceed according to Red - - VST of 1985. Markale is not convinced and speaks for STAC membership that prefers no disclosure. Presently STAC 5 is privately sympathetic to the position of Collins Elite; yet reiterates the position of CANDLE of 4 May 1991 that prior

196

A page from a 1998 draft-copy of The Collins Report

public of THE THEORY if STAC, NASA-TZER and WPAFB attempts to "close the door" are not satisfactory.

This writer concludes that if this hypothetical stage is reached disclosure and intense indoctrination of faith and values at planetary level to radically and rapidly alter current population mindset is the only alternative that may prove successful in thwarting plans of enemy.

This writer considers the disclosure to media and population of the Lincoln County fabrics, foils, parchments, chemical residuals and biological material to be crucial and integral in terms of revealing the "Trojan Horse" aspect of THE THEORY.

STAC-5 understands this too and agrees that only if present attempts by NASA-TZER and WPAFB-1T to prevent widespread infiltration and enemy deception fail that revelation, explanation of the "Trojan Horse" aspect of the Lincoln County fallings and indoctrination may be only viable alternatives. This writer is encouraged by confident comments from STAC-5 that if present and near-future operations fail to achieve success STAC and Collins Elite would provide a united front that would allow THE THEORY to be presented publicly and quickly and in a way that was acceptable to STAC.

For that reason and likelihood that enemy infiltration will not be thwarted by STAC and NASA-TZER methods [deleted] has prepared a unique briefing paper on the *Lincoln County Trojans* in the event that immediate and emergency dissemination of facts to media and population is required. **(3)**

Of course, those who believe literal extraterrestrials crashed near Roswell in 1947 might very well assert that even though the author of *The Collins Report* regarded the Roswell event as anomalous, the denial of a specifically alien angle to the whole affair should be interpreted as an attempt by insider sources to carefully spread disinformation designed to further hide the fact that E.T. really *did* crash at Roswell!

Certainly, documents and seemingly official Top Secret files of unclear origin and provenance have been made available to a number of players within the field of UFO research for decades, and have provoked unbridled controversy in the process. And those same files have successfully taken many a researcher on a wild ride that never ends, and down a pathway where the hard evidence that might confirm the legitimacy of the material is never, ever forthcoming—at least, not yet. The saga of the so-called Majestic 12 documents that dominated much of late-1980s and 1990s UFOlogy—as well as the valuable time and money of Stanton Friedman, Bill Moore, Dr. Robert Wood and his son, Ryan, and a number of others—is prime evidence of that. (4)

Perhaps, this is precisely what we are dealing with when it comes to *The Collins Report*, too. Unfortunately, for all my concerns about liaising with whistleblower sources and their treasure-trove-like collection of fantastic files and aging papers, I have to concede that I find it difficult to not at least address and dissect this material, such is its admittedly hypnotic allure.

So much for the strange debris found near Roswell in 1947, but what of the reports suggesting that "biological material" and unusual bodies may also have been recovered? To resolve that riddle, we have to delve deep into centuries-old rite and ritual and manufactured life-forms.

24

It's Alive!

One aspect of the 1998 *Collins Report* that I have deliberately not commented upon until now concerns the so-called "biological material" found at the Roswell crash site in early July 1947. Is it possible that some equally strange form of diabolical alchemy was at work to create not just the so-called memory-metal that a number of players in the Roswell saga described seeing, but also to generate a type of extraterrestrial Jackalope, a creature that looks real and that exhibits prime evidence of DNA, flesh, bone, and skin, but that is, in reality, nothing more than a brilliant piece of fakery?

To answer that question, we have to turn to a very well-known and renowned figure within the history of rocketry, one who was well-acquainted with Robert Goddard in Roswell; who was a work-colleague of, and even almost a father-figure to, Jack Parsons; and who maintained that a distant relative of his had succeeded in giving some form of rudimentary life to previously inanimate matter.

Theodore von Kármán was a Hungarian-American engineer and physicist active primarily in the fields of aeronautics and astronautics, and responsible for numerous important advances in aerodynamics, notably his work on the characterization of supersonic and hypersonic airflow. Concerned about the rise in fascism and Nazism in Europe, von Kármán accepted in 1930 the directorship of the Guggenheim Aeronautical Laboratory at the California Institute of Technology, emigrated to live in the United States and in 1936 founded Aerojet with Frank Malina and Jack Parsons. Nazi developments in rock-

Giving life to the Golem

etry during the Second World War encouraged the U.S. military to look into the potential use of rockets in warfare, a matter in which von Kármán played a significant role. For example, during the early part of 1943, the Experimental Engineering Division of the United States Army Air Forces Materiel Command worked closely with von Kármán on the status of Germany's rocket program.

In 1946, after the hostilities were over and Hitler and his cronies were firmly defeated, von Kármán became the first chairman of the Scientific Advisory Group, which studied aeronautical technologies for the United States Army Air Forces. He also helped found AGARD, the NATO aerodynamics research oversight group, the International Council of the Aeronautical Sciences, the International Academy of Astronautics, and the Von Karman Institute for Fluid Dynamics in Brussels. At the age of 81, von Kármán received the first National Medal of Science, bestowed in a White House ceremony by President John F. Kennedy. He was recognized specifically for "...his leadership in the science and engineering basic to aeronautics; for his effective teaching and related contributions in many fields of mechanics, for his distinguished counsel to the Armed Services, and for his promoting international cooperation in science and engineering." Von Kármán passed away on a trip to Aachen in 1963, and is buried in Pasadena, California. (1)

Perhaps most startling of all, von Kármán claimed until his dying day that an ancestor of his, one Rabbi Judah Loew ben Bezalel of Prague, had succeeded in creating a Golem, an artificial human being endowed with life, according to Hebrew folklore. A Golem, essentially, is an animated being created entirely out of inanimate matter; in the pages of the Bible, the word is used to refer to an embryonic or incomplete figure. The earliest stories of Golems date to ancient Judaism. For example, Adam is described in the *Talmud* as initially being created as a Golem when his dust was "kneaded into a shapeless hunk." Like Adam, all Golems are said to be modeled out of clay.

In many tales the Golem is inscribed with magic, or religious, words that ensure it remains animated. Writing one of the names of God on its forehead, placing a slip of paper in its mouth, or inscribing certain terms on its body, are all ways and means to instill and continue the life of a Golem. Another way of activating the creature is by writing a specific incantation using the owner's blood on calfskin parchment, and then placing it inside the Golem's mouth. Conversely, removing the parchment is said to deactivate the creation.

As for the tale of Rabbi Judah Loew ben Bezalel, it must be noted that many scholars who have studied the Golem controversy are convinced that the story of the 16th century Chief Rabbi of Prague is merely an entertaining piece of Jewish folklore. Nevertheless, it is worthy of examination. According to the legend, under Rudolf II, the Holy Roman Emperor who ruled from 1576 to 1612, the Jews in Prague were to be expelled from the city or outright slaughtered. In an effort to try and afford the Jewish community some protection, the rabbi constructed the Golem out of clay taken from the banks of the Vltava River and subsequently succeeded in bringing it to life via archaic rituals and ancient Hebrew incantations. As the Golem grew, it became increasingly violent, killing gentiles and spreading fear and dread all across the land.

The Emperor supposedly begged Rabbi Loew to destroy the Golem, promising in return to stop the persecution of the Jews. The rabbi agreed and quickly deactivated his creation by rubbing out the first letter of the word "emet" ("truth" or "reality") from the creature's forehead and leaving the Hebrew word "met," meaning death. The Emperor understood, however, that the Golem's body, stored in the attic of the Old New Synagogue in Prague, could be quickly restored to life again if it was ever needed. Accordingly, legend says, the body of Rabbi Loew's Golem still lies in the synagogue's attic to this very day, awaiting the time when it will once again be summoned to continue the work of its long-dead creator.

Regardless of whether or not the tale of the Golem is true, the mere fact that Jack Parsons was a very close friend and colleague of Von Kármán, that Von Kármán knew how inanimate matter might become animate, that he had met with the Roswell-based Robert Goddard, and that *The Collins Report* makes reference to a seemingly-classified Defense Intelligence Agency document of 1971 titled Parsons, von Karman and Goddard: A Door Unlocked, strongly and collectively suggests that some officials had linked not only Parsons and von Kármán with the UFO subject but even with the Lincoln County event and the curious biological materials reportedly recovered there, too. (2)

There are rumors that, on the day he died, Jack Parsons attempted to create life in Golem-like fashion. Filmmaker Renate Druks, who was an acquaintance of Marjorie Elizabeth Cameron, said in Nat Freedland's *The Occult Explosion*: "I have every reason to believe that Jack Parsons was working on some very strange experiments, trying to create what the old alchemists call a homunculus, *a tiny artificial man with magic powers* [emphasis mine]. I think that's what he was working on when the accident happened."(3)

Creating a Homunculus

Ancient alchemists had several methods of bringing these diminutive humanoids to life; one involved the mandrake. Popular, centuries-old belief holds that the mandrake plant grew on ground where semen ejaculated by hanged men had fallen to earth, and, as a result, its roots vaguely resemble those of a human being. To ensure a successful creation of the homunculus, the root is to be picked before dawn on a Friday morning by a black dog, then washed and nourished with milk and honey and, in some prescriptions, blood, whereupon it develops into a miniature human that will guard and protect its owner.

Another method, cited by Dr. David Christianus at the University of Giessen during the 18th century, was to take an egg laid by a black hen, poke a tiny hole through its shell, replace a bean-sized portion of the egg white with human semen, seal the opening with virgin parchment, and bury the egg in dung on the first day of the March lunar cycle. The ancient teachings suggested that a miniature humanoid would emerge from the egg after thirty days and, in return, help and protect its creator for a steady diet of lavender seeds and earthworms. (4)

How curious that both Parsons and von Karman, in roundabout ways, had links to stories of manufactured life-forms—and in Parsons' case, even to a "tiny artificial man with magic powers." That is precisely what the Collins Elite concluded about the biological material found at Roswell: that it was of alchemical origin, *not* extraterrestrial.

25

SOUL FOOD

Thus far, we have predominantly focused upon the theories, ideas, and conclusions of the Collins Elite as they relate to the perceived nature of the UFO presence. Those same theories, ideas, and conclusions do not stand alone, however. The fact is that, over time, numerous people in public UFO research have come to very similar conclusions.

Many students of the UFO riddle view alien abductions as involving extraterrestrial scientists, the Grays, secretly visiting the Earth to milk us of our DNA, eggs, and sperm. The purpose, supposedly, is to try and save their rapidly ailing race through cross breeding, creating beings that are part human and part extraterrestrial. In recent years, however, many UFO researchers have come to accept—just as the Collins Elite did—that the phenomenon is inextricably tied to the Human soul, and not always in a good way.

Howard Menger, one of the most well-known of the so-called contactees, claimed that, in 1956, he had been informed by one of his purported alien-contacts that there were both "good and bad space people" visiting the Earth; and, moreover, that "this Earth is the battlefield of Armageddon, and the battle is for men's minds and souls. Prayers, good thoughts and caution are your best insulation."(1)

The late John Keel said that Menger admitted, in letters to UFO investigator and author Gray Barker and *Saucer News* editor Jim Moseley, that his book "fiction-fact," and he "implied that the Pentagon had asked him to participate in an experiment to test the public's reaction to extraterrestrial contact." Perhaps this was simply Menger's idea of a little self-aggrandizing mischief; on the other hand, just maybe, it was part of an early attempt by the Collins Elite to inform the public of what it believed was *really* going down in the world of the UFO. (2)

In 1988, one year after his groundbreaking and bestselling book *Communion* was published, Whitley Strieber wrote with respect to the abduction phenomenon: "…it was clear to me that the soul was very much at issue. People experienced feeling as if their souls were being dragged from their bodies. I'd had an incident of total separation of soul and body. More than one person had seen the visitors in the context of a near-death experience. The visitors have said 'We recycle souls,' and—of the earth—that 'this is a school.' It may be exactly that—a place where souls are growing and evolving toward some form that we can scarcely begin to imagine. I can conceive that the fate of souls may be one of the great universal questions. It may be that we have emerged as a means of at once creating and answering this question."(3)

Seven years later, Strieber stated that one of his correspondents, who had had a particularly distressing encounter with a non-human creature, wrote to him as follows: "It was looking at me like it was hungry, and I got the idea that it wanted to eat my soul." Strieber commented: "I could not help but recall the words of the famous investigator of anomalous experiences, Charles Fort. He'd suggested, toward the end of his life, that our world might be like a barnyard, implying that we are ignorant animals here for the slaughter and incapable of seeing the greater and more terrible meanings that surround us."(4)

The late Professor John E. Mack, M.D. also uncovered some highly disturbing data that suggested a link between purported alien abductions and the soul. Mack stated starkly:

"Some abductees feel that certain beings seem to want to take their souls from them."

Commenting on the experience of an abductee named Greg, Mack said: "[Greg] told me that the terror of his encounters with certain reptilian beings was so intense that he feared being separated from his soul. 'If I were separated from my soul,' he said, 'I would not have any sense of being. I think all my consciousness would go. I would cease to exist. That would be the worst thing anyone could do to me.'"

About another abductee—Isabel—Mack noted: "She recalled vividly waking up once in the middle of the night to find 'one of the creatures right next to my bed, and another one bending over me trying to bring up as much fear in me' as possible. 'I knew instinctively that whatever that thing was that was next to me wanted to enter me.'"

Mack added: "She felt certain that what these beings were after is 'the human soul.' Perhaps, she speculated, this is because 'they don't possess a soul.' But 'they can't just take our souls, because they cannot come into this world physically. But they can fool you into handing it over.'" (5)

Then there is the illuminating experience of one Paul Inglesby, author of *UFOs and the Christian*. Dr. David Clarke and Andy Roberts, noted and respected English authorities on the UFO controversy, have highlighted Inglesby's views on the relationship between UFOs and the human soul: "Born in 1915, Inglesby is probably Britain's longest serving UFO theorist, with contacts at the highest level both in the church and the British establishment... Inglesby is also unique in that his interest began a whole decade before the flying saucer era. In 1938, while serving with the Royal Navy under Lord Mountbatten, he contracted a tropical disease and was left dangerously ill for three months. During this time he underwent a 'devastating spiritual experience,' during which he saw visions of a future atomic war and demonic forces controlling space ships and nuclear weapons. While tapped in this timeless limbo, '…not only did I witness future events, in a mental telepathic sort of way, but throughout the whole of this time a battle was raging for possession of my soul.'" (6)

Clarke and Roberts also note that towards the end of the 1970s, a number of leading figures in the British UFO Research Organization (BUFORA), including founding president Graham Knewstub and chairman Roger Stanway, became believers in the satanic theory for the UFO phenomenon. Certainly, Knewstub was very much to-the-point when he said: "their source may be in malignant spiritual intervention."

The story of Roger Stanway is even more alarming. Shortly after coming to accept that UFOs were the products of the Devil, Stanway had an unsettling experience in the bowels of the underground tube-station at Euston, London, England. He reported: "…as soon as I stepped onto the platform, I became alarmed to realize that there was, welling up within me, a very strong sub-conscious compulsion to throw myself onto the electric line…my legs became weak, my heart raced and I started to sweat profusely…I didn't dare move in case I could not prevent my legs taking me onto the line."(7)

It may not be coincidental that the unsettling feelings only vanished after Stanway recited lines from the Gospel of St. John. And, of course, Stanway's near-overwhelming compulsion to throw himself onto the tracks is *very* reminiscent of the 1973 account of Tammy Stone, who had to fight with all her might a compulsion to have a head-on collision with a truck, on a stretch of highway in Waco, Texas.

Without doubt one of the most controversial statements that may have bearing on the link between UFO activity and the human soul—and secret government data on the subject— came from a man named Robert Lazar. Lazar claims that from late 1988 to early 1989, while working at a location in the Nevada desert known as Area 51, he was allegedly shown a number of alien spacecraft that the U.S. Government had acquired under unclear circumstances. Lazar further maintained that while at Area 51 he read a variety of classified reports on UFOs that provided extensive background data on the alleged history of an alien presence on the Earth.

In an interview with George Knapp, an investigative journalist who works for KLAS-TV in Las Vegas, Nevada, Lazar said that the reports he read stated that humankind is the product of 65 genetic "corrections" by the aliens. Lazar admitted to being skeptical of the religious information he read in the briefing papers. "It's easier to swallow things you can put your hands on and touch and work with," he told Knapp. "That's no problem. But when you get a lot of spiritual stuff and religion...that we were made by progressive corrections in evolution and that sort of stuff...it's tough to accept without hardcore proof. The only hard-core thing is that there is an *extremely* classified document dealing with religion, and it's extremely thick. But why should there be *any* classified documents dealing with religion?"

When pressed further by Knapp, Lazar said that the documents he read described human-beings as "containers." Knapp asked for clarification on this odd terminology, to which Lazar replied: "That's supposedly how the aliens look at us; that we are nothing but containers. Maybe containers of souls. You can come up with whatever theory you want. But we're containers, and that's how we're mentioned in the documents; that religion was specifically created so we have some rules and regulations for the sole purpose of not damaging the containers."

Knapp pushed further: "We're containers for souls that they're going to use at some other point?"

"Right," replied Lazar. (8)

In a later interview, with researcher Michael Lindemann,

Lazar made a very similar comment: "What they were talking about was the desirability of containers, and that the containers were not damaged. Now, people speculate on containers. Are they talking about containers of souls, something bizarre like that; or is it the opposite? Is the container the soul, and it contains the body? That's too far out really for me to grasp, but they were talking about the preservation of the containers, and how unique they are. Extremely, extremely unique. Very difficult to find."(9)

26

"They come in the emperor's new clothes"

"The only alternative that may prove successful in thwarting plans of enemy," states the 1988 report of the Collins Elite, is through "…intense indoctrination of faith and values at planetary level to radically and rapidly alter current population mind-set."

These words are highly significant, as there are those within the UFO research community who—after careful study—have *also* determined that a belief in the power of the Christian God and Jesus Christ can indeed thwart the demonic assault that, the Collins Elite believes, currently manifests under the guise of alien abductors and hybridizers. One of those people is Joe Jordan.

Jordan, who has a keen interest in the abduction phenomenon and works as a safety specialist at the Kennedy Space Center, told me: "UFOs weren't even in my vocabulary until 1992. I was introduced to a local MUFON [Mutual UFO Network] state section director in Orlando, Florida, and became involved and went through the training. And I soon became a state-section director for MUFON. This is when I was introduced to the abduction experience: from some of the people coming to the monthly meetings. These people were claiming to be in contact with the so-called entities responsible for the UFO sightings. So, we decided to look at these reports. I told our investigators: 'We can continue to chase our tails by looking at lights-in-the-sky, or we can focus on people who are in the front-line.' And this seems to be the abductees."

Joe Jordan, Kennedy Space Center

About four years after his UFO research began, Jordan saw the light, so to speak. "In the fall of 1996," said Jordan, "I started dealing with two unusual, *very* bizarre cases. And I had a girlfriend at the time who was one of my investigators dealing with abductions. It was good having her with us because a lot of the abductees are female and, with some of the more personal aspects of abductions, they wanted to share them but felt uncomfortable sharing them with a man. So, she was able to do these sides of the investigations, and let me know what was going on.

"She was a Christian, and I was fine with that. She didn't push it on me in any way. But she pulled me aside one day and said: 'There's something very dark going on with these two cases, and I think you need some protection.' She handed me a Bible and said: 'It's in here.' I replied: 'No, it's got nothing to do with that.' But I took a look at it, and when I read what's called the Gospel Message, I chose to become a Christian. That was in November of 1996.

"I had two weeks time-off coming up and took part in a Bible-study group a friend was planning. I wanted to know what it was to be a Christian. And it was during these two weeks that something happened. I had a vision-like experience, which I had never had before. I was shown what these entities *really* were, to a point that I knew without a doubt what they were. I told my buddy: 'We don't need to be working in this field. This is something, as Christians, we should not be involved with.' And, we decided to put it away.

"But what we also did was to go back and look at a 2-hour video we had made of one of the guys involved in one of these two cases. And, when we went back, it was like at the time we hadn't heard what he said. It was amazing: here was the evidence. He had stated that during an experience he had—in sheer panic—called out: 'Jesus, Jesus; help me!' And the experience instantly, and abruptly, terminated. And he woke up in the bed. And, I realized that all the other abduction researchers were saying that stopping an experience was not possible. But, here, I have one, and he *did* stop the experience."

What followed next was very surprising, to say the least— given that the UFO research community is supposed to be exposing the facts, not suppressing them. "So, I called some of the top abduction researchers in the country at that time, and shared the details," said Jordan. "Each time I shared the case, they all would ask something like: 'Can we go off the record?' I said: 'Sure, that's fine.' They *all* agreed that they had come across similar cases, where people were using prayer or calling out and using the name and authority of Jesus Christ, and were able to stop an abduction experience.

"I said: 'If you have come across this, why have you not printed it, talked about it, and where people can see this?' And, I usually got one of two responses, or both, or something like: 'We really didn't know what to make of it.' I would have been fine with that, but they would always come out with this second reason: 'We were afraid to go there, because it might affect our credibility in the field.' That's interesting, and even like a cover-up, not giving all the information. Don't rock the boat. So, I told these guys: 'You just confirmed that this case I have is not unusual, that there are plenty more out there. So I'm going to take this piece of the puzzle and I'm going to run with it.' They all said: 'Please do, because we can't.'"

Thus was born Joe Jordan's research project to expose what he sees as the truth of the demonic abductions: "Now, today, I've worked on close to 400 cases—in the past 12 years—of people who have gone through this abduction experience and have been able to stop it, either in the act, or by being able to terminate it completely from ever happening again in their life, and being able to get their lives back on track. On my website I have more than 80 of those cases posted."

Of those many cases, one is from a man named Joel, whose story as told to Jordan is typical:

I am from the Island nation of Trinidad and Tobago and am a preacher's kid. So I've grown up in the church and seen a fare [sic] share of demonic attacks and the power of God at work against the forces of darkness. My first experience was at a very young age; I was under ten years old and one night while I was in bed asleep, I felt myself become paralyzed with FEAR to the point that I could not move a single muscle. The only part of my body that was active was my mind. I felt a force of some kind trying to pull me towards the window of my bedroom to OUTSIDE and all I could do to try to prevent it from happening was [to] scream for my mommy in my mind and eventually it stopped.

Well this unwelcome visit although very infrequent, went on for many years throughout my college years in Houston, TX and even during my professional career in San Francisco, CA. During this time I was old enough to know that when I had a visit, instead of calling for my mom in my mind, I called on the name of Jesus and they would leave but would still revisit me from time to time.

One night while in bed, I had a major breakthrough. I finally realized who I was in Christ and that no evil spirit should ever be bothering me like this. You see I finally understood that it was because of FEAR in my own life that gave these evil spirits a foothold and once I realized this, I was able to do something about it. That night I had another visit and this time I was able to muster up enough strength to move my lips and say: "By the blood of Jesus I rebuke you," and instantly they left me and to this day they never returned.

"Over the years," said Jordan, "I started seeing some patterns, and once I started posting the testimonies, I would have people come to me who had read them and ask me if I could help them stop the experience. Well, that changed the whole research completely. But, because I learned how other people had changed their lives, I was able to show these people coming to me what was happening, and how to make the process work. And, I've learned a lot more too. One of the things people ask is: 'Why is this happening to me?' Working on the approximately 400 cases I have, I've found three answers.

"The first one is there are people who have actually outright said: 'I'd like to have that experience.' They have consciously invited it into their lives. And I always warn people: 'Be careful what you ask for.' The second reason was that people had unknowingly opened a door to allow these entities in to harass them in their life. When I say opening of doors, all of these activities have been something related to being anti-Christian or anti-biblical, or anti-God, and going against the things in the Bible that God warns us not to be associated with, like dealing with different types of the occult, new-age, metaphysics, the paranormal—any of these types of activity seem to open that door. And people unknowingly open it, because they don't see the connection. And, working with these people I can find when that door was opened.

"Now, the third answer puzzled us for a while. I had adults telling me that they had had the abduction experience since being a little child. And I thought: a little child won't consciously ask for this experience. And I doubt they would unknowingly ask for it either because they're not associated with any of these things. But, what I *did* find—by asking the right questions—was that when looking into their family lives, we found the open doors came through the parents. And that starts a generational cycle. Those were the reasons for this possibly happening in someone's life."

And there was much more to come.

"There's another part to this: where these entities communicate with the experiencers. The experiencer often talks about the message being anti-God, anti-the Bible, anti-Jesus Christ. And it's real strange that if they were extraterrestrial they would come all this way just to bash one belief-system, and not all the others. In some cases, the people telling me this were people who were Christians, but who had gotten off-track with their faith. And so, again, the door was opened and these entities began their harassment.

"The purpose I see with these entities in their communication is that they're preaching a new gospel. And, the Bible warns of angels preaching gospel. I do believe they are a part of a demonic hierarchy, and the entities involved in the abduction experience are the elite of that hierarchy; it seems like we're dealing with fallen-angels. The abilities that the fallen-angels have are mirrored by these entities, but the message they come with is not that of the Judeo-Christian God. It's against them. I do not see that these are physical entities, in any way. You will see physical manifestation of the experience, like marks on the body, and evidence that looks like things have been disturbed in the home. But I do believe that the actual experience itself occurs in a whole other state."

Jordan elaborated on this point: "The people don't get taken to a ship; they are physically still in bed. I have a couple of cases where people had the abduction experience while in the presence of a witness who was awake. They didn't go anywhere. They almost went into an unconscious state. This was only for a few minutes, but they came out of it totally exhausted and could talk about what had happened to them, and it would take hours for them to tell it all. But it was just minutes. Like a time-displacement. I'm not sure I would call it a hallucination, maybe more of an apparition, something along the lines of a hologram, but it's still in the mind. These entities can create this experience in our minds and we can interact with it, and it can leave physical manifestations from the experience. And that's why this is so confusing."

Jordan's views as to why this is taking place accord closely with those of the Collins Elite: "The purpose of all this is to deny the reality of Christianity. And, they have probably the best propaganda machine I've ever seen or read about. I believe that's the purpose behind this whole experience. Look at the stories of old of gnomes, fairies and elves: we wouldn't believe that today. So they come in the emperor's new clothes. And they come in a guise that we will accept. But their purpose is to defeat us and to delude us, so that we will take our focus off the one true God. And if that happens, if the Bible is real, and if the message it shares is real, then the people who succumb to this, their souls are doomed. And I think that's what these entities are trying to do. That's their agenda. The demons *know* they're doomed to Hell; the Bible teaches that is what will happen to them. But when that time comes, they plan on trying to take as many of God's creation with them as they can. It's a cosmic war."

Jordan's final words could easily serve as a warning to officials—such as the colleagues of Ray Boeche's informants— who seek to bargain with the unholy entities in the hope of gaining something that could be used from a military or espionage perspective and advantage: "One of the seductions they use is the lure of advanced alien technology, but it's a false lure. But it becomes a hook, and you end up selling your soul to the Devil."(1)

27

WHAT INTELLIGENT EVIL WANTS

Michael S. Heiser, who earned an M.A. and Ph.D. in the Hebrew Bible and ancient Semitic languages from the University
of Wisconsin-Madison, has notable views that closely parallel
the beliefs of the Collins Elite, Ray Boeche's Department of
Defense informants, and Joe Jordan.

"Fundamentally," Heiser said to me, "whatever this is, it's
in it for itself. This is not altruistic. I look at it demonically
because of the human-rights issues: people being taken against
their will, nasty things done to them. Or even if things are not
literally done, they're implanted in their minds; they're mentally tormented. This is something inherently negative and
sinister. I've been in some settings where people have tried to
compare them to scientists and us to polar bears, or something
like that, that it's for our own good. Well, the analogy misses
something: we can't talk to the polar bear. If we could, we could
put the polar bear's fears at ease. Now that's a little trite, but if
we believe these people's experiences, these beings are perfectly
capable of communicating with us. And, as [Jacques] Vallee
pointed out years ago, the whole scenario—abductions, all the
elements of it—doesn't really sound like something that would
be done by a super-advanced, technological being. Vallee's observations of 20 or 30 years ago are still valid: this doesn't sound
like something that if we had this kind of technology that we
couldn't do better. So, I do view it in human-rights terms. I
view it in terms of it being unethical by whatever is doing it."

As for the final goal, Heiser added: "What they are trying
to do is to bring about a global, intellectual, and mental para-

Michael S. Heiser

digm shift. That is, they are pushing the idea that we—as human beings—are related to them, that we come from them and that they are responsible for making us what we are, even if they didn't initially create us. All of these ideas imply that they are progenitors, benefactors, gardeners, or whatever metaphor you want to use. The whole point, I think, is to work that into the consciousness of as many people as possible, all over the world. People become predisposed to those kinds of ideas.

"I view that as a stepping stone. This isn't just a targeting of Christianity. We tear down the belief in the truly supernatural, the idea that there is reality beyond the physical, material world. And what that does is it eliminates the need for the supernatural completely, and eliminates the need for a belief in God completely, too. What they get out of it is what they have always wanted: they want to place themselves in the position of authority, in the position of creatorship. They want us to believe that they are the ones that deserve to be worshipped, not the true God.

"They're essentially manipulators of human beings. That's the game: they want to usurp the higher authority, to usurp God for their own ends. And the way you do that is you create this paradigm shift, mentally, across the board and all over the globe. And, once this happens, the need to have a dualistic system and a single god is supplanted. And I think that's what intelligent evil wants.

"The dismissal of the dualistic worldview eliminates the need for salvation. If you don't believe you need spiritual salvation, then people are in trouble. If there is this intelligent evil that wants the souls of humanity to be damned, they are going to see significant victories. The hatred of the souls of humanity is what is behind the shifting of the paradigm. And if the stuff that is removed during this paradigm shift is the truth—and I believe it is—that's just a huge victory for the forces of evil. They win the day.

"But, I think souls are eternal. It's very clear that, at the end, because of the resurrection of Christ, Christian teaching is that everything is raised, good or evil. But, then, when everything is raised, you have the decision of who lives where forever. I view Heaven as what Revelation calls the New Heaven and the New Earth: it's physical, yet something that transcends the physical existence that we know now. It's a good one, a blissful one, which is why the Book of Revelation ends with the description of Eden. We steward and enjoy the creation as we were intended to do from the beginning, before our corruption. Those who don't get to participate in that, there's this teaching of eternal punishment. And that's what these beings want: to take us with them when the end comes."

Heiser has a few words for those who might be tempted to follow the path taken by Jack Parsons: "There are people like Parsons inside what would become the military-industrial complex who are devoted—in a worship sense—to certain entities and who thought they would get more information and reward. But they're just lackeys."(1)

You have been warned.

28

THE MAN FROM ROSWELL

Echoing these views, and in particular those of Joe Jordan, is Guy Malone—a respected UFO researcher who makes his home in Roswell, New Mexico, with his wife, the aforementioned Nicole Malone.

"For much of my life," said Malone when I interviewed him, "until about age 23, I would best be described as a card-carrying New Ager, practicing astrology and astral projection, believing in reincarnation, and even carrying crystals. While I wanted to believe the visitors were 'good guys,' here to help save the planet, a long honest look was enough to convince me that these beings were not benevolent. In fact, I think the only thing most credible UFO researchers agree on across the board is that whatever they are, or aren't, they're liars.

"Upon becoming a Christian, the first thing I was told about UFOs and aliens is that they're really demons. Among Christians who *don't* study the topic, that's the prevailing view. It's not entirely off-base. But I've since found that that answer is way oversimplified. The angelic view of Genesis 6 at least begins to fit what both secular ufologists and modern theologians know of angels and aliens. And the Book of Enoch begins to answer the questions related to advanced technology given by the visitors, because this text describes the same thing happening in the ancient world.

"Joe Jordan's work in stopping abductions for so many people moves these theological ideas into the real world, proving that the true nature of the visitors is indeed spiritual, rather than physical. Otherwise, why would a deliverance, or exor-

Guy Malone

cism, have any effect? Surely it's not just a case of hurting the aliens' feelings?"

It was when Malone relocated to live in Roswell in 1999, he revealed, that things began to change on a large scale for him: "Upon moving, I had no real plan other than to get my book placed in the more popular tourist locations. Given the enormous profits generated by UFO-related tourism, however, I was not at all well-received or popular in Roswell, among either the secular or church community. For starters, the well-known International UFO Museum would not carry the book 'because it dealt with religion'—a policy, they said. Then, oddly enough, the Christian bookstore would not carry it either—'because it dealt with UFOs.' Caught between a rock and a hard place, and stymied for quite some time by the lack of a venue, I simply got a job waiting tables and opened Alien Resistance HQ as a non-profit bookstore almost a year after moving there.

"The simple rationale was always: If Roswell is the place the whole world looks to for the truth on this subject, then Biblical perspectives should be allowed in the mix for them to choose from. In the beginning, I viewed my target audience as people who looked to UFOs and aliens as a religion—such as Heaven's Gate or the Raelians—but soon saw that many more people, *not* affiliated with specific cults, were being influenced to some very specific UFO-cult belief systems by Hollywood, and by popular authors such as Erich von Daniken and Zechariah Sitchin. For the most part, even the Christian church is more influenced by these other factors on the questions of aliens and UFOs, than by the Bible itself.

"Currently, I believe that the best course of action is to increase public awareness of the UFO-abduction phenomena, both via secular views and venues and Biblical teaching. Put simply, until a person believes the phenomena are real, they do not care about what they are, or what the Bible may or may not say about them. The essence of the struggle here from a Fundamental Christian worldview is that of trying to reconcile the reality of alien encounters with what the Bible teaches very clearly. It has absolutely *nothing* to do with whether life could possibly exist on other planets or not. It *all* has to do with the fact that the extremely well documented messages of beings claiming to be aliens repeatedly attack this doctrine and claim that Jesus is not really God Incarnate, but is simply an advanced alien.

"The common questions that Christians arrive at when they examine the documented teaching of aliens are quite logically along the lines of: Why would authentic extraterrestrial biological entities travel 90 billion light years just to attack one specific religion? Why don't they ever go after or work so hard to change what people believe about Buddha, or Mohammed? Why do they make such a concentrated effort to convince people that Jesus Christ is not true the Deity, or God Incarnate? Given their powers and abilities, the Christian truly is left with no choice but to identify these creatures as deceiving spirits.

"To summarize, the reported activities of UFOs and aliens, do indeed have *exact* parallels in the Bible of exactly what fallen angels are capable of. To the Fundamentalist Christian, who really knows his or her Bible and what it says, when they examine the messages of aliens, they seem exactly like what the Bible says deceiving spirits would say. And we are, in fact, warned through an unfailing chain of prophecy to expect. Most people don't have a problem making the jump either, that when an entity comes and walks through your walls with the express purpose of tormenting you, and teaching you these doctrines as part of the lifelong process, but they leave in Jesus' name if you're a follower of His, that's likely *not* a genuine biological entity.

"And with all that Christians have going for the argument that the entities claiming to be from other planets are really just lying spirits—who can't offer *any* proof or evidence that they really are from those other planets—the Christian argues that the burden of proof is really shifted more to the side of those who claim that aliens are *not* fallen angels."

As for what the future may bring, Malone believes we may be in for turbulent times. "Most in this field feel that a major event is on the horizon," he said. "Some might call it Disclosure, while others might prefer Art Bell's term, The Quickening. Phrases like The Coming, or The Arrival, or simply First Contact are all Hollywood terms influencing general thought. New Agers and Christians may disagree over whether what's to come is best described as an awakening, of some sort, of grand delusion. But I feel it is essential for people to become aware of the credible information—secular and biblical—regarding this phenomenon now. And especially to make an educated decision about what they are and why they're here before a major event occurs. Once that happens, society may experience a collective state of shock and will be completely at the mercy of what the visitors themselves—and/or what our governments and religious leaders—say they are. None of these groups have a great track record for truth-telling however, and even the most sincere humans can be misled, duped, or have ulterior motives, which will skew what they do and don't disclose.

"Research by John Mack, Karla Turner, David Jacobs, Budd Hopkins, and many other prominent abduction researchers bears out that visions of the end of the world—or at least some massive future apocalypse—is one the major themes that contactees experience in their interactions with aliens. They also often speak of how the aliens will help mankind survive this period.

"The Bible says a great deal about the End of the Age, however, and the disasters that will come on the Earth before Jesus Christ's return—specifically in Matthew 24 and the Book of Revelation. But, the documented fact is that aliens' messages routinely contradict the biblical messages of destruction and recreation of a New Heaven and a New Earth by God, followed by Jesus' 1000 year-reign from Jerusalem. But this well researched point by Dr. Mack, and so many others, makes the messages and the promises of aliens suspect from the very beginning.

"Research shows that aliens routinely promise deliverance from the disasters foretold in the End-Times in a variety of ways—including but not limited to cloning, reincarnation, or by lifting those who follow the aliens off the planet just in the nick of time. It's a wide enough variety, in fact, that you yourself would not trust the aliens if you study the larger picture of how many different methods they promise this alleged deliverance.

"So, the Bible actually tells people to expect, in the last days, many people falling away from the faith partly on the basis of believing human teachers of false doctrines, and very specifically because of seducing spirits that teach the doctrines of devils. Even if one were to accept the entities as genuine extraterrestrials rather than seducing spirits, their messages reveal themselves to be promoting the doctrines of devils."

And as the countdown begins, Malone outlined to me what he saw taking place in the final days: "Trying to be succinct, I believe that all of this activity—man-made or supernatural—is largely the workings-together of fallen angels and globalists to bring about a one-world government under [the] Antichrist... Fallen angels and demons are creating a completely false but ingeniously crafted worldwide belief system that aliens are visiting Earth—and have been since biblical times. People are being conditioned to re-interpret the Bible itself as 'the greatest UFO story ever told' and to accept some the coming aliens as our friends, benefactors, superiors, and saviors here to help us fight off the so-called 'bad aliens' and usher humanity into a New Golden Age of peace and spiritual harmony with the deified universe—all the while lying about helping us escape the coming horrors of the tribulation period and sure judgment at the return of Jesus Christ.

"I think that what will happen is that there will be a worldwide disclosure and a revealing of an alien presence here, which will be a lie, their lie, the fallen-angels' lie. Belief in alien life forms here on Earth, whether they're real or not, demands that we become a united world, and that is exactly what the Bible describes will happen.

"What I believe is that the disclosure will be the catalyst that unites the world under that one-world leader, the Antichrist. He will be the leader of the one-world government, one religion, and one economy. What we're getting into here is eschatology. We are talking about the futuristic view of revelations, where you believe that what is in the Book of Revelation describes the future, the end of the age, and a final confrontation between good and evil. And this is why we have these UFO deceptions; it's leading to the final battle described in Revelation, the final judgment on our souls, and these entities working at the end to seduce as many of us, our souls, as they can.

"People commonly believe the Lake of Fire to represent eternal torment, which—in my theological interpretation that I know goes against the grain of much of Christendom—is not true. The Lake of Fire is indeed the intended destiny of wicked angels. But for unsaved humans, it is also called in Revelation 'the second death.' One natural death of the body, then one of the spirit/soul, a.k.a. annihilation, which I believe is probably more accurate. I don't believe in eternal torment at the hand of God. People need to understand all of this now so that when the curtain is unveiled, they already have made their choice about which God to serve."(1)

29

When Time Runs Out

The Last Judgment, Judgment Day, the Final Judgment, or the Day of the Lord—to describe its various names—is the period of time in which the Bible predicts the dead will be resurrected and the second-coming of Jesus Christ will occur. Within Roman Catholicism, the belief is that at the moment of death each human soul undergoes what is known as the Particular Judgment, which—depending on the person and how he or she has lived their life—dictates if the ultimate destination of the soul is Heaven, Hell, or Purgatory, the latter being a place of purification or temporary punishment. At the moment of Final Judgment, however, the fate of everyone who has ever lived will be judged. Those already in Heaven will remain there. Those in Hell will do likewise. And everyone in Purgatory will be given a place in Heaven. This will coincide with the reuniting of soul and body and—after Final Judgment—the renewal of the Universe and the creation of a new Heaven and Earth, many of the details of which can be found in the Book of the Revelation of John, or Revelation, as it is more commonly known. (1)

Revelation is the very last book of the New Testament. It is the only one that is wholly composed of apocalyptic literature. The specific nature, time, and outcome of the perceived coming apocalypse, however, is a matter of deep debate amongst Christians—chiefly because there exist a number of theories, some of which are at variance with each other.

Preterism is a variant of Christian eschatology which teaches that the majority, or perhaps all, of the biblical prophecies that relate to the end of days refer not to events in the future, but to matters that have already occurred, namely, in the first century after Christ's birth. (2)

Then there is the Futurist interpretation on the apocalypse. Generally speaking, this is a prediction pointing to the resurrection of the dead and a rapture of the living, at which point all true Christians, as well as those who have not reached an age of accountability, are gathered together at the time of Christ's return. The Futurist view also holds that a violent tribulation will occur—which is usually described as a seven-year-long period of time when the Antichrist will appear in our midst, when Christians will be persecuted on a worldwide scale but who will ultimately be purified and strengthened by the assault. But even among Futurists, there are differences of opinion. Some take the view that rapture will take place before tribulation; others believe that it will be at the mid-point of the end-times that rapture occurs. Then here are those who believe rapture can only occur when tribulation reaches its end. (3)

Taking a different approach are the Pretribulationists, whose belief system is that all true Christians will undergo the rapture before the end-times begin, in much the same way that the Bible tells of Noah being given safe-haven prior to when God judged the antediluvian world. Meanwhile, the Mid-tribulationist view is that a Christian rapture will take place roughly halfway through the tribulation. In other words, after it begins, but before things reach truly apocalyptic levels. As for the Post-tribulationists, they take the approach that Christians will not be taken up into Heaven early on, or as the events unfold, but will be received into God's realm at the end of the tribulation. (4)

One thing that the proponents of all these views generally adhere to, however, is the scenario of Israel unwittingly signing a seven-year-long peace treaty with the Antichrist, something that will trigger the beginning of the final events. Perhaps, at this stage, we should not forget that Jack Parsons once proclaimed himself the Antichrist and had plans to relocate to Israel before his violent death in 1952 changed all that.

It should be noted that the various views on tribulation are actually a subset of three theological interpretations referred to in Revelation 20: Premillennialism, Amillennialism, and Postmillennialism. The first teaches that Jesus will return to Earth, bind Satan, and reign for 1,000 years, with the city of Jerusalem acting as his capital. Amillennialism, which is considered to be the traditional view for Roman Catholicism, adheres to the idea that the 1,000-year period should not be taken literally. Whereas Postmillennialism supporters conclude that Jesus will return to the Earth after tribulation. All, however, are bound by the beliefs that the ultimate future war between good and evil, between the powers of God and those of Satan, as well as the judgment of our souls, are sure to come true. (5)

Ray Boeche's two DoD sources had their own views on what the final events might bring. "They didn't just think that this was a spiritual deception," recalls Boeche, "but that it was possibly something leading to a *final* deception. In their view—which, theologically, I don't particularly hold—they viewed things much more like that of [Tim] LaHaye and [Jerry B.] Jenkins in the *Left Behind* book-series: the Antichrist will appear, then we are fooled, and Armageddon will then be triggered. That seemed to be their personal feeling about the whole scenario."

Boeche has his own position on Armageddon. "I tend to take the view," he told me, "that many of the prophecies in the Book of Revelation were fulfilled with Rome's destruction of Jerusalem. Orthodox Christianity teaches a physical return of Christ, but that is always considered to be the church's great hope: Christ's returning, a triumphant return. So, from that point of view, the *Left Behind* mentality—that Armageddon is a terrible thing and that you want to push it off as long as possible—to me doesn't really hold, at least in the historical sense. Christ's eventual return is the culmination of this age and this world, so it's not something to fear. It's something to be welcomed. But, it *was* viewed by the DoD like that, as a final battle scenario. Their other big fear in the whole thing was: if you have these types of entities who will present themselves as extraterrestrial beings, how is that going to affect the spiritual outlook of the people? Will it sway people from a belief in Christ? Would it have that sort of a spiritual effect?" (6)

And then there is Dan T. Smith, an enigmatic figure on the UFO research scene, whose father was Harvard economist Dan Throop Smith, the Treasury Department's number-one tax advisor during the Eisenhower administration. Researcher Gary Bekkum said of Dan T. Smith: "His personal meetings have included former and present representatives of the U.S. Government intelligence community and their political associates, like Chris Straub, a former member of the Senate Select Committee on Intelligence."(7)

Researcher Vince Johnson, who had the opportunity to speak with Smith on a number of occasions about his ufological views and insider contacts, stated: "According to Smith, UFOs are primarily a psychological/metaphysical phenomenon which are both preparing us and pressuring us to develop our own psi abilities. Not that UFOs are a single type of entity; Smith asserts that there are 'powers and principalities' at work—presumably supernatural entities like angels and demons.

"Furthermore, he said that a radical program of parapsychological research and development is currently underway near Los Alamos, New Mexico. This group's development of psychokinesis, and psychotronics (a term used to denote psychic warfare techniques) represents a danger of eschatological proportions. 'These techniques have been available, but controlled, throughout history. Now, other entities are forcing the issue,' said Smith."

Johnson added: "[Smith] reported that his governmental sources 'hinted at' an eschatological emergency... When I asked why the CIA was interested in eschatology, he replied that the ramifications of the eschaton event represented a serious threat to national security, and thus, fell into the purview of the intelligence agencies. Smith also revealed that the eschatological issues he raised related directly to the biblical prophecies of the Book of Revelation."(8)

The Collins Elite had their own view of how the end game will play out.

30

Seeing is Believing

The Collins Elite still exists today, in 2010, albeit, apparently, in a *very* different format than that of earlier years and decades, and with a radically altered agenda, too. It seems to be the case today that all of the group's research programs—such as those focusing on abductions—are either on hold or are in closed status. Why? Because in the minds of the membership, they have proved the validity of their theories and beliefs; they understand what the future and the ancient biblical prophecies will both bring. They now see the end looming perilously close, and as a consequence, they see no further need to study either the demonic agenda or how it seeks to achieve its deceptive aims.

Rather, the focus of attention today is upon two issues: (A) how to best convince the U.S. military that the Collins Elite theories are the absolute truth, and (B) how to convert the mindset of the people of the planet to a deep, radical, fundamentalist, Christian way of thinking, as part of a concerted effort to save their souls—even via the use of large-scale, forced indoctrination and trickery, if such a situation is deemed necessary.

From their present perspective, the only viable way to help convert and save those hundreds of millions of people who do not currently subscribe to a Christian way of life from everlasting damnation in fiery Hell is to give birth of a kind of New World Order, based around, and arguably controlled by, the beliefs, prophecies, and teachings of The Old Testament and those of Revelation.

In November 2009—thanks to an introduction made by Robert Manners—I had the opportunity to speak with a former member of the Collins Elite who left the project in 2006, "disgusted" at the way in which matters were rapidly moving forward. That disgust was apparently prompted by one controversial plan in particular. It was the plan that seemingly, and finally, unified the Collins Elite with the group to which Ray Boeche's Department of Defense sources were tied, as well as with the mysterious STAC organization, and the personnel stationed at Wright-Patterson Air Force Base who were—at least as late as 1998, as *The Collins Report* of that year demonstrated—studying the nature and origin of the strange materials collected at Roswell, New Mexico, in 1947.

"What do you think might happen if Jesus Christ *doesn't* return as quickly as certain people want him to?" the elderly man asked me, as we sat in the bar at Las Vegas' Flamingo hotel along with Robert Manners and an attractive woman named Vicki, whose hand Manners clutched tight throughout much of the meeting.

"I don't know. Life goes on as normal?" I replied, as Manners carefully scrutinized us back and forth with a look of distinct fear on his face.

The man shook his head: "He will be *made* to return quickly, because he *has* to return quickly."

Seeing my puzzled frown, the man explained that in the immediate aftermath of the tragedy of 9-11, a highly covert plan—the roots of which went back decades—was "given a second-look" by senior elements of the Bush administration who ultimately persuaded the Collins Elite of its worthiness. He told me that there were, and still are, those within the government who "call themselves Christians, but who are really bullying thugs who have hijacked it and represent *nothing* of what Christianity should really be."

And their attitude to enforcing a planned, strict Christian

doctrine on the entire American population in the near future is said to be near-dictatorial, "which goes against all and everything I stand for," said the man. "There's free-will; that's what we were taught, and that's how it should be." Following what happened on 9-11, those same figures within the Bush administration and their newfound allies in the Collins Elite, saw the destruction of the World Trade Center towers as the commencement of the countdown to the last great battle, good and evil facing off against each other one final time, and just before the events detailed in Revelation come to pass.

As I sat and listened evermore intently, the man informed me that "an idea was discussed" for a covert arm of the U.S. military—that was being "cleverly swamped with ideas to make it seem justified"—to explode a small atomic device within a major U.S. city in the near future—"or to encourage it and let it happen." The result would be martial law, nightly curfews, the complete deconstruction of freedom of speech, the total closing of borders, and widespread surveillance of the populace.

Then, with the media controlled, and with the population held in the vice-like grip of those who drew up that overwhelming atrocity known as the Patriot Act, the collective forces within the military, intelligence community, and government would play their ace card. On a date still to be designated, the skies of North America would be filled with huge images of Jesus Christ—or at least, with imagery that reflects how he is generally portrayed within biblical publications. But the man told me, if the operation ever comes to pass, it would all be a terrible ruse.

"Have you ever heard of Project Blue Beam?" he asked me. (1)

I had. Blue Beam Project is said to be a secret operation designed to ensure the fulfillment of certain biblical, End-Times prophecies through stage-managed fakery and elaborate holograms. In essence, space-based laser-generating satellites would project simultaneous images of a whole plethora of deities, including Mohammed, Krishna, Jesus Christ and Buddha—to the four corners of the planet, and in every language and dialect.

Those images would then merge into one dreaded entity, the Antichrist, who would explain to the shocked people of the world that the various scriptures faithfully recorded and digested throughout history have all been misunderstood and misinterpreted, and that the religions of old are responsible for turning brother against brother, and nation against nation. Therefore religion must be abolished in favor of a distinctly new age, new world religion, represented by the Antichrist. Of course, this fabricated series of events would result in civil disorder and chaos on a massive scale, thus allowing New World Order proponents—working under the Antichrist—to take control of the populace and usher in a terrible, new era designed to seduce the Human Race and pit it against the Christian God. Or, at least, that is what the rumors on the Internet tell us. (2)

But my source assured me that "in its name and goal of creating a *new* religion under the Antichrist, Project Blue Beam is nothing but internet gossip and distortion, and a *lot* of hoaxing and people just grabbing at straws. It's *not* real. No one I know wants to see the Antichrist running the planet."

But, he was careful to add, "If you know where to look, there are a few, just a few, good nuggets in the story. And although the Blue Beam story was originally around in the '90s's, some of the later nuggets, in the 2000s, that were added to the story *did* have their place in that meeting, and somehow got picked up later by people spreading the Blue Beam stories. How, someone got hold of them, I don't know, but they did. So there is no real Blue Beam; there never was. But, there *was* a very real idea in the [President George W.] Bush world that had a similar theme, to look at faking a significant religious event to influence the American people, if it could be done, and if it might succeed."

He then thought for a moment and chose his next words carefully: "I don't want you to think the satellites are ready and up there, or there are thousands of people in government and the military ready and waiting to go on this, just waiting for the order and hit the button and the skies are filled with God, angels. It's nothing like that. The idea of getting this implemented and making sure there would be no failures, or it doesn't get blown wide open and exposed, would require incredible planning — *incredible*. It was just an idea discussed around a table—notes, presentations, Power-Point, whatever—and whether it was possible, or worth looking at further. As far as I know, they still see the idea as a winner, if it's needed. But, actually doing it and getting away with it, that's *definitely* something else."

The mere discussion of such a plan was enough to make the man leave the Collins Elite, never to return. Trying to expose deceptive entities via the creation of another deception "was not where I wanted to go," the man told me. The irony of all this, he said, was that the ruse of trying to save the souls of the people of Earth via the implementation of a staged-managed, religious charade designed to convert one and all to Christianity, might ultimately only help fulfill the ancient prophecies by unwittingly opening the door for the Antichrist to take control of a New World Order-style future. In other words, what the bogus Project Blue Beam stories foretell could actually occur.

The man suggested that after decades of investigating, trying to understand, and fending off the UFO-demonic deception, the now-radically-altered Collins Elite might be the very people who—as a result of their own deceptive plans—are destined to allow the old prophecies to reach their final stages. "Possibly that's how it's always supposed to have been. Perhaps we were *always* part of the plan," the man reflected, already beaten and defeated by the apocalyptic and unstoppable future he believes is rapidly heading our way.

"And that, my friend," said Robert Manners to me, "is why we're talking."(3)

Admittedly, the scenario sounds like something one might expect to see on one of the wilder episodes of *The X-Files*, but it is not easily dismissed. It's also worth noting that Offutt Air Force Base, Nebraska—from where I received a phone-call that ultimately led me to Richard Duke and Robert Manners—was where President George W. Bush conducted one of the first major strategy sessions to plan a response to the attacks of September 11, 2001. (4) How curious that Offutt AFB should have had a connection to both the post-9-11 events and to the Collins Elite. Of course, if the man Robert Manners introduced me to was speaking truthfully about 9-11, about the Collins Elite, and about a planned religious charade designed to control the nation, then the connection may not so curious at all.

I have saved until now one aspect of Ray Boeche's story that may have some significance for this highly controversial scenario.

Between the nights of December 26 and 28, 1980, a series of almost science-fiction-like events occurred in Rendlesham Forest, Suffolk, England, a densely treed area adjacent to the joint Royal Air Force/U.S. Air Force military complex of Bentwaters-Woodbridge. Essentially, what many believe took place over the course of several nights was nothing less than the landing of a craft—or multiple craft—from another world from which small, humanoid entities reportedly emerged. It was tracked on radar, deposited traces of radiation within the forest, avoided capture and made good its escape—and created a controversy that rages to this day. (5)

It just so happens that one of those who tried to get to the bottom of the Rendlesham mystery was none other than Ray Boeche. He spent a great deal of time digging into the puzzle and even approached the office of the Honorable James J. Exon, United States Senate, in an effort to uncover the cloak of secrecy surrounding the affair. It was largely and unfortunately to no avail, however, and Rendlesham continues to remain the enigma today that it was 30 years ago—although not to everyone, it seems, specifically not to Ray Boeche's two whistleblower sources from the Department of Defense.

In 1994 Boeche's informants advised researcher Linda Howe that: "We had become aware of [Boeche] through his work on the British incident (Bentwaters Dec. 26-28, 1980), when his probings began to bother a number of high level people within our government."

To which Boeche commented: "I found it interesting that they would mention Rendlesham at the meeting. They said there was a sense that this was maybe, in some sense, staged. Or that some of the senior people there were more concerned with the reaction of the men—how they responded to the situation, rather than what was actually going on. That this was some sort of psychotronic device, a hologram, to see what sort of havoc they can wreak with people. But even if it was a type of hologram, they said it could interact with the environment. The tree marks and the pod marks at the landing site were indications of that. But how can you have a projected thing like a hologram that also has material, physical capabilities? They wouldn't elaborate on this."(6)

Also in 1992, British UFO researcher Jenny Randles met with Boeche in Lincoln, Nebraska, and later offered her views on this aspect of Boeche's experiences with his clandestine informants: "This is a device which manipulates the subatomic basis of matter at a quantum level and builds a bridge between mind and physical substance. If I understood it correctly, this supposedly stimulated the mind into having vivid hallucinations but, at the same time, created physical effects in the real world which could take on a semblance of the appearance of the hallucinated images. In other words, what was seen was mostly in the mind—and certainly a production of the subconscious imagination—but it was not entirely without physical form and partially substantial in the same way that a hologram is real, but has no weight or solidity. *The result is a terrifying apparition*"(emphasis mine). (7)

Boeche realizes that "The probability of disinformation here seems very high—why shift the emphasis on Bentwaters to psychotronic warfare?" (8) But the very fact that Boeche's sources were talking about using sophisticated 3D-like holograms that could actually interact with their environment to fool U.S. military personnel and to gauge their reactions sounds astonishingly like a very early, small-scale operation of the type that the Collins Elite discussed using on a much larger scale in the near future. Only this time, a gigantic Jesus Christ in the skies would replace the diminutive aliens in the woods.

Note also that the reference to this projection-style technology at Rendlesham Forest having the ability to interact physically with its environment (in the form of landing-traces and damage to trees in the woods) eerily echoes the words of Joe Jordan, of the Kennedy Space Center. He believes that the illusions weaved by the demonic entities as a part of their alien abduction deception can similarly result in physical manifestations, such as marks on the skin and physical disturbances in the home. In view of this, one might justifiably be inclined to conclude that, way back in 1980, colleagues of the DoD operatives who approached Ray Boeche in 1992 had succeeded in duplicating the strange technology which the demonic ones were themselves using to fabricate alien abductions—but, at the time, elected to test it on their own nation's unwitting military personnel, albeit on British soil.

The controversy does not end there. In the early 1960s, Robert Manners told me, the CIA mused upon the idea of trying something very similar over Cuba, namely, to project hologram-style images of Jesus Christ onto clouds that would appear in conjunction with U.S. forces invading the island—thus giving the impression to Fidel Castro and the Cuban people that the American military had the mighty support of God himself. And although the operation did not come to fruition, we might be wise to consider the possibility that, today, someone at an official level may very well be considering capitalizing on such a scenario, but on a far grander, more intricate, and far-reaching scale. (9)

Is this all reality or disinformation? And even if the basics of the story are true, it may well be—as I was certainly told—that the plan was simply a theoretical one and no more; a plan that was borne out of a strange meeting of minds in some darkened corner of the Pentagon or in a secure, underground bunker. But the issue of false-flags and sophisticated holograms aside, there can be no denying that there certainly is a very concerted effort underway today to increase the presence of Christianity within the U.S. military—and a good deal of that indoctrination most assuredly *is* based around the Book of Revelation and the final days.

31

ONWARD, CHRISTIAN SOLDIERS

In January 2010, the mainstream American media focused a wealth of attention on a startling and weird revelation: namely, that coded biblical messages were being inscribed on high-powered rifle sights designated for use by the U.S. military. The maker of the sights, a Michigan-based outfit called Trijicon, signed a $650 million, multi-year contract to provide up to 800,000 such sights to the Marine Corps. Trijicon was founded by one Glyn Bindon, a devout Christian who was killed in a plane crash in South Africa in 2003.

Although Army regulations specifically and absolutely prohibit the proselytizing of any religion in Iraq and Afghanistan – specifically to lay to rest any claims that the U.S. military is on some sort of religious "crusade" – this did not stop the sights from being distributed and utilized. One of the citations on the gun sights read: "For God, who commanded the light to shine out of darkness, hath shined in our hearts, to give the light of the knowledge of the glory of God in the face of Jesus Christ." Very notably, other messages on the rifle sights come from the End-Times-dominated Book of Revelation.

Michael Weinstein of the Military Religious Freedom Foundation (MRFF) said of the "Jesus Rifles": "It's literally pushing fundamentalist Christianity at the point of a gun against the people that we're fighting. We're emboldening an enemy." Rather disturbingly, U.S. military personnel told Weinstein that their commanders were referring to these weapons as "spiritually transformed firearm[s] of Jesus Christ."

As a result of the publicity and condemnation afforded

the affair, Trijicon announced it would remove the messages from those weapons in its factory and would also "provide 100 modification kits to forces in the field to remove the reference on the already forward deployed optical sights." In response to this development, Haris Tarin, Director of the Washington, D.C. office of the Muslim Public Affairs Council, said: "We must ensure that incidents like these are not repeated, so as not to give the impression that our country is involved in a religious crusade, which hurts America's image abroad and puts our soldiers in harm's way."(1)

This is not the first time that religion and the U.S. military have crossed paths in the post 9-11 era. In 2003, intelligence briefings on the war in Iraq sent to the White House by the Pentagon were delivered with cover pages that quoted from the books of Psalms and Ephesians and the epistles of Peter. For example, the cover page of a report dated March 31, 2003, read: "Therefore put on the full armor of God, so that when the day of evil comes, you may be able to stand your ground, and after you have done everything, to stand."

Similarly, a Pentagon report of April 10, 2003, included this quote from Psalms on its front page: "Behold, the eye of the Lord is on those who fear Him...To deliver their soul from death." It was accompanied by a photograph of a statue of Saddam Hussein being pulled to the ground in Baghdad, Iraq. (2)

In response to these revelations, the Reverend Barry W. Lynn, Executive Director of Americans United for Separation of Church and State, said that American soldiers "are not Christian crusaders, and they ought not be depicted as such. Depicting the Iraq conflict as some sort of holy war is completely outrageous." Try telling that to the people who want us to believe that a holy war is exactly what is afoot. (3)

The BBC noted – also in 2003 – that when Lieutenant General William Boykin gave speeches at churches, and while in his uniform no less, that disparaged Islam and that defined the War on Terror in a specifically fundamentalist End-Times scenario, he was not fired but promoted. In an unofficial acknowledgment of that view, "U.S. Defense Secretary Donald Rumsfeld," noted the BBC, "has declined to criticize a senior army officer who told audiences the war on terror is a battle with Satan."(4)

Michael Weinstein of the Military Religious Freedom Foundation (MRFF) said: "There's an eschatology obsessed version of Christianity…that is trying to make American foreign policy conterminous with their Biblical worldview," and added that there is: "…improper pressure within the military command structure to make members join them."(5)

The MMRF also learned that, in 2007, an evangelical group called Operation Stand Up was preparing to mail "freedom packages" to soldiers in Iraq as part of an Army program. Along with socks and snacks, the packages were set to include copies of an apocalyptic video game titled "Left Behind: Eternal Forces." Only when the details of the plan were publicized by those who saw such actions as fundamentally wrong did the Pentagon grudgingly announce that the operation would be shelved. (6)

In February 2010 I asked Robert Manners why the U.S. military was apparently being indoctrinated into an army of literal Christian soldiers with a solid acceptance of End-Times scenarios. After all, I said to him, in the wars in Iraq and Afghanistan – and who knows where next – wouldn't the military just go ahead and follow orders anyway, even if they weren't of a fundamentalist and End-Times dominated mindset?

Manners looked grim. "They would," he said, "that's what they're trained to do: follow orders. But you're missing the point. The whole point of creating an army of God has less to do with the Middle East and more to do with preparing the troops for the day they come home, when religious fascism – the New World Order, the hologram things we told you about – comes right here, to the U.S.

"If – and, okay, it *is* still an if – our country becomes enslaved under a government that's going to use religious fear to control the population and lock us down from the rest of the world, the people running the show will need someone to run that control, no matter what. And that's what they're doing right now; they're slowly grooming and creating an army of God's soldiers that are going to police the U.S., and – as they see it – keep the invaders, the demons, at bay.

"Can you imagine the entire country – maybe ten years from now and after the next 9-11, a dirty-bomb in a big city, maybe – policed and controlled by the U.S. military, an army totally convinced and believing that what they're doing is according to what God wants and that will save the U.S. from a satanic threat? That's the crux of what's going on; indoctrinate the troops today for when they're needed here tomorrow. I call it Biblical Big-Brother. Just watch, ten years from now the U.S. military will be indistinguishable from religious warriors. That's the plan: save the country by keeping it under a religious iron-fist and enforcing Christianity on everyone. But if that's to be the future of Christianity, I'm not sure it's worth it. It's not the Christianity *I* want taught."

It remains to be seen whether this is all indeed a growing agenda to carefully indoctrinate the military and the populace with the End-Times views of the Collins Elite, as part of an utterly misguided plan to save our souls from what they perceive as being the clutches of Lucifer's minions.

Final Thoughts

Four years have passed since I first embarked upon the strange and surreal journey that began with the revelations of Ray Boeche and that ended—for now at least—with the ominous words of Robert Manners. The journey has been a strange one. It overflows with claims that the end is drawing ever-nearer and strongly held assertions that we face deception from all sides: from non-human, soul-devouring entities that the Collins Elite believe masquerade as aliens, and from factions of the official world who seem prepared to do just about whatever it takes to rewire the collective mindset of the world's population to a radical, fundamentalist way of thinking.

If the story should prove to be bogus, then a tremendous amount of effort and time has been utilized to convince both Ray Boeche and me of its validity—and that surely begs the question of why? Could it be to further confuse the nature, origin, and intent of the intelligences behind what we call UFOs? Might the demonic theory actually be a cover story to steer people away from the extraterrestrial angle? Is this all part of some deceitful and nefarious plot to have us believe that hostile, demonic forces are lining up for the final battle, one that will result in the careful ushering in a New World Order driven and controlled by an overwhelming fear of non-existing fallen-angels; bogus, hate-filled demons; and a fictional Antichrist? On the other hand, if the overall story of the Collins Elite is absolutely true, then we may be in for some very turbulent times.

And, of course, I have to ask: why me? Did some of the

Collins Elite just want to test the waters before running into the offices of the *Washington Post* or the *New York Times* and blowing the whole thing wide open in the near future? I don't know. Perhaps the passage of time will answer that question. But one thing I *do* know: if all those in the Collins Elite who expressed their views to me *were* speaking truthfully, and if Ray Boeche's sources were being honest with him, then it may not be long before we have all the answers. The nightmarish final events may already be under way.

Sources

Introduction

1. Interview with Ray Boeche, January 22, 2007

Chapter 1: *The Quest Begins*

1. *The Lay of the Last Minstrel*, Sir Walter Scott, 1805, http://www.theotherpages.org/poems/minstrel.html

Chapter 2: *Sympathy for the Devil*

1. *The Wickedest Man in the World*, John Bull, *Sunday Express*, March 24, 1923; *Perdurabo: The Life of Aleister Crowley*, Richard Kaczynski, New Falcon Publications, 2002; *The Beast 666: The Life of Aleister Crowley*, John Symonds, St. Martin's Press, 1997; *A Magick Life: The Life of Aleister Crowley*, Martin Booth, Coronet Books, 2000; *Do What Thou Wilt: A Life of Aleister Crowley*, Lawrence Sutin, Pindar Press, 2000

2. *Boleskine House*, Thelemapedia, http://www.thelemapedia.org/index.php/Boleskine_House; *Aleister Crowley - Black Magic at Boleskine House?* http://www.mysteriouspeople.com/Aleister_Crowley.htm

3. *The Beast of Adam Gorightly*, Adam Gorightly, Virtualbookworm Publishing, 2005; *Ritual Magic, Mind Control and the UFO Phenomenon*, Adam Gorightly, 2001, http://www.conspiracyarchive.com/UFOs/UFO_Ritual_Magic.htm; *Aleister Crowley and the Lam Statement*, Ian Blake, 1996, *The*

228

Excluded Middle, http://www.excludedmiddle.com/LAM-statement.html;

The Alamantrah Working, http://www.sacred-texts.com/oto/lib97.txt;

Did Magicians Cause UFO Sightings? Whitley Strieber's Unknown Country, July 20, 2005, http://www.unknowncountry.com/mindframe/opinion/?id=199

4. *Sex and Rockets: The Occult World of Jack Parsons*, John Carter, Feral House, 1999

5. *Jack Parsons and the Fall of Babalon,* http://www.excludedmiddle.com/jack_parsons.htm;

The Magical Father of American Rocketry, Brian Doherty, 2005, http://reason.com/archives/2005/05/01/the-magical-father-of-american;

Strange Angel: The Otherworldly Life of Rocket Scientist John Whiteside Parsons, George Pendle, Harcourt, 20005;

Jet Propulsion Laboratory: Early History, NASA, http://www.jpl.nasa.gov/jplhistory/early/index.php;

Jack Parsons, Thelemapedia, http://www.thelemapedia.org/index.php/Jack_Parsons

Chapter 3: *"Be careful, they bite"*

1. *Sex and Rockets*, John Carter, Feral House, 2000;

Jack Parsons and the Curious Tale of Rocketry in the 1930s, George Pendle, The *Naked Scientists*, March 2006, http://www.thenakedscientists.com/HTML/articles/article/georgependlecolumn1.htm;

JPL – The Occult Roots of NASA, http://www.bariumblues.com/jpl.htm

John Whiteside Parsons, Colin Bennett, *Fortean Times*, March 2000;

2. Ibid.

3. Ibid.

4. *Arroyo Seco (Los Angeles County)*, http://en.wikipedia.org/

wiki/Arroyo_Seco_(Los_Angeles_County)

5. *Dr. Robert H. Goddard, American Rocketry Pioneer*, http://www.nasa.gov/centers/goddard/about/dr_goddard.html; *Robert Goddard and his Rockets*, http://www-istp.gsfc.nasa.gov/stargaze/Sgoddard.htm

6. *L. Ron Hubbard: The Founder of Scientology*, http://www.aboutlronhubbard.org; *L. Ron Hubbard: Scientology's Esteemed Founder*, Michael Crowley, *Slate*, July 15, 2005; *L. Ron Hubbard: A Profile*, http://www.lronhubbardprofile.org/profile/index.htm; *L. Ron Hubbard: Founder of Dianetics and Scientology*, http://www.theta.com/goodman/lrh.htm; *Battlefield Earth (novel)*, http://en.wikipedia.org/wiki/Battlefield_Earth_(novel); *Books by L. Ron Hubbard*, http://www.biblio.com/author_biographies/2098631/L_Ron_Hubbard.html; *Babalon*, http://en.wikipedia.org/wiki/Babalon; *JPL -- The Occult Roots of NASA*, http://www.bariumblues.com/jpl.htm; *Hubbard's Magic*, Craig Branch, *Watchman*, http://www.watchman.org/Sci/hubmagk2.htm

7. *The Coming of the Saucers*, Kenneth Arnold & Ray Palmer, Legend Press, 1996

8. *The Beast of Adam Gorightly*, Adam Gorightly, Virtualbookworm Publishing, 2005; *Ritual Magic, Mind Control and the UFO Phenomenon*, Adam Gorightly, 2001, http://www.conspiracyarchive.com/UFOs/UFO_Ritual_Magic.htm

9. *U.S. Air Force Project Blue Book Fact Sheet*, 1996

10. *Body Snatchers in the Desert*, Nick Redfern, Paraview-Pocket Books, 2005; *Crash at Corona*, Stanton T. Friedman & Don Berliner, Paragon House, 1992; *The Truth about the UFO Crash at Roswell*, Kevin D. Randle & Donald R. Schmitt, M. Evans, 1994; *UFO Crash at Roswell*, Kevin D. Randle & Donald R. Schmitt, Avon, 1991;

Roswell in Perspective, Karl Pflock, Fund for UFO Research, 1994

11. *The Roswell Incident*, Charles Berlitz & William L. Moore, Granada Publishing, 1980
12. *Ritual Magic, Mind Control and the UFO Phenomenon*, Adam Gorightly, 2001, http://www.conspiracyarchive.com/UFOs/ UFO_Ritual_Magic.htm

Chapter 4: *The Parsons Files*

1. Interview with Ralph Summers, February 2, 2007
2. Conversation with representative of Offutt Air Force Base, February 14, 2007
3. Interview with Richard Duke, February 25, 2007
4. Documentation declassified under the terms of the United States' Freedom of Information act by the Federal Bureau of Investigation; Department of State; Department of the Army; and the Department of the Air Force

Chapter 5: *The Coming of the Collins Elite*

1. *L. Ron Hubbard: The Founder of Scientology*, http://www. aboutlronhubbard.org;
   L. Ron Hubbard: Scientology's Esteemed Founder, Michael Crowley, *Slate*, July 15, 2005;
   L. Ron Hubbard: A Profile, http://www.lronhubbardprofile. org/profile/index.htm;
   L. Ron Hubbard: Founder of Dianetics and Scientology, http://www.theta.com/goodman/lrh.htm;
2. *The Psychic Battlefield: A History of the Military-Occult Complex*, W. Adam Mandelbaum, St. Martin's Griffin, 2002
3. *The Truth about Charles Taze Russell*, http://www.angelfire. com/journal2/adrianbiblestudents/russell.html;
   The Biography of Pastor Russell, http://www.heraldmag.org/

olb/contents/history/bio%20ctr.htm;

4. *Sex and Rockets*, John Carter, Feral House, 2000

5. *Town of Collins,* http://history.rays-place.com/ny/collins. htm

6. Interview with Richard Duke, February 25, 2007

Chapter 6: *1952: Invasion*

1. Interview with Richard Duke, February 27, 2007

2. Documentation declassified under the terms of the United States' Freedom of Information Act by the Federal Bureau of Investigation; and the Department of the Army

Chapter 7: *Occult Space-Brothers*

1. Documentation on George Van Tassel declassified under the terms of the Freedom of Information Act by the Federal Bureau of Investigation;
   The Council of Seven Lights, George Van Tassel, DeVorss and Co., 1958;
   When Stars Look Down, George Van Tassel, Kruckeberg Press, 1976;
   I Rode a Flying Saucer! George Van Tassel, New Age, 1952;
   Religion and Science Merged, George Van Tassel, Ministry of Universal Wisdom, 1958

2. *Out of the Stars*, Robert Short, Infinity Publishing, 2003

3. Ibid.

4. *The Council of Seven Lights*, George Van Tassel, DeVorss and Co., 1958

5. Documentation on George Van Tassel declassified under the terms of the Freedom of Information Act by the Federal Bureau of Investigation

6. Documentation on George Adamski declassified under the terms of the Freedom of Information Act by the Federal

Bureau of Investigation

7. *Flying Saucers Have Landed*, George Adamski & Desmond Leslie, Werner Laurie, 1953

8. *Flying Saucerers*, David Clarke & Andy Roberts, Heart of Albion Press, 2007;

    Out of the Shadows, David Clarke & Andy Roberts, Piatkus, 2002;

    Desmond Leslie, Philip Hoare, *Independent Obituaries*, March 10, 2001, http://www.independent.co.uk/news/obituaries/desmond-leslie-728888.html

9. *The Saucers Speak!*, George Hunt Williamson & Alfred C. Bailey, New Age, 1954;

    Other Tongues – Other Flesh, George Hunt Williamson, Forgotten Books, 2008;

    Secret Places of the Lion, George Hunt Williamson, Neville Spearman, 1969;

    Star Guests, William Dudley Pelley, Soulcraft Chapels, 1950; "Tracks in the Desert," Alec Hiddell, http://tinyurl.com/2dug3tl

10. *Parapsychology in Intelligence*, Dr. Kenneth A. Kress, Central Intelligence Agency, Office of Technical Services, *Studies in Intelligence*, Winter 1977

11. Interview with Richard Duke, February 27, 2007

Chapter 8: *UFOs, Crowley and Ouija*

1. *Unmasking the Enemy: Visions Around the World and Global Deception in the End Times*, Nelson S. Pacheco & Tommy R. Blann, Bendan Press, Inc., 1993

2. *The Sacred Mushroom: Key to the Door of Eternity*, Andrija Puharich, Doubleday, 1974

3. *A History of Ouija and Intelligence Applications*, Central Intelligence Agency, February 1954

4. *The Museum of Talking Boards,* http://www.museumoftalkingboards.com/WebOuija.html;

The Official Website of William Fuld, http://www.william-fuld.com/

5. *Aleister Crowley and the Ouija Board,* J. Edward Cornelius, Feral House, 2005

6. *UFO: End Time Delusion,* David Allen Lewis & Robert Shreckhise, New Leaf Press, 1991

Chapter 9: *The Maine Events*

1. Documentation declassified under the terms of the Freedom of Information Act by the Federal Bureau of Investigation; Department of the Army; and Department of the Air Force;

2. Interview with Richard Duke, February 27, 2007

3. *Canadian UFO Director gets an Alien Letter,* Grant Cameron, August 20, 2009,
    http://www.presidentialufo.com/the-canadian-cover-up/237-canadian-ufo-director-gets-an-alien-letter;
    Captured! The Betty and Barney Hill UFO Experience: The True Story of the World's First Documented Alien Abduction, Stanton T. Friedman & Kathleen Marden, New Page Books, 2007;
    President John F. Kennedy, Grant Cameron, July 30, 2009,
    http://www.presidentialufo.com/john-f-kennedy/72-president-john-f-kennedy

4. Documentation declassified under the terms of the Freedom of Information Act by the Federal Bureau of Investigation

5. *Canadian UFO Director gets an Alien Letter,* Grant Cameron, August 20, 2009,
    http://www.presidentialufo.com/the-canadian-cover-up/237-canadian-ufo-director-gets-an-alien-letter;
    Captured! The Betty and Barney Hill UFO Experience: The True Story of the World's First Documented Alien Abduction, Stanton T. Friedman & Kathleen Marden, New Page Books, 2007;

President John F. Kennedy, Grant Cameron, July 30, 2009, http://www.presidentialufo.com/john-f-kennedy/72-president-john-f-kennedy

6. Documentation declassified under the terms of the Freedom of Information Act by the Federal Bureau of Investigation
7. *The Sacred Mushroom: Key to the Door of Eternity*, Andrija Puharich, Doubleday, 1974
8. *UFO's Past, Present & Future*, Robert Emenegger, Ballantine Books, 1978

Chapter 10: *The Montgomery Affair*

1. *Ruth Montgomery*, http://www.near-death.com/experiences/paranormal04.html
2. *UFO: End Time Delusion*, David Allen Lewis & Robert Shreckhise, New Leaf Press, 1991
3. *New York Journal American*, June 14, 1960
4. Documentation declassified under the terms of the Freedom of Information Act by the Federal Bureau of Investigation
5. Ibid.
6. Ibid.
7. *New York Journal American*, June 14, 1960
8. Interview with Richard Duke, February 25, 2007

Chapter 11: *The Arrival of the Kidnappers*

1. *The Interrupted Journey*, John G. Fuller, Souvenir Press, Ltd., 1980
2. *Captured! The Betty and Barney Hill UFO Experience: The True Story of the World's First Documented Alien Abduction*, Stanton T. Friedman & Kathleen Marden, New Page Books, 2007
3. Documentation declassified under the terms of the Free-

dom of Information Act by the Department of the Air Force
4. National Archive file: AIR 2/16918;
Interview with Robert Manners, June 15, 2007

Chapter 12: *Late Night Liaisons*

1. National Archive file: AIR 2/16918
2. National Archive file: AIR 2/17984
3. *Canadian UFO Director gets an Alien Letter*, Grant Cameron, August 20, 2009,
   http://www.presidentialufo.com/the-canadian-cover-up/237-canadian-ufo-director-gets-an-alien-letter
4. *Captured! The Betty and Barney Hill UFO Experience: The True Story of the World's First Documented Alien Abduction*, Stanton T. Friedman & Kathleen Marden, New Page Books, 2007;
   The Interrupted Journey, John G. Fuller, Souvenir Press, Ltd., 1980

Chapter 13: *The Black Sorcerer*

1. *Unmasking the Enemy: Visions Around the World and Global Deception in the End Times*, Nelson S. Pacheco & Tommy R. Blann, Bendan Press, Inc., 1993
2. *Sidney Gottlieb*, http://www.spartacus.schoolnet.co.uk/JFKgottlieb.htm
3. *Operation Often: Satanism in the CIA*, http://coverthistory. blogspot.com/2007/12/operation-often-satanism-in-cia-this. html;
   MKUlTRA, http://ensemble.va.com.au/tableau/suzy/TT_ResearchProjects/Hexen2039/PsyO/mkultra.html
4. *Journey into Madness*, Gordon Thomas, Corgi, 1988
5. *The James Cameron Conspiracy Theory*, http://www.whale. to/b/james_cameron.html
6. *Operation Often: Satanism in the CIA*, http://coverthistory.

blogspot.com/2007/12/operation-often-satanism-in-cia-this.
html;
MKUlTRA, http://ensemble.va.com.au/tableau/suzy/TT_
ResearchProjects/Hexen2039/PsyO/mkultra.html
7. Interview with Robert Manners, June 15, 2007
8. *Project Blue Book (The End)*, http://en.wikipedia.org/wiki/
Project_Blue_Book#The_End
9. *UFOs and Related Subjects*, Lynn E. Catoe, U.S. Government Printing Office, 1969

Chapter 14: *Soul Factories*

1. *Journey into Madness*, Gordon Thomas, Corgi, 1988;
Interview with Robert Manners, June 15, 2007
2. *Near Death Experiences and the Afterlife*, http://www.near-death.com/;
Near Death Experience Research Foundation, http://www.nderf.org/
3. *Beyond the Reality Barrier*, Gareth J. Medway, *Magonia*, No. 94, January 2007
4. *X-File Archive: Communion with Whitley Strieber*, Jon King, http://www.consciousape.com/articles/x-file-archive-communion-with-whitley-strieber/
5. Interview with Robert Manners, June 15, 2007

Chapter 15: *The Sorceress and the Spies*

1. *Sybil Leek – The South's White Witch*, BBC, October 28, 2002, http://www.bbc.co.uk/insideout/south/series1/sybil-leek.shtml;
Sybil Leek, http://lovestarz.com/leek.html;
Sybil Leek, http://www.solsticepoint.com/astrologersmemorial/leek.html
2. Interview with Robert Manners, September 4, 2007

Chapter 16: *Demons, Souls and Fallen Angels*

1. *Soul*, http://en.wikipedia.org/wiki/Soul
2. *Psyche*, Erwin Rohde, Routledge & Keegan Paul Ltd., 1925
3. *De Anima*, Aristotle, 350 BC, translated by J.A. Smith, http://classics.mit.edu/Aristotle/soul.html
4. *Avicenna*, http://en.wikipedia.org/wiki/Avicenna
5. *Ibn-al-Nafis*, http://en.wikipedia.org/wiki/Ibn_al-Nafis
6. *Saint Thomas Aquinas*, Ralph McInerny, *Stanford Encyclopedia of Philosophy*, July 12, 1999, http://plato.stanford.edu/entries/aquinas/#BodSou
7. *The Holy Bible: English Standard Version*, Crossway Bibles, 2003
8. *Whistling in the Dark*, Frederick Buechner, HarperOne, 1993
9. *The Greatness of the Soul*, St. Augustine, Paulist Press, 1978
10. *Soul – Definition*, http://www.wordiq.com/definition/Soul
11. *Catechism of the Catholic Church*, http://www.vatican.va/archive/ccc_css/archive/catechism/p1s2c1p6.htm
12. *Soul*, http://en.wikipedia.org/wiki/Soul
13. *Evil and the Demonic*, Paul Oppenheimer, New York University Press, 1996;
    Demonology, http://www.jewishencyclopedia.com/view.jsp?artid=245&letter=D
14. *The Holy Bible: English Standard Version*, Crossway Bibles, 2003
15. *The Book of Enoch*, http://www.israel-a-history-of.com/the-book-of-enoch.html
16. *The Holy Bible: English Standard Version*, Crossway Bibles, 2003
17. Ibid.
18. Ibid.
19. *Evidence for a Spiritual View of the UFO Phenomenon*, Guy Malone, 2009, http://www.alienresistance.org/demonsandaliens.htm

20. *Who were the Nephilim?* http://www.nwcreation.net/nephilim.html

21. *Sexuality in Christian Demonology*, http://en.wikipedia.org/wiki/Sexuality_in_Christian_demonology

22. *The Holy Bible*: *English Standard Version*, Crossway Bibles, 2003

23. *Contactees: A History of Alien-Human Interaction*, Nick Redfern, New Page Books, 2009

24. *The Holy Bible*: *English Standard Version*, Crossway Bibles, 2003

25. Ibid.

26. Ibid.

27. *The Complete Book of Devils and Demons*, Leonard R.N. Ashley, Robson Books, Ltd., 1998

Chapter 17: "*I dreamed I was dead in bed*"

1. *Coyne Helicopter Incident*, Jennie Zeidman, http://www.nicap.org/coyne.htm;
Captain Lawrence Coyne UFO Helicopter Case 1973,
http://www.paranominal.com/ufo/36816/captain-lawrence-coyne-ufo-helicopter-case-1973.html/comment-page-1;
A Helicopter-UFO Encounter over Ohio, Jennie Zeidman, Center for UFO Studies, 1979;
UFOs and the National Security State, An Unclassified History, Volume One: 1941 – 1973, Keyhole Publishing Company, 2000;
UFO Beams Green Light onto Helicopter, http://www.ufoevidence.org/Cases/CaseSubarticle.asp?ID=106;
Cincinnati Enquirer, October 22, 1973

2. *Soviet and Czechoslovakian Parapsychology Research*, Defense Intelligence Agency, 1975

3. *Psychic Discoveries Behind the Iron Curtain*, Sheila Ostrander & Lynn Schroeder, Prentice-Hall, 1984

4. *Soviet and Czechoslovakian Parapsychology Research*, Defense

Intelligence Agency, 1975

5. Interview with Robert Manners, January 9, 2008

Chapter 18: *Out-of-Body Abductions*

1. Interview with Tammy Stone, May 8, 2005
2. Documentation declassified under the terms of the Freedom of Information Act by the Federal Bureau of Investigation
3. *Project Beta: The Story of Paul Bennewitz, National Security, and the Creation of a Modern UFO Myth*, Greg Bishop, Paraview-Pocket Books, 2005

Chapter 19: *Project Abduction*

1. Interview with Dr. Mandor, March 19, 2009
2. *Clear Intent: The Government Cover-Up of the UFO Experience*, Lawrence Fawcett & Barry Greenwood, Prentice-Hall, 1984
3. *Missing Time*, Budd Hopkins, Ballantine Books, 1989;
    Abducted! Debbie Jordan & Kathy Mitchell, Carroll & Graf, 1994;
    Intruders, Budd Hopkins, Sphere Books, Ltd., 1988
4. *MILABS: Military Mind Control & Alien Abduction*, Helmutt Lammer & Marion Lammer, IllumiNet Press, 1999
5. *Into the Fringe: A True Story of Alien Abduction*, Karla Turner, Berkeley Books, 1992;
    Taken: Inside the Alien-Human Abduction Agenda, Karla Turner, Kelt Works, 1994
6. *Wake Up Down There! The Excluded Middle Collection*, edited by Greg Bishop, Adventures Unlimited Press, 2000
7. Interview with Alison, August 14, 2003
8. *MILABS: Military Mind Control & Alien Abduction*, Helmutt Lammer & Marion Lammer, IllumiNet Press, 1999

Chapter 20: *Reagan's Doomsday White House*

1. *Science Fiction Secrets: From Government Files and the Para-normal*, Nick Redfern, Anomalist Books, 2009
2. *The Interrupted Journey*, John G. Fuller, Souvenir Press, Ltd., 1980;
   Missing Time, Budd Hopkins, Ballantine Books, 1989;
   Beyond Earth: Man's Contact with UFOs, Ralph & Judy Blum, Bantam Books, 1974;
   Interview with Dr. Mandor, March 19, 2009
3. *Intruders*, Budd Hopkins, Ballantine Books, 1992
4. Interview with Brian Parks, March 12, 2007
5. Interview with Dr. Mandor, March 19, 2009;
   Journey into Madness, Gordon Thomas, Corgi, 1988;
   The Late Great Planet Earth, Hal Lindsay, Bantam Books, 1973;
   Scofield Reference Bible, Oxford University Press, 1945
6. *Good Heavens! An Astrologer Dictating the President's Sched-ule? Time*, May 16, 1988;
   What Does Joan Say? My Seven Years as White House Astrolo-ger to Nancy and Ronald Reagan, Joan Quigley, Carol Pub-lishing Group, 1990;
   For the Record: From Wall Street to Washington, Donald Re-gan, Harcourt, 1988
7. *Unmasking the Enemy: Visions Around the World and Global Deception in the End Times*, Nelson S. Pacheco & Tommy R. Blann, Bendan Press, Inc., 1993
8. *The Bible, Physics, and the Abilities of Fallen Angels: The Alien Abduction Phenomenon*, Nicole Malone, http://www.Para-doxBrown.com, 2009

Chapter 21: *Whistle-Blowing*

1. *Glimpses of Other Realities: High Strangeness, Volume II,*

Linda Moulton Howe, Linda Moulton Howe Productions, 2001

2. Communication to Linda Moulton Howe from Ray Boeche, reproduced in Howe's *Glimpses of Other Realities: High Strangeness, Volume II*

3. *Wholeness and the Implicate Order*, David Bohm, Routledge Classics, 2002

4. *Outside the Box: A Social Study of the UFO*, Mike Good, *UFO Magazine,* Vol. 23, No. 11, December 2009

Chapter 22: *Ancient Knowledge*

1. *Devils and Evil Spirits of Babylonia*, Reginald Campbell Thompson, Kessinger Publishing, 2003

2. *Joseph McCabe (1867-1955)*, http://www.infidels.org/library/historical/joseph_mccabe/;
   The Story of Religious Controversy, Joseph McCabe, the Stratford Company, 1929

3. *Lilu, Lilitu, and Ardat-Lili, Obsidian*, http://www.realmagick.com/articles/52/1352.html

4. *Communion*, Whitley Strieber, Avon, 1988

5. Ibid.

6. *Friends and Fellow UFO Experiencers, Whitley Strieber's Unknown Country*, June 22, 2004, http://www.unknowncountry.com/mindframe/opinion/?id=149

7. *Quinn's Story: Profile of an Abductee,* http://www.pararesearchers.org/Alien_Abduction/aa_2/aa_2.html

8. *The Story of the Strix*, Professor Samuel Grant Oliphant, American Philological Association, 1913

9. *Unger's Undoing*, Miles J. Stanford, http://withchrist.org/mjs/ungerm.htm

10. *Demons in the World Today*, Merrill F. Unger, Tynedale House, 1995

11. *What Demons Can Do to Saints*, Merrill F. Unger, Moody Press, 1977

12. *Occult ABC*, Kurt Koch, Literature Mission Aglasterhausen Inc., 1980;
    Occult Bondage and Deliverance, Kurt Koch, Kregel Publications, 1972
13. *The Mothman Prophecies*, John A. Keel, E.P. Dutton & Co., 1975
14. *Principalities and Powers*, John Warwick Montgomery, Canadian institute for Law, Theology and Public Policy, Inc., 2001
15. *Victory over the Darkness*, Neil T. Anderson, Regal, 2000
16. *Taken: Inside the Alien-Human Abduction Agenda*, Karla Turner, Kelt Works, 1994
17. *Angels and Demons According to Lactantius*, Emil Schneweis, Catholic University of America Press, 1944

Chapter 23: *Trojans in the Desert*

1. *The Collins Report, Deception and UFOs: What we Believe and Why*, Collins Elite, 1998
2. Interview with Ray Boeche, January 22, 2007
3. *The Collins Report, Deception and UFOs: What we Believe and Why*, Collins Elite, 1998
4. *Majic Eyes Only*, Ryan S. Wood, Wood & Wood Enterprises, 2005;
   Top Secret Majic, Stanton T. Friedman, Marlowe & Co., 1996

Chapter 24: *It's Alive!*

1. *Theodore von Karman*, http://www.nationalacademies.org/history/members/karman.html;
   Theodore von Karman, http://www.csupomona.edu/~nova/scientists/articles/vonk.html
2. *The Golem*, Alden Oreck, Jewish Virtual Library, http://www.jewishvirtuallibrary.org/jsource/Judaism/Golem.html;

The Golem of Prague, Gershon Winkler, Judaica Press, 1980;
Golem: Jewish Magical and Mystical Traditions on the Artificial Anthropoid, Mosche Idel, State University of New York Press, 1990

3. *The Occult Explosion*, Nat Freedland, Berkeley Books, 1972
4. *The Lore of the Homunculus*, S. Maconius, Red Lion Publications, 1980;
    In Search of Frankenstein, Radu Florescu, New York Graphic Society, 1975

Chapter 25: *Soul Food*

1. *From Outer Space to You*, Howard Menger, Saucerian Books, 1959
2. *Operation Trojan Horse*, John Keel, Souvenir Press, Ltd., 1971
3. *Transformation*, Whitley Strieber, William Morrow & Co., 1988
4. *Breakthrough*, Whitley Strieber, Harper-Collins, 1995
5. *Abduction*, John E. Mack, Scribner, 1994;
    Passport to the Cosmos, John E. Mack, Thorsons, 2000
6. *Flying Saucerers*, David Clarke & Andy Roberts, Heart of Albion Press, 2007
7. Ibid.
8. *Alien Liaison*, Timothy Good, Arrow, 1991
9. *UFOs and the Alien Presence*, Michael Lindemann, Blue Water Publishing, 1995

Chapter 26: *"They come in the Emperor's new clothes"*

1. Interview with Joe Jordan, February 4 2010;
    CE4 Research Group, http://www.alienresistance.org/ce4.htm

Chapter 27: *What Intelligent Evil Wants*

   1.   Interview with Michael Heiser, March 8, 2007

Chapter 28: *The Man from Roswell*

   1.   Interview with Guy Malone, December 6, 2009;
      Evidence for a Spiritual View of the UFO Phenomenon, Guy Malone, 2009, http://www.alienresistance.org/demonsan-daliens.htm

Chapter 29: *When Time Runs Out*

   1.   *Last Judgment*, http://en.wikipedia.org/wiki/Last_Judg-ment
   2.   *What is the Preterist View of Bible Prophecy?* International Preterist Association, http://www.preterist.org/whatispret-erism.asp
   3.   *Eschatology: A Futurist View*, L. Thomas Holdcroft, CeeTec Publishing, 2001;
      Are you a Preterist or a Futurist? http://www.theberencall.org/node/2015
   4.   *Tribulation*, http://en.wikipedia.org/wiki/Tribulation
   5.   *Millennialism*, www.bu.edu/mille/people/.../millennialism-mw-encyl.html
   6.   Interview with Ray Boeche, January 22, 2007
   7.   *Is the Sky Falling Over Chicken Little?* Gary S. Bekkum, *Spies, Lies and Polygraph Tape*, May 3, 2007, http://star-gate007.blogspot.com/2007_05_03_archive.html
   8.   *The Aviary, the Aquarium and Eschatology*, Vince Johnson, http://www.think-aboutit.com/ufo/aviary_the_aquarium.htm

Chapter 30: *Seeing is Believing*

1. Interview with Robert Manners and source, November 8, 2009
2. *NOW Project Blue Beam: False Holographic Second Coming*, http://2012poleshift.wetpaint.com/page/NWO+Project+Bl ue+Beam%3A+False+Holographic+Second+Coming;
    Project Blue Beam, Serge Monast, 1994, http://educate-your-self.org/cn/projectbluebeam25jul05.shtml;
    Has Project "BlueBeam" Begun? http://www.rumormill-news.com/cgi-bin/archive.cgi?read=42593
3. Interview with Robert Manners and source, November 8, 2009
4. *Profile: Offutt Air Force Base*, http://www.historycommons. org/entity.jsp?entity=offutt_air_force_base
5. Interview with Ray Boeche, January 22, 2007
6. Ibid.
7. *UFO Crash Landing?* Jenny Randles, Blandford, 1998
8. Interview with Ray Boeche, January 22, 2007
9. Interview with Robert Manners and source, November 8, 2009

Chapter 31: *Onward, Christian Soldiers*

1. *U.S. Military Weapons Inscribed with Secret "Jesus" Bible Codes*, Joseph Rhee, Tahman Bradley and Brian Ross, ABC News, January 18, 2010,
    http://abcnews.go.com/Blotter/us-military-weapons-in-scribed-secret-jesus-bible-codes/story?id=9575794&page=1;
    Muslims Angry Over U.S. Military "Jesus" Rifles, Fox News, January 21, 2010,
    http://www.foxnews.com/us/2010/01/21muslims-angry-military-jesus-rifles/;
    No More "Jesus" Rifles, Luis Martinez, Joseph Rhee and

Mark Schone, ABC News, http://abcnews.go.com/Blotter/jesus-rifles/story?id=9618791

2. *Pentagon Briefings no Longer Quote Bible*, Associated Press, May 18, 2009

3. Ibid.

4. *US is "Battling Satan" Says General*, BBC, October 17, 2003, http://news.bbc.co.uk/2/hi/americas/3199212.stm

5. *Building God's (Christian) Army*, Jane Lampman, *Christian Science Monitor*, October 19, 2007

6. Ibid.

Acknowledgments

I would like to offer my very sincere thanks to the following people, without whom the writing and publication of this book would not have been possible: Ray Boeche, Adam Gorightly, Guy and Nicole Malone, Greg Bishop, Tammy Stone, Joe Jordan, Michael Heiser, Anne Henson, Brian Parks, Richard Duke, Ralph Summers, Robert Manners, Dr. Mandor, and Patrick Huyghe and Dennis Stacy of Anomalist Books.

Index

About the Author

Nick Redfern works full-time as an author, lecturer and journalist. He writes about a wide range of unsolved mysteries, including Bigfoot, UFOs, the Loch Ness Monster, alien encounters, and government conspiracies. He is a regular contributor to *UFO Magazine, Fate, Fortean Times*, and *Paranormal Magazine*. He has also written for *Military Illustrated*, the British *Daily Express* newspaper, and *Penthouse*. His previous books include *Science Fiction Secrets; There's Something in the Woods; On the Trail of the Saucer Spies*; and *Strange Secrets*. Nick has appeared on numerous television shows, including the BBC's *Out of this World*; History Channel's *Monster Quest* and *UFO Hunters*; the National Geographic Channel's *Paranatural*; MSNBC's *Countdown* with Keith Olbermann; and the SyFy Channel's *Proof Positive*. He is the co-host with Raven Meindel of the weekly radio-show *Exploring All Realms*. Nick Redfern lives in Arlington, Texas with his wife, Dana. He can be contacted at nickredfern.com.

Lightning Source UK Ltd.
Milton Keynes UK
07 April 2011

170521UK00008B/59/P